THE NEW MEDITERRANEAN DIET COOKBOOK 2021

A Delicious Collection of 700+ Easy, Quick and Affordable Recipes to Help You Reset Your Metabolism and Change Your Eating Habits for a Healthy Lifestyle.

Michelle Johnson

© Copyright Michelle Johnson 2021 - All rights reserved.

The content contained within this book may not be reproduced, duplicated or transmitted without direct written permission from the author or the publisher.

Under no circumstances will any blame or legal responsibility be held against the publisher, or author, for any damages, reparation, or monetary loss due to the information contained within this book. Either directly or indirectly.

Legal Notice:

This book is copyright protected. This book is only for personal use. You cannot amend, distribute, sell, use, quote or paraphrase any part, or the content within this book, without the consent of the author or publisher.

Disclaimer Notice:

By reading this document, the reader agrees that under no circumstances is the author responsible for any losses, direct or indirect, which are incurred as a result of the use of information contained within this document, including, but not limited to, — errors, omissions, or inaccuracies.

Table of Contents

Introduction 1

Chapter 1: Breakfast Recipes 4

1. Ham Muffins 4
2. Morning Pizza with Sprouts 4
3. Banana Quinoa 5
4. Egg Casserole with Paprika 5
5. Cauliflower Fritters 5
6. Creamy Oatmeal with Figs 5
7. Baked Oatmeal with Cinnamon 6
8. Almond Chia Porridge 6
9. Cocoa Oatmeal 6
10. Avocado Egg Scramble 6
11. Breakfast Tostadas 7
12. Parmesan Omelet 7
13. Watermelon Pizza 7
14. Cinnamon Roll Oats 8
15. Pumpkin Oatmeal with Spices 8
16. Mediterranean Pita Breakfast 8
17. Hummus Deviled Egg 9
18. Apple Cheese Scones 9
19. Bacon and Egg Wrap 9
20. Orange-Blueberry Muffin 10
21. Baked Ginger Oatmeal with Pear Topping 10
22. Greek-Style Veggie Omelet 10
23. Ham & Egg Pitas 10
24. Breakfast Couscous 11
25. Peach Breakfast Salad 11
26. Savory Oats 11
27. Tahini & Apple Toast 12
28. Scrambled Basil Eggs 12
29. Greek Potatoes & Eggs 12
30. Vegetable Frittata 12
31. Mini Lettuce Wraps 13
32. Curry Apple Couscous 13
33. Herb Flounder 13
34. Cauliflower Quinoa 14
35. Spinach Omelet 14
36. Almond Pancakes 14
37. Buckwheat Buttermilk Pancakes 15
38. French Toast with Almonds and Peach Compote 15
39. Mixed Berries Oatmeal with Sweet Vanilla Cream 15
40. Choco-Strawberry Crepe 16
41. No Crust Asparagus-Ham Quiche 16
42. Barley Porridge 17
43. Yogurt with Blueberries, Honey, and Mint 17
44. Berry and Yogurt Parfait 17
45. Oatmeal with Berries and Sunflower Seeds 17
46. Almond and Maple Quick Grits 18
47. Banana Oats 18
48. Breakfast Sandwich 18
49. Morning Couscous 18
50. Mini Frittatas 19
51. Sun-dried Tomatoes Oatmeal 19
52. Breakfast Egg on Avocado 19
53. Brekky Egg-Potato Hash 19
54. Cranberry Bulgur Mix 20
55. Apple Crisp with Oatmeal 20
56. Jamaican Cornmeal Porridge 20
57. Blueberry Muffins 21
58. Strawberry Muffins 21
59. Savory Spinach Feta and Sweet Pepper Muffins 21

Chapter 2: Appetizers and Snacks 23

60. Zucchini Chips 23
61. Egg Cupcakes 23
62. Grilled Spiced Turkey Burger 24
63. Tomato Tea Party Sandwiches 24
64. Mediterranean Flatbread with Toppings 24
65. Smoked Salmon and Goat Cheese Bites .. 25
66. Hummus Snack Bowl 25
67. Greek Spinach Yogurt Artichoke Dip ... 26
68. Sautéed Apricots 26
69. Spiced Kale Chips 26
70. Turkey Spheroids with Tzatziki Sauce ... 27
71. Cheesy Caprese Salad Skewers 27
72. Leafy Lacinato Tuscan Treat 27
73. Portable Packed Picnic Pieces 28
74. Perfect Pizza & Pastry 28
75. Zucchini Fritters 28
76. Cucumber Bites 29
77. Stuffed Avocado 29
78. Wrapped Plums 29
79. Cucumber Sandwich Bites 29
80. Cucumber Rolls 30

81. Olives and Cheese Stuffed Tomatoes 30
82. Veggie Shish Kebabs 30
83. Crispy Falafel... 30
84. Onion Fried Eggs 31
85. Black Bean Cake with Salsa 31
86. Pickled Apple... 32
87. Baked Clams Oreganata 32
88. Tuna Tartare 32
89. Cod Cakes 33
90. Mixed Mushroom Palermitani Pasta 33
91. Mediterranean Macaroni with Seasoned Spinach................................. 33
92. Frittata Filled with Zesty Zucchini & Tomato Toppings 34
93. Grilled Vegetable Kebabs........................ 34
94. Vegetable Fritters 34
95. Baba Ghanoush 35
96. Sfougato 35
97. Skordalia 35
98. Pinto Bean Dip with Avocado Pico 36
99. Margherita Mediterranean Model 36
100. Fowl & Feta Fettuccini 36
101. Very Vegan Patras Pasta 37
102. Scrumptious Shrimp Pappardelle Pasta . 37
103. Mediterranean Chicken Bites 38
104. Turkey Wrapped Eggs............................. 38
105. Grilled Pineapple Sandwich 38
106. Roasted Green Beans............................... 39
107. Smoked Salmon, Avocado and Cucumber Bites 39
108. Roasted Almonds..................................... 39
109. Pistachio Balls 39
110. Healthy & Quick Energy Bites............... 40
111. Tuna Sandwiches...................................... 40
112. Pepperoni Eggs... 40
113. Flatbread Sandwiches.............................. 40

Chapter 3: Main Meals 42

114. Cacciatore Black Olive Chicken 42
115. Mustard Green Chicken........................... 42
116. Chickpea Spiced Chicken 43
117. Vegetable Rice Chicken 43
118. Chicken Shawarma................................... 44
119. Caprese Chicken Dinner 44
120. Pork Loin with Peach Sauce................... 44
121. Mushroom Tomato Beef.......................... 45
122. Black Olive Sea Bass............................... 45
123. Broccoli Soy Salmon 46
124. Shrimp Fennel Pasta 46
125. Fish with Farro & Green Beans.............. 47
126. Spinach Mackerel 47
127. Instant Pot Beef Gyros 47
128. Instant Pot Lasagna Hamburger Helper.. 48
129. Salmon Salad Wraps 48
130. Scallops in Citrus Sauce 48
131. Trout & Greens 49
132. Healthy Instant Pot Mediterranean Chicken... 49
133. Mediterranean Instant Pot Chicken and Potatoes 50
134. Instant Pot Moroccan Chicken............... 50
135. Mediterranean Instant Pot Shredded Beef 51
136. Instant Pot Orzo with Shrimp, Tomatoes, And Feta................................. 51
137. Instant Pot Mediterranean Chicken Wings 51
138. Honey Almond–Crusted Chicken Tenders 52
139. Romesco Poached Chicken 52
140. Roasted Red Pepper Chicken with Lemony Garlic Hummus.......................... 53
141. Sheet Pan Lemon Chicken and Roasted Artichokes................................... 53
142. Parmesan Chicken Wraps........................ 54
143. Cod & Green Bean Dinner 54
144. Easy Grilled Catfish 54
145. Garlic & Orange Shrimp.......................... 55
146. Kale & Tuna Bowl 55
147. Tuna with Lettuce and Chickpeas 55
148. Chicken with Salsa & Cilantro 56
149. Lime Chicken with Black Beans 56
150. Turkey Verde with Brown Rice 56
151. Turkey with Basil & Tomatoes 57
152. Turkey Lasagna 57
153. Tuna with Lemon Butter Sauce.............. 57
154. Mediterranean Cod 57
155. Shrimp with Honeydew and Feta 58
156. Spicy Seared Mussels 58
157. Zucchini and Chicken 59
158. Shrimp with Tomatoes & Feta................. 59
159. Mussels in Garlic Butter Sauce 59
160. Fish Stew with Tomatoes & Olives 59
161. Rosemary Salmon..................................... 60
162. Salmon with Tahini Sauce 60
163. Fish & Potatoes... 60
164. Sautéed Shrimp with Garlic Couscous .. 61
165. Seafood Garlic Couscous......................... 61
166. Crusty Grilled Clams 61
167. Lemon-Thyme Chicken........................... 62
168. Mediterranean Chicken Quinoa Bowl .. 62

169. Blue Cheese-Topped Pork Chops 62
170. Greek Beef Steak and Hummus Plate 63
171. Linguine with Shrimp 63
172. Oysters with Vinaigrette 63
173. Grilled Chicken Wraps 64
174. Pork Chops and Relish 64
175. Glazed Pork Chops 64
176. Pork Chops and Cherries Mix 65
177. Pork Chops and Herbed Tomato Sauce ... 65
178. Black Bean & Turkey Skillet 65
179. Beef and Cheese Gratin 65
180. Greek Beef and Veggie Skewers 66
181. Pork Tenderloin with Orzo 66
182. Moroccan Lamb Flatbreads 66
183. Greek Lamb Burgers 67
184. Broiled Swordfish with Oven-Roasted Tomato Sauce 67
185. Pan-Seared Citrus Shrimp 68
186. Spicy Mexican Casserole 68
187. Succulent Baked Salmon 68
188. Coconut Chicken Curry 69
189. Blue Cheese Pasta 69
190. Quinoa and Halibut Bowl 70
191. Barramundi in Parchment with Lemons, Dates, and Toasted Almonds 70
192. Sardine Fish Cakes 70
193. Baked Salmon Tacos 71
194. No-Drain Pasta alla Norma 71
195. Zucchini with Bow Ties 72
196. Roasted Asparagus Caprese Pasta 72
197. Speedy Tilapia with Red Onion and Avocado 73
198. Grilled Fish on Lemons 73
199. Weeknight Sheet Pan Fish Dinner 74
200. Crispy Polenta Fish Sticks 74
201. Salmon Skillet Supper 74
202. Orange and Garlic Shrimp 75
203. Lamb Chops with Herb Butter 75
204. Healthy Lasagna 76
205. Chicken Alfredo 76
206. Fried Halloumi & Avocados 77
207. Chicken Korma 77
208. Mediterranean Tuna Noodle Casserole 78
209. Acquapazza Snapper 78
210. Eggplant Brown Rice Bowl 78
211. Extra-Crispy Veggie-Packed Pizza 79
212. Greek Turkey Burgers 79
213. Beef and Lamb Kofta Lettuce Wraps 80
214. Chicken Souvlaki 80
215. Spicy Chicken Shawarma 81
216. Lemon Chicken Pita Burgers with Spiced Yogurt Sauce 81
217. Lamb Chop with Pistachio Gremolata ... 81
218. Pita Salad with Cucumber, Fennel, and Chicken 82
219. Halibut with Lemon-Fennel Salad 82
220. Cabbage Roll Casserole with Veal 82
221. Slow-Cooked Daube Provencal 83
222. Osso Bucco 83
223. Slow Cooker Beef Bourguignon 83
224. Balsamic Beef 84
225. Veal Pot Roast 84
226. Mediterranean Rice and Sausage 85
227. Spanish Meatballs 85
228. Lamb Shanks with Red Wine 85
229. Leg of Lamb with Rosemary and Garlic .. 86
230. Lemon Honey Lamb Shoulder 86
231. Italian Shredded Pork Stew 86
232. Rosemary-Lemon Snapper Baked in Parchment 87
233. Shrimp in Creamy Pesto over Zoodles 87
234. Nut-Crusted Baked Fish 87
235. Pesto Walnut Noodles 88
236. Tomato Tabbouleh 88
237. Lemon Faro Bowl 89
238. Chickpea & Red Pepper Delight 89
239. Eggplant Rolls 89
240. Heavenly Quinoa 90
241. Mediterranean Lettuce Wraps 90
242. Greek Salad Nachos 90
243. Sirloin with Sweet Bell Peppers 91
244. Quinoa and Spinach Salad with Figs and Balsamic Dressing 91
245. Greek-Style Tuna Salad in Pita 91
246. Delicious Broccoli Tortellini Salad 92
247. Tuna and Cheese Bake 92
248. Instant Pot Potato Salad 92
249. Veggie Hummus Sandwich 93
250. Spicy Potato Salad 93
251. Tomato and Halloumi Platter 93
252. Bean Lettuce Wraps 93
253. Red Bean & Green Salad 94
254. Chickpea Patties 94
255. Red Onion Tilapia 95
256. Chicken & Asparagus 95
257. Beef Kofta 95
258. Raisin Rice Pilaf 96
259. Lebanese Delight 96
260. Flavorful Braised Kale 96
261. Tomato and Wine-Steamed Mussels 97

262. Tangy Tilapia Fish Fillets with Crusty Coating 97
263. Feta-Fused Mussels Marmite 97
264. Sauced Shellfish in White Wine 98
265. Couscous with Tuna and Pepperoncini .. 98
266. Lemon Chicken with Asparagus............. 99
267. Cilantro Lime Chicken 99
268. Shrimp and Leek Spaghetti 99
269. Lamb and Beet Meatballs 100
270. Chicken Wings Platter........................ 100
271. Spicy Sweet Red Hummus 100
272. Dill Relish on White Sea Bass 101
273. Mustard Chops with Apricot-basil Relish 101
274. Seafood and Veggie Pasta 101
275. Creamy Alfredo Fettuccine 102
276. Walnut-Rosemary Crusted Salmon 102
277. Quick Tomato Spaghetti..................... 102
278. Crispy Italian Chicken 103
279. Chili Oregano Baked Cheese 103
280. Sea Bass in a Pocket 103
281. Shrimp, Avocado and Feta Wrap 104
282. Broiled Tilapia Parmesan 104
283. Italian Herb Grilled Chicken 104
284. Mediterranean Grilled Shrimp 105
285. Italian Breaded Shrimp....................... 105
286. Fried Fresh Sardines........................... 105
287. White Wine–Sautéed Mussels 106
288. Paprika-Spiced Fish 106
289. Citrus-Herb Scallops 106
290. Whole Trout Baked with Lemon and Herbs 106
291. Skillet Cod with Fresh Tomato Salsa . 107
292. Broiled Flounder with Nectarine and White Bean Salsa 107
293. Trout with Ruby Red Grapefruit Relish 107
294. Classic Pork Tenderloin Marsala......... 108
295. Chili-Spiced Lamb Chops 108
296. Greek Herbed Beef Meatballs 109
297. Chicken in Tomato-Balsamic Pan Sauce 109
298. Seasoned Buttered Chicken 109
299. Shrimps with Lemon and Pepper 110
300. Breaded and Spiced Halibut 110
301. Curry Salmon with Mustard 110
302. Mediterranean Lamb Chops................ 111
303. Pasta Salad with Chicken Club 111
304. Alfredo Peppered Shrimp 111
305. Blackened Salmon Fillets 112
306. Cajun Seafood Pasta 112
307. Scrumptious Salmon Cakes 112
308. Easy Tuna Patties 113
309. Brown Butter Perch 113
310. Fish in Foil.. 113
311. Herby Juicy Chicken Fillets 114
312. Wild Rice Pilaf with Beans 114
313. Arroz con Pollo with a Twist 114
314. Mackerel Fillets with Authentic Skordalia Sauce 115
315. Spanish Repollo Guisado 115
316. Spring Wax Beans with New Potatoes 115
317. Sweet Sausage Marsala....................... 116
318. Feta Chicken Burgers 116
319. Baked Salmon with Dill 117
320. Herb-Crusted Halibut 117
321. Marinated Tuna Steak........................ 117
322. Niçoise-Style Tuna Salad with Olives & White Beans 117
323. Tilapia with Avocado & Red Onion...... 118
324. Mixed Spice Burgers 118
325. Delicious Pork & Orzo........................ 119
326. Mezze Platter with Toasted Za'atar Pita Bread 119
327. Mediterranean Whole Wheat Pizza ... 119
328. Lamb & Vegetable Bake 120
329. Southwest Chipotle Chili 120
330. Mediterranean Chicken and Tomato Dish 120
331. Beef Tartar....................................... 121
332. Cabbage and Beef Stir Fry 121
333. Simple Pork Stir Fry 121

Chapter 4: Vegetarian Recipes 123

334. Roasted Portobello Mushrooms with Kale and Red Onion 123
335. Balsamic Marinated Tofu with Basil and Oregano........... 124
336. Ricotta, Basil, and Pistachio–Stuffed Zucchini 124
337. Farro with Roasted Tomatoes and Mushrooms 124
338. Baked Orzo with Eggplant, Swiss Chard, and Mozzarella........... 125
339. Barley Risotto with Tomatoes............. 125
340. Chickpeas and Kale with Spicy Pomodoro Sauce........... 126
341. Roasted Feta with Kale and Lemon Yogurt........... 126
342. Roasted Eggplant and Chickpeas with Tomato Sauce 127
343. Baked Falafel Sliders.......................... 127

- 344. Portobello Caprese 127
- 345. Mushroom and Cheese Stuffed Tomatoes 128
- 346. Tabbouleh 128
- 347. Spicy Broccoli Rabe And Artichoke Hearts 129
- 348. Cauliflower Steaks with Olive Citrus Sauce 129
- 349. Pistachio Mint Pesto Pasta 129
- 350. Burst Cherry Tomato Sauce with Angel Hair Pasta 130
- 351. Baked Tofu with Sun-Dried Tomatoes and Artichokes 130
- 352. Baked Mediterranean Tempeh with Tomatoes and Garlic 131
- 353. Shakshuka 131
- 354. Spanakopita 132
- 355. Tagine 132
- 356. Citrus Pistachios and Asparagus 133
- 357. Tomato and Parsley Stuffed Eggplant 133
- 358. Ratatouille 133
- 359. Gemista 134
- 360. Stuffed Cabbage Rolls 134
- 361. Brussels Sprouts with Balsamic Glaze 135
- 362. Spinach Salad with Citrus Vinaigrette 135
- 363. Simple Celery and Orange Salad 135
- 364. Rice with Vermicelli 136
- 365. Fava Beans and Rice 136
- 366. Buttered Fava Beans 136
- 367. Freekeh 137
- 368. Fried Rice Balls with Tomato Sauce 137
- 369. Spanish-Style Rice 137
- 370. Zucchini with Rice and Tzatziki 138
- 371. Cannellini Beans with Rosemary and Garlic Aioli 138
- 372. Jeweled Rice 138
- 373. Bulgur with Tomatoes and Chickpeas . 139
- 374. Chickpea Medley 139
- 375. Moroccan Couscous 139
- 376. Lemony Asparagus Pasta 140
- 377. Moroccan Tempeh 140
- 378. Pasta with Lemon and Artichokes 141
- 379. Roasted Pine Nut Orzo 141
- 380. Greek Flatbreads 141
- 381. Mediterranean Macro Plate 142
- 382. The Athena Pizza 142
- 383. Mujadara 142
- 384. Briam 143
- 385. Zucchini Boats with Couscous Stuffing 143
- 386. Pasta with Creamy Tomato Sauce 144
- 387. Spicy Eggplant Polenta 144
- 388. Greek Tostadas 145
- 389. Asparagus Risotto 145
- 390. Vegetable Paella 145
- 391. Eggplant and Rice Casserole 146
- 392. Many Vegetable Couscous 146
- 393. Kushari 147
- 394. Italian Oven Roasted Vegetables 147
- 395. Pesto with Basil and Spinach 148
- 396. Broiled Mushrooms Burgers and Goat Cheese 148
- 397. Whole Grain Pita Bread Stuffed with Olives and Chickpeas 148
- 398. Simple Penne Anti-Pasto 149
- 399. Broiled Tomatoes with Feta 149
- 400. Sautéed Dark Leafy Greens 149
- 401. Alethea's Lemony Asparagus Pasta 150
- 402. Herbed Roasted Tomato with Feta Cheese 150
- 403. Roasted Tomato Pita Pizzas 150

Chapter 5: Salads 152

- 404. Olives and Lentils Salad 152
- 405. Lime Spinach and Chickpeas Salad 152
- 406. Minty Olives and Tomatoes Salad 152
- 407. Beans and Cucumber Salad 153
- 408. Tomato and Avocado Salad 153
- 409. Arugula Salad 153
- 410. Chickpea Salad 153
- 411. Chopped Israeli Mediterranean Pasta Salad 154
- 412. Feta Tomato Salad 154
- 413. Greek Pasta Salad 154
- 414. Pork and Greens Salad 155
- 415. Mediterranean Duck Breast Salad 155
- 416. Creamy Chicken Salad 155
- 417. Chicken and Cabbage Salad 155
- 418. Roasted Broccoli Salad 156
- 419. Tomato Salad 156
- 420. Feta Beet Salad 156
- 421. Chicken and Quinoa Salad 157
- 422. Melon Salad 157
- 423. Bean and Toasted Pita Salad 157
- 424. Goat Cheese 'n Red Beans Salad 158
- 425. Peppers and Lentils Salad 158
- 426. Cashews and Red Cabbage Salad 158
- 427. Apples and Pomegranate Salad 158

428. Chickpeas, Corn and Black Beans Salad 158
429. Celery Citrus Salad 159
430. Broccoli Crunch Salad 159
431. Summer Tomato Salad 159
432. Cheese Beet Salad 160
433. Cauliflower and Cherry Tomato Salad 160
434. Watermelon Salad 160
435. Orange Celery Salad 160
436. Cauliflower & Tomato Salad 160
437. Quinoa Fruit Salad 161
438. Spinach Salad with Grilled Mediterranean Vegetables 161
439. Fava Bean Salad 161
440. Salmon & Avocado Salad 162
441. Tuna and Potato Salad 162
442. Brown Rice, Feta, Fresh Pea, and Mint Salad 162
443. Tortellini Salad with Broccoli 163

Chapter 6: Soups and Stews 164

444. Mediterranean Beef Stew 164
445. Italian Meatball Soup 164
446. Tuscan White Bean Soup with Sausage and Kale 165
447. Vegetable Soup 165
448. Vegetable Lover's Chicken Soup 166
449. Spring Faro Plate 166
450. Greek Style Spring Soup 166
451. Healthy Vegetable Soup 167
452. Delicious Okra Chicken Stew 167
453. Tuscan Beef Stew 167
454. Sorghum Stew 168
455. Moroccan Lentil Soup 168
456. Roasted Red Pepper and Tomato Soup .. 168
457. Minestrone Soup 169
458. Chicken Wild Rice Soup 169
459. Chicken Noodle Soup 170
460. Cucumber Soup 170
461. Squash and Turmeric Soup 170
462. Leek, Potato and Carrot Soup 170
463. Roasted Red Pepper Soup 171
464. Yucatan Soup 171
465. Zesty Taco Soup 171
466. Southwestern Posole 172
467. Spring Vegetable Soup 172
468. Seafood Corn Chowder 172
469. Beef Sage Soup 172
470. Cabbage Borscht 173
471. Ground Beef Soup 173
472. Slow Cooker BBQ Chicken Pizza Soup .. 173
473. Slow Cooker Beef Round Stew 174
474. Slow Cooker Chicken Pot Pie Stew 174
475. Slow Cooker Mediterranean Stew 175
476. Easy Lemon Chicken Soup 175
477. Basil Zucchini Soup 175
478. Roasted Tomatoes Soup 176
479. Southern Style Beef Stew 176
480. Spicy Black Bean and Quinoa Soup 176
481. Spicy Chicken Noodle Soup 177
482. Spicy Chicken Vegetable Soup 177
483. Spicy Chicken and Jicama Stew 177
484. Spring Vegetable Noodle Soup 178
485. Stuffed Pepper Soup 178
486. Tender Pork Stew with Beans 178
487. Garlic Squash Broccoli Soup 179
488. Chicken Rice Soup 179
489. Mussels Soup 179
490. Creamy Chicken Soup 180
491. Cheesy Chicken Soup 180
492. Italian Chicken Stew 180
493. Creamy Carrot Tomato Soup 181
494. Basil Broccoli Soup 181
495. Shredded Chicken Soup 181
496. Mediterranean Rabbit Soup 182
497. Mushroom Cream Soup 182
498. Creamy Salmon Soup 182
499. Basil and Tomato Soup 182
500. Kale Chicken Soup 183
501. Ajoblanco (Cold Spanish Almond Soup) 183
502. Mixed Seafood Stew 183
503. Wild Rice Soup & Creamy Chicken 184

Chapter 7: Side Dishes 185

504. Instant Pot® Salsa 185
505. Garlic Rice 185
506. Roasted Garlic Hummus 186
507. Tomato Salsa 186
508. Black Bean Dip 186
509. Easy Hummus 187
510. Tasty Lasagna Rolls 187
511. Red Pepper Hummus 187
512. Classic Hummus 188
513. Greek Eggplant Dip 188
514. Chickpea, Parsley, and Dill Dip 188
515. Yogurt Dip 189
516. Sage Barley Mix 189
517. Chickpeas and Beets Mix 189
518. Creamy Sweet Potatoes Mix 189
519. Cabbage and Mushrooms Mix 190

520. Lemon Mushroom Rice 190
521. Paprika and Chives Potatoes 190
522. Bulgur, Kale and Cheese Mix 190
523. Spicy Green Beans Mix 191
524. Beans and Rice 191
525. Artichoke ala Romana 191
526. Balsamic Asparagus 192
527. Lime Cucumber Mix 192
528. Walnuts Cucumber Mix 192
529. Rosemary Beets 192
530. Squash and Tomatoes Mix 193
531. Eggplant Carpaccio 193
532. Beans and Escarole 193
533. Escarole ala Mediterranean 194
534. Puglia Green Beans 194
535. Bean Cream 194
536. Tzatziki 195
537. Mashed Potatoes 195
538. Genovese Pesto 195
539. Sicilian Pesto 196
540. Cocktail Sauce 196
541. Baked Potatoes 196
542. Homemade Whole Wheat Pita Bread .. 197
543. Crisp Spiced Cauliflower with Feta Cheese 197
544. Spring Peas and Beans with Zesty Thyme Yogurt Sauce 197
545. Loaded Mediterranean Cauliflower Fries 198
546. Mediterranean Succotash 198
547. Mediterranean Chicken Samosas with Apple Cumin Chutney 199
548. Toasted Israeli Couscous with Vegetables and Lemon-Balsamic Vinaigrette 199
549. Elbow Macaroni with Pine Nuts, Lemon and Fennel 200
550. Vegetable Couscous 200
551. Eggplant Pesto 201
552. Aioli Sauce 201
553. Power Pods & Hearty Hazelnuts with Mustard-y Mix 201
554. Peppery Potatoes 202
555. Greek Guacamole Hybrid Hummus 202
556. Minty Melon & Fruity Feta with Cool Cucumber 202
557. Limassolian Lemony Steamed Spears with Cheese Chips 203
558. Mediterranean Minestrone 203
559. Sour Cream Broccoli Casserole 203
560. Salsa Verde 203
561. Mediterranean Chickpea Bowl 204
562. Carrot Spread 204
563. Carrot Rice 204
564. Tomato Cream Sauce 205
565. Butternut Squash Hummus 205

Chapter 8: Drinks 206

566. Sweet Kale Smoothie 206
567. Gingerbread & Pumpkin Smoothie 206
568. Walnut & Date Smoothie 207
569. Avocado-Blueberry Smoothie 207
570. Cranberry-Pumpkin Smoothie 207
571. Avocado and Apple Smoothie 207
572. Green Juice 208
573. Sweet Cranberry Nectar 208
574. Hearty Pear and Mango Smoothie 208
575. Strawberry Rhubarb Smoothie 208
576. Breakfast Almond Milk Shake 209
577. Raspberry Vanilla Smoothie 209
578. Mango Pear Smoothie 209
579. Blueberry Banana Protein Smoothie .. 209
580. Chocolate Banana Smoothie 209
581. Fruit Smoothie 210
582. Mango-Pear Smoothie 210
583. Strawberry-Rhubarb Smoothie 210
584. Chia-Pomegranate Smoothie 210
585. Honey and Wild Blueberry Smoothie . 211
586. Oats Berry Smoothie 211
587. Kale-Pineapple Smoothie 211
588. Moroccan Avocado Smoothie 211
589. Mediterranean Smoothie 211
590. Anti-Inflammatory Blueberry Smoothie 212
591. Pina Colada Smoothie 212
592. Avocado & Honey Smoothie 212
593. Kiwi Smoothie 212
594. Summer Smoothie 212

Chapter 9: Desserts 214

595. Orange Butterscotch Pudding 214
596. Mixed Berry and Orange Compote 214
597. Streuselkuchen with Peaches 215
598. Fig and Honey Buckwheat Pudding 215
599. Zingy Blueberry Sauce 215
600. Chocolate Almond Custard 216
601. Honey Stewed Apples 216
602. Greek-Style Compote with Yogurt 216
603. Butterscotch Lava Cakes 216
604. Vanilla Bread Pudding with Apricots 217
605. Mediterranean-Style Carrot Pudding 217
606. Oatmeal Cakes with Mango 218

- 607. Rice Pudding 218
- 608. Ripe Banana Pudding 218
- 609. Picositos Brownies 219
- 610. Fruit Crepes 219
- 611. Crème Caramel 220
- 612. Galaktoboureko 220
- 613. Kourabiedes Almond Cookies 220
- 614. Ekmek Kataifi 221
- 615. Revani Syrup Cake 221
- 616. Almonds and Oats Pudding 222
- 617. Chocolate Cups 222
- 618. Mango Bowls 222
- 619. Cocoa and Pears Cream 222
- 620. Pineapple Pudding 223
- 621. Vanilla Cake 223
- 622. Vanilla Pastry Cream 223
- 623. Small Pumpkin Pastry Cream 224
- 624. Tapioca Pudding 224
- 625. Mango Mug Cake 224
- 626. Chocolate Coffee Pots de Crème .. 224
- 627. Almond Cherry Crumble Cake 225
- 628. Black Forest 225
- 629. Greek Cheesecake with Yogurt 226
- 630. Greek Yogurt and Honey Walnuts .. 226
- 631. Healthy Coconut Blueberry Balls . 226
- 632. Chocolate Matcha Balls 227
- 633. Creamy Yogurt Banana Bowls 227
- 634. Chocolate Mousse 227
- 635. Decadent Croissant Bread Pudding. 227
- 636. Poached Apples with Greek Yogurt and Granola 228
- 637. Jasmine Rice Pudding with Cranberries 228
- 638. Orange and Almond Cupcakes 229
- 639. Bread Pudding 229
- 640. Ruby Pears 229
- 641. Lemon Marmalade 230
- 642. Peach Jam 230
- 643. Raspberry Curd 230
- 644. Pear Jam 230
- 645. Berry Compote 231
- 646. Key Lime Pie 231
- 647. Fruit Cobbler 231
- 648. Stuffed Peaches 232
- 649. Peach Compote 232
- 650. Chocolate Pudding 232
- 651. Refreshing Curd 232
- 652. The Best Jam Ever 233
- 653. Pistachio and Fruits 233
- 654. Avocado Sorbet 233
- 655. Cioccolata Calda 233
- 656. Chocolate Pudding in a Mug 234
- 657. Healthy Fruit Salad with Yogurt Cream 234
- 658. Banana Shake Bowls 235
- 659. Cold Lemon Squares 235
- 660. Strawberries Cream 235
- 661. Sweetened Grapes 235
- 662. Compote Dipped Berries Mix 235
- 663. Popped Quinoa Bars 236
- 664. Almond Orange Pandoro 236
- 665. Mint Chocolate Chip Nice Cream .. 236
- 666. Creamy Berry Crunch 236
- 667. Creme Brûlée with a Gingerbread Twist 237
- 668. Mandarin Cream 237
- 669. Pumpkin Cream 237
- 670. Minty Coconut Cream 237
- 671. Watermelon Cream 238
- 672. Chocolate Lava Cake 238
- 673. Coffee Mocha Ice Cream 238
- 674. Chocolate & Pecan Thins 239
- 675. Banana Blueberry Blast 239
- 676. Sweet Yogurt Bulgur Bowl 239

Conclusion 240

Introduction

The Mediterranean diet refers to the traditional eating habits and lifestyles of people living around the Mediterranean Sea – Italy, Spain, France, Greece, and some North African countries. The Mediterranean diet has become very popular in recent times, as people from these regions have better health and suffer from fewer ailments, such as cancer and cardiovascular issues. Food plays a key role in this.

Research has uncovered the many benefits of this diet. According to the results of a 2013 study, many overweight and diabetic patients showed a surprising improvement in their cardiovascular health after eating the Mediterranean diet for 5 years. The study was conducted among 7000 people in Spain. There was a marked 30% reduction in cardiovascular disease in this high-risk group.

The report took the world by storm after the New England Journal of Medicine published the findings. Several studies have indicated its many health benefits – the Mediterranean diet may stabilize the level of blood sugar, prevent Alzheimer's disease, reduce the risk of heart disease and stroke, improve brain health, ease anxiety and depression, promote weight loss, and even lower the risk of certain types of cancer.

The diet differs from country to country, and even within the regions of these countries because of cultural, ethnic, agricultural, religious, and economic differences. So, there is no one standard Mediterranean diet. However, there are several common factors.

The Mediterranean Diet Pyramid

The Mediterranean diet food pyramid is a nutritional guide to help people eat the right foods in the correct quantities and the prescribed frequency as per the traditional eating habits of people from the Mediterranean coast countries.

The pyramid was developed by the World Health Organization, Harvard School of Public Health, and the old ways Preservation Trust in 1993.

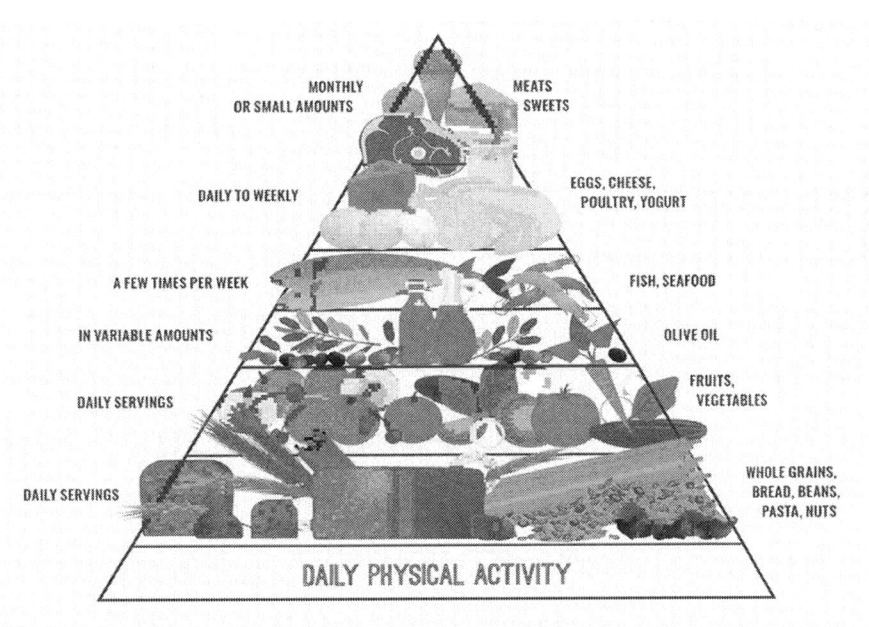

There are 6 food layers in the pyramid with physical activity at the base, which is an important element to maintain a healthy life.

Just above it is the first food layer, consisting of whole grains, bread, beans, pasta, and nuts. It is the strongest layer having foods that are recommended by the Mediterranean diet. Next comes fruits and vegetables. As you move up the pyramid, you will find foods that must be eaten less and less, with the topmost layer consisting of foods that should be avoided or restricted.

The Mediterranean diet food pyramid is easy to understand. It provides an easy way to follow the eating plan.

The Food Layers

- *Whole Grains, Bread, Beans* – The lowest and the widest layer with foods that are strongly recommended. Your meals should be made of mostly these items. Eat whole-wheat bread, whole-wheat pita, whole-grain roll and bun, whole-grain cereal, whole-wheat pasta, and brown rice. 4 t0 6 servings a day will give you plenty of nutrition.

- *Fruits, Vegetables* – Almost as important as the lowest layer. Eat non-starchy vegetables daily like asparagus, broccoli, beets, tomatoes, carrots, cucumber, cabbage, cauliflower, turnips 4 to 8 servings daily. Take 2 to 4 servings of fruits every day. Choose seasonal fresh fruits.

- *Olive oil* – Cook your meals preferably in extra-virgin olive oil. Daily consumption. Healthy for the body, it lowers the low-density lipoprotein cholesterol (LDL) and total cholesterol level. Up to 2 tablespoons of olive oil is allowed. The diet also allows for canola oil.

- *Fish* – Now we come to the food layers that must be consumed weekly and not daily. You can have fish 2 to 3 times a week. Best is fatty sea fish like tuna, herring, salmon, and sardines. Sea fish will give you heart-healthy omega-3 fatty acids and plenty of proteins. Shellfish, including mussels, oysters, shrimp, and clams are also good.

- *Poultry, cheese, yogurt* – The diet should include cheese, yogurt, eggs, chicken, and other poultry products, but in moderation. Maximum 2-3 times a week. Low-fat dairy is best. Soy milk, cheese, or yogurt is better.

- *Meats, sweets* – This is the topmost layer consisting of foods that are best avoided. You can have them once or twice in a month max. Remember, the Mediterranean diet is plant-based. There is very little room for meat, especially red meat. If you cannot live without it, then take red meat in small portions. Choose lean cuts. Have sweets only to celebrate. For instance, you can have a couple of sweets after following the diet for a month.

Recommended Foods

For example, most people living in the region eat a diet rich in whole grains, vegetables, fruits, nuts, seeds, fish, fats, and legumes. It is not a restrictive diet like the many low-fat eating plans. Fat is encouraged, but only from healthy sources, such as polyunsaturated fat (omega-3 fatty acids) that you will get from fish and monounsaturated fat from olive oil.

It is strongly plant-based, but not exclusively vegetarian. The diet recommends limiting the intake of saturated fats and trans fats that you get from red meat and processed foods. You must also limit the intake of dairy products.

- *Fruits and vegetables* – Eat daily. Try to have 7-10 servings every day. Meals are strongly based on plant-based foods. Eat fresh fruits and vegetables. Pick from seasonal varieties.

- *Whole grains* – Eat whole-grain cereal, bread, and pasta. All parts of whole grains – the germ, bran, and endosperm provide healthy nutrients. These nutrients are lost when the grain is refined into white flour.

- *Healthy fats only* – Avoid butter for cooking. Switch to olive oil. Dip your bread in flavored olive oil instead of applying margarine or butter on bread. Trans fats and saturated fats can cause heart disease.
- *Fish* – Fish is encouraged. Eat fatty fish like herring, mackerel, albacore tuna, sardines, lake trout, and salmon. Fatty fish will give you plenty of healthy omega-3 fatty acids that reduce inflammation. Omega-3 fatty acids also reduce blood clotting, decreased triglycerides, and improves heart health. Eat fresh seafood two times a week. Avoid deep-fried fish. Choose grilled fish.
- *Legumes* – Provides the body with minerals, protein, complex carbohydrates, polyunsaturated fatty acids, and fiber. Eat daily.
- *Dairy and poultry* – You can eat eggs, milk products, and chicken throughout the week, but in moderation. Restrict cheese. Go for plain or low-fat Greek yogurt instead of cheese.
- *Nuts and seeds* – 3 or more servings every week. Eat a variety of nuts, seeds, and beans. Walnuts and almonds are all allowed.
- *Red meat* – The Mediterranean diet is not meat-based. You can still have red meat, but only once or twice a week max. If you love red meat, then make sure that it is lean. Take small portions only. Avoid processed meats like salami, sausage, and bologna.
- *Olive Oil* – The key source of fat. Olive oil will give you monounsaturated fat that lowers the LDL or low-density lipoprotein cholesterol and total cholesterol level. Seeds and nuts will also provide you monounsaturated fat. You can also have canola oil but no cream, butter, mayonnaise, or margarine. Take up to 4 tablespoons of olive oil a day. For best results, only take extra-virgin olive oil.
- *Wine* – Red wine is allowed, but with moderation. Don't take more than a glass of red wine daily. Best take only 3-4 days a week.
- *Desserts* – Say no to ice cream, sweets, pies, and chocolate cake. Fresh fruits are good.

Main Components

Focus on natural foods – Avoid processed foods as much as you can

Be flexible – Plan to have a variety of foods

Consume fruits, vegetables, healthy fats, and whole grains daily

Have weekly plans for poultry, fish, eggs, and beans

Take dairy products moderately

Limit red meat intake

Take water instead of soda. Only take wine when you are having a meal.

Chapter 1: Breakfast Recipes

1. Ham Muffins

Preparation Time: 10 minutes | **Cooking time:** 15 minutes | **Servings:** 4

Ingredients:
3 oz ham, chopped
4 eggs, beaten
2 tablespoons coconut flour
½ teaspoon dried oregano
¼ teaspoon dried cilantro
Cooking spray

Directions:
Spray the muffin's molds with cooking spray from inside. In the bowl mix up together beaten eggs, coconut flour, dried oregano, cilantro, and ham. When the liquid is homogenous, pour it into the prepared muffin molds.
Bake the muffins for 15 minutes at 360F. Chill the cooked meal well and only after this remove it from the molds.

Nutrition:
128 Calories | 7.2g Fat | 2.9g Fiber | 10.1g protein

2. Morning Pizza with Sprouts

Preparation Time: 15 minutes | **Cooking time:** 20 minutes | **Servings:** 6

Ingredients:
½ cup wheat flour, whole grain
2 tablespoons butter, softened
¼ teaspoon baking powder
¾ teaspoon salt
5 oz chicken fillet, boiled
2 oz Cheddar cheese, shredded
1 teaspoon tomato sauce
1 oz bean sprouts

Directions:
Make the pizza crust: mix up together wheat flour, butter, baking powder, and salt. Knead the soft and non-sticky dough. Add more wheat flour if needed. Leave the dough for 10 minutes to chill. Then place the dough on the baking paper. Cover it with the second baking paper sheet.
Roll up the dough with the help of the rolling pin to get the round pizza crust. After this, remove the upper baking paper sheet. Transfer the pizza crust to the tray.
Spread the crust with tomato sauce. Then shred the chicken fillet and arrange it over the pizza

crust. Add shredded Cheddar cheese. Bake pizza for 20 minutes at 355F. Then top the cooked pizza with bean sprouts and slice it into servings.

Nutrition:
157 Calories | 8.8g Fat | 0.3g Fiber | 10.5g protein

3. Banana Quinoa

Preparation Time: 10 minutes | **Cooking time:** 12 minutes | **Servings:** 4

Ingredients:
1 cup quinoa
2 cup milk
1 teaspoon vanilla extract
1 teaspoon honey
2 bananas, sliced
¼ teaspoon ground cinnamon

Directions:
Pour milk into the saucepan and add quinoa. Close the lid and cook it over medium heat for 12 minutes or until quinoa will absorb all liquid. Then chill the quinoa for 10-15 minutes and place in the serving mason jars.
Add honey, vanilla extract, and ground cinnamon. Stir well. Top quinoa with banana and stir it before serving.

Nutrition:
279 Calories | 5.3g Fat | 4.6g Fiber | 10.7g protein

4. Egg Casserole with Paprika

Preparation Time: 10 minutes | **Cooking time:** 28 minutes | **Servings:** 4

Ingredients:
2 eggs, beaten
1 red bell pepper, chopped
1 chili pepper, chopped
½ red onion, diced
1 teaspoon canola oil
½ teaspoon salt
1 teaspoon paprika
1 tablespoon fresh cilantro, chopped
1 garlic clove, diced
1 teaspoon butter, softened
¼ teaspoon chili flakes

Directions:
Brush the casserole mold with canola oil and pour beaten eggs inside. After this, toss the butter in the skillet and melt it over medium heat. Add chili pepper and red bell pepper.
After this, add red onion and cook the vegetables for 7-8 minutes over medium heat. Stir them from time to time. Transfer the vegetables to the casserole mold.
Add salt, paprika, cilantro, diced garlic, and chili flakes. Stir gently with the help of a spatula to get a homogenous mixture. Bake the casserole for 20 minutes at 355F in the oven. Then chill the meal well and cut into servings. Transfer the casserole to the serving plates with the help of the spatula.

Nutrition:
68 Calories | 4.5g Fat | 1g Fiber | 3.4g protein

5. Cauliflower Fritters

Preparation Time: 10 minutes | **Cooking time:** 10 minutes | **Servings:** 2

Ingredients:
1 cup cauliflower, shredded
1 egg, beaten
1 tablespoon wheat flour, whole grain
1 oz Parmesan, grated
½ teaspoon ground black pepper
1 tablespoon canola oil

Directions:
In the mixing bowl mix up together shredded cauliflower and egg. Add wheat flour, grated Parmesan, and ground black pepper. Stir the mixture with the help of the fork until it is homogenous and smooth.
Pour canola oil into the skillet and bring it to a boil. Make the fritters from the cauliflower mixture with the help of the fingertips or use a spoon and transfer in the hot oil. Roast the fritters for 4 minutes from each side over medium-low heat.

Nutrition:
167 Calories | 12.3g Fat | 1.5g Fiber | 8.8g protein

6. Creamy Oatmeal with Figs

Preparation Time: 10 minutes | **Cooking time:** 20 minutes | **Servings:** 5

Ingredients:
2 cups oatmeal

1 ½ cup milk
1 tablespoon butter
3 figs, chopped
1 tablespoon honey

Directions:
Pour milk into the saucepan. Add oatmeal and close the lid. Cook the oatmeal for 15 minutes over medium-low heat. Then add chopped figs and honey.
Add butter and mix up the oatmeal well. Cook it for 5 minutes more. Close the lid and let the cooked breakfast rest for 10 minutes before serving.

Nutrition:
222 Calories | 6g Fat | 4.4g Fiber | 7.1g protein

7. Baked Oatmeal with Cinnamon

Preparation Time: 10 minutes | **Cooking time:** 25 minutes | **Servings:** 4

Ingredients:
1 cup oatmeal
1/3 cup milk
1 pear, chopped
1 teaspoon vanilla extract
1 tablespoon Splenda
1 teaspoon butter
½ teaspoon ground cinnamon
1 egg, beaten

Directions:
In the big bowl mix up together oatmeal, milk, egg, vanilla extract, Splenda, and ground cinnamon. Melt butter and add it to the oatmeal mixture. Then add chopped pear and stir it well. Transfer the oatmeal mixture to the casserole mold and flatten gently. Cover it with foil and secure edges. Bake the oatmeal for 25 minutes at 350F.

Nutrition:
151 Calories | 3.9g Fat | 3.3g Fiber | 4.9g protein

8. Almond Chia Porridge

Preparation Time: 10 minutes | **Cooking time:** 30 minutes | **Servings:** 4

Ingredients:
3 cups organic almond milk
1/3 cup chia seeds, dried
1 teaspoon vanilla extract
1 tablespoon honey
¼ teaspoon ground cardamom

Directions:
Pour almond milk into the saucepan and bring it to boil. Then chill the almond milk to room temperature (or appx. For 10-15 minutes). Add vanilla extract, honey, and ground cardamom. Stir well. After this, add chia seeds and stir again. Close the lid and let chia seeds soak the liquid for 20-25 minutes. Transfer the cooked porridge into the serving ramekin's.

Nutrition:
150 Calories | 7.3g Fat | 6.1g Fiber | 3.7g protein

9. Cocoa Oatmeal

Preparation Time: 10 minutes | **Cooking time:** 15 minutes | **Servings:** 2

Ingredients:
1 ½ cup oatmeal
1 tablespoon cocoa powder
½ cup heavy cream
¼ cup of water
1 teaspoon vanilla extract
1 tablespoon butter
2 tablespoons Splenda

Directions:
Mix up together oatmeal with cocoa powder and Splenda. Transfer the mixture to the saucepan. Add vanilla extract, water, and heavy cream. Stir it gently with the help of the spatula.
Close the lid and cook it for 10-15 minutes over medium-low heat. Remove the cooked cocoa oatmeal from the heat and add butter. Stir it well.

Nutrition:
230 Calories | 10.6g Fat | 3.5g Fiber | 4.6g protein

10. Avocado Egg Scramble

Preparation Time: 8 minutes | **Cooking time:** 15 minutes | **Servings:** 4

Ingredients:
4 eggs, beaten
1 white onion, diced
1 tablespoon avocado oil
1 avocado, finely chopped
½ teaspoon chili flakes

1 oz Cheddar cheese, shredded
½ teaspoon salt
1 tablespoon fresh parsley

Directions:
Pour avocado oil into the skillet and bring it to a boil. Then add diced onion and roast it until it is light brown. Meanwhile, mix up together chili flakes, beaten eggs, and salt.
Pour the egg mixture over the cooked onion and cook the mixture for 1 minute over medium heat. After this, scramble the eggs well with the help of the fork or spatula. Cook the eggs until they are solid but soft.
After this, add chopped avocado and shredded cheese. Stir the scrambled eggs well and transfer them to the serving plates. Sprinkle the meal with fresh parsley.

Nutrition:
236 Calories | 20g Fat | 4g Fiber | 8.6g Protein

11.   Breakfast Tostadas

Preparation Time: 15 minutes | **Cooking time:** 6 minutes | **Servings:** 6

Ingredients:
½ white onion, diced
1 tomato, chopped
1 cucumber, chopped
1 tablespoon fresh cilantro, chopped
½ jalapeno pepper, chopped
1 tablespoon lime juice
6 corn tortillas
1 tablespoon canola oil
2 oz Cheddar cheese, shredded
½ cup white beans, canned, drained
6 eggs
½ teaspoon butter
½ teaspoon Sea salt

Directions:
Make Pico de Galo: in the salad bowl, combine diced white onion, tomato, cucumber, fresh cilantro, and jalapeno pepper. Then add lime juice and a ½ tablespoon of canola oil. Mix up the mixture well. Pico de Galo is cooked. After this, preheat the oven to 390F. Line the tray with baking paper. Arrange the corn tortillas on the baking paper and brush with remaining canola oil from both sides. Bake the tortillas for 10 minutes or until they start to be crunchy. Chill the cooked crunchy tortillas well. Meanwhile, toss the butter in the skillet.
Crack the eggs in the melted butter and sprinkle them with sea salt. Fry the eggs until the egg whites become white (cooked). Approximately for 3-5 minutes over medium heat. After this, mash the beans until you get a puree texture. Spread the bean puree on the corn tortillas. Add fried eggs. Then top the eggs with Pico de Galo and shredded Cheddar cheese.

Nutrition:
246 Calories | 11g Fat | 4.7g Fiber | 13.7g protein

12.   Parmesan Omelet

Preparation Time: 5 minutes | **Cooking time:** 10 minutes | **Servings:** 2

Ingredients:
1 tablespoon cream cheese
2 eggs, beaten
¼ teaspoon paprika
½ teaspoon dried oregano
¼ teaspoon dried dill
1 oz Parmesan, grated
1 teaspoon coconut oil

Directions:
Mix up together cream cheese with eggs, dried oregano, and dill. Place coconut oil in the skillet and heat it until it will coat all the skillet. Then pour the egg mixture into the skillet and flatten it. Add grated Parmesan and close the lid. Cook omelet for 10 minutes over low heat. Then transfer the cooked omelet to the serving plate and sprinkle with paprika.

Nutrition:
148 Calories | 11.5g Fat | 0.3g Fiber | 10.6g protein

13.   Watermelon Pizza

Preparation Time: 10 minutes | **Cooking time:** 0 minute | **Servings:** 2

Ingredients:
9 oz watermelon slice
1 tablespoon Pomegranate sauce
2 oz Feta cheese, crumbled
1 tablespoon fresh cilantro, chopped

Directions:
Place the watermelon slice on a plate and sprinkle it with crumbled Feta cheese. Add fresh cilantro. After this, sprinkle the pizza with Pomegranate juice generously. Cut the pizza into servings.

Nutrition:
143 Calories | 6.2g Fat | 0.6g Fiber | 5.1g protein

14. Cinnamon Roll Oats

Preparation Time: 7 minutes | **Cooking time:** 10 minutes | **Servings:** 4

Ingredients:
½ cup rolled oats
1 cup milk
1 teaspoon vanilla extract
1 teaspoon ground cinnamon
2 teaspoon honey
2 tablespoons Plain yogurt
1 teaspoon butter

Directions:
Pour milk into the saucepan and bring it to a boil. Add rolled oats and stir well. Close the lid and simmer the oats for 5 minutes over medium heat. The cooked oats will absorb all milk.
Then add butter and stir the oats well. In the separated bowl, whisk together Plain yogurt with honey, cinnamon, and vanilla extract. Transfer the cooked oats to the serving bowls. Top the oats with the yogurt mixture in the shape of the wheel.

Nutrition:
243 Calories | 20.2g Fat | 1g Fiber | 13.3g protein

15. Pumpkin Oatmeal with Spices

Preparation Time: 10 minutes | **Cooking time:** 13 minutes | **Servings:** 6

Ingredients:
2 cups oatmeal
1 cup of coconut milk
1 cup milk
1 teaspoon Pumpkin pie spices
2 tablespoons pumpkin puree
1 tablespoon Honey
½ teaspoon butter

Directions:
Pour coconut milk and milk into the saucepan. Add butter and bring the liquid to a boil. Add oatmeal, stir well with the help of a spoon, and close the lid.
Simmer the oatmeal for 7 minutes over medium heat. Meanwhile, mix up together honey, pumpkin pie spices, and pumpkin puree. When the oatmeal is cooked, add pumpkin puree mixture, and stir well. Transfer the cooked breakfast to the serving plates.

Nutrition:
232 Calories | 12.5g Fat | 3.8g Fiber | 5.9g protein

16. Mediterranean Pita Breakfast

Preparation Time: 22 minutes | **Cooking time:** 3 minutes | **Servings:** 2

Ingredients:
1/4 cup of sweet red pepper, chopped
1/4 cup of chopped onion
1 cup of egg substitute
1/8 teaspoon of salt
1/8 teaspoon of pepper
1 small chopped tomato
1/2 cup of fresh torn baby spinach
1-1/2 teaspoons of minced fresh basil
2 whole size pita bread
2 tablespoons of crumbled feta cheese

Directions:
Coat a small size non-stick skillet with a cooking spray. Stir in the onion and red pepper for 3 minutes over medium heat. Add your egg substitute and season with salt and pepper. Stir cook until it sets. Mix the torn spinach, chopped tomatoes, and mince basil. Scoop onto the pitas. Top vegetable mixture with your egg mixture. Sprinkle with crumbled feta cheese and serve immediately.

Nutrition:
267 Calories | 41g Carbohydrates | 3g Fiber | 20g Protein

17. Hummus Deviled Egg

Preparation Time: 10 minutes | **Cooking time:** 0 minute | **Servings:** 6

Ingredients:
1/4 cup of finely diced cucumber
1/4 cup of finely diced tomato
2 teaspoons of fresh lemon juice
1/8 teaspoon salt
6 hard-cooked peeled eggs, sliced half lengthwise
1/3 cup of roasted garlic hummus or any hummus flavor
Chopped fresh parsley (optional)

Directions:
Combine the tomato, lemon juice, cucumber, and salt then gently mix. Remove the yolks from the halved eggs and store them for later use. Scoop a heaping teaspoon of hummus in each half egg. Top with parsley and half-teaspoon tomato-cucumber mixture. Serve immediately

Nutrition:
40 Calories | 3g Carbohydrates | 1g Fiber | 4g Protein

18. Apple Cheese Scones

Preparation Time: 20 minutes | **Cooking time:** 15 minutes | **Servings:** 10

Ingredients:
1 cup of all-purpose flour
1 cup whole wheat flour, white
3 tablespoons sugar
1 1/2 teaspoons of baking powder
1/2 teaspoon salt
1/2 teaspoon of ground cinnamon
1/4 teaspoon of baking soda
1 diced Granny Smith apple
1/2 cup shredded sharp Cheddar cheese, reduced-Fat | 1/3 cup applesauce, natural or unsweetened
1/4 cup milk, fat-free (skim)
3 tablespoons of melted butter
1 egg

Directions:
Preheat your oven to 425 degrees F. Prepare the baking sheet by lining it with parchment paper. Combine all dry ingredients in a bowl and mix. Stir in the cheese and apple. Set aside. Whisk all the wet ingredients together. Pour over the dry mixture until blended and turns like a sticky dough.
Knead the dough on a floured surface about 5 times. Pat and then stretch into an 8-inch circle. Slice into 10 diagonal cuts.
Place on the baking sheet and spray top with cooking spray. Bake for 15 minutes or until lightly golden. Serve.

Nutrition:
169 Calories | 26g Carbohydrates | 2g Fiber | 5g Protein

19. Bacon and Egg Wrap

Preparation Time: 15 minutes | **Cooking time:** 15 minutes | **Servings:** 4

Ingredients:
1 cup egg substitute, cholesterol-free
1/4 cup Parmesan cheese, shredded
2 slices diced Canadian bacon
1/2 teaspoon red hot pepper sauce
1/4 teaspoon of black pepper
4x7-inch whole wheat tortillas
1 cup of baby spinach leaves

Directions:
Preheat your oven at 325 degrees F. Combine the first five ingredients to make the filling. Pour the mixture into a 9-inch glass dish sprayed with butter-flavored cooking spray.
Bake for 15 minutes or until the egg sets. Remove from the oven. Place the tortillas for a minute in the oven. Cut baked egg mixture into quarters. Arrange one quarter at the center of each tortilla and top with ¼-cup spinach. Fold tortilla from the bottom to the center and then both sides to the center to enclose. Serve immediately.

Nutrition:
195 Calories | 20g Carbohydrates | 3g Fiber | 15g Protein

20. Orange-Blueberry Muffin

Preparation Time: 10 minutes | **Cooking time:** 20 - 25 minutes | **Servings:** 12

Ingredients:
1 3/4 cups of all-purpose flour
1/3 cup sugar
2 1/2 teaspoons of baking powder
1/2 teaspoon of baking soda
1/2 teaspoon salt
1/2 teaspoon of ground cinnamon
3/4 cup milk, fat-free (skim)
1/4 cup butter, (1/2 stick) melted and cooled
1 egg, large, lightly beaten
3 tablespoons thawed orange juice concentrate
1 teaspoon vanilla
3/4 cup fresh blueberries (or thawed frozen but it takes longer to bake)

Directions:
Preheat your oven to 400 degrees F. Follow steps 2 to 5 of Buckwheat Apple-Raisin Muffin Fill up the muffin cups ¾-full of the mixture and bake for 20 to 25 minutes. Let it cool for 5 minutes and serve warm.

Nutrition:
149 Calories | 24g Carbohydrates | 3g Fiber

21. Baked Ginger Oatmeal with Pear Topping

Preparation Time: 10 minutes | **Cooking time:** 15 minutes | **Servings:** 2

Ingredients:
1 cup of old-fashioned oats
3/4 cup milk, fat-free (skim)
1 egg white
1 1/2 teaspoons grated ginger, fresh or 3/4 teaspoon of ground ginger
2 tablespoons brown sugar, divided
1/2 ripe diced pear

Directions:
Spray 2x6 ounce ramekins with a non-stick cooking spray. Start preheating the oven to 350 degrees F. Combine the first four ingredients and a tablespoon of sugar then mix well. Pour evenly between the 2 ramekins. Top with pear slices and the remaining tablespoon of sugar. Bake for 15 minutes. Serve warm.

Nutrition:
268 Calories | 2g Carbohydrates | 5g Fiber | 10g Protein

22. Greek-Style Veggie Omelet

Preparation Time: 10 minutes | **Cooking time:** 20 minutes | **Servings:** 2

Ingredients:
4 large eggs
2 tablespoons of fat-free milk
1/8 teaspoon salt
3 teaspoons of olive oil, divided
2 cups baby Portobello, sliced
1/4 cup of finely chopped onion
1 cup of fresh baby spinach
3 tablespoons feta cheese, crumbled
2 tablespoons ripe olives, sliced
Freshly ground pepper

Directions:
Whisk together the first three ingredients. Heat 2 tablespoons of oil in a non-stick skillet over medium-high heat. Sauté the onions and mushroom for 5-6 minutes or until golden brown. Add in the spinach and cook until wilted. Remove mixture from pan.
Using the same pan, heat over medium-low heat the remaining oil. Pour your egg mixture and as it starts to set, push the edges towards the center to let the uncooked mixture flow underneath. When eggs are set scoop the veggie mixture on one side. Sprinkle with olives and feta then fold the other side to close. Cut in half and sprinkle with pepper to serve.

Nutrition:
271 Calories | 7g Carbohydrates | 2g Fiber | 18g Protein

23. Ham & Egg Pitas

Preparation Time: 5 minutes | **Cooking time:** 15 minutes | **Servings:** 4

Ingredients:
6 Eggs
2 Shallots, Chopped
1 Teaspoon Olive Oil
1/3 Cup Smoked Ham, Chopped
1/3 Cup Sweet Green Pepper, Chopped
1/4 Cup Brie Cheese

Sea Salt & Black Pepper to Taste
4 Lettuce Leaves
2 Pita Breads, Whole Wheat

Directions:
Start by heating your olive oil in a pan using medium heat. Add in your shallots and green pepper, letting them cook for five minutes while stirring frequently.
Get out a bowl and whisk your eggs, sprinkling in your salt and pepper. Make sure your eggs are well beaten. Pour the eggs into the pan, and then add the ham and cheese. Stir well, and cook until your mixture thickens. Slice the pitas in half, and open the pockets. Spread a teaspoon of mustard in each pocket, and add a lettuce leaf in each one. Spread the egg mixture in each one and serve.

Nutrition:
610 Calories | 41g Protein | 21g Fats

24. Breakfast Couscous

Preparation Time: 5 minutes | **Cooking time:** 15 minutes | **Servings:** 4

Ingredients:
3 Cups Milk, Low Fat | 1 Cinnamon Stick
1/2 Cup Apricots, Dried & Chopped
1/4 Cup Currants, Dried
1 Cup Couscous, Uncooked
Pinch Sea Salt, Fine
4 Teaspoons Butter, Melted
6 Teaspoons Brown Sugar

Directions:
Heat a pan up with milk and cinnamon using medium-high heat. Cook for three minutes before removing the pan from heat.
Add in your apricots, couscous, salt, currants, and sugar. Stir well, and then cover. Leave it to the side, and let it sit for fifteen minutes.
Throw out the cinnamon stick, and divide between bowls. Sprinkle it with brown sugar before serving.

Nutrition:
520 Calories | 39g Protein | 28g Fats

25. Peach Breakfast Salad

Preparation Time: 10 minutes | **Cooking time:** 0 minute | **Servings:** 1

Ingredients:
1/4 Cup Walnuts, Chopped & Toasted
1 Teaspoon Honey, Raw
1 Peach, Pitted & Sliced
1/2 Cup Cottage Cheese, Nonfat & Room Temperature
1 Tablespoon Mint, Fresh & Chopped
1 Lemon, Zested

Directions:
Place your cottage cheese in a bowl, and top with peach slices and walnuts. Drizzle with honey and top with mint.
Sprinkle on your lemon zest before serving immediately.

Nutrition:
280 Calories | 39g Protein | 11g Fats

26. Savory Oats

Preparation Time: 10 minutes | **Cooking time:** 10 minutes | **Servings:** 2

Ingredients:
1/2 Cup Steel Cut Oats
1 Cup Water
1 Tomato, Large & Chopped
1 Cucumber, Chopped
1 Tablespoon Olive Oil
Sea Salt & Black Pepper to Taste
Flat Leaf Parsley, Chopped to Garnish
Parmesan Cheese, Low Fat & Freshly Grated

Directions:
Bring your oats and a cup of water to a boil using a saucepan over high heat. Stir often until your water is completely absorbed, which will take roughly fifteen minutes. Divide between two bowls, and top with tomatoes and cucumber. Drizzle with olive oil and top with parmesan. Garnish with parsley before serving.

Nutrition:
408 Calories | 28g Protein | 13g Fats

27. Tahini & Apple Toast

Preparation Time: 15 minutes | **Cooking time:** 0 minute | **Servings:** 1

Ingredients:
2 Tablespoons Tahini
2 Slices Whole Wheat Bread, Toasted
1 Teaspoon Honey, Raw
1 Apple, Small, Cored & Sliced Thin

Directions:
Start by spreading the tahini over your toast, and then lay your apples over it. drizzle with honey before serving.

Nutrition:
366 Calories | 29g Protein | 13g Fats

28. Scrambled Basil Eggs

Preparation Time: 5 minutes | **Cooking time:** 10 minutes | **Servings:** 2

Ingredients:
4 Eggs, Large
2 Tablespoons Fresh Basil, Chopped Fine
2 Tablespoons Gruyere Cheese, Grated
1 Tablespoon Cream
1 Tablespoon Olive Oil
2 Cloves Garlic, Minced
Sea Salt & Black Pepper to Taste

Directions:
Get out a large bowl and beat your basil, cheese, cream, and eggs together. Whisk until it's well combined. Get out a large skillet over medium-low heat, and heat your oil. Add in your garlic, cooking for a minute. It should turn golden.
Pour the egg mixture into your skillet over the garlic, and then continue to scramble as they cook so they become soft and fluffy. Season with salt and pepper, and serve warm.

Nutrition:
360 Calories | 29g Protein | 14g Fats

29. Greek Potatoes & Eggs

Preparation Time: 10 minutes | **Cooking time:** 30 minutes | **Servings:** 2

Ingredients:
3 tomatoes, seeded & roughly chopped
2 tablespoons basil, fresh & chopped
1 clove garlic, minced
2 tablespoons + ½ cup olive oil, divided
sea salt & black pepper to taste
3 russet potatoes, large
4 eggs, large
1 teaspoon oregano, fresh & chopped

Directions:
Start by getting out your food processor and place your tomatoes in, pureeing them with the skin on.
Add your garlic, two tablespoons of oil, salt, pepper, and basil. Pulse until it's well combined. Place this mixture in a skillet, cooking while covered for twenty to twenty-five minutes over low heat. Your sauce should be thickened as well as bubbly.
Dice your potatoes into cubes, and then place them in a skillet with a ½ a cup of olive oil in a skillet using medium-low heat.
Fry your potatoes until crisp and browned. This should take five minutes, and then cover the skillet, reducing the heat to low. Steam them until your potatoes are done.
Crack your eggs into the tomato sauce, and cook using low heat for six minutes. Your eggs should be set.
Remove the potatoes from your pan, and drain using paper towels. Place them in a bowl. Sprinkle in your salt, pepper, and oregano, and then serve your eggs with potatoes. Drizzle your sauce over the mixture, and serve warm.

Nutrition:
348 Calories | 27g Protein | 12g Fats

30. Vegetable Frittata

Preparation Time: 5 minutes | **Cooking time:** 10 minutes | **Servings:** 2

Ingredients:
1/2 baby eggplant, peeled & diced
1 handful baby spinach leaves
1 tablespoon olive oil
3 eggs, large
1 teaspoon almond milk
1-ounce goat cheese, crumbled
1/4 small red pepper, chopped
sea salt & black pepper to taste

Directions:
Start by heating the broiler in your oven, and then beat the eggs together with almond milk. Make sure it's well combined, and then get out a nonstick, ovenproof skillet. Place it over medium-high heat, and then add in your olive oil.

Once your oil is heated, add in your eggs. Spread your spinach over this mixture in an even layer, and top with the rest of your vegetables.

Reduce your heat to medium, and sprinkle with salt and pepper. Allow your vegetables and eggs to cook for five minutes. The bottom half of your eggs should be firm, and your vegetables should be tender. Top with goat cheese, and then broil on the middle rack for three to five minutes. Your eggs should be all the way done, and your cheese should be melted. Slice into wedges and serve warm.

Nutrition:
340 Calories | 16g Fats | 37g protein

31. Mini Lettuce Wraps

Preparation Time: 15 minutes | **Cooking time:** 0 minute | **Servings:** 4

Ingredients:
1 cucumber, diced
1 red onion, sliced
1-ounce feta cheese, low fat & crumbed
1 lemon, juiced
1 tomato, diced
1 tablespoon olive oil
12 small iceberg lettuce leaves
sea salt & black pepper to taste

Directions:
Combine your tomato, onion, feta, and cucumber in a bowl. Mix your oil and juice, and season with salt and pepper.

Fill each leaf with the vegetable mixture, and roll them tightly. Use a toothpick to keep them together to serve.

Nutrition:
291 Calories | 27g Protein | 10g Fats

32. Curry Apple Couscous

Preparation Time: 20 minutes | **Cooking time:** 5 minutes | **Servings:** 4

Ingredients:
2 teaspoons olive oil
2 leeks, white parts only, sliced
1 apple, diced
2 tablespoons curry powder
2 cups couscous, cooked & whole wheat
1/2 cup pecans, chopped

Directions:
Heat your oil in a skillet using medium heat. Add the leeks, and cook until tender, which will take five minutes. Add in your apple, and cook until soft.

Add in your curry powder and couscous, and stir well. Remove from heat, and mix in your nuts before serving immediately.

Nutrition:
330 Calories | 30g Protein | 12g Fats

33. Herb Flounder

Preparation Time: 20 minutes | **Cooking time:** 1 hour and 5 minutes | **Servings:** 4

Ingredients:
1/2 cup flat-leaf parsley, lightly packed
1/4 cup olive oil
4 cloves garlic, peeled & halved
2 tablespoons rosemary, fresh
2 tablespoons thyme leaves, fresh
2 tablespoons sage, fresh
2 tablespoons lemon zest, fresh
4 flounder fillets
sea salt & black pepper to taste

Directions:
Start by heating your oven to 350, and then put all the ingredients except for the flounder in the processor. Blend until it forms a thick paste. Put your fillets on a baking sheet, and brush them down with the paste. Allow them to chill in the fridge for an hour. Bake for ten minutes. Season with salt and pepper, and serve warm.

Nutrition:
307 Calories | 11g Fats | 34g protein

34. Cauliflower Quinoa

Preparation Time: 15 minutes | **Cooking time:** 10 minutes | **Servings:** 4

Ingredients:
1 1/2 cups quinoa, cooked
3 tablespoons olive oil
3 cups cauliflower florets
2 spring onions, chopped
1 tablespoon red wine vinegar
sea salt & black pepper to taste
1 tablespoon red wine vinegar
1 tablespoon chives, chopped
1 tablespoon parsley, chopped

Directions:
Start by heating a pan over medium-high heat. Add your oil. Once your oil is hot, add in your spring onions and cook for about two minutes. Add in your quinoa and cauliflower, and then add in the rest of the ingredients. Mix well, and cover. Cook for nine minutes over medium heat, and divide between plates to serve.

Nutrition:
290 Calories | 26g Protein | 14g Fats

35. Spinach Omelet

Preparation Time: 10 minutes | **Cooking time:** 20 minutes | **Servings:** 4

Ingredients:
3 tablespoons olive oil
1 onion, small & chopped
1 clove garlic, minced
4 tomatoes, large, cored & chopped
1 teaspoon sea salt, fine
8 eggs, beaten
¼ teaspoon black pepper
2 ounces feta cheese, crumbled
1 tablespoon flat-leaf parsley, fresh & chopped

Directions:
Start by heating your oven to 400, and then place your olive oil in an ovenproof skillet. Place your skillet over high heat, adding in your onions. Cook for five to seven minutes. Your onions should soften.
Add your tomatoes, salt, pepper, and garlic in. simmer for another five minutes, and then pour in your beaten eggs. Mix lightly, and cook for three to five minutes. They should be set at the bottom. Put the pan in the oven, baking for five minutes more. Remove from the oven, topping with parsley and feta. Serve warm.

Nutrition:
280 Calories | 19g Fats | 31g protein

36. Almond Pancakes

Preparation Time: 15 minutes | **Cooking time:** 15 minutes | **Servings:** 6

Ingredients:
2 cups almond milk, unsweetened & room temperature
2 eggs, large & room temperature
½ cup coconut oil, melted + more for greasing
2 teaspoons honey, raw
¼ teaspoon sea salt, fine
½ teaspoon baking soda
1 ½ cups whole wheat flour
½ cup almond flour
1 ½ teaspoons baking powder
¼ teaspoon cinnamon, ground

Directions:
Get out a large bowl and whisk your coconut oil, eggs, almond milk, and honey, blending until it's mixed well.
Get a medium bowl out and sift together your baking powder, baking soda, almond flour, sea salt, whole wheat flour, and cinnamon. Mix well. Add your flour mixture to your milk mixture, and whisk well.
Get out a large skillet and grease it using your coconut oil before placing it over medium-high heat. Add in your pancake batter in ½ cup measurements.
Cook for three minutes or until the edges are firm. The bottom of your pancake should be golden, and bubbles should break the surface. Flip and cook for two minutes on the other side. They should be cooked all the way through, and then get out a plate to put them on.
Wipe your skillet with a clean paper towel, and repeat until all your batter is used. Make sure to re-grease your skillet, and top with fresh fruit if desired.

Nutrition:
205 Calories | 16g Fats | 36g protein

37. Buckwheat Buttermilk Pancakes

Preparation Time: 2 minutes | **Cooking time:** 18 minutes | **Servings:** 9

Ingredients:
1/2 cup of buckwheat flour
1/2 cup of all-purpose flour
2 teaspoons of baking powder
1 teaspoon of brown sugar
2 tablespoons of olive oil
2 large eggs
1 cup of reduced-fat buttermilk

Directions:
Combine the first four ingredients in a bowl. Add the oil, buttermilk, and eggs and mix until thoroughly blended. Place a skillet or griddle over medium heat and spray with non-stick cooking spray. Pour ¼ cup of the batter over the skillet and cook for 1-2 minutes on each side or until they turn golden brown. Serve immediately.

Nutrition:
108 Calories | 12g Carbohydrates | 1g Fiber | 4g Protein

38. French Toast with Almonds and Peach Compote

Preparation Time: 10 minutes | **Cooking time:** 15 minutes | **Servings:** 4

Ingredients:
Compote:
3 tablespoons of sugar substitute, sucralose-based
1/3 cup + 2 tablespoons of water, divided
1 1/2 cups of fresh peeled or frozen, thawed and drained sliced peaches
2 tablespoons peach fruit spread, no-sugar-added
1/4 teaspoon of ground cinnamon
Almond French toast
1/4 cup of (skim) fat-free milk
3 tablespoons of sugar substitute, sucralose-based
2 whole eggs
2 egg whites
1/2 teaspoon of almond extract
1/8 teaspoon salt
4 slices of multigrain bread
1/3 cup of sliced almonds

Directions:
To make the compote, dissolve 3 tablespoons sucralose in 1/3 cup of water in a medium saucepan over high-medium heat. Stir in the peaches and bring to a boil. Reduce the heat to medium and continue to cook uncovered for another 5 minutes or until the peaches softened. Combine remaining water and fruit spread then stir into the peaches in the saucepan. Cook for another minute or until syrup thickens. Remove from heat and stir in the cinnamon. Cover to keep warm.

To make the French toast. Combine the milk and sucralose in a large size shallow dish and whisk until it completely dissolves. Whisk in the egg whites, eggs, almond extract, and salt. Dip both sides of the bread slices for 3 minutes in the egg mixture or until completely soaked. Sprinkle both sides with sliced almonds and press firmly to adhere.

Spray a non-stick skillet or griddle with cooking spray and place over medium-high heat. Cook bread slices on a griddle for 2 to 3 minutes on both sides or until it turns light brown. Serve topped with the peach compote.

Nutrition:
277 Calories | 31g Carbohydrates | 7g Fiber | 12g Protein

39. Mixed Berries Oatmeal with Sweet Vanilla Cream

Preparation Time: 5 minutes | **Cooking time:** 5 minutes | **Servings:** 4

Ingredients:
2 cups of water
1 cup of quick-cooking oats
1 tablespoon of sucralose-based sugar substitute
1/2 teaspoon of ground cinnamon
1/8 teaspoon salt
Cream
3/4 cup of fat-free half-and-half
3 tablespoons of sucralose-based sugar substitute
1/2 teaspoon of vanilla extract

1/2 teaspoon of almond extract
Toppings
1 1/2 cups of fresh or frozen and thawed blueberries
1/2 cup of fresh or frozen and thawed raspberries

Directions:
Boil water in high-heat and stir in the oats. Reduce heat to medium while cooking oats, uncovered for 2 minutes or until thick. Remove from heat and stir in sugar substitute, salt, and cinnamon. In a medium-size bowl, combine all the cream ingredients until well blended. Scoop cooked oatmeal into 4 equal portions and pour the sweet cream over. Top with the berries and serve.

Nutrition:
150 Calories | 30g Carbohydrates | 5g Fiber | 5g Protein

40. Choco-Strawberry Crepe

Preparation Time: 5 minutes | **Cooking time:** 10 minutes | **Servings:** 4

Ingredients:
1 cup of wheat all-purpose flour
2/3 cup of low-fat (1%) milk
2 egg whites
1 egg
3 tablespoons sugar
3 tablespoons of unsweetened cocoa powder
1 tablespoon of cooled melted butter
1/2 teaspoon salt
2 teaspoons of canola oil
3 tablespoons of strawberry fruit spread
3 1/2 cups of sliced thawed frozen or fresh strawberries
1/2 cup of fat-free thawed frozen whipped topping
Fresh mint leaves (if desired)

Directions:
Whisk the first eight ingredients in a large size bowl until smooth and thoroughly blended.
Brush ¼-teaspoon oil on a small size non-stick skillet over medium heat. Pour ¼-cup of the batter onto the center and swirl to coat the pan with batter.
Cook for a minute or until crêpe turns dull and the edges dry. Flip on the other side and cook for another half a minute. Repeat the process with the remaining mixture and oil.
Scoop ¼-cup of thawed strawberries at the center of the crepe and roll up to cover the filling. Top with 2 tablespoons whipped cream and garnish with mint before serving.

Nutrition:
334 Calories | 58g Carbohydrates | 5g Fiber | 10g Protein

41. No Crust Asparagus-Ham Quiche

Preparation Time: 5 minutes | **Cooking time:** 42 minutes | **Servings:** 6

Ingredients:
2 cups 1/2-inch sliced asparagus
1 red chopped bell pepper
1 cup milk, low-fat (1%)
2 tablespoons of wheat all-purpose flour
4 egg whites
1 egg, whole
1 cup cooked chopped deli ham
2 tablespoons fresh chopped tarragon or basil
1/2 teaspoon of salt (optional)
1/4 teaspoon of black pepper
1/2 cup Swiss cheese, finely shredded

Directions:
Preheat your oven to 350 degrees F. Microwave bell pepper and asparagus in a tablespoon of water on HIGH for 2 minutes. Drain. Whisk flour and milk, and then add egg and egg whites until well combined. Stir in the vegetables and the remaining ingredients except for the cheese. Pour in a 9-inch size pie dish and bake for 35 minutes. Sprinkle cheese over the quiche and bake for another 5 minutes or until the cheese melts. Let it cool for 5 minutes then cut into 6 wedges to serve.

Nutrition:
138 Calories | 8g Carbohydrates | 1g Fiber | 13g Protein

42. Barley Porridge

Preparation Time: 10 minutes | **Cooking time:** 20 minutes | **Servings:** 4

Ingredients:
1 cup wheat berries
1 cup barley
2 cups almond milk, unsweetened + more for serving
½ cup blueberries
½ cup pomegranate seeds
2 cups water
½ cup hazelnuts, toasted & chopped
¼ cup honey, raw

Directions:
Get out a saucepan and put it over medium-high heat, and then add in your almond milk, water, barley, and wheat berries. Bring it to a boil before reducing the heat to low, and allow it to simmer for twenty-five minutes. Stir frequently. Your grains should become tender.
Top each serving with blueberries, pomegranate seeds, hazelnuts, a tablespoon of honey, and a splash of almond milk.

Nutrition:
150 Calories | 10g Fats | 29g protein

43. Yogurt with Blueberries, Honey, and Mint

Preparation Time: 5 minutes | **Cooking time:** 0 minute | **Servings:** 2

Ingredients:
2 cups unsweetened nonfat plain Greek yogurt
1 cup blueberries
3 tablespoons honey
2 tablespoons fresh mint leaves, chopped

Directions:
Apportion the yogurt between 2 small bowls. Top with blueberries, honey, and mint.

Nutrition:
126 Calories | 12g Fats | 37g protein

44. Berry and Yogurt Parfait

Preparation Time: 5 minutes | **Cooking time:** 0 minute | **Servings:** 2

Ingredients:
1 cup raspberries
1½ cups unsweetened nonfat plain Greek yogurt
1 cup blackberries
¼ cup chopped walnuts

Directions:
In 2 bowls, layer the raspberries, yogurt, and blackberries. Sprinkle with the walnuts.

Nutrition:
119 Calories | 13g Fats | 28g protein

45. Oatmeal with Berries and Sunflower Seeds

Preparation Time: 5 minutes | **Cooking time:** 10 minutes | **Servings:** 4

Ingredients:
1¾ cups water
½ cup unsweetened almond milk
Pinch sea salt
1 cup old-fashioned oats
½ cup blueberries
½ cup raspberries
¼ cup sunflower seeds

Directions:
In a medium saucepan over medium-high heat, heat the water, almond milk, and sea salt to a boil.
Stir in the oats. Reduce the heat to medium-low and cook, stirring occasionally, for 5 minutes. Cover, and let the oatmeal stand for 2 minutes more. Stir and serve topped with blueberries, raspberries, and sunflower seeds.

Nutrition:
106 Calories | 9g Fats | 29g protein

46. Almond and Maple Quick Grits

Preparation Time: 5 minutes | **Cooking time:** 10 minutes | **Servings:** 4

Ingredients:
1 ½ cups water
½ cup unsweetened almond milk
Pinch sea salt
½ cup quick-cooking grits
½ teaspoon ground cinnamon
¼ cup pure maple syrup
¼ cup slivered almonds

Directions:
In a medium saucepan over medium-high heat, heat the water, almond milk, and sea salt until it boils.
Stirring constantly with a wooden spoon, slowly add the grits. Continue stirring to prevent lumps and bring the mixture to a slow boil. Reduce the heat to medium-low. Simmer for 5 to 6 minutes, stirring frequently, until the water is completely absorbed.
Stir in the cinnamon, syrup, and almonds. Cook for 1 minute more, stirring.

Nutrition:
126 Calories | 10g Fats | 28g protein

47. Banana Oats

Preparation Time: 10 minutes | **Cooking time:** 10 minutes | **Servings:** 2

Ingredients:
1 banana, peeled and sliced
¾ c. almond milk
½ c. cold-brewed coffee
2 pitted dates
2 tbsps. cocoa powder
1 c. rolled oats
1 ½ tbsps. chia seeds

Directions:
Using a blender, add in all ingredients. Process well for 5 minutes and serve.

Nutrition:
288 Calories | 4.4g Fat | 5.9g

48. Breakfast Sandwich

Preparation Time: 5 minutes | **Cooking time:** 20 minutes | **Servings:** 4

Ingredients:
4 multigrain sandwich thins
4 tsps. olive oil
4 eggs
1 tbsp. Rosemary, fresh
2 c. baby spinach leaves, fresh
1 tomato, sliced
1 tbsp. of feta cheese
Pinch of kosher salt
Ground black pepper

Directions:
Turn on the oven and preheat to 375 F/190 C. Brush the thins' sides with 2 tsps. of olive oil and set on a baking sheet. Set in the oven and toast for 5 minutes or until the edges are lightly brown.
In a skillet, add in the rest of the olive oil and rosemary to heat over high heat. Break and place whole eggs one at a time into the skillet. The yolk should still be runny, but the egg whites should be set.
Break yolks up with a spatula. Flip the egg and cook on another side until done. Remove eggs from heat. Place toasted sandwich thins on 4 separate plates. Divide spinach among the thins. Top each thin with two tomato slices, cooked egg, and 1 tbsp. of feta cheese. Lightly sprinkle with salt and pepper for flavoring. Place remaining sandwich thin halves over the top and they are ready to serve.

Nutrition:
241 Calories | 12.2g Fat | 602g Fiber

49. Morning Couscous

Preparation Time: 10 minutes | **Cooking time:** 8 minutes | **Servings:** 4

Ingredients:
3 c. low-fat milk
1 c. whole-wheat couscous, uncooked
1 cinnamon stick
½ chopped apricot, dried
¼ c. currants, dried
6 tsps. brown sugar
¼ tsp. salt

4 tsps. melted butter

Directions:
Take a large saucepan and combine milk and cinnamon stick and heat over medium. Heat for 3 minutes or until microbubbles form around the edges of the pan. Do not boil. Remove from heat, stir in the couscous, apricots, currants, salt, and 4 tsps. brown sugar. Cover the mixture and allow it to sit for 15 minutes. Remove and throw away the cinnamon stick. Divide couscous among 4 bowls, and top each with 1 tsp. melted butter and ½ tsp. brown sugar. Ready to serve.

Nutrition:
306 Calories | 6g Fat | 5g Fiber

50. Mini Frittatas

Preparation Time: 10 minutes | **Cooking time:** 20 minutes | **Servings:** 8

Ingredients:
1 chopped yellow onion
1 c. grated parmesan
1 chopped yellow bell pepper
1 chopped red bell pepper
1 chopped zucchini
Salt and black pepper
A drizzle of olive oil
8 whisked eggs
2 tbsps. chopped chives

Directions:
Set a pan over medium-high heat. Add in oil to warm. Stir in all ingredients except chives and eggs. Sauté for around 5 minutes.
Put the eggs on a muffin pan and top with the chives. Set oven to 350 F/176 C. Place the muffin pan into the oven and bake for about 10 minutes. Serve the eggs on a plate with sautéed vegetables.

Nutrition:
55 Calories | 3g Fat | 0.7g Fiber

51. Sun-dried Tomatoes Oatmeal

Preparation Time: 10 minutes | **Cooking time:** 25 minutes | **Servings:** 4

Ingredients:
3 c. water
1 c. almond milk
1 tbsp. olive oil
1 c. steel-cut oats
¼ c. chopped tomatoes, sun-dried
A pinch of red pepper flakes

Directions:
Using a pan, add water and milk to mix. Set on medium heat and allow to boil. Set up another pan on medium-high heat. Warm oil and add oats to cook for 2 minutes. Transfer to the first pan plus tomatoes then stir. Let simmer for approximately 20 minutes. Set in serving bowls and top with red pepper flakes. Enjoy.

Nutrition:
170 Calories | 17.8g Fat | 1.5g Fiber

52. Breakfast Egg on Avocado

Preparation Time: 5 minutes | **Cooking time:** 15 minutes | **Servings:** 6

Ingredients:
1 tsp. garlic powder
½ tsp. sea salt
¼ c. shredded Parmesan cheese
¼ tsp. black pepper
3 pitted avocados, halved
6 eggs

Directions:
Prepare muffin tins and preheat the oven to 350 F/176 C. Split the avocado. To ensure that the egg would fit inside the cavity of the avocado, lightly scrape off 1/3 of the meat.
Place avocado on a muffin tin to ensure that it faces with the top-up. Evenly season each avocado with pepper, salt, and garlic powder. Add one egg on each avocado cavity and garnish tops with cheese. Set in your oven to bake until the egg white is set, about 15 minutes. Serve and enjoy.

Nutrition:
252 Calories | 20g Fat | 2g Fiber

53. Brekky Egg- Potato Hash

Preparation Time: 10 minutes | **Cooking time:** 25 minutes | **Servings:** 2

Ingredients:
1 zucchini, diced
½ c. chicken broth

½ lb. or 220 g cooked chicken
1 tbsp. olive oil
4 oz. or 113g shrimp
Salt and black pepper
1 diced sweet potato
2 eggs
¼ tsp. cayenne pepper
2 tsps. garlic powder
1 c. fresh spinach

Directions:
In a skillet, add the olive oil. Fry the shrimp, cooked chicken, and sweet potato for 2 minutes. Add the cayenne pepper, garlic powder and toss for 4 minutes. Add the zucchini and toss for another 3 minutes.
Whisk the eggs in a bowl and add to the skillet. Season using salt and pepper. Cover with the lid. Cook for 1 more minute and mix in the chicken broth.
Cover and cook for another 8 minutes on high heat. Add the spinach, toss for 2 more minutes, and serve.

Nutrition:
198 Calories | 0.7g Fat | 7g Fiber

54. Cranberry Bulgur Mix

Preparation Time: 10 minutes | **Cooking time:** 0 minutes | **Servings:** 4

Ingredients:
1 and ½ cups hot water
1 cup bulgur
Juice of ½ lemon
4 tablespoons cilantro, chopped
½ cup cranberries
1 and ½ teaspoons curry powder
¼ cup green onions
½ cup red bell peppers
½ cup carrots, grated
1 tablespoon olive oil

Directions:
Put bulgur into a bowl, add the water, stir, cover, leave aside for 10 minutes, fluff with a fork, and transfer to a bowl. Add the rest of the ingredients, toss, and serve cold.

Nutrition:
300 Calories | 6.4g Fat | 13g Protein

55. Apple Crisp with Oatmeal

Preparation Time: 5 minutes | **Cooking time:** 20 minutes | **Servings:** 4

Ingredients:
4 cups peeled apples and slices
1 tablespoon lemon juice
½ cup quick-cooking oatmeal
¼ cup brown sugar
2 tablespoons flour
1 teaspoon cinnamon
2 tablespoons soft butter
2 cups of water

Directions:
Spray apples with lemon juice. Combine oatmeal, brown sugar, flour, and cinnamon.
Cut and add the butter to the oatmeal mixture until a lumpy dough forms. Place the apples in an oiled bowl that fits comfortably in the pot. Spray the oatmeal mixture evenly over the apples. Cover the bowl firmly with the foil.
Pour the water into the pot. Position the bowl on the rack of the pot. Close and secure the lid.
Place the pressure regulator on the vent tube and cook for 20 minutes once the pressure regulator begins to slowly swing. Cool the pot quickly.

Nutrition:
Calories: 209

56. Jamaican Cornmeal Porridge

Preparation Time: 5 minutes | **Cooking time:** 16 minutes | **Servings:** 6

Ingredients:
4 separate cups of water
1 cup of milk
1 cup fine yellow cornmeal
2 cinnamon sticks
3 pepper berries
1 teaspoon vanilla extract
½ teaspoon ground nutmeg
½ cup sweetened condensed milk

Directions:
Add 3 cups of water and 1 cup of milk to the instant pot and stir. In a separate bowl, beat 1 cup of water and cornmeal until completely combined.

Add to the instant pot. Add cinnamon sticks, pepper berries, vanilla extract, and nutmeg. Cover and cook on porridge for 6 minutes. Once the timer is turned off, allow it to release naturally for at least 10 minutes, then quickly release any remaining pressure.
Once done with natural release, open Instant Pot and beat to remove any lump. Add sweetened condensed milk to sweeten. Enjoy!!

Nutrition:
Calories: 424

57. Blueberry Muffins

Preparation Time: 5 minutes | **Cooking time:** 20 minutes | **Servings:** 24

Ingredients:
2 cups all-purpose flour
2 cups whole wheat flour
2/3 cup sugar
6 teaspoons baking powder
1 teaspoon salt
2 cups blueberries
2 free-range eggs
2/3 cup olive oil
2 cups milk

Directions:
Preheat your oven to 400°F and line a muffin tin with paper cases.
Grab a large bowl and add the dry ingredients. Stir well to combine.
Add the blueberries and stir through.
Take a medium bowl and add the wet ingredients. Stir well then pour into the dry ingredients.
Pour the muffin batter into the muffin cases and pop it into the oven.
Bake for 18 minutes.
Remove from the oven and allow to cool slightly before enjoying.

Nutrition:
Calories: 179 | Net Carbs: 24g | Fat: 7g | Protein: 4g

58. Strawberry Muffins

Preparation Time: 5 minutes | **Cooking time:** 25 minutes | **Servings:** 8

Ingredients:
2 cup Wheat flour
1 cup Strawberry
1/2 cup Milk
2 fl. oz Olive oil
1 Egg
2 tsp Baking powder | Sugar: and salt, to taste

Directions:
In a bowl, mix the baking powder, sugar, and flour. In another bowl, beat the egg with milk and olive oil.
Mix both mixtures and mix well. Add a glass of sliced strawberries and mix gently, without damaging the berries.
Grease the muffin pan with butter or put a paper mold in each hole. Fill two-thirds doughs and bake for 20-25 minutes in an oven preheated to 375 degrees until cooked.
Allow to cool in shape, then shift to a platter.

Nutrition:
Calories: 284 Kcal | Fat: 8 g. | Protein: 5.3 g | Carbs: 48 g.

59. Savory Spinach Feta and Sweet Pepper Muffins

Preparation Time: 10 minutes | **Cooking time:** 25 minutes | **Servings:** 10

Ingredients:
2 and ½ cups of flour
2 tbsp. of baking powder
A ¼ cup of sugar
¾ tbs. salt
1 tbs. paprika
A ¾ cup of milk
2 fresh eggs
½ cup olive oil
A ¾ cup of feta (crumbled)
1 and ¼ cups of sliced spinach
1/3 cup of Florina peppers

Directions:
As the muffins will be baked in the oven, you need to preheat them to a temperature of 190 degrees.

Take a deep and large container. In this, put in the sugar, baking powder, salt, and flour. Mix all these dry ingredients properly and make sure there are no lumps.

In a separate container, you need to pour in the milk, eggs, and olive oil. Stir these ingredients so that they form one smooth liquid.

Carefully pour in the liquids in the container that has the dry ingredients. Use your hand to mix everything well, so that a thick and smooth dough is formed.

Then it is time to put in the crumbled feta, pepper, and sliced spinach into the dough. Then spend some time with it to ensure that the new ingredients have mixed evenly into the muffin dough.

You can get muffin trays at the market. In such a tray, scoop out portions of the dough and place it into the muffin tray depressions.

Put in this pan inside the oven for 25 minutes. After cooling, the muffins will be ready for consumption.

Nutrition:
Carbohydrate – 15g | Protein: – 10g | Fat: – 20g | Calories: 240

Chapter 2: Appetizers and Snacks

60. Zucchini Chips

Preparation Time: 5 minutes | **Cooking time:** 15 minutes | **Servings:** 4

Ingredients:
1 pound (½ kg) zucchini, sliced
1 cup mayonnaise
½ cup sour cream
1 tablespoon sriracha sauce (or hot chili sauce), or to taste
2 tablespoons honey
½ cup chives (scallion/green onion), chopped
½ cup of breadcrumbs
½ cup parmesan cheese
1 teaspoon red paprika (paprika)
2 eggs
1 teaspoon of water

Directions:
Slice the zucchini. Reserve.
In the 2-Quart Mixing Bowl, add mayonnaise, sour cream, sriracha, honey, and chives. Combine well with the help of the Balloon Whisk, cover, and refrigerate.
In the 3-quart Mixing Bowl, beat the eggs with a teaspoon of water; reservation.
In the 1-quarter Mixing Bowl, mix the ground bread, Parmesan cheese, and paprika. Reserve separately.
Dip the zucchini slices in the beaten egg, then cover them with the ground bread mixture. Place each slice in the Cookie Tray.
Preheat the oven to 400 F / 204 C. Place the tray inside the oven and cook for 8 minutes. Flip the chips with the help of the Spatula and bake for 7 more minutes.
Serve with the honey and sriracha sauce.

Nutrition:
Calories: 344 | Carbohydrates: 46g | Fat: 9.3g | Protein: 18g | Sugar: 4.8g | Cholesterol: 0mg

61. Egg Cupcakes

Preparation Time: 10 minutes | **Cooking time:** 20 minutes | **Servings:** 6

Ingredients:
1 pack of bacon (12 ounces)
6 eggs
2 tablespoons of milk
1 c. Melted butter
1/4 teaspoon dried parsley
1/4 teaspoon salt
1/4 teaspoon ground black pepper
1/2 cup diced ham
1/4 cup grated mozzarella cheese
6 slices gouda

Directions:
Preheat the oven to 175 °C (350 °F).
Place the bacon in a large frying pan and cook over medium heat, occasionally turning until brown, about 5 minutes. Drain the bacon slices on kitchen paper.
Cover 6 cups of the non-stick muffin pan with slices of bacon.
Cut the remaining bacon slices and sprinkle the bottom of each cup.
In a large bowl, beat eggs, milk, butter, parsley, salt, and pepper. Stir in the ham and mozzarella cheese.
Pour the egg mixture into cups filled with bacon; garnish with Gouda cheese.
Bake in the preheated oven until Gouda cheese is melted and the eggs are tender for about 15 minutes.

Nutrition: (Per Serving)
310 calories | 22.9 g of fat | 2.1 g carbohydrates | 23.1 g of protein | 249 mg of cholesterol | 988 mg of sodium.

62. Grilled Spiced Turkey Burger

Preparation Time: 15 minutes | **Cooking time:** 20 minutes | **Servings:** 3

Ingredients:
Onion (1.8 oz, chopped fine)
Extra Virgin Olive Oil (1/3 tbsp)
Turkey (14.4 oz, ground)
Salt (1/3 tbsp)
Curry powder (1/3 tbsp)
Lemon zest (2/5 tsp, grated)
Pepper (1/8 tsp)
Cinnamon (1/8 tsp)
Coriander (1/4 tsp, ground)
Cumin (1/8 tsp, ground)
Cardamom (1/8 tsp, ground)
Water (1.2 Fl oz)
Tomato Raisin Chutney (as desired)
Cilantro leaves (as desired)

Directions:
Cook the onions in the oil. Cool completely.
Combine the turkey, onions, spices, water, and salt in a bowl. Toss.
Divide the mixture into 5 oz portions (or as desired). Form each portion into a thick patty. Broil but do not overcook it.
Plate the burgers. Put a spoonful of chutney on top of each.

Nutrition:
250 Calories | 14g Fat | 27g Protein

63. Tomato Tea Party Sandwiches

Preparation Time: 15 minutes | **Cooking time:** 0 minute | **Servings:** 4

Ingredients:
Whole wheat bread (4 slices)
Extra virgin olive oil (4 1/3 tbsp)
Basil (2 1/8 tbsp., minced)
Tomato slices (4 thick)
Ricotta cheese (4 oz)
Dash of pepper

Directions:
Toast bread to your preference.
Spread 2 tsp. olive oil on each slice of bread. Add the cheese.
Top with tomato, then sprinkle with basil and pepper.
Serve with lemon water and enjoy it!

Nutrition:
239 Calories | 16.4g Fat | 6g Protein

64. Mediterranean Flatbread with Toppings

Preparation Time: 10 minutes | **Cooking time:** 15 minutes | **Servings:** 10

Ingredients:
2 medium tomatoes
5 black olives (diced)
8 ounces of crescent rolls
1 clove of garlic (finely chopped)
1 red onion (sliced)
¼ tbs. salt
4 tbs. olive oil
¼ tbs. pepper powder
1 and ½ tbs. Italian seasoning
Parmesan cheese as per requirement

Directions:
Wash and clean the tomatoes properly. Then make very thin and round slices with a sharp knife. You must ensure that the tomato juices

drain out. So, place these on a dry piece of linen cloth.

You will get crescent rolls or flatbread dough in the market. Unroll these and keep these on a big baking tray. Make sure the surface of the baking dish has no grease or water.

Then roll the dough into several portions, which will not be more than 14x10 inches in measurement.

With the help of a rolling pin, shape these into rectangular flatbreads.

Place the tomato slices, diced black olive, and onion slices on these flatbreads.

Add the Italian seasoning, olive oil, pepper powder, salt, and chopped garlic together and mix well.

Take the mixture and apply an even coat on all the flatbreads. This mixture will add flavor to the toppings and flatbreads.

Put the baking tray in the microwave oven and set the temperature at 375°.

After 15 minutes, remove the plate from the oven and enjoy your crunchy Mediterranean flatbread with toppings with a glass of red wine.

Nutrition:
Carbohydrate – 9g | Protein - 2g | Fat: – 6g | Calories: 101

65. Smoked Salmon and Goat Cheese Bites

Preparation Time: 10 minutes | **Cooking time:** 15 minutes | **Servings:** 12

Ingredients:
8 ounces of goat cheese
1 tbs. of fresh rosemary
2 tbsp. of oregano
2 tbsp. of basil (fresh)
2 cloves of garlic (chopped)
4 ounces fresh smoked salmon
½ tbs. salt
½ tbs pepper

Directions:
Put the three herbs on the chopping board and run a knife vigorously through them. Once the herbs have been mixed well, transfer them to a medium-sized bowl

Add goat cheese (grated), chopped garlic, pepper, and salt in the bowl and mix properly. Keep this mixture for some time to rest.

There are two ways of serving salmon-goat cheese bites. Either you can place a flat piece of smoked salmon on the tray and top it with a dollop of goat cheese and seasoning mix.

The other way is to make small balls with the goat cheese and seasoning mix and wrap a wide stripe of smoked salmon around the ball.

One can also sprinkle some additional Italian seasoning on the final salmon bites to enhance the taste. This step is optional, and omitting it will not mar the original richness of the salmon-cheese bites.

Nutrition:
Carbohydrate – 17.33g | Protein - 54.83g | Fat: – 53.33g | Calories: 739

66. Hummus Snack Bowl

Preparation Time: 5 minutes | **Cooking time:** 5 minutes | **Servings:** 2

Ingredients:
8 tbsp of hummus
½ cup fresh spinach (coarsely chopped)
½ cups of carrots (shredded)
1 big tomato (diced)
¼ tbs. salt
¼ tbs. chili powder
¼ tbs. pepper
6 sweet olives (3 green, 3 black, chopped)

Directions:
Take a large bowl and put in 6 spoonfuls of hummus into it. In this, put in chopped olives, shredded carrots, spinach leaves, and diced tomatoes.

Coat these vegetables with hummus properly.

After mixing the vegetables and hummus paste for at least five minutes, add in the chili powder. Make sure that it is evenly spread into the whole salad.

Lastly, add pepper powder and salt to the hummus-veggies mixture. You can taste the mixture and check the balance of all the ingredients.

Some also drizzle on some extra virgin olive oil onto the salad. This step is optional and can be omitted.

The Hummus Snack Bowl is a complete snack on its own. If you desire to add some texture to it, some freshly baked flatbreads or bread will complement the salad.

Nutrition:
Carbohydrate – 43g | Protein: – 12g | Fat: – 10g | Calories: 280

67. Greek Spinach Yogurt Artichoke Dip

Preparation Time: 10 minutes | **Cooking time:** 10 minutes | **Servings:** 2

Ingredients:
1 tbs. olive oil
9-ounces spinach (roughly chopped)
¼ cup Parmesan cheese (grated)
14 ounces artichoke hearts (chopped)
½ tbsp. pepper powder
½ tbs. onion powder
½ tbs. garlic powder
8 ounces sliced chestnuts
2 cups of Greek yogurt (fat-free)

Directions:
Preheat the oven to 350°F.
Chop artichoke hearts into bite-sized pieces. Mix all ingredients and season with a pinch of salt; pour into a small casserole or oven-safe dish (about 1-quart). Sprinkle the top with extra mozzarella cheese.
Bake for 20-22 minutes, or until heated through and the cheese on top is melted. Serve warm with pita or tortilla chips.

Nutrition:
Carbohydrate – 20.9 g | Protein – 16.3 g | Fat: – 2.9 g | Calories: 170

68. Sautéed Apricots

Preparation Time: 5 minutes | **Cooking time:** 15 minutes | **Servings:** 4

Ingredients:
2 Tablespoons Olive Oil
1 Cup Almonds, Blanched, Skinless & Unsalted
½ Teaspoon Sea Salt, Fine
1/8 Teaspoon Red Pepper Flakes
1/8 Teaspoon Cinnamon, Ground
½ Cup Apricots, Dried & Chopped

Directions:
Place a frying pan over high heat, adding in your almonds, salt, and olive oil. Sauté until the almonds turn light gold, which will take five to ten minutes. Make sure to stir often because they burn easily.
Spoon your almonds into a serving dish, adding in your cinnamon, red pepper flakes, and chopped apricot.
Allow it to cool before serving.

Nutrition:
Calories: 207 | Protein: 5 Grams | Fat: 19 Grams | Carbs: 7 Grams

69. Spiced Kale Chips

Preparation Time: 5 minutes | **Cooking time:** 35 minutes | **Servings:** 4

Ingredients:
1 Tablespoon Olive Oil
½ Teaspoon Chili Powder
¼ Teaspoon Sea Salt, Fine
3 Cups Kale, Stemmed, Washed & Torn into 2 Inch Pieces

Directions:
Start by heating your oven to 300, and then get out two baking sheets. Line each baking sheet with parchment paper before placing them to the side.
Dry your kale off completely before placing it in a bowl, and add in your olive oil. Make sure the kale is thoroughly coated before seasoning it.
Spread your kale out on your baking sheets in a single layer, baking for twenty-five minutes. Your kale will need roasted halfway through, and it should turn out dry and crispy.
Allow them to cool for at least five minutes before serving.

Nutrition:
Calories: 56 | Protein: 2 Grams | Fat: 4 Grams | Carbs: 5 Grams

70. Turkey Spheroids with Tzatziki Sauce

Preparation Time: 10 minutes | **Cooking time:** 20 minutes | **Servings:** 8

Ingredients:
For Meatballs:
2-lbs ground turkey
2-tsp salt
2-cups zucchini, grated
1-tbsp lemon juice
1-cup crumbled feta cheese
1½-tsp pepper
1½-tsp garlic powder
1½-tbsp oregano
¼-cup red onion, finely minced
For Tzatziki Sauce:
1-tsp garlic powder
1-tsp dill
1-tbsp white vinegar
1-tbsp lemon juice
1-cup sour cream
½-cup grated cucumber
Salt and pepper

Directions:
Preheat your oven to 350 ºF.
For the Meatballs:
Incorporate all the meatball ingredients in a large mixing bowl. Mix well until fully combined. Form the turkey mixture into spheroids, using ¼-cup of the mixture per spheroid.
Heat a non-stick skillet placed over high heat. Add the meatballs, and sear for 2 minutes.
Transfer the meatballs to a baking sheet. Situate the sheet in the oven, and bake for 15 minutes.
For the Tzatziki Sauce:
Combine and whisk together all the sauces ingredients in a medium-sized mixing bowl. Mix well until fully combined. Refrigerate the sauce until ready to serve and eat.

Nutrition:
280 Calories | 16g Fats | 26.6g Protein

71. Cheesy Caprese Salad Skewers

Preparation Time: 15 minutes | **Cooking time:** 0 minute | **Servings:** 10

Ingredients:
8-oz cherry tomatoes, sliced in half
A handful of fresh basil leaves, rinsed and drained
1-lb fresh mozzarella, cut into bite-sized slices
Balsamic vinegar
Extra virgin olive oil
Freshly ground black pepper

Directions:
Sandwich a folded basil leaf and mozzarella cheese between the halves of tomato onto a toothpick.
Drizzle with olive oil and balsamic vinegar for each skewer. To serve, sprinkle with freshly ground black pepper.

Nutrition:
94 Calories | 3.7g Fats | 2.1g Protein

72. Leafy Lacinato Tuscan Treat

Preparation Time: 10 minutes | **Cooking time:** 0 minute | **Servings:** 1

Ingredients:
1-tsp Dijon mustard
1-tbsp light mayonnaise
3-pcs medium-sized Lacinato kale leaves
3-oz. cooked chicken breast, thinly sliced
6-bulbs red onion, thinly sliced
1-pc apple, cut into 9-slices

Directions:
Mix the mustard and mayonnaise until fully combined.
Spread the mixture generously on each of the kale leaves. Top each leaf with 1-oz. chicken slices, 3-apple slices, and 2-red onion slices. Roll each kale leaf into a wrap.

Nutrition:
370 Calories | 14g Fats | 29g Protein

73. Portable Packed Picnic Pieces

Preparation Time: 5 minutes | **Cooking time:** 0 minute | **Servings:** 1

Ingredients:
1-slice of whole-wheat bread, cut into bite-size pieces
10-pcs cherry tomatoes
¼-oz. aged cheese, sliced
6-pcs oil-cured olives

Directions:
Pack each of the ingredients in a portable container to serve you while snacking on the go.

Nutrition:
197 Calories | 9g Fats | 7g Protein

74. Perfect Pizza & Pastry

Preparation Time: 35 minutes | **Cooking time:** 15 minutes | **Servings:** 10

Ingredients:
For Pizza Dough:
2-tsp honey
¼-oz. active dry yeast
1¼-cups warm water (about 120 ºF)
2-tbsp olive oil
1-tsp sea salt
3-cups whole grain flour + ¼-cup, as needed for rolling
For Pizza Topping:
1-cup pesto sauce (refer to Perky Pesto recipe)
1-cup artichoke hearts
1-cup wilted spinach leaves
1-cup sun-dried tomato
½-cup Kalamata olives
4-oz. feta cheese
4-oz. mixed cheese of equal parts low-fat mozzarella, asiago, and provolone
Optional:
Bell pepper
Chicken breast, strips
Fresh basil
Pine nuts

Directions:
For the Pizza Dough:
Preheat your oven to 350 ºF.
Combine the honey and yeast with the warm water in your food processor with a dough attachment. Blend the mixture until fully combined. Allow the mixture to rest for 5 minutes to ensure the activity of the yeast through the appearance of bubbles on the surface.
Pour in the olive oil. Add the salt, and blend for half a minute. Add gradually 3 cups of flour, about half a cup at a time, blending for a couple of minutes between each addition.
Let your processor knead the mixture for 10 minutes until smooth and elastic, sprinkling it with flour whenever necessary to prevent the dough from sticking to the processor bowl's surfaces.
Take the dough from the bowl. Let it stand for 15 minutes, covered with a moist, warm towel.
6.Using a rolling pin, roll out the dough to a half-inch thickness, dusting it with flour as needed. Poke holes indiscriminately on the dough using a fork to prevent crust bubbling.
Place the perforated, rolled dough on a pizza stone or baking sheet. Bake for 5 minutes.
For Pizza Topping:
Lightly brush the baked pizza shell with olive oil. Pour over the pesto sauce and spread thoroughly over the pizza shell's surface, leaving out a half-inch space around its edge as the crust.
Top the pizza with artichoke hearts, wilted spinach leaves, sun-dried tomatoes, and olives. Cover the top with the cheese.
Place the pizza directly on the oven rack. Bake for 10 minutes. Set aside for 5 minutes before slicing.

Nutrition:
242.8 Calories | 15g Fats | 14g Protein

75. Zucchini Fritters

Preparation Time: 5 minutes | **Cooking time:** 30 minutes | **Servings:** 6

Ingredients:
2 Zucchinis, Peeled & Grated
1 Sweet Onion, Diced Fine
2 Cloves Garlic, Minced
1 Cup Parsley, Fresh & Chopped
½ Teaspoon Sea Salt, Fine
½ Teaspoon Black Pepper
½ Teaspoon Allspice, Ground
2 Tablespoons Olive Oil

4 Eggs, Large

Directions:
Get out a plate and line it with paper towels before setting it to the side.
Get out a large bowl and mix your onion, parsley, garlic, zucchini, pepper, allspice, and sea salt.
Get out a different bowl and beat your eggs before adding them to your zucchini mixture. Make sure it's mixed well.
Get out a large skillet and place it over medium heat. Heat your olive oil, and then scoop ¼ cup at a time into the skillet to create your fritters. Cook for three minutes or until the bottom sets. Flip and cook for an additional three minutes. Transfer them to your plate so they can drain. Serve with pita bread or on their own.

Nutrition:
Calories: 103 | Protein: 5 Grams | Fat: 8 Grams | Carbs: 5 Grams

76. Cucumber Bites

Preparation Time: 10 minutes | **Cooking time:** 0 minutes | **Servings:** 12

Ingredients:
1 English cucumber, sliced into 32 rounds
10 ounces hummus
16 cherry tomatoes, halved
1 tablespoon parsley, chopped
1-ounce feta cheese, crumbled

Directions:
Spread the hummus on each cucumber round, divide the tomato halves on each, sprinkle the cheese and parsley on to, and serve as an appetizer.

Nutrition:
Calories 162, | Fat: 3.4 | Fiber 2 | Carbs 6.4, | Protein: 2.4

77. Stuffed Avocado

Preparation Time: 10 minutes | **Cooking time:** 0 minutes | **Servings:** 2

Ingredients:
1 avocado, halved and pitted
10 ounces of canned tuna, drained
2 tablespoons sun-dried tomatoes, chopped
1 and ½ tablespoon basil pesto
2 tablespoons black olives, pitted and chopped
Salt and black pepper to the taste
2 teaspoons pine nuts, toasted and chopped
1 tablespoon basil, chopped

Directions:
In a bowl, combine the tuna with the sun-dried tomatoes and the rest of the ingredients except the avocado and stir.
Stuff the avocado halves with the tuna mix and serve as an appetizer.

Nutrition:
Calories 233, | Fat: 9 | Fiber 3.5 | Carbs 11.4, | Protein: 5.6

78. Wrapped Plums

Preparation Time: 5 minutes | **Cooking time:** 0 minutes | **Servings:** 8

Ingredients:
2 ounces prosciutto, cut into 16 pieces
4 plums, quartered
1 tablespoon chives, chopped
A pinch of red pepper flakes, crushed

Directions:
Wrap each plum quarter in a prosciutto slice, arrange them all on a platter, sprinkle the chives and pepper flakes all over, and serve.

Nutrition:
Calories 30, | Fat: 1 | Fiber 0 | Carbs 4, | Protein: 2

79. Cucumber Sandwich Bites

Preparation Time: 5 minutes | **Cooking time:** 0 minutes | **Servings:** 12

Ingredients:
1 cucumber, sliced
8 slices whole-wheat bread
2 tablespoons cream cheese, soft
1 tablespoon chives, chopped
¼ cup avocado, peeled, pitted, and mashed
1 teaspoon mustard
Salt and black pepper to the taste

Directions:
Spread the mashed avocado on each bread slice, also spread the rest of the ingredients except the cucumber slices.

Divide the cucumber slices into the bread slices, cut each slice in thirds, arrange on a platter, and serve as an appetizer.

Nutrition:
Calories 187, | Fat: 12.4 | Fiber 2.1 | Carbs 4.5, | Protein: 8.2

80. Cucumber Rolls

Preparation Time: 5 minutes | **Cooking time:** 0 minutes | **Servings:** 6

Ingredients:
1 big cucumber, sliced lengthwise
1 tablespoon parsley, chopped
8 ounces canned tuna, drained and mashed
Salt and black pepper to the taste
1 teaspoon lime juice

Directions:
Arrange cucumber slices on a working surface, divide the rest of the ingredients, and roll.
Arrange all the rolls on a platter and serve as an appetizer.

Nutrition:
Calories 200, | Fat: 6 | Fiber 3.4 | Carbs 7.6, | Protein: 3.5

81. Olives and Cheese Stuffed Tomatoes

Preparation Time: 10 minutes | **Cooking time:** 0 minutes | **Servings:** 24

Ingredients:
24 cherry tomatoes, top cut off, and insides scooped out
2 tablespoons olive oil
¼ teaspoon red pepper flakes
½ cup feta cheese, crumbled
2 tablespoons black olive paste
¼ cup mint, torn

Directions:
In a bowl, mix the olives paste with the rest of the ingredients except the cherry tomatoes and whisk well.
Stuff the cherry tomatoes with this mix, arrange them all on a platter, and serve as an appetizer.

Nutrition:
Calories 136, | Fat: 8.6 | Fiber 4.8 | Carbs 5.6, | Protein: 5.1

82. Veggie Shish Kebabs

Preparation Time: 10 minutes | **Cooking time:** 0 minute | **Servings:** 3

Ingredients:
Cherry tomatoes (9)
Mozzarella balls (9 low-fat)
Basil leaves (9)
Olive oil (1 tsp.)
Zucchini (3, sliced)
Dash of pepper
Whole Wheat Bread (6 slices)

Directions:
Stab 1 cherry tomato, low-fat mozzarella ball, zucchini, and basil leaf onto each skewer. Situate skewers on a plate and drizzle with olive oil. Finish with a sprinkle of pepper.
Set your bread to toast. Serve 2 bread slices with 3 kebobs.

Nutrition:
349 Calories | 5.7g Fat | 15g Protein

83. Crispy Falafel

Preparation Time: 20 minutes | **Cooking time:** 8 minutes | **Servings:** 3

Ingredients:
Chickpeas (1 cup, drained and rinsed)
Parsley (½ cup, chopped with stems removed)
Cilantro (1/3 cup, chopped with stems removed)
Dill (¼ cup, chopped with stems removed)
Cloves garlic (4, minced)
Sesame seeds (1 tbsp., toasted)
Coriander (½ tbsp.)
Black pepper (½ tbsp.)
Cumin (½ tbsp.)
Baking powder (½ tsp.)
Cayenne (½ tsp.)

Directions:
Thoroughly dry your chickpeas with a paper towel.
Place the parsley, cilantro, and dill in a food processor.

Mix chickpeas, garlic, coriander, black pepper, cumin, baking powder, and cayenne.

Transfer the mixture to an airtight container and chill for about an hour.

Take out from the refrigerator and mix the baking powder and sesame seeds.

Scoop the mixture into a pan with 3 inches of olive oil over medium heat to create patties. Keep in mind as you create the patties that you are aiming to make 12 with the mixture.

Let the falafel patties fry for 1-2 minutes on each side.

Once your falafel patties are nicely browned, transfer them to a plate lined with paper towels to finish crisping.

Dip, dunk, fill, and enjoy!

Nutrition:
328 Calories | 10.8g Fat | 24g Protein

84. Onion Fried Eggs

Preparation Time: 15 minutes | **Cooking time:** 91 minutes | **Servings:** 4

Ingredients:
Eggs (11)
White mushroom (1 cup)
Feta cheese (4 oz, crumbled)
Sun-dried tomatoes (1/2 cup, chopped)
Onion (2 large, sliced)
Garlic clove (2, minced)
Olive oil (2.5 tbsp.)

Directions:
Put a pan with the olive oil over medium-low heat.

Once hot, stir onions and mushrooms into the oil.

Allow the onion and mushroom mix to cook for about one hour. Stir them every 5-7 minutes to ensure they cook evenly.

After the onions have browned, add the sun-dried tomatoes and garlic, and let cook for 2 minutes.

Once the sun-dried tomatoes and garlic are fragrant, spread all the ingredients out into an even thin layer across the pan.

Crack the eggs overtop the ingredients already in the pan.

Sprinkle your feta cheese and pepper over top of the eggs.

Cover the pan with its corresponding lid and let the eggs sit to cook for about 10-12 minutes. Gently shake the pan at 10 minutes to check on the consistency of the egg yolks. Continue to cook until they reach your desired level of doneness.

Remove pan from heat and divide the mixture between two plates.

Nutrition:
360 Calories | 27g Fat | 20g Protein

85. Black Bean Cake with Salsa

Preparation Time: 15 minutes | **Cooking time:** 18 minutes | **Servings:** 10

Ingredients:
Olive oil (1 Fl oz)
Onion (16 oz,)
Garlic (2-4 cloves)
Jalapenos
Ground cumin (2 tsp)
Black beans (32 oz.)
Oregano (1 tsp)
Salsa cruda (450 ml)

Directions:
Heat the olive oil in a sauté pan over low heat.

Add the garlic and onions, cook until soft. Do not brown.

Add the ground cumin and jalapeño. Cook for a few more minutes.

Add the oregano and beans. Cook until they are heated through.

Place the mixture in a food processor and blend in a puree.

Season well.

Divide the mixture into 2 oz portions. Form into small, flat cakes.

Brown the cakes lightly on both sides in hot olive oil in a sauté pan.

Serve 2 cakes per portion with 1 ½ Fl oz salsa.

Nutrition:
260 Calories | 12g Fat | 9g Protein

86. Pickled Apple

Preparation Time: 10 minutes | **Cooking time:** 20 minutes | **Servings:** 6

Ingredients:
Water (1/2 cup)
Maple syrup (3 ½ oz)
Cider vinegar (1/2 cup)
Sachet:
Peppercorns (3-4)
Mustard seed (1/4 tsp)
Coriander seed (1/4 tsp)
Salt (1/4 tsp)
Granny smith apple (2,)
Italian parsley (1 tbsp,)

Directions:
Combine the water, maple syrup, vinegar, sachet, and salt in a saucepan. Bring to a boil.
Pour the liquid and the sachet over the apples in a nonreactive container.
Let it be refrigerated for 3-4 hours or overnight.
Drain the apples before serving and toss with the parsley.

Nutrition:
50 Calories | 0.1g Fat | 0.3g Protein

87. Baked Clams Oreganata

Preparation Time: 30 minutes | **Cooking time:** 13 minutes | **Servings:** 10

Ingredients:
Cherrystone clams (30)
Olive oil (2 Fl oz)
Onions (1 oz, chopped fine)
Garlic (1 tsp, finely chopped)
Lemon juice (1 Fl oz)
Fresh breadcrumbs (10 oz)
Parsley (1 tbsp, chopped)
Oregano (3/4 tsp, dried)
White pepper (1/8 tsp)
Parmesan cheese (1/3 cup)
Paprika (as needed)
Lemon wedges (10)

Directions:
Open the clams. Catch the juice in a bowl.
Remove the clams from the shell. Place them in a strainer over the bowl of juice. Let them drain for 15 minutes in the refrigerator. Save the 30 best half-shells.
Chop the clams into small pieces.
Heat the oil in a sauté pan. Add the onion and garlic. Sauté about 1 minute, but do not brown.
Use half of the clam juice, then reduce it over high heat by three-fourths.
Remove from the heat and add the crumbs, parsley, lemon juice, white pepper, and oregano.
Mix gently to avoid making the crumbs pasty.
If necessary, adjust the seasonings.
Once the mixture has cooled. Mix in the chopped clams.
Place the mixture in the 30 clamshells. Sprinkle with parmesan cheese and (very lightly) with paprika.
Place on a sheet pan and refrigerate until needed.
For each order, bake 3 clams in a hot oven (450 F) until they are hot and the top brown.
Garnish with a lemon wedge.

Nutrition:
180 Calories | 8g Fat | 10g Protein

88. Tuna Tartare

Preparation Time: 15 minutes | **Cooking time:** 0 minute | **Servings:** 8

Ingredients:
Sashimi quality tuna (26.5 g, well-trimmed)
Shallots (1 oz, minced)
Parsley (2 tbsp, chopped)
Fresh tarragon (2 tbsp, chopped)
Lime juice (2 tbsp)
Dijon-style mustard (1 Fl oz)
Olive oil (2 Fl oz)

Directions:
Use a knife to mince the tuna.
Mixed the rest of the ingredients with the chopped tuna.
Use a ring mold to make a beautifully presented tuna tartare.
Season to taste with pepper and salt.

Nutrition:
200 Calories | 12g Fat | 21g Protein

89. Cod Cakes

Preparation Time: 25 minutes | **Cooking time:** 30 minutes | **Servings:** 12

Ingredients:
Cod (12 oz, cooked)
Turnips puree (12 oz.)
Whole eggs (2 ½ oz, beaten)
Egg yolk (1 yolk, beaten)
Salt (to taste)
White pepper (to taste)
Ground ginger (pinch)
Standard Breading Procedure:
Whole wheat flour
Egg wash
Breadcrumbs
Tomatoes sauce

Directions:
Shred the fish.
Combine with the turnips, egg, and egg yolk.
Season with salt, pepper, and ground ginger.
Divide the mixture into 2 ½ oz portions. Shape the mixture into a ball and then slightly flatten the mixture cakes.
Put the mixture through the Standard Breading Procedure.
Deep-fry at 350 F until golden brown.
Serve 2 cakes per portion. Accompany with tomato sauce.

Nutrition:
280 Calories | 6g Fat | 23g Protein

90. Mixed Mushroom Palermitani Pasta

Preparation Time: 5 minutes | **Cooking time:** 30 minutes | **Servings:** 8

Ingredients:
5-quarts salted water
3-tbsp olive oil
26-oz. assorted wild mushrooms
4-cloves garlic, minced
1-bulb red onion, diced
1-tsp sea salt
2-tbsp sherry cooking wine
2½-tsp fresh thyme, diced
1-lb. linguine pasta
¾-cup reserved liquid from cooked pasta
6-oz. goat cheese
¼-cup hazelnuts

Directions:
Bring the salted water to a boil for cooking the pasta.
In the meantime, heat the olive oil in a large skillet placed over medium-high heat. Add the mushrooms and sauté for 10 minutes until they brown.
Add the garlic, onions, and salt. Sauté for 4 minutes.
Stir in the wine, and cook down until the liquid evaporates. Sprinkle with thyme, and set aside.
Cook pasta in boiling water per the manufacturer's specifications.
Before draining the pasta completely, reserve ¾-cup of the pasta liquid.
Transfer the cooked pasta to a large serving bowl and combine with the mushroom mixture, pasta liquid, and goat cheese. Toss gently to combine fully until the goat cheese melts completely.
To serve, top the pasta with chopped hazelnuts.

Nutrition:
331 Calories | 12g Fats | 13g Protein

91. Mediterranean Macaroni with Seasoned Spinach

Preparation Time: 5 minutes | **Cooking time:** 20 minutes | **Servings:** 4

Ingredients:
2-tbsp olive oil
2-cloves garlic
1-pc yellow onion
10-oz. fresh baby spinach
2-pcs fresh tomatoes
¼-cup skim mozzarella cheese
½-cup crumbled feta cheese
½-cup white cheddar cheese, cubed
1-cup low-sodium vegetable broth
2-cups elbow whole-grain macaroni
1-cup unsweetened almond milk
½-tsp organic Italian Seasoning

Directions:
Heat olive oil in a large pan placed over medium-high heat. Add the garlic, onions, and a pinch of salt, and sauté for 3 minutes.
Add the spinach, tomatoes, cheese, vegetable broth, macaroni, milk, and seasonings. Mix well

until fully combined. Bring the mixture to a boil, stirring frequently.
Lower heat to medium-low, and cover the pan. Cook further for 15 minutes, stirring every 3 minutes to prevent the pasta mixture from sticking on the pan's surfaces.
Remove the pasta from the heat and stir. To serve, garnish the pasta with parsley.

Nutrition:
544 Calories | 23g Fats | 22g Protein

92. Frittata Filled with Zesty Zucchini & Tomato Toppings

Preparation Time: 10 minutes | **Cooking time:** 15 minutes | **Servings:** 4

Ingredients:
8-pcs eggs
¼-tsp red pepper, crushed
¼-tsp salt
1-tbsp olive oil
1-pc small zucchini
½-cup red or yellow cherry tomatoes
1/3-cup walnuts, coarsely chopped
2-oz. bite-sized fresh mozzarella balls (bocconcini)

Directions:
Preheat your broiler. Meanwhile, whisk together the eggs, crushed red pepper, and salt in a medium-sized bowl. Set aside.
In a 10-inch broiler-proof skillet placed over medium-high heat, heat the olive oil. Arrange the slices of zucchini in an even layer on the bottom of the skillet. Cook for 3 minutes, turning them once, halfway through.
Top the zucchini layer with cherry tomatoes. Pour the egg mixture over the vegetables in the skillet. Top with walnuts and mozzarella balls. Switch to medium heat. Cook for 5 minutes. By using a spatula, lift the frittata for the uncooked portions of the egg mixture to flow underneath. Place the skillet on the broiler. Broil the frittata 4-inches from the heat for 5 minutes until the top is set. To serve, cut the frittata into wedges.

Nutrition:
281 Calories | 14g Fats | 17g Protein

93. Grilled Vegetable Kebabs

Preparation Time: 12 minutes | **Cooking time:** 13 minutes | **Servings:** 6

Ingredients:
Zucchini (6 oz, trimmed)
Yellow Summer Squash (6 oz, trimmed)
Bell pepper (6 oz, red or orange, cut into 1 ½ in. squares)
Onion (12 oz, red, large dice)
Mushroom caps (12, medium)
Olive oil (12 Fl oz)
Garlic (1/2 oz, crushed)
Rosemary (1 ½ tsp, dried)
Thyme (1/2 tsp, dried)
Salt (2 tsp)
Black pepper (1/2 tsp)

Directions:
Cut the zucchini and yellow squash into 12 equal slices each.
Arrange the vegetables on 12 bamboo skewers. Give each skewer an equal arrangement of vegetable pieces.
Place the skewers in a single layer in a hotel pan. Mix the oil, garlic, herbs, salt, and pepper to make a marinade.
Pour the marinade over the vegetables, turning them to coat completely.
Marinate for 1 hour. Turn the skewers once or twice during margination to ensure the vegetables are coated.
Remove the skewers from the marinade and let the excess oil drip off.

Nutrition:
50 Calories | 3g Fat | 1g Protein

94. Vegetable Fritters

Preparation Time: 15 minutes | **Cooking time:** 6 minutes | **Servings:** 5

Ingredients:
Egg (3, beaten)
Milk (8 Fl oz)
Whole wheat flour (8 oz)
Baking powder (1 tbsp)
Salt (½ tsp)
Maple syrup (1/2 oz)
Vegetables:
Carrot (12 oz,)

Baby lima beans (12 oz)
Asparagus (12 oz)
Celery (12 oz)
Turnip (12 oz)
Eggplant (12 oz)
Cauliflower (12 oz)
Zucchini (12 oz)
Parsnips (12 oz)

Directions:
Combine the eggs and milk.
Mix the flour, baking powder, salt, and maple syrup. Add to the milk and eggs and mix until smooth.
Let the batter stand for several hours in a refrigerator.
Stir the cold, cooked vegetables into the batter.
Drop with a No. 24 scoop into deep fat at 350 F. Toss the content from the scoop carefully in the hot oil. Fry until golden brown.
Drain well and serve.

Nutrition:
140 Calories | 6g Fat | 4g Protein

95. Baba Ghanoush

Preparation Time: 9 minutes | **Cooking time:** 11 minutes | **Servings:** 8

Ingredients:
2 tablespoons extra-virgin olive oil
1 large eggplant
3 cloves garlic
½ cup water
3 tablespoons fresh flat-leaf parsley
½ teaspoon salt
¼ teaspoon smoked paprika
2 tablespoons lemon juice
2 tablespoons tahini

Directions:
Press the Sauté button on the Instant Pot® and add 1 tablespoon oil. Add eggplant and cook until it begins to soften about 5 minutes. Add garlic and cook for 30 seconds.
Add water and close lid, click steam release to Sealing, select Manual, and time to 6 minutes. Once the timer rings, quick-release the pressure. Select Cancel and open the lid.
Strain cooked eggplant and garlic and add to a food processor or blender along with parsley, salt, smoked paprika, lemon juice, and tahini.
Add remaining 1 tablespoon oil and process. Serve warm or at room temperature.

Nutrition:
79 Calories | 6g Fat | 2g Protein

96. Sfougato

Preparation Time: 9 minutes | **Cooking time:** 13 minutes | **Servings:** 4

Ingredients:
½ cup crumbled feta cheese
¼ cup bread crumbs
1 medium onion
4 tablespoons all-purpose flour
2 tablespoons fresh mint
½ teaspoon salt
½ teaspoon ground black pepper
1 tablespoon dried thyme
6 large eggs, beaten
1 cup water

Directions:
In a medium bowl, mix cheese, bread crumbs, onion, flour, mint, salt, pepper, and thyme. Stir in eggs.
Spray an 8" round baking dish with nonstick cooking spray. Pour egg mixture into the dish.
Place the rack in the Instant Pot® and add water. Fold a long piece of foil in half lengthwise. Lay foil over the rack to form a sling and top with a dish. Cover loosely with foil. Seal lid, put the steam release in Sealing, select Manual, and time to 8 minutes.
When the timer alarms, release the pressure. Uncover. Let stand for 5 minutes, then remove the dish from the pot.

Nutrition:
274 Calories | 14g Fat | 17g Protein

97. Skordalia

Preparation Time: 7 minutes | **Cooking time:** 11 minutes | **Servings:** 16

Ingredients:
1-pound russet potatoes
3 cups plus ¼ cup water
2 teaspoons salt
8 cloves garlic
¾ cup blanched almonds

½ cup extra-virgin olive oil
2 tablespoons lemon juice
2 tablespoons white wine vinegar
½ teaspoon ground black pepper

Directions:
Place potatoes, 3 cups water, and 1 teaspoon salt in the Instant Pot® and stir well. Close, set steam release to Sealing, click the Manual button, and set to 10 minutes.

While potatoes cook, place garlic and remaining 1 teaspoon salt on a cutting board. With the side of a knife, press garlic and salt until it forms a paste. Transfer the garlic paste into a food processor along with almonds and olive oil. Purée into a paste. Set aside.

When the timer beeps, quick-release the pressure. Select the Cancel button and open the lid. Drain potatoes and transfer to a medium bowl. Add garlic mixture and mash with a potato masher until smooth. Stir in lemon juice, vinegar, and pepper. Stir in ¼ cup water a little at a time until the mixture is thin enough for dipping. Serve warm or at room temperature.

Nutrition:
115 Calories | 10g Fat | 2g Protein

98. Pinto Bean Dip with Avocado Pico

Preparation Time: 6 minutes | **Cooking time:** 52 minutes | **Servings:** 16

Ingredients:
1 cup dried pinto beans
4 cups water
4 tablespoons cilantro, divided
3 tablespoons extra-virgin olive oil
1 teaspoon ground cumin
1 clove garlic, peeled and minced
½ teaspoon salt
1 medium avocado
1 large ripe tomato
1 small jalapeño pepper
½ medium white onion
2 teaspoons lime juice

Directions:
Place beans, water, and 2 tablespoons of cilantro in the Instant Pot®. Close lid, place steam release to Sealing, click Bean, and set default time of 30 minutes.

When the timer rings, let the pressure release naturally. Open then check the beans are tender. Drain off excess water. Crush beans with a fork. Add oil, cumin, garlic, and salt and mix well.

Toss the remaining 2 tablespoons of cilantro with avocado, tomato, jalapeño, onion, and lime juice. Spoon topping over bean dip. Serve.

Nutrition:
59 Calories | 4g Fat | 1g Protein

99. Margherita Mediterranean Model

Preparation Time: 15 minutes | **Cooking time:** 15 minutes | **Servings:** 10

Ingredients:
1-batch pizza shell
2-tbsp olive oil
½-cup crushed tomatoes
3-Roma tomatoes, sliced ¼-inch thick
½-cup fresh basil leaves, thinly sliced
6-oz. block mozzarella
½-tsp sea salt

Directions:
Preheat your oven to 450 ºF.

Lightly brush the pizza shell with olive oil. Thoroughly spread the crushed tomatoes over the pizza shell, leaving a half-inch space around its edge as the crust.

Top the pizza with the Roma tomato slices, basil leaves, and mozzarella slices. Sprinkle salt over the pizza.

Place the pizza directly on the oven rack. Bake for 15 minutes. Put aside for 5 minutes before slicing.

Nutrition:
251 Calories | 8g Fats | 9g Protein

100. Fowl & Feta Fettuccini

Preparation Time: 5 minutes | **Cooking time:** 30 minutes | **Servings:** 6

Ingredients:
2-tbsp extra-virgin olive oil
1 ½-lb chicken breasts
¼-tsp freshly ground black pepper
1-tsp kosher salt
2-cups water

2-14.5-oz. cans tomatoes with garlic, oregano, and basil
1-lb whole-wheat fettuccini pasta
4-oz. reduced-fat feta cheese
Fresh basil leaves, finely chopped (optional)

Directions:

Heat olive oil for 1 minute in your Dutch oven placed over high heat for 1 minute. Add the chicken, and sprinkle over with freshly ground black pepper and half a teaspoon of kosher salt. Cook the chicken for 8 minutes, flipping once. Sprinkle over with the remaining salt after flipping each chicken on its side. Cook further for 5 minutes until the chicken cooks through.

Pour in the water, and add the tomatoes. Stir in the fettuccini pasta, cook for 5 minutes, uncovered. Cover the dish, and cook further for 10 minutes.

Uncover the dish, and stir the pasta. Add 3-oz. of the feta cheese, and stir again. Cook further for 5 minutes, uncovered.

To serve, sprinkle over with the chopped basil and the remaining feta cheese.

Nutrition:
390 Calories | 11g Fats | 19g Protein

101. Very Vegan Patras Pasta

Preparation Time: 5 minutes | **Cooking time:** 10 minutes | **Servings:** 6

Ingredients:
4-quarts salted water
10-oz. gluten-free and whole-grain pasta
5-cloves garlic, minced
1-cup hummus
Salt and pepper
1/3 cup water
½-cup walnuts
½-cup olives
2-tbsp dried cranberries (optional)

Directions:

Bring the salted water to a boil for cooking the pasta.

In the meantime, prepare for the hummus sauce. Combine the garlic, hummus, salt, and pepper with water in a mixing bowl. Add the walnuts, olive, and dried cranberries, if desired. Set aside.

Put pasta in boiling water. Cook the pasta according to the package's specifications. Drain the pasta.

Transfer the pasta to a large serving bowl and combine with the sauce.

Nutrition:
329 Calories | 12.6g Fats | 12g Protein

102. Scrumptious Shrimp Pappardelle Pasta

Preparation Time: 10 minutes | **Cooking time:** 20 minutes | **Servings:** 4

Ingredients:
3-quarts salted water
1-lb. jumbo shrimp
½-tsp kosher salt
¼-tsp black pepper
3-tbsp olive oil
2-cups zucchini
1-cup grape tomatoes
1/8 tsp red pepper flakes
2-cloves garlic
1 tsp zest of 1-pc lemon
2-tbsp lemon juice
1-tbsp Italian parsley, chopped
8-oz. fresh pappardelle pasta

Directions:

Bring the salted water to a boil for cooking the pasta.

In the meantime, prepare for the shrimp. Combine the shrimp with salt and pepper. Set aside.

Heat a tablespoon of oil in a large sauté pan placed over medium heat. Add the zucchini slices and sauté for 4 minutes.

Add the grape tomatoes and sauté for 2 minutes. Stir in the salt to combine with the vegetables. Transfer the cooked vegetables to a medium-sized bowl. Set aside.

In the same sauté pan, pour in the remaining oil. Switch the heat to medium-low. Add the red pepper flakes and garlic. Cook for 2 minutes.

Add the seasoned shrimp, and keep the heat on medium-low. Cook the shrimp for 3 minutes on each side until they turn pinkish.

Stir in the zest of lemon and the lemon juice. Mix cooked vegetables back to the pan. Stir to combine with the shrimp. Set aside.

Situate pasta in the boiling water. Cook following the manufacturer's specifications until al dente texture. Drain the pasta.
Transfer the cooked pasta to a large serving bowl and combine it with the lemony-garlic shrimp and vegetables.

Nutrition:
474 Calories | 15g Fats | 37g Protein

103. Mediterranean Chicken Bites

Preparation Time: 10 minutes | **Cooking time:** 10 minutes | **Servings:** 4

Ingredients:
20 ounces canned pineapple slices
A drizzle of olive oil
3 cups chicken thighs
A tablespoon of smoked paprika

Directions:
Situate pan over medium-high heat, add pineapple slices, cook them for a few minutes on each side, transfer to a cutting board, cool them down, and cut into medium cubes.
Heat another pan with a drizzle of oil over medium-high heat, rub chicken pieces with paprika, add them to the pan and cook for 5 minutes on each side.
Arrange chicken cubes on a platter, add a pineapple piece on top of each and stick a toothpick in each, and serve.

Nutrition:
120 Calories | 3g Fat | 2g Protein

104. Turkey Wrapped Eggs

Preparation Time: 5 minutes | **Cooking time:** 17 minutes | **Servings:** 6

Ingredients:
6 cooked eggs, without shell
1 uncooked egg
1 pound (½ kg) ground turkey meat low Fat | ¼ cup finely chopped onion
¼ cup finely chopped jalapeños
¼ cup of ground bread
Mustard Dressing:
½ cup chicken broth
½ cup double cream (heavy cream)
1 teaspoon Dijon mustard
1 teaspoon tarragon leaves
1 teaspoon fine cornmeal (cornstarch) — optional

Directions:
In the pot, mix the chicken broth, double cream, mustard, and tarragon leaves. Cook at medium-high temperature until the dressing begins to thicken, in about 8 minutes. Stir occasionally. If you want the sauce to be thicker, you can add 1 teaspoon of fine cornmeal, and beat well until all the lumps are dissolved.
In a bowl, combine turkey, onion, jalapenos, and a raw egg. Add the breadcrumbs, and season with salt and pepper to taste.
Make 6 thin burgers with the meat mixture and use them to wrap the cooked eggs.
Preheat a skillet at medium-high temperature for about 3 minutes or until, after spraying a few drops of water, they roll on the surface without evaporating. Immediately reduce the temperature to medium, and cook the wrapped eggs for 4 minutes, with the lid ajar.
Turn and cook for 5 more minutes with the lid closed. Make sure the meat is fully cooked before removing the eggs from the stove. Serve with the dressing.

Nutrition:
Calories:150 | Carbohydrates: 21g | Fat: 7g | Protein: 2g | Sugar: 20g | Cholesterol: 5mg

105. Grilled Pineapple Sandwich

Preparation Time: 10 minutes | **Cooking time:** 7 minutes | **Servings:** 4

Ingredients:
8 slices of pineapple
½ cup macadamia nuts, chopped
½ cup chocolate cream and hazelnut spread
¼ cup double cream
½ cup mascarpone Italian cheese
1 teaspoon whipped cream
4 cherries

Directions:
Preheat the skillet at medium heat for 3 minutes. Add the macadamia nuts and roast them for 3 minutes, stirring constantly.
Preheat the Round Grill at medium-high heat for 3 minutes. Add the pineapple slices and roast each side for 2 minutes.

In a bowl, add the chocolate cream, double cream, and mascarpone cheese; stir until a uniform mixture is achieved. Spread four slices of pineapple with the mixture and cover with the remaining slices to form the sandwiches. Garnish with cream, cherries, and nuts.

Nutrition:
Calories: 344 | Carbohydrates: 46g | Fat: 9.3g | Protein: 18g | Sugar: 4.8g | Cholesterol: 0mg

106. Roasted Green Beans

Preparation Time: 10 minutes | **Cooking time:** 15 minutes | **Servings:** 4

Ingredients:
1 lb green beans
4 tbsp parmesan cheese
2 tbsp olive oil
¼ tsp garlic powder
Pinch of salt

Directions:
Preheat the oven to 400 F.
Add green beans to a large bowl.
Add remaining ingredients on top of green beans and toss to coat.
Spread green beans onto the baking tray and roast in a preheated oven for 15 minutes. Stir halfway through.
Serve and enjoy.

Nutrition:
Calories 101, | Fat: 7.5g, | Carbohydrates: 8.3g, | Sugar: 1.6g, | Protein: 2.6g, | Cholesterol: 1mg

107. Smoked Salmon, Avocado and Cucumber Bites

Preparation Time: 5 minutes | **Cooking time:** 10 minutes | **Servings:** 12 bites

Ingredients:
1 large avocado, peeled and pit removed
1 medium cucumber
6 oz. smoked salmon
½ tablespoon lime juice
chives
black pepper

Directions:
Cut the cucumber into ¼ inch thick pieces and lay flat on a plate.
Add the lime juice and the avocado to a bowl and mash with a fork until creamy.
Spread avocado on each cucumber and add a slice of salmon on top.
Add black pepper and chives to each bite.
Once cooked, serve.

Nutrition:
46 calories | 3 g fat | 2 g total carbs | 3 g protein

108. Roasted Almonds

Preparation Time: 10 minutes | **Cooking time:** 20 minutes | **Servings:** 12

Ingredients:
2 ½ cups almonds
¼ tsp cayenne
¼ tsp ground coriander
¼ tsp cumin
¼ tsp chili powder
1 tbsp fresh rosemary, chopped
1 tbsp olive oil
2 ½ tbsp maple syrup
Pinch of salt

Directions:
Preheat the oven to 325 F.
Spray a baking tray with cooking spray and set it aside.
In a mixing bowl, whisk together oil, cayenne, coriander, cumin, chili powder, rosemary, maple syrup, and salt.
Add almond and stir to coat.
Spread almonds onto the prepared baking tray.
Roast almonds in a preheated oven for 20 minutes. Stir halfway through.
Serve and enjoy.

Nutrition:
Calories 137, | Fat: 11.2g, | Carbohydrates: 7.3g, | Sugar: 3.3g, | Protein: 4.2g, | Cholesterol: 0mg

109. Pistachio Balls

Preparation Time: 10 minutes | **Cooking time:** 5 minutes | **Servings:** 16

Ingredients:
½ cup pistachios, unsalted
1 cup dates, pitted
½ tsp ground fennel seeds
½ cup raisins

Pinch of pepper

Directions:
Add all ingredients into the food processor and process until well combined.
Make small balls and place them onto the baking tray.
Serve and enjoy.

Nutrition:
Calories 55, Fat 0.9g, | Carbohydrates: 12.5g, | Sugar: 9.9g, | Protein: 0.8g, | Cholesterol: 0mg

110. Healthy & Quick Energy Bites

Preparation Time: 10 minutes | **Cooking time:** 0 minutes | **Servings:** 20

Ingredients:
2 cups cashew nuts
¼ tsp cinnamon
1 tsp lemon zest
4 tbsp dates, chopped
1/3 cup unsweetened shredded coconut
¾ cup dried apricots

Directions:
Line the baking tray with parchment paper and set it aside.
Add all ingredients to a food processor and process until the mixture is crumbly and well combined.
Make small balls from the mixture and place them on a prepared baking tray.
Serve and enjoy.

Nutrition:
Calories 100, | Fat: 7.5g, | Carbohydrates: 7.2g, | Sugar: 2.8g, | Protein: 2.4g, | Cholesterol: 0mg

111. Tuna Sandwiches

Preparation Time: 30 minutes | **Cooking time:** 0 minutes | **Servings:** 4

Ingredients:
1½ Tbsp Lemon Juice, fresh
1 Tbsp Olive Oil
Sea Salt & Black Pepper to taste
½ Clove Garlic, minced
2½ oz. Canned Tuna, drained
Ounce Canned Olives, sliced
½ cup Fennel, fresh & chopped
4 Slices Whole Grain Bread

Directions:
In a bowl, whisk lemon juice, garlic, pepper, and oil before adding in fennel, olive sand tuna.
Use a fork to separate it into chunks before mixing everything.
Divide between four slices of bread.
Serve it.

Nutrition:
Calories: 332 | Protein: 29 Grams | Fat: 12 Grams | Carbs: 27 Grams

112. Pepperoni Eggs

Preparation Time: 10 minutes | **Cooking time:** 15 minutes | **Servings:** 2

Ingredients:
1 cup of egg substitute
1 egg
3 green onions, minced
8 slices of pepperoni, diced
1/2 teaspoon of garlic powder
1 teaspoon melted butter
1/4 cup grated Romano cheese
1 pinch of salt and ground black pepper to taste

Directions:
Combine the egg substitute, egg, green onions, pepperoni slices, and garlic powder in a bowl.
Heat the butter in a non-stick frying pan over low heat. Add the egg mixture, cover the pan, and cook until the eggs are set, 10 to 15 minutes.
Sprinkle Romano cheese on eggs and season with salt and pepper.

Nutrition: (Per Serving)
266 Calories | 16.2 g Fat | 3.7 grams of Carbohydrates | 25.3 g of Protein | 124 mg of Cholesterol | 586 mg of sodium

113. Flatbread Sandwiches

Preparation & Cooking time: 20 minutes | **Servings:** 6

Ingredients: Needed:
Olive oil (1 tbsp.)
7-Grain pilaf (8.5 oz. pkg.)
English seedless cucumber (1 cup)
Seeded tomato (1 cup)
Crumbled feta cheese (.25 cup)
Fresh lemon juice (2 tbsp.)

Freshly cracked black pepper (.25 tsp.)
Plain hummus (7 oz. container)
Whole grain white flatbread wraps (3 @ 2.8 oz. each)

Directions:
Cook the pilaf as directed on the package instructions and cool.
Chop and combine the tomato, cucumber, cheese, oil, pepper, and lemon juice. Fold in the pilaf.
Prepare the wraps with the hummus on one side. Spoon in the pilaf and fold.
Slice into a sandwich and serve.

Nutrition:
Calories: 310 | Protein: 10 grams | Fat: 9 grams

Chapter 3: Main Meals

114. Cacciatore Black Olive Chicken

Preparation Time: 10 minutes | **Cooking time:** 15 minutes | **Servings:** 4-6

Ingredients:
6–8 bone-in chicken drumsticks or mixed drumsticks and thighs
1 cup chicken stock
1 bay leaf
½ cup black olives, pitted
1 medium yellow onion, roughly chopped
1 teaspoon dried oregano
1 teaspoon garlic powder
1 (28-ounce) can stewed tomato puree

Directions:
Open the top lid of your Instant Pot.
Add the stock, bay leaf, and salt; stir to combine with a wooden spatula.
Add the chicken, tomato puree, onion, garlic powder, and oregano; stir again.
Close the lid and make sure that the valve is sealed properly.
Press MANUAL and set the timer to 15 minutes.
The Instant Pot will start building pressure; allow the mixture to cook for the set time.
When the timer reads zero, press NPR for natural pressure release. It will take 8–10 minutes to release the pressure.
Open the lid and remove the bay leaf.
Serve warm with the black olives on top.

Nutrition:
Calories 309, | Fat: 16.5 g | Carbs 9 g, | Protein: 30.5 g, | Sodium: 833 mg

115. Mustard Green Chicken

Preparation Time: 10 minutes | **Cooking time:** 15 minutes | **Servings:** 4

Ingredients:
1 bunch mustard greens, washed and chopped
Juice of 1 lemon
⅓ cup extra-virgin olive oil
4–5 boneless, skinless chicken thighs
3 cloves garlic, minced
1 cup white wine
1 teaspoon Dijon mustard
1 teaspoon honey
½ cup cherry tomatoes
½ cup green olives, pitted
Salt and pepper to taste

Directions:
Open the top lid of your Instant Pot.

Add the mustard greens and then add the chicken thighs on top; season to taste with salt and pepper.
Top with garlic, tomatoes, olives, mustard, and honey followed by lemon juice, olive oil, and wine.
Close the lid and make sure that the valve is sealed properly.
Press MANUAL and set the timer to 15 minutes.
The Instant Pot will start building pressure; allow the mixture to cook for the set time.
When the timer reads zero, press QPR for quick pressure release.
Open the lid and take out the prepared recipe.
Serve warm.

Nutrition:
Calories 314, | Fat: 19 g | Carbs 14.5 g, | Protein: 17 g, | Sodium: 745 mg

116. Chickpea Spiced Chicken

Preparation Time: 10 minutes | **Cooking time:** 15 minutes | **Servings:** 4

Ingredients:
2 red peppers, cut into chunks
1 large onion
1 (15-ounce) can chickpeas
4 cloves garlic
2 Roma tomatoes, cut into chunks
1 tablespoon olive oil
1–2 pounds boneless chicken thighs, trimmed and cut into large chunks
1 teaspoon cumin
½ teaspoon coriander powder
1 teaspoon salt
½ teaspoon pepper
1 teaspoon dried parsley
½ teaspoon red pepper flakes
1 cup tomato sauce

Directions:
Open the top lid of your Instant Pot and press SAUTÉ.
Add the olive oil to the pot and heat it.
Add the onions and garlic and stir cook for 4–5 minutes until soft and translucent.
Add chicken chunks; stir-cook for 4–5 minutes on each side to evenly brown.
Add the remaining ingredients and stir gently.
Close the lid and make sure that the valve is sealed properly.
Press MANUAL and set the timer to 10 minutes.
The Instant Pot will start building pressure; allow the mixture to cook for the set time.
When the timer reads zero, press QPR for quick pressure release.
Open the lid and take out the prepared recipe.
Serve warm with grilled pita (optional).

Nutrition:
Calories 371, | Fat: 15 g | Carbs 26.5 g, | Protein: 33 g, | Sodium: 1279 mg

117. Vegetable Rice Chicken

Preparation Time: 10 minutes | **Cooking time:** 4 minutes | **Servings:** 4

Ingredients:
1 medium red onion, diced
4 cloves garlic, minced
2 tablespoons olive oil
3 chicken breasts, diced
3 tablespoons lemon juice
1½ cups chicken broth
1 each red and yellow bell pepper, chopped
1 zucchini, sliced
1 cup dry white rice
¼ cup parsley, finely chopped
1 tablespoon oregano
½ teaspoon each salt and pepper
¼ cup feta cheese, crumbled (optional)

Directions:
Open the top lid of your Instant Pot.
Add the olive oil, garlic, onions, chicken, lemon juice, oregano, salt, and pepper; stir to combine with a wooden spatula.
Add the broth and rice; stir again.
Close the lid and make sure that the valve is sealed properly.
Press MANUAL and set the timer to 4 minutes.
The Instant Pot will start building pressure; allow the mixture to cook for the set time.
When the timer reads zero, press QPR for quick pressure release.
Open the lid and stir in the bell peppers, zucchini, and parsley. Close the lid and allow it to settle for 5–10 minutes.
Serve warm with the feta cheese on top (optional).

Nutrition:
Calories 293, | Fat: 11 g | Carbs 33.5 g, | Protein: 16 g, | Sodium: 951 mg

118. Chicken Shawarma

Preparation Time: 10 minutes | **Cooking time:** 15 minutes | **Servings:** 2-4

Ingredients:
1–1½ pounds boneless skinless chicken thighs, cut into strips
1–1½ pounds boneless skinless chicken breasts, cut into strips
½ teaspoon turmeric
1 teaspoon ground cumin
1 teaspoon paprika
¼ teaspoon granulated garlic
⅛ teaspoon ground cinnamon
¼ teaspoon ground allspice
¼ teaspoon chili powder
Salt and pepper to taste
1 cup chicken broth or stock

Directions:
Combine the spices in a mixing bowl. Add the strips and coat well. Season to taste with salt and pepper.
Open the top lid of your Instant Pot.
Add the broth and chicken strips; stir to combine with a wooden spatula.
Close the lid and make sure that the valve is sealed properly.
Press MANUAL and set the timer to 15 minutes.
The Instant Pot will start building pressure; allow the mixture to cook for the set time.
When the timer reads zero, press QPR for quick pressure release.
Open the lid and take out the prepared recipe. Serve warm with cooked veggies of your choice (optional).

Nutrition:
Calories 273, | Fat: 9 g| Carbs 12.5 g | Protein: 39.5 g | Sodium: 1149 mg

119. Caprese Chicken Dinner

Preparation Time: 10 minutes | **Cooking time:** 20 minutes | **Servings:** 6

Ingredients:
¼ cup maple syrup or honey
¼ cup chicken stock or water
¼ cup balsamic vinegar
1½ pounds boneless skinless chicken thighs, fat trimmed
8 slices mozzarella cheese
3 cups cherry tomatoes
½ cup basil leaves, torn

Directions:
Open the top lid of your Instant Pot.
Add the stock, balsamic vinegar, and maple syrup; stir to combine with a wooden spatula.
Add the chicken thighs and combine well.
Close the lid and make sure that the valve is sealed properly.
Press MANUAL and set the timer to 10 minutes.
The Instant Pot will start building pressure; allow the mixture to cook for the set time.
When the timer reads zero, press QPR for quick pressure release.
Open the lid, remove the chicken thighs, and place them on a baking sheet. Top each thigh with a cheese slice.
Press SAUTÉ; cook the sauce mixture for 4–5 minutes. Add the tomatoes and simmer for 1–2 minutes. Mix in the basil.
Add the baking sheet to a broiler and heat until the cheese melts. Serve warm with the sauce drizzled on top.

Nutrition:
Calories 311, | Fat: 13 g | Carbs 15 g, | Protein: 31 g | Sodium: 364 mg

120. Pork Loin with Peach Sauce

Preparation Time: 10 minutes | **Cooking time:** 10 minutes | **Servings:** 4

Ingredients:
1 (15-ounce) can peaches, diced (liquid reserved)
¼ cup beef stock
1 pound pork loin, cut into chunks
2 tablespoons white wine
2 tablespoons sweet chili sauce
2 tablespoons soy sauce
2 tablespoons honey
¼ cup water combined with 2 tablespoons cornstarch

Directions:
Open the top lid of your Instant Pot.

Add the wine, soy sauce, beef stock, peach can liquid, and chili sauce; stir to combine with a wooden spatula.
Add the pork and stir again.
Close the lid and make sure that the valve is sealed properly.
Press MANUAL and set the timer to 5 minutes.
The Instant Pot will start building pressure; allow the mixture to cook for the set time.
When the timer reads zero, press NPR for natural pressure release. It will take 8–10 minutes to release the pressure.
Open the lid and mix in the cornstarch mixture.
Press SAUTÉ; cook for 4–5 minutes. Mix in the peach pieces.
Serve warm.

Nutrition:
Calories 277, | Fat: 4.5 g | Carbs 28 g | Protein: 24 g | Sodium: 1133 mg

121. Mushroom Tomato Beef

Preparation Time: 10 minutes | **Cooking time:** 18 minutes | **Servings:** 4

Ingredients:
1 pound beef steaks
1 bay leaf
1 tablespoon dried thyme
6 ounces cherry tomatoes
1 pound button mushrooms, thinly chopped
2 tablespoons extra-virgin olive oil or avocado oil
½ teaspoon pepper
1 teaspoon salt

Directions:
Rub the steaks with salt, pepper, and thyme.
Open the top lid of your Instant Pot.
Add the bay leaf, 3 cups of water, and the steaks; stir to combine with a wooden spatula.
Close the lid and make sure that the valve is sealed properly.
Press MANUAL and set the timer to 13 minutes.
The Instant Pot will start building pressure; allow the mixture to cook for the set time.
When the timer reads zero, press QPR for quick pressure release.
Open the lid and take out the prepared recipe.
Add the olive oil to the pot and SAUTÉ the tomatoes and mushrooms for 4–5 minutes.

Add the steak and stir-cook to evenly brown. Serve warm.

Nutrition:
Calories 384, | Fat: 21 g | Carbs 11 g, | Protein: 23.5 g, | Sodium: 664 mg

122. Black Olive Sea Bass

Preparation Time: 10 minutes | **Cooking time:** 4 minutes | **Servings:** 4

Ingredients:
12 cherry tomatoes
12 black olives
2 tablespoons marinated baby capers
¼ cup water
4 frozen sea bass or other white fish fillets, halved
½ teaspoon salt
Pinch of chili flakes
⅓ cup roasted red peppers, sliced
2 tablespoons olive oil
Fresh parsley or basil, chopped, to serve

Directions:
Open the top lid of your Instant Pot.
Add the water and frozen fish. Add the remaining ingredients and top with olive oil, sea salt, and chili flakes.
Close the lid and make sure that the valve is sealed properly.
Press MANUAL and set the timer to 4 minutes.
The Instant Pot will start building pressure; allow the mixture to cook for the set time.
When the timer reads zero, press NPR for natural pressure release. It will take 8–10 minutes to release the pressure.
Open the lid and take out the prepared recipe.
Serve warm with basil or parsley on top.
Note: If using fresh fish, set the timer to 5 minutes at LOW pressure.

Nutrition:
Calories 224, | Fat: 12.5 g | Carbs 4.5 g, | Protein: 24 g, | Sodium: 824 mg

123. Broccoli Soy Salmon

Preparation Time: 10 minutes | **Cooking time:** 2 minutes | **Servings:** 4

Ingredients:
1-pound Alaskan salmon, cut into four 4-ounce fillets
Salt and pepper to taste
Dressing:
1 pound broccoli, cut into florets
2 tablespoons raw apple cider vinegar
6 tablespoons extra-virgin olive oil
2 tablespoons soy sauce or tamari
3 tablespoons maple syrup
1 teaspoon toasted sesame oil
1 tablespoon fresh ginger, minced
1 clove garlic
Sesame seeds and chopped green onions for garnish

Directions:
Blend the sesame oil, olive oil, ginger, garlic, soy sauce, vinegar, and maple syrup in a blender. Set aside.
Open the top lid of your Instant Pot.
Add 1 cup of water to the cooking pot; arrange the trivet/steamer basket.
Place the salmon fillets skin side down over the steamer basket/trivet. Season with salt and pepper.
Close the lid and make sure that the valve is sealed properly.
Press MANUAL and set the timer to 1 minute.
The Instant Pot will start building pressure; allow the mixture to cook for the set time.
When the timer reads zero, press QPR for quick pressure release.
Open the lid and place the broccoli over the salmon.
Close the lid and make sure that the valve is sealed properly.
Press MANUAL and set the timer to 1 minute.
The Instant Pot will start building pressure; allow the mixture to cook for the set time.
When the timer reads zero, press QPR for quick pressure release.
Open the lid and serve warm with the dressing, green onions, and sesame seeds on top.

Nutrition:
Calories 395, | Fat: 26 g | Carbs 14 g | Protein: 27 g | Sodium: 654 mg

124. Shrimp Fennel Pasta

Preparation Time: 10 minutes | **Cooking time:** 12 minutes | **Servings:** 6

Ingredients:
1 small fennel bulb
1 tablespoon olive oil
½ cup chopped onion
6 cloves garlic, minced
1 (28-ounce) can crushed tomatoes
½–1 teaspoon crushed red pepper
2¾ cups water
⅓ cup cognac or brandy
1-pound raw jumbo shrimp, peeled and deveined
1-pound dried whole wheat trottole pasta or corkscrews
2 tablespoons chopped parsley
Salt and pepper to taste
3 tablespoons heavy cream

Directions:
Open the top lid of your Instant Pot and press SAUTÉ.
Add the oil to the pot and heat it.
Add the fennel, garlic, onions, and red pepper and stir cook for 3–5 minutes to soften.
Add the cognac, salt, and pepper, tomatoes, water, and pasta. Stir the mixture.
Close the lid and make sure that the valve is sealed properly.
Press MANUAL and set the timer to 4 minutes.
The Instant Pot will start building pressure; allow the mixture to cook for the set time.
When the timer reads zero, press QPR for quick pressure release.
Open the lid and mix in the cream, shrimp, and parsley.
Press SAUTÉ; cook the mixture for 2–3 minutes. Serve warm.

Nutrition:
Calories 491 | Fat: 7 g | Carbs 61 g, | Protein: 28 g | Sodium: 797 mg

125. Fish with Farro & Green Beans

Preparation Time: 10 minutes | **Cooking time:** 12 minutes | **Servings:** 4

Ingredients:
4 skinless trout fillets
½ pound green beans
1 cup farro
2 cups water
1 tablespoon olive oil
1 teaspoon salt (divided)
1 teaspoon pepper (divided)
½ tablespoon sugar
¼ cup melted butter
½ teaspoon dried rosemary
2 cloves garlic, minced
½ teaspoon dried thyme
½ tablespoon lemon juice

Directions:
In a mixing bowl, combine the green beans, olive oil, ½ teaspoon of the pepper, and ½ teaspoon of the salt.
In another bowl, combine the remaining salt and pepper with butter, sugar, garlic, lemon juice, and rosemary. Add the fish and coat well.
Open the top lid of your Instant Pot.
Add the water and farro; season with some salt. Arrange the trivet/steamer basket. Place the trout fillets and green beans over it.
Close the lid and make sure that the valve is sealed properly.
Press MANUAL and set the timer to 12 minutes.
The Instant Pot will start building pressure; allow the mixture to cook for the set time.
When the timer reads zero, press QPR for quick pressure release.
Open the lid and take out the prepared recipe. Serve warm.

Nutrition:
Calories 331, | Fat: 16.5 g | Carbs 36 g, | Protein: 12 g, | Sodium: 602 mg

126. Spinach Mackerel

Preparation Time: 10 minutes | **Cooking time:** 12 minutes | **Servings:** 4

Ingredients:
5 potatoes, peeled and chopped
¼ cup olive oil
4 mackerels, skin on
1 pound spinach, torn
1 teaspoon dried rosemary, chopped
2 cloves garlic, crushed
1 lemon, juiced
2 sprigs mint leaves, chopped
Salt to taste

Directions:
Open the top lid of your Instant Pot and press SAUTÉ.
Add the olive oil to the pot and heat it.
Add the garlic and rosemary; stir-cook for 1–2 minutes until fragrant.
Add the spinach and a pinch of salt and cook for 4–5 minutes, until the spinach wilts. Remove the spinach and set it aside.
Add the potatoes and fish and top with sea salt and lemon juice.
Add 1 cup of water.
Close the lid and make sure that the valve is sealed properly.
Press STEAM and set the timer to 7 minutes.
The Instant Pot will start building pressure; allow the mixture to cook for the set time.
When the timer reads zero, press QPR for quick pressure release.
Open the lid and take out the prepared recipe. Serve the fish warm with the spinach on top.

Nutrition:
Calories 289 | Fat: 12 g | Carbs 13.5 g | Protein: 21 g | Sodium: 733 mg

127. Instant Pot Beef Gyros

Preparation Time: 10 minutes | **Cooking time:** 15 minutes | **Servings:** 6

Ingredients:
2 pounds beef roast, thinly sliced
1 tablespoon dried parsley
1 teaspoon salt
3 cloves minced garlic
1 teaspoon black pepper
1 sliced red onion
4 tablespoons oil of choice
1 teaspoon olive oil
½ cup vegetable broth
1 tablespoon lemon juice
For the Tzatziki sauce:

1 cup plain yogurt
1 clove minced garlic
2 tablespoon fresh dill
½ cup cucumber, peeled, seeded, and chopped finely

Directions:
Turn on the instant pot and then add oil to the bottom.
Add meat, seasonings, garlic, and onion to sear and soften the onions.
Pour the lemon juice and broth over the meat, and then stir it, lock the lid into place, and then use meat/stew and cook it for 9 minutes.
Let it naturally release pressure for 3 minutes before quickly releasing.
Mix the Tzatziki sauce and if you want vegetable toppings or apple cider vinegar over this, you can.
You can also put lettuce at the bottom of naan or pita bread before adding meat and toppings.

Nutrition:
Calories: 395, | Fat: 27g | Carbs: 4gNet | Carbs: 4g | Protein: 32g | Fiber: 0g. | Sodium: 38%

128. Instant Pot Lasagna Hamburger Helper

Preparation Time: 2 minutes | **Cooking time:** 5 minutes | **Servings:** 4

Ingredients:
1 box 16 oz, pasta
8 oz. Ricotta cheese
½ pound ground beef
1 jar pasta sauce
8 oz. Mozzarella cheese
½ pound ground sausage
4 cups water

Directions:
Put the pot in a sauté mode and cook the meat till brown and crumbled.
Add in the rest of the ingredients, turn it on high pressure for five minutes.
Quick-release it, and then put in half the cheese and half the mozzarella, and then put into a baking pan with more mozzarella. You can cook it for another 2-3 minutes till the cheese melts.

Nutrition:
Calories: 537 | Fat: 33g | Carbs: 25 g | Protein: 34g | Fiber: 4g | Sodium: 36%

129. Salmon Salad Wraps

Preparation Time: 20 minutes | **Cooking time:** 0 minutes | **Servings:** 2

Ingredients:
½ lb. Salmon Fillet, cooked & flaked
½ cup Carrots, diced
½ cup Celery, diced
1 Tbsp Red Onion, diced
1 Tbsp Dill, fresh & diced
1 Tbsp Capers
½ Tbsp Aged Balsamic Vinegar
½ Tbsp Olive Oil
½ a dash of salt
½ a dash of pepper
2 Whole Wheat Flatbread Wraps

Directions:
Mix carrots, dill, celery, salmon, red onions, oil, vinegar, pepper, capers, and salt together in the bowl.
Divide between flatbread, and fold up to serve.

Nutrition:
Calories: 336 | Protein: 32 Grams | Fat: 16 Grams | Carbs: 23 Grams

130. Scallops in Citrus Sauce

Preparation Time: 10 minutes | **Cooking time:** 10 minutes | **Servings:** 2

Ingredients:
2 tsp olive oil
½ shallot, minced
10 sea scallops, cleaned
½ tsp lime zest
½ tbsp lemon zest
2 tsp orange zest
½ tbsp fresh basil, chopped
½ cup fresh orange juice
½ tbsp fresh lemon juice
½ tbsp raw honey
½ tbsp plain Greek yogurt
½ tsp fine sea salt
1 tbsp Provencal herbs

Directions:
In a large skillet, pour olive oil and heat over medium-high heat.
Add in minced shallot and sauté for 1 minute.
Add shallots and cook until soft.
In cold water, rinse scallops and pat dry with a towel. In the skillet, pour 1 tablespoon of olive oil, sprinkle with salt and Provencal herbs.
Add scallops in and sear for 2 minutes.
Turn once during this time. They should be tender.
Push scallops to the edge of the skillet, stirring in three zests, basil, lemon juice, and orange juice.
It will boil and the scallops will absorb the flavorful liquid.
Let the scallops stay in the pan for exactly 2 minutes with the juice and turn off the heat.
Cook in a saucepan for 2 minutes on medium heat.
Coat scallops in the sauce before serving warm.

Nutrition:
Calories: 207 | Protein: 26 Grams | Fat: 4 Grams | Carbs: 17 Grams

131. Trout & Greens

Preparation Time: 30 minutes | **Cooking time:** 0 minutes | **Servings:** 2

Ingredients:
½ tsp Olive Oil (plus extra for greasing)
1 cup Swiss Chard, chopped
1 cup Kale, chopped
¼ Sweet Onion, thinly sliced
1 5-oz Trout Fillet, skin on
¼ Lemon, zested
Pinch of Fine Salt
Pinch of Black Pepper
½ a bunch of parsley
Pinch of Black Pepper

Directions:
Preheat the oven to 395 degrees.
Defrost trout if frozen, rinse, cut fins, head, and tail.
Dry with paper towels.
Slice lemons and halve each slice.
Finely chop parsley.
Rub the fish inside and out with ground black pepper.
Fill the trout abdomen with greens.
Make diagonal cuts on one side of the trout.
Insert a half cup of lemon into each of them.
Sprinkle fish with lemon juice and olive oil.
Grease a 9x13 inch baking dish using olive oil.
Lay out on a baking dish Swiss chard, kale, and onion.
Put the fish on top of vegetables.
Make sure the skin side is up.
Serve with lemon zest after seasoning.

Nutrition:
Calories: 120 | Protein: 17 Grams | Fat: 5 Grams | Carbs: 0 Grams

132. Healthy Instant Pot Mediterranean Chicken

Preparation Time: 5 minutes | **Cooking time:** 20 minutes | **Servings:** 4

Ingredients:
4 chicken breasts, skinless and boneless
1 can tomatoes with no salt, diced
½ onion, diced
2 tablespoons garlic, minced
25 kalamata or black olives, pitted
2 tablespoons extra virgin olive oil
2 tablespoons Greek seasoning
fresh oregano sprigs for garnish

Directions:
Cut each chicken breast into 4-5 large pieces.
Turn the instant pot to the sauté setting.
Add the olive oil, onion, and garlic to the pot.
Cook for 3-4 minutes.
Sprinkle Greek seasoning on both sides of chicken pieces.
Take ½ of chicken breasts and place them in the instant pot. Brown on both sides, which will take about 3 minutes. Remove this first batch of chicken and add in the second. Once this chicken is done, remove it from the pot.
Add the tomatoes, olives, and dried oregano.
Nestle the chicken breasts into the olive oil mixture.
Set the instant pot to Manual high for 15 minutes.
Allow to self-release for 10 minutes and then pressure release until all the steam is gone.
Serve this chicken over your favorite rice.

Nutrition:
Calories: 228 | Protein: 11.1 grams | Total Fat: 10.7 grams | Carbohydrates: 25 grams

133. Mediterranean Instant Pot Chicken and Potatoes

Preparation Time: 5 minutes | **Cooking time:** 14 minutes | **Servings:** 6

Ingredients:
2 tablespoons of olive oil
½ teaspoon of ground pimento
1 teaspoon of smoked paprika
6 chicken thighs, bone-in and skin on
1 cup of chicken broth
1 teaspoon of garlic puree
juice from 1 lemon
2 tablespoons of honey
1 pound of potatoes, cut in half
1 teaspoon of fresh oregano

Directions:
In a bowl, combine 1 tablespoon of olive oil with salt, smoked paprika, and pimento.
Add in the chicken thighs and coat well with the sauce.
Take the other tablespoon of olive oil in the instant pot using the sauté setting. Add the chicken thighs and brown on both sides, about 6 minutes.
Turn the instant pot off. Remove any excess oil before going further.
Pour in chicken broth.
Add in remaining ingredients, put on the lid, and lock. Set the valve to the sealing position.
Set the instant pot to pressure cook, high pressure for 8 minutes.
Allow for 5 minutes of natural pressure release, then perform quick pressure release for remaining.

Nutrition:
Calories: 273 | Protein: 24 grams | Total Fat: 10 grams | Carbohydrates: 21 grams

134. Instant Pot Moroccan Chicken

Preparation Time: 5 minutes | **Cooking time:** 25 minutes | **Servings:** 4

Ingredients:
1 teaspoon paprika
1 teaspoon turmeric
1 teaspoon ground cumin
½ teaspoon salt
¼ teaspoon black pepper
3 tablespoons olive oil
1 ½ pounds chicken thighs, boneless and skinless
1 ½ cups chicken broth
2 garlic cloves, minced
½ cup onions, diced
1 teaspoon ginger, minced
¾ cup quinoa, uncooked
1 can chickpeas, drained
½ cup dried cherries
chopped cilantro leaves

Directions:
Mix paprika, turmeric, cumin, salt, and pepper in a small bowl.
Coat the chicken thighs with the spice rub. Set aside.
Add 2 tablespoons of olive oil to the bottom of the instant pot.
Select the sauté mode.
Add chicken to the instant pot and cook both sides until slightly brown. Remove from the instant pot and set aside on a plate.
Add another tablespoon of olive oil to the bottom of the pot.
Add garlic, onions, and ginger, then sauté for 2 minutes while stirring slowly.
Add quinoa, dried cherries, chickpeas, chicken broth, and the browned chicken.
Close the lid and seal.
Press poultry and set for 10 minutes.
At the end of the 10 minutes, use tongs to carefully turn the knob for quick release of pressure.
Once the pressure is released, carefully open the lid.
Check the chicken and make sure it is 165 degrees F before serving.
Serve on a plate with cilantro garnish.

Nutrition:
Calories: 194.2 | Protein: 28.1 grams | Total Fat: 6.7 grams | Carbohydrates: 5.3 grams

135. Mediterranean Instant Pot Shredded Beef

Preparation Time: 5 minutes | **Cooking time:** 25 minutes | **Servings:** 8

Ingredients:
2 pounds Chuck beef roast
1 teaspoon salt
1 cup white onion, chopped
¾ cup carrots, chopped
¾ cup yellow bell pepper, chopped
14.5 ounce can of fire-roasted tomatoes
2 tablespoons red wine vinegar
1 tablespoon garlic, minced
1 tablespoon Italian seasoning blend
1/2 tablespoon dried red pepper flakes

Directions:
Cut the beef roast into small chunks, and trim away any excess fat. Season with salt.
Place the small beef cubes into the instant pot and then top with onions, carrots, and yellow bell peppers.
Open the can of fire-roasted tomatoes and stir in the vinegar, garlic, Italian dressing, and red pepper flakes. Pour mixture over the beef in the instant pot.
Secure the lid and set the vent to seal. Set for 20 minutes in the high-pressure setting.
When the timer goes off, quickly release the pressure, remove the lid carefully, and let it stand for 5-10 minutes.
Use a large fork to shred beef into bite-sized pieces and then serve.

Nutrition:
Calories: 190.2 | Protein: 23.5 grams | Total Fat: 6.3 grams | Carbohydrates: 8.9 grams

136. Instant Pot Orzo with Shrimp, Tomatoes, And Feta

Preparation Time: 5 minutes | **Cooking time:** 28 minutes | **Servings:** 4

Ingredients:
1 tablespoon olive oil
1 medium onion, diced
2 cloves garlic, minced
2, 14-ounce cans diced tomatoes
2 tablespoons fresh parsley
2 tablespoons fresh dill
1-¼ pounds medium shrimp, peeled and deveined
¼ teaspoon salt
¼ teaspoon freshly ground black pepper
⅔ cup of feta cheese, crumbled
1-¼ cups chicken stock
¾ cup orzo

Directions:
Set your instant pot to sauté. Then add the olive oil, onion, and garlic. Cook, stirring until softened and translucent, which takes about 3 minutes. Deglaze with a splash of water to prevent sticking.
Next, add the tomatoes and chicken stock and bring to a boil, and stir.
Add the orzo, dill, and parsley and mix well.
Add shrimp and season with salt and pepper and add feta cheese.
Set instant pot on manual high pressure for 3 minutes.
After 3 minutes, press the quick release to avoid overcooking the shrimp and orzo. Serve.

Nutrition:
Calories: 395 | Protein: 38 grams | Total Fat: 11 grams | Carbohydrates: 33 grams

137. Instant Pot Mediterranean Chicken Wings

Preparation Time: 5 minutes | **Cooking time:** 13 minutes | **Servings:** 2

Ingredients:
1 pound of chicken wings
1 tablespoon garlic puree
3 tablespoons coconut oil
6 tablespoons white wine
1 tablespoon chicken seasoning
3 tablespoons tarragon
1 tablespoon oregano
1 tablespoon basil
salt and pepper to taste
1 cup of water

Directions:
Split the marinade ingredients between two foil sheets.
Split the chicken wings between the two parcels and rub well into the mixture. Seal each package up and shake so everything has a good coating.
Add one cup of water to your instant pot and place the steaming shelf on top.
Place chicken wing packets on top of the steaming shelf.
Place the lid on your instant pot and set the valve to seal, then press the manual button for 10 minutes.
Ready to serve in foil packets.

Nutrition:
Calories: 545 | Protein: 26 grams | Total Fat: 42 grams | Carbohydrates: 8 grams

138. Honey Almond–Crusted Chicken Tenders

Preparation Time: 10 minutes | **Cooking time:** 10 minutes | **Servings:** 4

Ingredients:
Nonstick cooking spray
1 tablespoon honey
1 tablespoon whole-grain or Dijon mustard
¼ teaspoon kosher or sea salt
¼ teaspoon freshly ground black pepper
1-pound boneless, skinless chicken breast tenders or tenderloins
1 cup almonds (about 3 ounces)

Directions:
Preheat the oven to 425°F. Line a large, rimmed baking sheet with parchment paper. Place a wire cooling rack on the parchment-lined baking sheet, and coat the rack well with nonstick cooking spray.
In a large bowl, combine the honey, mustard, salt, and pepper. Add the chicken and stir gently to coat. Set aside.
Use a knife or a mini food processor to roughly chop the almonds; they should be about the size of sunflower seeds. Dump the nuts onto a large sheet of parchment paper and spread them out. Press the coated chicken tenders into the nuts until evenly coated on all sides. Place the chicken on the prepared wire rack.
Bake for 15 to 20 minutes, or until the internal temperature of the chicken measures 165°F on a meat thermometer and any juices run clear. Serve immediately.

Nutrition:
Per serving | Calories: 263 | Total fat: 12g | Saturated fat: 1g | Cholesterol: 65mg | Sodium: 237mg | Potassium: 85mg | Total Carbohydrates: 9g | Fiber: 3g | Protein: 31g

139. Romesco Poached Chicken

Preparation Time: 5 minutes | **Cooking time:** 20 minutes | **Servings:** 6

Ingredients:
1½ pounds boneless, skinless chicken breasts, cut into 6 pieces
1 carrot, halved
1 celery stalk, halved
½ onion, halved
2 garlic cloves, smashed
3 sprigs fresh thyme or rosemary
1 cup Romesco Dip
2 tablespoons chopped fresh flat-leaf (Italian) parsley
¼ teaspoon freshly ground black pepper

Directions:
Put the chicken in a medium saucepan. Fill with water until there's about one inch of liquid above the chicken. Add the carrot, celery, onion, garlic, and thyme. Cover and bring it to a boil. Reduce the heat to low (keeping it covered), and cook for 12 to 15 minutes, or until the internal temperature of the chicken measures 165°F on a meat thermometer and any juices run clear.
Remove the chicken from the water and let sit for 5 minutes.
When you're ready to serve, spread ¾ cup of romesco dip on the bottom of a serving platter. Arrange the chicken breasts on top, and drizzle with the remaining romesco dip. Sprinkle the tops with parsley and pepper.

Nutrition:
Per serving | Calories: 237 | Total fat: 11g | Saturated fat: 1g | Cholesterol: 65mg | Total Carbohydrates: 8g | Fiber: 4g | Protein: 28g

140. Roasted Red Pepper Chicken with Lemony Garlic Hummus

Preparation Time: 10 minutes | **Cooking time:** 10 minutes | **Servings:** 6

Ingredients:
1¼ pounds boneless, skinless chicken thighs, cut into 1-inch pieces
½ sweet or red onion, cut into 1-inch chunks (about 1 cup)
2 tablespoons extra-virgin olive oil
½ teaspoon dried thyme
¼ teaspoon freshly ground black pepper
¼ teaspoon kosher or sea salt
1 (12-ounce) jar roasted red peppers, drained, and chopped
Lemony Garlic Hummus, or a 10-ounce container prepared hummus
½ medium lemon
3 (6-inch) whole-wheat pita bread, cut into eighths

Directions:
Line a large, rimmed baking sheet with aluminum foil. Set aside. Set one oven rack about 4 inches below the broiler element. Preheat the broiler to high.
In a large bowl, mix the chicken, onion, oil, thyme, pepper, and salt. Spread the mixture onto the prepared baking sheet.
Place the chicken under the broiler and broil for 5 minutes. Remove the pan, stir in the red peppers, and return to the broiler. Broil for another 5 minutes, or until the chicken and onion just start to char on the tips. Remove from the oven.
Spread the hummus onto a large serving platter, and spoon the chicken mixture on top. Squeeze the juice from half a lemon over the top, and serve with the pita pieces.

Nutrition:
Per serving | Calories: 324 | Total fat: 11g | Saturated fat: 2g | Cholesterol: 54mg | Sodium: 625mg | Total Carbohydrates: 29g | Fiber: 6g | Protein: 29g

141. Sheet Pan Lemon Chicken and Roasted Artichokes

Preparation Time: 10 minutes | **Cooking time:** 20 minutes | **Servings:** 4

Ingredients:
2 large lemons
3 tablespoons extra-virgin olive oil, divided
½ teaspoon kosher or sea salt
2 large artichokes
4 (6-ounce) bone-in, skin-on chicken thighs

Directions:
Put a large, rimmed baking sheet in the oven. Preheat the oven to 450°F with the pan inside. Tear off four sheets of aluminum foil about 8-by-10 inches each; set aside.
Using a Microplane or citrus zester, zest 1 lemon into a large bowl. Halve both lemons and squeeze all the juice into the bowl with the zest. Whisk in 2 tablespoons of oil and the salt. Set aside.
Rinse the artichokes with cool water, and dry with a clean towel. Using a sharp knife, cut about 1½ inches off the tip of each artichoke. Cut about ¼ inch off each stem. Halve each artichoke lengthwise so each piece has equal amounts of the stem. Immediately plunge the artichoke halves into the lemon juice and oil mixture (to prevent browning) and turn to coat on all sides. Lay one artichoke half flat-side down in the center of a sheet of aluminum foil, and close loosely to make a foil packet. Repeat the process with the remaining three artichoke halves. Set the packets aside.
Put the chicken in the remaining lemon juice mixture and turn to coat.
Using oven mitts, carefully remove the hot baking sheet from the oven and pour on the remaining tablespoon of oil; tilt the pan to coat. Carefully arrange the chicken, skin-side down, on the hot baking sheet. Place the artichoke packets, flat-side down, on the baking sheet as well. (Arrange the artichoke packets and chicken with space between them so air can circulate them.)
Roast for 20 minutes, or until the internal temperature of the chicken measures 165°F on a meat thermometer and any juices run clear. Before serving, check the artichokes for

doneness by pulling on a leaf. If it comes out easily, the artichoke is ready.

Nutrition:
Per serving | Calories: 372 | Total fat: 11g | Saturated fat: 29g | Cholesterol: 98mg | Sodium: 381mg | Total Carbohydrates: 11g | Fiber: 5g | Protein: 20g

142. Parmesan Chicken Wraps

Preparation Time: 25 minutes | **Cooking time:** 5 minutes | **Servings:** 2

Ingredients:
½ Lb. Chicken breasts, boneless & skinless
2/3 cup whole-wheat panko bread crumbs
½ egg, large
¼ cup buttermilk
½ cup parmesan cheese, grated
¾ tsp garlic powder, divided
½ cup tomatoes, salt-free & crushed
½ tsp oregano
2 whole wheat tortilla, 8 inches each
½ cup mozzarella cheese, fresh & sliced
1 cup flat-leaf parsley, loosely packed, fresh & chopped

Directions:
Preheat the oven to 425 ° F. Cover the baking sheet with foil. Put the wire rack on top of it. Coat a wire rack in nonstick spray then set it to the side.
Put the chicken breasts in a zipper-top plastic bag. Pound chicken so that it's ¼ inch thick with a rolling pin or meat mallet. Slice it into 2 portions.
Whisk egg and buttermilk together in a shallow bowl.
Mix parmesan, panko crumbs, and garlic powder together in another shallow bowl.
Dip chicken into the egg mixture and then the crumb mixture. Press the crumbs into the chicken, and then place them on the wire rack.
Bake for fifteen to eighteen minutes, and then slice diagonally
In a microwave-safe bowl, mix tomatoes, remaining garlic powder, and oregano together. Microwave for 1 minute and set it to the side.
Wrap tortillas with a damp paper towel and then microwave for thirty seconds.

Assemble with chicken and cheese, and then spread warm tomato sauce over each one. Serve warm.

Nutrition:
Calories: 174 | Protein: 18 Grams | Fat: 4 Grams | Carbs: 16 Grams

143. Cod & Green Bean Dinner

Preparation Time: 10 minutes | **Cooking time:** 10 minutes | **Servings:** 2

Ingredients:
1 Tbsp Olive Oil
½ Tbsp Balsamic Vinegar
2 Cod Fillets, 4 oz. Each
1 ½ Cups Green Beans
½ Pint Cherry Grapes

Directions:
Heat oven to 390° F, and get out two rimmed baking sheets. Coat them with nonstick cooking spray.
Whisk vinegar and oil together in the bowl before setting it to the side.
Place two pieces of fish on each baking sheet.
Get out a bowl and combine tomatoes and beans. Pour the oil and vinegar over it, and toss to coat.
Pour half of the green bean mixture over the fish on one baking sheet and the remaining fish and green beans on the other.
Turn the fish over, and coat it with the oil mixture.
Bake for five to eight minutes.

Nutrition:
Calories: 440 | Protein: 14 Grams | Fat: 22 Grams | Carbs: 48 Grams

144. Easy Grilled Catfish

Preparation Time: 10 minutes | **Cooking time:** 15 minutes | **Servings:** 4

Ingredients:
2 Lemons
2 Catfish Fillets, 4 oz. Each
½ Tbsp Olive Oil
Sea Salt & Black Pepper to Taste

Directions:
Pat fish dry with paper towels, and allow it to stand at room temperature for ten minutes.

Coat the grill with cooking spray, and preheat it to 375° F.
Cut one of the lemons in half, and then set half of it aside.
Slice one half into ¼ inch slices.
Get out a bowl and squeeze a tablespoon of juice from the reserved half.
Mix lemon juice and oil in a bowl, and brush fish with it.
Season with salt and pepper.
Place the lemon slices on the grill, and place fish fillets on each one.
Turn the fish halfway through.
Serve with lemon.

Nutrition:
Calories: 323 | Protein: 56 Grams | Fat: 10 Grams | Carbs: 0 Grams

145. Garlic & Orange Shrimp

Preparation Time: 10 minutes | **Cooking time:** 10 min | **Servings:** 2

Ingredients:
3 Cloves Garlic, minced
Sea Salt & Black Pepper to taste
2 ½ oz. Shrimp, Fresh & Raw, de-shelled & tails removed
½ Tbsp Thyme, fresh & chopped
½ Tbsp Rosemary, fresh & chopped
1 ½ Tbsp Olive Oil, divided
½ Orange, large

Directions:
Zest orange. In a zipper-top bag, combine zest with 1 Tbsp of oil and rosemary. Add in garlic, pepper, salt, and thyme.
Add in shrimp, and seal. Massage the seasoning into the shrimp and set aside.
Heat a grill, and then brush the remaining oil onto shrimp.
Cook for 4-6 minutes in a grill pan, and flip halfway through.
Transfer to a serving bowl, and then chop orange.
Serve with shrimp.

Nutrition:
Calories: 327 | Protein: 31 Grams | Fat: 5 Grams | Carbs: 40 Grams

146. Kale & Tuna Bowl

Preparation Time: 5 minutes | **Cooking time:** 15 minutes | **Servings:** 2

Ingredients:
½ lb. Kale, Chopped
1 ½ Tbsp Olive Oil
1 oz. Olives, Canned & Drained
1 ½ Cloves Garlic, Minced
½ cup Onion, Chopped
¼ cup Capers
¼ Tsp Crushed Red Pepper
1 Tsp Sugar
1 Cans Tuna in Olive Oil, Undrained & 6 oz. Each1
7 Ounce Can Cannellini Beans, Drained & Rinsed
½ a dash of salt
½ a dash of pepper

Directions:
Fill a large stockpot three-quarters full of water. Bring it to a boil and cook kale for 2 minutes. Drain in a colander before setting it aside.
Place the empty pot over medium heat, and then add in oil.
Add in onion, and cook for 4 minutes. Stir often and cook garlic for a minute more.
Stir often, and then add the olives, crushed red pepper, capers, and cook for 1 minute. Stir often, and add kale and sugar in. Stir well, and cook for 8 minutes while covered.
Remove from heat, and mix in tuna, pepper, salt, and beans.
Serve warm.

Nutrition:
Calories: 265 | Protein: 16 Grams | Fat: 12 Grams | Carbs: 26 Grams

147. Tuna with Lettuce and Chickpeas

Preparation Time: 25 minutes | **Cooking time:** 0 min | **Servings:** 2

Ingredients:
½ head green lettuce, washed and cut in thin strips
½ cup chopped watercress
½ cucumber, peeled and chopped
½ tomato, diced

½ can tuna, drained and broken into small chunks
¼ cup chickpeas, from a can
3-4 radishes, sliced
1½-2 spring onions, chopped
juice of half a lemon
1½- Tbsp extra-virgin olive oil

Directions:
Mix green lettuce, watercress, cucumber, tomato, radishes, spring onion in a large bowl. Add to the vegetables the tuna and the chickpeas. Toss over with lemon juice, oil, and salt to taste.

Nutrition:
Calories: 290 | Protein: 14 Grams | Fat: 22 Grams | Carbs: 8 Grams

148. Chicken with Salsa & Cilantro

Preparation Time: 10 minutes | **Cooking time:** 15 minutes | **Servings:** 6

Ingredients:
1 ½ lb. chicken breast fillets
2 cups salsa verde
1 teaspoon garlic, minced
1 teaspoon cumin
2 tablespoons fresh cilantro, chopped

Directions:
Put the chicken breast fillets inside the Instant Pot.
Pour the salsa, garlic, and cumin on top.
Seal the pot.
Set it to poultry.
Release the pressure quickly.
Remove the chicken and shred.
Put it back in the pot.
Stir in the cilantro.

Nutrition:
Calories 238 | Total Fat: 8.7g | Saturated Fat: 2.3g | Cholesterol: 101mg | Sodium: 558mg | Total Carbohydrate: 3.8g | Dietary Fiber: 0.4g | Total Sugars: 1.2g | Protein: 34g | Potassium: 285mg

149. Lime Chicken with Black Beans

Preparation Time: 10 minutes | **Cooking time:** 10 minutes | **Servings:** 8

Ingredients:
8 chicken thighs (boneless and skinless)
3 tablespoons lime juice
1 cup black beans
1 cup canned tomatoes
4 teaspoons garlic powder

Directions:
Marinate the chicken in a mixture of lime juice and garlic powder.
Add the chicken to the Instant Pot.
Pour the tomatoes on top of the chicken.
Seal the pot.
Set it to manual.
Cook at high pressure for 10 minutes.
Release the pressure naturally.
Stir in the black beans.
Press sauté to simmer until black beans are cooked.

Nutrition:
Calories 370 | Total Fat: 11.2g | Saturated Fat: 3.1g | Cholesterol: 130mg | Sodium: 128mg | Total Carbohydrate: 17.5g | Dietary Fiber: 4.1g | Total Sugars: 1.5g | Protein: 47.9g | Potassium: 790mg

150. Turkey Verde with Brown Rice

Preparation Time: 5 minutes | **Cooking time:** 25 | **Servings:** 5

Ingredients:
2/3 cup chicken broth
1 1/4 cup brown rice
1 1/2 lb. turkey tenderloins
1 onion, sliced
1/2 cup salsa verde

Directions:
Add the chicken broth and rice to the Instant Pot.
Top with the turkey, onion, and salsa.
Cover the pot.
Set it to manual.
Cook at high pressure for 18 minutes.
Release the pressure naturally.

Wait for 8 minutes before opening the pot.

Nutrition:
Calories 336 | Total Fat: 3.3g | Saturated Fat: 0.3g | Cholesterol: 54mg | Sodium: 321mg | Total Carbohydrate: 39.4g | Dietary Fiber: 2.2g | Total Sugars: 1.4g | Protein: 38.5g | Potassium: 187mg

151. Turkey with Basil & Tomatoes

Preparation Time: 5 minutes | **Cooking time:** 10 minutes | **Servings:** 4

Ingredients:
4 turkey breast fillets
1 tablespoon olive oil
1/4 cup fresh basil, chopped
1 1/2 cups cherry tomatoes, sliced in half
1/4 cup olive tapenade

Directions:
Season the turkey fillets with salt.
Add the olive oil to the Instant Pot.
Set it to sauté.
Cook the turkey until brown on both sides.
Stir in the basil, tomatoes, and olive tapenade.
Cook for 3 minutes, stirring frequently.

Nutrition:
Calories 188 | Total Fat: 5.1g | Saturated Fat: 1g | Cholesterol: 0mg | Sodium: 3mg | Total Carbohydrate: 2.8g | Dietary Fiber: 1.6g | Total Sugars: 1.9g | Protein: 33.2g | Potassium: 164mg

152. Turkey Lasagna

Preparation Time: 20 minutes | **Cooking time:** 10 minutes | **Servings:** 4

Ingredients:
4 tortillas
1 1/4 cup salsa
1/2 can refried beans
1 1/2 cups cooked turkey
1 1/4 cup cheddar cheese, shredded

Directions:
Spray a small pan with oil.
Spread the refried beans on each tortilla.
Place the first tortilla inside the pan.
Add layers of turkey, salsa, and cheese.
Place another tortilla and repeat the layers.
Pour 1 cup of water inside the Instant Pot.
Place the layers on top of a steamer basket.
Place the basket inside the Instant Pot.
Choose the manual setting.
Cook at high pressure for 10 minutes.

Nutrition:
Calories 335 | Total Fat: 15.5g | Saturated Fat: 8.6g | Cholesterol: 79mg | Sodium: 849mg | Total Carbohydrate: 21.1g | Dietary Fiber: 4.5g | Total Sugars: 3g | Protein: 28.5g | Potassium: 561mg

153. Tuna with Lemon Butter Sauce

Preparation Time: 10 minutes | **Cooking time:** 5 minutes | **Servings:** 4

Ingredients:
4 tuna fillets
1/4 cup lemon juice
1 tablespoon fresh dill
1 tablespoon butter

Directions:
Pour 1 cup water and lemon juice into the Instant Pot.
Add the steamer basket.
Put the tuna fillet on top of the basket.
Season with salt and pepper and dill.
Seal the pot.
Choose the manual setting.
Cook at high pressure for 5 minutes.
Release the pressure quickly.
Remove from the pot.
Place the butter on top.
Let it melt and then serve.

Nutrition:
Calories 213 | Total Fat: 18.5g | Saturated Fat: 1.9g | Cholesterol: 8mg | Sodium: 25mg | Total Carbohydrate: 0.8g | Dietary Fiber: 0.2g | Total Sugars: 0.3g | Protein: 10.8g | Potassium: 46mg

154. Mediterranean Cod

Preparation Time: 10 minutes | **Cooking time:** 10 minutes | **Servings:** 6

Ingredients:
6 cod fillets
1 onion, sliced
1 tablespoon lemon juice
1 teaspoon oregano

28 oz. canned diced tomatoes

Directions:
Season the cod with salt and pepper.
Add 2 tablespoons of olive oil into the Instant Pot.
Set it to sauté.
Add the cod and cook for 3 minutes per side.
Add the rest of the ingredients. Mix well.
Cover the pot.
Choose manual function.
Cook at high pressure for 5 minutes.
Release the pressure quickly.
Pour the sauce over the cod before serving.

Nutrition:
Calories 123 | Total Fat: 1.3g | Saturated Fat: 0.1g | Cholesterol: 55mg | Sodium: 78mg | Total Carbohydrate: 7.1g | Dietary Fiber: 2.1g | Total Sugars: 4.3g | Protein: 21.4g | Potassium: 348mg

155. Shrimp with Honeydew and Feta

Preparation Time: 10 minutes | **Cooking time:** 4 minutes | **Servings:** 4

Ingredients:
30 big shrimp, peeled and deveined
Salt and black pepper to taste
A pinch of cayenne pepper
¼ cup olive oil
2 tablespoons shallots, chopped
1 teaspoon lime zest
4 teaspoons lime juice
½ pound frisee or curly endive, torn into small pieces
1 honeydew melon, peeled, seeded, and chopped
¼ cup mint, chopped
8 ounces feta cheese, crumbled
1 tablespoon coriander seeds

Directions:
Heat a pan with 2 tablespoons oil over medium-high heat, add shrimp, cook for 1 minute, and flip.
Add lime zest, 1 teaspoon lime juice, shallots, and some salt, stir, cook for 1 minute and take off the heat.
In a bowl, mix the remaining oil with the rest of the lime juice, salt, and pepper to taste.
Add honeydew and frisee, stir and divide into plates.

Add shrimp, coriander seeds, mint, and feta on top and serve.

Nutrition:
Calories 245, | Fat: 23 | Fiber 3 | Carbs 23, | Protein: 45

156. Spicy Seared Mussels

Preparation Time: 10 minutes | **Cooking time:** 15 minutes | **Servings:** 4

Ingredients:
1 and ½ cups green grapes, cut in quarters
Zest from 1 lemon, chopped
Juice of 1 lemon
Salt and black pepper to taste
2 scallions, chopped
¼ cup olive oil
2 tablespoons mint, chopped
2 tablespoons cilantro, chopped
1 teaspoon cumin, ground
1 teaspoon paprika
½ teaspoon ginger, ground
¼ teaspoon cinnamon, ground
1 teaspoon turmeric, ground
½ cup water
1 and ½ pounds sea scallops

Directions:
Heat a pan with the water, some salt, and the lemon zest over medium-high heat and simmer for 10 minutes.
Drain lemon zest and transfer to a bowl.
Mix with grapes, 2 tablespoons oil, cilantro, mint, and scallions, and stir well.
In another bowl, mix cumin with turmeric, paprika, cinnamon, and ginger and stir.
Season scallops with salt and pepper, coat with the spice mix, and place them on a plate.
Heat a pan with remaining oil over medium-high heat, add scallops, cook for 2 minutes on each side and transfer to a plate.
Divide scallops on 4 plates, pour lemon juice over them, and serve with grape relish.

Nutrition:
Calories 320, | Fat: 12 | Fiber 2 | Carbs 18, | Protein: 28

157. Zucchini and Chicken

Preparation Time: 10 minutes | **Cooking time:** 15 minutes | **Servings:** 4

Ingredients:
1 pound chicken breasts, cut into medium chunks
12 ounces zucchini, sliced
2 tablespoons olive oil
2 garlic cloves, minced
2 tablespoons parmesan, grated
1 tablespoon parsley, chopped
Salt and black pepper to taste

Directions:
In a bowl, mix chicken pieces with 1 tablespoon oil, some salt, and pepper, and toss to coat.
Heat a pan over medium-high heat, add chicken pieces, brown for 6 minutes on all sides, transfer to a plate and leave aside.
Heat the pan with the remaining oil over medium heat, add zucchini slices and garlic, stir, and cook for 5 minutes.
Return chicken pieces to the pan, add parmesan on top, stir, take off heat, divide between plates and serve with some parsley on top.

Nutrition:
Calories 212 | Fat: 4 | Fiber 3 | Carbs 4 | Protein: 7

158. Shrimp with Tomatoes & Feta

Preparation Time: 10 minutes | **Cooking time:** 10 minutes | **Servings:** 4

Ingredients:
2 tablespoons butter
1 tablespoon garlic, minced
1 lb. shrimp, peeled and deveined
14 oz. canned crushed tomatoes
1 cup feta cheese, crumbled

Directions:
Set the Instant Pot to sauté.
Add the butter.
Wait for it to melt.
Add the garlic and cook until fragrant.
Add the shrimp and tomatoes.
Seal the pot.
Set it to manual.
Cook at low pressure for 1 minute.
Release the pressure quickly.
Top with the feta cheese.

Nutrition:
Calories 218 | Total Fat: 10.5g | Saturated Fat: 6.6g | Cholesterol: 192mg | Sodium: 618mg | Total Carbohydrate: 7.9g | Dietary Fiber: 2.2g | Total Sugars: 4.7g | Protein: 22.5g | Potassium: 150mg

159. Mussels in Garlic Butter Sauce

Preparation Time: 10 minutes | **Cooking time:** 10 minutes | **Servings:** 4

Ingredients:
2 tablespoons butter
4 cloves garlic, minced
1/2 cup broth
1/2 cup white wine
2 lb. mussels, cleaned and beard removed

Directions:
Add the butter and garlic to the Instant Pot.
Switch it to sauté.
Cook until fragrant.
Pour in the broth and wine.
Add the mussels.
Cover the pot.
Set it to manual.
Cook at high pressure for 5 minutes.
Release the pressure quickly.

Nutrition:
Calories 280 | Total Fat: 11g | Saturated Fat: 4.7g | Cholesterol: 79mg | Sodium: 787mg | Total Carbohydrate: 10.3g | Dietary Fiber: 0.1g | Total Sugars: 0.4g | Protein: 27.9g | Potassium: 795mg

160. Fish Stew with Tomatoes & Olives

Preparation Time: 5 minutes | **Cooking time:** 10 minutes | **Servings:** 4

Ingredients:
1 1/2 lb. halibut fillet
4 cloves garlic, minced
1 cup cherry tomatoes, sliced in half
3 cups tomato soup
1 cup green olives, pitted and sliced

Directions:
Season the fish with salt and pepper.
Pour 1 tablespoon olive oil into the Instant Pot.
Add the garlic and cook until fragrant.
Add the fish.
Cook for 3 minutes per side.
Add the rest of the ingredients.
Cover the pot.
Select the manual function.
Cook at low pressure for 3 minutes.
Release the pressure quickly.

Nutrition:
Calories 245 | Total Fat: 3.7g | Saturated Fat: 0.6g | Cholesterol: 35mg | Sodium: 1098mg | Total Carbohydrate: 28g | Dietary Fiber: 2.9g | Total Sugars: 16.5g | Protein: 26.3g | Potassium: 1040mg

161. Rosemary Salmon

Preparation Time: 10 minutes | **Cooking time:** 5 minutes | **Servings:** 3

Ingredients:
1 lb. salmon fillets
10 oz. fresh asparagus
1 sprig fresh rosemary
1/2 cup cherry tomatoes, sliced in half
Dressing (a mixture of 1 tablespoon olive oil and 1 tablespoon lemon juice)

Directions:
Add 1 cup of water into the Instant Pot.
Place the steamer rack inside.
Put the salmon fillets on the rack.
Add the rosemary and asparagus on top of the salmon.
Cover the pot.
Select the manual setting.
Cook at high pressure for 3 minutes.
Release the pressure quickly.
Transfer to a plate.
Place the tomatoes on the side.
Drizzle with the dressing.

Nutrition:
Calories 267 | Total Fat: 14.3g | Saturated Fat: 2.1g | Cholesterol: 67mg | Sodium: 71mg | Total Carbohydrate: 5.2g | Dietary Fiber: 2.5g | Total Sugars: 2.7g | Protein: 31.7g | Potassium: 853mg

162. Salmon with Tahini Sauce

Preparation Time: 5 minutes | **Cooking time:** 5 minutes | **Servings:** 2

Ingredients:
1 lb. salmon fillets
3 tablespoons tahini sauce
2 lemon slices
2 sprigs fresh rosemary

Directions:
Add the water to the Instant Pot.
Place a steamer basket inside.
Put the salmon on top of the basket.
Season with salt and pepper.
Place rosemary and lemon slices on top.
Cover the pot.
Set it to manual.
Cook at high pressure for 3 minutes.
Release the pressure quickly.
Drizzle the tahini sauce on top before serving.

Nutrition:
Calories 306 | Total Fat: 14.2g | Saturated Fat: 2.1g | Cholesterol: 100mg | Sodium: 101mg | Total Carbohydrate: 1.4g | Dietary Fiber: 0.7g | Total Sugars: 0.2g | Protein: 44.1g | Potassium: 892mg

163. Fish & Potatoes

Preparation Time: 5 minutes | **Cooking time:** 10 minutes | **Servings:** 4

Ingredients:
1 lb. cod fillets, sliced into strips.
1 onion, chopped
1 lb. potatoes, sliced into cubes
4 cups vegetable broth
1 teaspoon old bay seasoning

Directions:
Season the salmon fillets with salt and pepper.
Pour 1 tablespoon olive oil in the Instant Pot.
Add the onion.
Cook for 3 minutes.
Add the salmon and cook for 1 minute per side.
Pour in the broth and add the potatoes and seasoning.
Seal the pot.
Turn it to manual.
Cook at high pressure for 3 minutes.

Release the pressure quickly.

Nutrition:
Calories 278 | Total Fat: 8.5g | Saturated Fat: 1.4g | Cholesterol: 50mg | Sodium: 981mg | Total Carbohydrate 21.3g | Dietary Fiber: 3.3g | Total Sugars: 3.2g | Protein: 29.1g | Potassium: 1144mg

164. Sautéed Shrimp with Garlic Couscous

Preparation Time: 5 minutes | **Cooking time:** 5 minutes | **Servings:** 4

Ingredients:
1 lb. shrimp, peeled and deveined
1/2 cup fresh chives, chopped
1/2 cup fresh parsley, chopped
1 tablespoon scallions, chopped
10 oz. garlic-flavored couscous

Directions:
Choose the sauté function in the Instant Pot.
Add 2 tablespoons of olive oil.
Add the shrimp and herbs.
Cook for 3 minutes, stirring frequently.
Serve with the couscous.

Nutrition:
Calories 615 | Total Fat: 8.3g | Saturated Fat: 0.6g | Cholesterol: 239mg | Sodium: 1556mg | Total Carbohydrate: 95g | Dietary Fiber: 8g | Total Sugars: 2.7g | Protein: 43.8g | Potassium: 256mg

165. Seafood Garlic Couscous

Preparation Time: 10 minutes | **Cooking time:** 20 minutes | **Servings:** 8

Ingredients:
8 scallions, sliced
4 (5.4-oz.) boxes garlic-flavored couscous, boiled and drained
1-pound raw shrimp, peeled, deveined, and coarsely chopped
1 cup fresh parsley, chopped
4 tablespoons olive oil
2 pounds codfish, cut into 1-inch pieces
1 cup fresh chives, chopped
Hot sauce, to taste
1-pound bay scallops
Salt and black pepper, to taste

Directions:
Mix shrimps, scallions, codfish, scallops, parsley, chives, salt, and black pepper in a bowl.
Heat oil in a deep skillet and add the seafood mixture.
Sauté until golden and pour in the hot sauce.
Lower the heat and cover with a lid.
Divide the couscous into the serving plates and top evenly with the seafood mixture.
Dish out and serve immediately.

Nutrition:
Calories 476 | Total Fat 9 g | Saturated Fat 1.4 g | Cholesterol 138 mg | Total Carbs 68 g | Dietary Fiber 4.9 g | Sugar: 0.8 g | Protein: 32.9 g

166. Crusty Grilled Clams

Preparation Time: 5 minutes | **Cooking time:** 10 minutes | **Servings:** 4

Ingredients:
4 tablespoons garlic and parsley butter
2 cups toasted bread crumbs
Fresh herbs, to garnish
2 pounds clams, rinsed and debearded
Chopped tomatoes, to garnish
2 lemons, zested

Directions:
Boil clams in water for about 3 minutes in a large pot.
Preheat the grill and lightly grease a baking sheet.
Mix zest and bread crumbs in a bowl.
Drizzle butter on top of the clams and place them shell side down on the baking sheet.
Top the breadcrumbs mixture on the clams and transfer to the grill.
Cover the grill for about 4 minutes and let it cook.
Serve garnished with tomato and parsley.

Nutrition:
Calories 510 | Total Fat 19.5 g | Saturated Fat 8.9 g | Cholesterol 94 mg | Total Carbs 47.3 g | Dietary Fiber 2.4 g | Sugar: 3.4 g | Protein: 34.3 g

167. Lemon-Thyme Chicken

Preparation Time: 5 minutes | **Cooking time:** 25 minutes | **Servings:** 8

Ingredients:
½ teaspoon black pepper
2 teaspoons crushed dried thyme, divided
8 small skinless, boneless chicken breast halves
2 lemons, thinly sliced
1 teaspoon salt
4 garlic cloves, minced
8 teaspoons extra-virgin olive oil, divided
2 pounds fingerling potatoes, halved lengthwise

Directions:
Heat half of olive oil in a skillet over medium heat and add ½ teaspoon thyme, potatoes, salt, and black pepper.
Cover and cook for about 12 minutes, while stirring occasionally.
Push the potatoes to the side and add the rest of the olive oil and chicken.
Sear the chicken for about 5 minutes per side and season with thyme.
Arrange lemon slices over the chicken and cover the pan.
Cook for about 10 minutes and dish out to serve hot.

Nutrition:
Calories 483 | Total Fat 9.4 g | Saturated Fat 0.7 g | Cholesterol 195 mg | Total Carbs 18.8 g | Dietary Fiber 2.1 g | Sugar: 1.2 g | Protein: 80.3 g

168. Mediterranean Chicken Quinoa Bowl

Preparation Time: 10 minutes | **Cooking time:** 15 minutes | **Servings:** 8

Ingredients:
½ cup almonds, slivered
1/8 teaspoon black pepper
2 tablespoons extra-virgin olive oil, divided
1/8 teaspoon crushed red pepper
1 tablespoon fresh parsley, finely chopped
1 cup cooked quinoa
1/8 cup feta cheese, crumbled
½ teaspoon salt
1 small garlic clove, crushed
½ pound boneless, skinless chicken breasts, trimmed
½ (7-ounce) jar roasted red peppers, rinsed
½ teaspoon paprika
1/8 cup pitted Kalamata olives, chopped
½ cup cucumber, diced
¼ teaspoon ground cumin
1/8 cup red onions, finely chopped

Directions:
Preheat the oven on a broiler setting and lightly grease a baking sheet.
Sprinkle the chicken with salt and black pepper.
Transfer it to the baking sheet and broil for about 15 minutes.
Let the chicken cool for about 5 minutes and transfer to a cutting board.
Shred the chicken and keep it aside.
Put almonds, paprika, black pepper, garlic, half of the olive oil, red pepper, and cumin in a blender.
Blend until smooth and dish out in a bowl.
Toss quinoa, red onions, 2 tablespoons oil, quinoa, and olives in a bowl.
Divide the quinoa mixture in the serving bowls and top with cucumber, red pepper sauce, and chicken.
Garnish with feta cheese and parsley to immediately serve.

Nutrition:
Calories 741 | Total Fat 33.7 g | Saturated Fat 6.7 g | Cholesterol 109 mg | Total Carbs 62.1 g | Dietary Fiber 8.2 g | Sugar: 3.6 g | Protein: 48.4 g

169. Blue Cheese-Topped Pork Chops

Preparation Time: 10 minutes | **Cooking time:** 15 minutes | **Servings:** 8

Ingredients:
4 tablespoons fat-free Italian salad dressing
½ cup reduced-fat blue cheese, crumbled
2 pinches cayenne pepper
8 (6-ounce) bone-in pork loin chops
2 tablespoons fresh rosemary, snipped

Directions:
Preheat the oven at broiler settings and line a broiler tray with a foil sheet.
Mix the Italian salad dressing with cayenne pepper.
Brush the dressing mixture on both sides of the pork chops.

Place the pork chops on the broiler tray and broil the pork chops for about 10 minutes, flipping in between.
Top the chops with blue cheese and rosemary to serve.

Nutrition:
Calories 506 | Total Fat 21.6 g | Saturated Fat 3.7 g | Cholesterol 193 mg | Total Carbs 3.3 g | Dietary Fiber 0.9 g | Sugar: 1.6 g | Protein: 70.8 g

170. Greek Beef Steak and Hummus Plate

Preparation Time: 10 minutes | **Cooking time:** 15 minutes | **Servings:** 8

Ingredients:
2 tablespoons plus 2 teaspoons garlic, minced
2 cups hummus
½ cup fresh oregano leaves, chopped
2 medium cucumbers, thinly sliced
½ teaspoon black pepper
2 pounds beef sirloin steaks, boneless, cut 1 inch thick
2 teaspoons black pepper
4 tablespoons Romesco Sauce
2 tablespoons lemon peel, grated
6 tablespoons fresh lemon juice

Directions:
Preheat a grill on medium heat and lightly grease a grill grate.
Mix all the dry spices and rub on both sides of the beef steaks.
Grill the steaks for about 15 minutes.
Mix sliced cucumber, lemon juice, and black pepper in a bowl.
Slice the grilled steak and sprinkle with salt and black pepper.
Serve with Romesco sauce, hummus, and cucumber strips.

Nutrition:
Calories 463 | Total Fat 37.7 g | Saturated Fat 7.6 g | Cholesterol 28 mg | Total Carbs 68.7 g | Dietary Fiber 14.5 g | Sugar: 19.7 g | Protein: 36.4 g

171. Linguine with Shrimp

Preparation Time: 10 minutes | **Cooking time:** 15 minutes | **Servings:** 4

Ingredients:
3 tablespoons extra virgin olive oil
12 ounces linguine
1 tablespoon garlic, minced
30 large shrimp, peeled and deveined
A pinch of red pepper flakes, crushed
1 cup green olives, pitted and chopped
3 tablespoons lemon juice
1 teaspoon lemon zest, grated
¼ cup parsley, chopped

Directions:
Put some water in a large saucepan, add water, bring to a boil over medium-high heat, add linguine, cook according to instructions, take off heat, drain and put in a bowl, and reserve ½ cup cooking liquid.
Heat a pan with 2 tablespoons oil over medium-high heat, add shrimp, stir, and cook for 3 minutes.
Add pepper flakes and garlic, stir, and cook 10 seconds more.
Add remaining oil, lemon zest, and juice and stir well.
Add pasta and olives, reserved cooking liquid and parsley, stir, cook for 2 minutes more, take off heat, divide between plates and serve.

Nutrition:
Calories 500 | Fat: 20 | Fiber 5 | Carbs 45 | Protein: 34

172. Oysters with Vinaigrette

Preparation Time: 10 minutes | **Cooking time:** 6 minutes | **Servings:** 4

Ingredients:
2 tablespoons shallots, finely chopped
½ cup sherry vinegar
A pinch of saffron threads
½ cup olive oil
1 tablespoon olive oil
Salt and black pepper to taste
1 pound chorizo sausage, chopped
1 pound fennel bulbs, thinly sliced lengthwise
24 oysters, shucked

Directions:
In a bowl, mix shallots with vinegar, saffron, salt, pepper, and ½ cup olive oil and stir well.
Heat a pan with the remaining oil over medium-high heat, add sausage, cook for 4 minutes, transfer to a paper towel, drain grease, and put on a plate.
Add fennel on top, spoon vinaigrette into each oyster and place them on the platter as well, drizzle the rest of the vinaigrette on top and serve.

Nutrition:
Calories 113, | Fat: 1 | Fiber 3 | Carbs 10, | Protein: 7

173. Grilled Chicken Wraps

Preparation Time: 10 minutes | **Cooking time:** 12 minutes | **Servings:** 4

Ingredients:
4 chicken breast halves, skinless and boneless
Salt and black pepper to taste
4 teaspoons olive oil
1 small cucumber, sliced
3 teaspoons cilantro, chopped
4 Greek whole wheat tortillas
4 tablespoons peanut sauce

Directions:
Heat a grill pan over medium-high heat, season chicken with salt and pepper, rub with the oil, add to the grill, cook for 6 minutes on each side, transfer to a cutting board, leave to cool down for 5 minutes, slice, and leave aside.
In a bowl, mix cilantro with cucumber and stir.
Heat a pan over medium heat, add each tortilla, heat up for 20 seconds, and transfer them to a working surface.
Spread 1 tablespoon peanut sauce on each tortilla, divide chicken and cucumber mix on each, fold, arrange on plates and serve.

Nutrition:
Calories 321, | Fat: 3 | Fiber 4 | Carbs 7 | Protein: 9

174. Pork Chops and Relish

Preparation Time: 15 minutes | **Cooking time:** 14 minutes | **Servings:** 6

Ingredients:
6 pork chops, boneless
7 ounces marinated artichoke hearts, chopped and their liquid reserved
A pinch of salt and black pepper
1 teaspoon hot pepper sauce
1 and ½ cups tomatoes, cubed
1 jalapeno pepper, chopped
½ cup roasted bell peppers, chopped
½ cup black olives, pitted and sliced

Directions:
In a bowl, mix the chops with the pepper sauce, reserved liquid from the artichokes, cover, and keep in the fridge for 15 minutes.
Heat a grill over medium-high heat, add the pork chops and cook for 7 minutes on each side.
In a bowl, combine the artichokes with the peppers and the remaining ingredients, toss, divide on top of the chops and serve.

Nutrition:
Calories 215, | Fat: 6 | Fiber 1 | Carbs 6, | Protein: 35

175. Glazed Pork Chops

Preparation Time: 10 minutes | **Cooking time:** 20 minutes | **Servings:** 4

Ingredients:
¼ cup apricot preserves
4 pork chops, boneless
1 tablespoon thyme, chopped
½ teaspoon cinnamon powder
2 tablespoons olive oil

Directions:
Heat a pan with the oil over medium-high heat, add the apricot preserves and cinnamon, whisk, bring to a simmer, cook for 10 minutes, and take off the heat.
Heat your grill over medium-high heat, brush the pork chops with some of the apricot glaze, place them on the grill and cook for 10 minutes. Flip the chops, brush them with more apricot glaze, cook for 10 minutes more, and divide between plates.

Sprinkle the thyme on top and serve.

Nutrition:
Calories 225, | Fat: 11 | Fiber 0 | Carbs 6 | Protein: 23

176. Pork Chops and Cherries Mix

Preparation Time: 10 minutes | **Cooking time:** 12 minutes | **Servings:** 4

Ingredients:
4 pork chops, boneless
Salt and black pepper to the taste
½ cup cranberry juice
1 and ½ teaspoons spicy mustard
½ cup dark cherries, pitted and halved
Cooking spray

Directions:
Heat a pan greased with the cooking spray over medium-high heat, add the pork chops, cook them for 5 minutes on each side, and divide between plates.
Heat the same pan over medium heat, add the cranberry juice and the rest of the ingredients, whisk, bring to a simmer, cook for 2 minutes, drizzle over the pork chops and serve.

Nutrition:
Calories 262 | Fat: 8 | Fiber 1 | Carbs 16, | Protein: 30

177. Pork Chops and Herbed Tomato Sauce

Preparation Time: 10 minutes | **Cooking time:** 10 minutes | **Servings:** 4

Ingredients:
4 pork loin chops, boneless
6 tomatoes, peeled and crushed
3 tablespoons parsley, chopped
2 tablespoons olive oil
¼ cup kalamata olives pitted and halved
1 yellow onion, chopped
1 garlic clove, minced

Directions:
Heat a pan with the oil over medium heat, add the pork chops, cook them for 3 minutes on each side, and divide between plates.
Heat the same pan again over medium heat, add the tomatoes, parsley, and the rest of the ingredients, whisk, simmer for 4 minutes, drizzle over the chops and serve.

Nutrition:
Calories 334, | Fat: 17 | Fiber 2 | Carbs 12, | Protein: 34

178. Black Bean & Turkey Skillet

Preparation Time: 20 minutes | **Cooking time:** 10 minutes | **Servings:** 6

Ingredients:
1 tablespoon olive oil
20 oz. lean ground turkey
2 medium zucchinis, cut into slices
1 medium onion, chopped
2 banana peppers, seeded and chopped
3 garlic cloves, minced
1/2 teaspoon dried oregano
1 x 15 oz. can black beans, rinsed and drained
1 x 14.5 oz. can diced tomatoes, undrained
1 tablespoon balsamic vinegar
1/2 teaspoon salt

Directions:
Grab a large skillet, add the oil, and pop over medium heat.
Add the turkey, zucchini, onion, peppers, garlic, and oregano, and cook for 10 minutes.
Stir through the remaining ingredients and cook long enough to heat through then serve and enjoy.

Nutrition:
Calories: 259 | Net Carbs: 6g | Fat: 10g | Protein: 24g

179. Beef and Cheese Gratin

Preparation Time: 10 minutes | **Cooking time:** 10 minutes | **Servings:** 4

Ingredients:
1 ½ lb. steak mince
2/3 cup beef stock
3 oz. mozzarella or cheddar cheese, grated
3 oz. butter, melted
7 oz. breadcrumbs
1 tablespoon extra-virgin olive oil
1 x roast vegetable pack
1 x red onion, diced
1 x red pepper, diced

1 x 14 oz. can chopped tomatoes
1 x zucchini, diced
3 cloves garlic, crushed
1 tablespoon Worcestershire sauce
For the topping…
Fresh thyme

Directions:
Pop a skillet over medium heat and add the oil.
Add the red pepper, onion, zucchini, and garlic. Cook for 5 minutes.
Add the beef and cook for five minutes.
Throw in the tinned tomatoes, beef stock, and Worcestershire sauce then stir well.
Bring to the boil then simmer for 6 minutes.
Divide between the bowl and top with the thyme.
Serve and enjoy.

Nutrition:
Calories: 678 | Net Carbs: 24g | Fat: 45g | Protein: 48g

180. Greek Beef and Veggie Skewers

Preparation Time: 5 minutes | **Cooking time:** 30 minutes | **Servings:** 6-8

Ingredients:
For the beef skewers…
1 ½ lb. skirt steak, cut into cubes
1 teaspoon grated lemon zest
½ teaspoon coriander seeds, ground
½ teaspoon salt
2 garlic cloves, chopped
2 tablespoons olive oil
2 bell peppers, seeded and cubed
4 small green zucchinis, cubed
24 cherry tomatoes
2 tablespoons extra virgin olive oil
To serve…
Store-bought hummus
1 lemon, cut into wedges

Directions:
Grab a large bowl and add all the ingredients. Stir well.
Cover and pop into the fridge for at least 30 minutes, preferably overnight.
Preheat the grill to high and oil the grate.
Take a medium bowl and add the peppers, zucchini, tomatoes, and oil. Season well

Just before cooking, start threading everything onto the skewers. Alternate veggies and meat as you wish.
Pop into the grill and cook for 5 minutes on each side.
Serve and enjoy.

Nutrition:
Calories: 938 | Net Carbs: 65g | Fat: 25g | Protein: 87g

181. Pork Tenderloin with Orzo

Preparation Time: 10 minutes | **Cooking time:** 10 minutes | **Servings:** 6

Ingredients:
1-1/2 lb. pork tenderloin
1 teaspoon coarsely ground pepper
2 tablespoons extra virgin olive oil
3 quarts water
1 1/4 cups uncooked orzo pasta
1/4 teaspoon salt
6 oz. fresh baby spinach
1 cup grape tomatoes, halved
3/4 cup crumbled feta cheese

Directions:
Place the pork onto a flat surface and rub with the pepper.
Cut into the 1" cubes.
Place a skillet over medium heat and add the oil.
Add the pork and cook for 10 minutes until no longer pink.
Fill a Dutch oven with water and place over medium heat. Bring to a boil.
Stir in the orzo and cook uncovered for 8-10 minutes.
Stir through the spinach then drain.
Add the tomatoes to the pork, heat through then stir through orzo and cheese.

Nutrition:
Calories: 372 | Net Carbs: 34g | Fat: 11g | Protein: 31g

182. Moroccan Lamb Flatbreads

Preparation Time: 5 minutes | **Cooking time:** 25 minutes | **Servings:** 6

Ingredients:
1 ½ lb. ground lamb

1 ½ cups chopped zucchini
1 ¼ cups medium salsa
2 cups julienned carrots, divided
1/2 cup dried apricots, coarsely chopped
2 tablespoons apricot preserves
1 tablespoon grated lemon zest
1 tablespoon Moroccan seasoning (ras el hanout)
1/2 teaspoon garlic powder
To serve…
3 naan flatbreads
1/3 cup crumbled feta cheese
2 tablespoons chopped fresh mint

Directions:
Find a large skillet and place over medium heat.
Add the lamb and cook for 10 minutes until no longer pink, stirring and breaking up as it cooks.
Drain away any excess fat.
Add the remaining ingredients then stir and cook for 7-10 minutes.
Place the naan onto plates, spoon over the lamb mixture then top with the feta and mint.
Cut into wedges then serve and enjoy.

Nutrition:
Calories: 423 | Net Carbs: 15g | Fat: 19g | Protein: 24g

183. Greek Lamb Burgers

Preparation Time: 5 minutes | **Cooking time:** 30 minutes | **Servings:** 8

Ingredients:
2 lb. ground lamb
1 small red onion, grated
2 garlic cloves, minced
1 cup chopped fresh parsley
10 mint leaves, chopped
2 ½ teaspoons dry oregano
2 teaspoons ground cumin
½ teaspoon paprika
½ teaspoon cayenne pepper, optional
Salt and pepper, to taste
Extra virgin olive oil
To serve…
Greek pita bread or buns
Tzatziki sauce
Sliced tomatoes
Sliced green bell pepper
Sliced cucumbers
Sliced red onions
Pitted Kalamata olives, sliced
Crumbled feta

Directions:
Preheat your outdoor grill on medium whilst you prepare your burgers.
Grab a large mixing bowl and add the lamb, onions, garlic, herbs, oregano, cumin, paprika, and cayenne.
Season well, drizzle with olive oil and mix everything using your hands.
Shape into 8 balls then press into patties. Use your thumb to make a small depression into the middle of each.
Oil the grill and place the burger patties on top.
Cook for 5-10 minutes until cooked, turning halfway through.
Leave to rest for 5-10 minutes then serve and enjoy.

Nutrition:
Calories: 77 | Net carbs: 6g | Fat: 5g | Protein: 3g

184. Broiled Swordfish with Oven-Roasted Tomato Sauce

Preparation Time: 5 minutes | **Cooking time:** 25 minutes | **Servings:** 4

Ingredients:
4 x 4 oz. fresh or frozen swordfish steaks, cut about 1" thick
Extra virgin olive oil
1 lb. Roma tomatoes, cored and quartered
½ small onion, peeled and quartered
3 cloves garlic, peeled
¼ teaspoon salt
¼ teaspoon crushed red pepper
2 tablespoons tomato paste
1 teaspoon snipped fresh rosemary
½ cup vegetable broth
2 tablespoons heavy cream
1 tablespoon olive oil
½ teaspoon freshly ground black pepper
2 tablespoons finely snipped fresh basil or Italian parsley

Directions:
Preheat the broiler and lightly grease a 15 x 10" baking pan with olive oil.
Place the tomatoes, onion, and garlic into the pan and then season well.

Broil for 10 minutes.
Add the tomato paste and stir well to coat.
Broil for 5 more minutes.
Place the tomatoes into your food processor with the rosemary then cover and blend until smooth.
Pour into a saucepan and stir through the broth.
Bring to a boil, stirring often.
Reduce the heat then cook for 15 minutes.
Add the heavy cream then stir through. Cover with the lid and keep warm.
Cover a broiler pan with foil.
Next season both sides of the fish with oil, season well with pepper, and place onto the broiler pan.
Broil for 10-12 minutes until cooked.
Serve the fish with the sauce then enjoy!

Nutrition:
Calories: 254 | Net carbs: 7g | Fat: 12g | Protein: 24g

185. Pan-Seared Citrus Shrimp

Preparation Time: 10 minutes | **Cooking time:** 15 minutes | **Servings:** 4

Ingredients:
1 tablespoon olive oil
Juice of 2 oranges
Juice of 3 lemons
5 garlic cloves, minced or pressed
1 tablespoon finely chopped red onion or shallot
1 tablespoon chopped fresh parsley
Pinch red pepper flakes
Salt and pepper, to taste
3 lb. medium shrimp peeled and deveined
1 medium orange, cut into wedges or slices
1 medium lemon, cut into wedges

Directions:
Find a medium bowl and add the olive oil, orange juice, lemon juice, garlic, onion, 2 teaspoons of parsley, and a pinch of red pepper flakes. Stir well to combine.
Pour the mixture into a large skillet and place over medium heat.
Bring to a simmer and cook for 5-8 minutes until reduced to half.
Add the shrimp, season well then cover and cook for about 5 minutes until no longer pink.
Top with the rest of the parsley and with the lemon and orange slices, then serve and enjoy.

Nutrition:
Calories: 262 | Net carbs: 18g | Fat: 6g | Protein: 38g

186. Spicy Mexican Casserole

Preparation Time: 5 minutes | **Cooking time:** 10 minutes | **Servings:** 4

Ingredients:
25oz beef, ground
2oz butter
3tbsp Mexican seasoning (Tex Mex works well)
7oz tomatoes, crushed
2oz jalapeños (you can use pickled)
7oz cheese, shredded
1 cup sour cream
1 chopped scallion
5oz iceberg lettuce
Large baking dish, greased

Directions:
Preheat the oven to 200°C
Add the butter to a pan and cook the beef
Add the Mexican seasoning and the tomatoes and cover well
Simmer for 5 minutes and season if necessary
Add the mixture into a baking dish (greased)
Add the peppers and cheese on top
Place in the oven for 20 minutes
In a separate bowl, combine the scallion and sour cream
Remove the casserole and allow to cool a little
Serve with the dip on the side

Nutrition:
Carbs - 8g | Fat: - 70g | Protein - 50g | Calories - 870

187. Succulent Baked Salmon

Preparation Time: 5 minutes | **Cooking time:** 5 minutes | **Servings:** 4

Ingredients:
1 tbsp olive oil
2lb salmon
1 tsp salt
7oz butter
1 lemon

A little pepper
Large oven-safe dish

Directions:
Preheat your oven to 200°C
Take a large oven-safe dish and grease it with oil
Arrange the salmon into the dish, with the skin facing upwards
Add salt and pepper
Slice the lemon and butter thinly and place over the top of the salmon
Place into the oven for half an hour
Take the rest of the butter and place into a pan, melting until it bubbles
Stir in a little lemon juice and pour over the salmon
Serve!

Nutrition:
Carbs - 1g | Fat: - 49g | Protein - 31g | Calories - 573

188. Coconut Chicken Curry

Preparation Time: 5 minutes | **Cooking time:** 10 minutes | **Servings:** 4

Ingredients:
2 tbsp coconut oil
1 tbsp curry powder
2 lemongrass stalks
20oz boneless chicken thighs
1 small piece of fresh ginger, grated
2 cloves of garlic
1 sliced red bell pepper
14oz coconut cream
0.5 chopped red chili pepper

Directions:
Cut the lemongrass with a knife, to release the flavor
Cut the chicken up into chunks
Add the coconut oil to a large frying pan and allow to heat up
Cook the ginger, lemongrass, and curry powder for a few minutes
Add half of the cut chicken into the pan and cook over a medium temperature
Add salt and pepper and combine
Place the contents of the pan to one side and add the rest of the chicken to the pan
Add the rest of the vegetables to the pan and cook for a few minutes
Add the coconut cream, the other batch of chicken and combine everything
Allow to simmer for around 10 minutes before serving

Nutrition:
Carbs - 8g | Fat: - 66g | Protein - 29g | Calories - 736

189. Blue Cheese Pasta

Preparation Time: 5 minutes | **Cooking time:** 10 minutes | **Servings:** 4

Ingredients:
8 eggs
10oz cream cheese
1 tsp salt
5.5 tbsp psyllium husk powder
7oz blue cheese
7oz cream cheese
2oz butter
2 small pinches of black pepper
Baking tray lined with parchment paper

Directions:
Preheat the oven to 150°C
In a bowl, combine the eggs, salt, and cream cheese
Add the psyllium husk a small amount at a time and continue to combine
Allow the bowl to sit to one side for a couple of minutes
Line a baking tray with parchment paper
Spread the batter over the paper and place another piece of parchment over the top
Place in the oven and cook for 12 minutes
Once cooled, remove the paper
Cut into strips with a pizza slicer or a pair of scissors
Take a saucepan and heat over a medium temperature
Add the blue cheese and stir until melted
Add the butter and stir
Pour over the pasta and enjoy

Nutrition:
Carbs - 10g | Fat: - 87g | Protein: 0 37g | Calories - 981

190. Quinoa and Halibut Bowl

Preparation Time: 5 minutes | **Cooking time:** 20 minutes | **Servings:** 4

Ingredients:
2 tablespoons extra virgin olive oil
2 teaspoons ground cumin
1 teaspoon dried rosemary
1 tablespoon ground coriander
2 teaspoons dried oregano
2 teaspoons ground cinnamon
1 teaspoon salt
For the bowl…
2 cups cooked quinoa
1 avocado, sliced
1 cup cherry tomatoes, cut in half
1/2 cup pitted kalamata olives, sliced
1 cucumber, cubed cucumber
Greek dressing
1 lemon

Directions:
Preheat your oven to 435°F.
Find a small bowl and add the cumin, rosemary, coriander, oregano, cinnamon, and salt. Stir well.
Place the halibut onto a flat surface and rub with the spice mix.
Find a skillet, add enough olive oil to cover the bottom, and then sear the halibut.
Once brown, pop into the oven and cook for about 5 minutes.
Meanwhile, place the quinoa, salad ingredients into the bowl and drizzle with the dressing.
Remove the fish from the oven then place it on top of the quinoa.
Serve and enjoy.

Nutrition:
Calories: 608 | Net carbs: 75g | Fat: 29g | Protein: 16g

191. Barramundi in Parchment with Lemons, Dates, and Toasted Almonds

Preparation Time: 5 minutes | **Cooking time:** 22 minutes | **Servings:** 2

Ingredients:
2 x 6 oz. barramundi fillets
1 whole lemon
1 medium shallot, peeled and thinly sliced
6 oz. baby spinach
2 tablespoons extra virgin olive oil
1/4 cup unsalted almonds, coarsely chopped
4 Medjool dates, pitted and finely chopped
1/4 cup fresh flat-leaf parsley, chopped
Salt and pepper, to taste

Directions:
Preheat the oven to 400°F.
Season the barramundi with salt and pepper then pop to one side.
Remove the zest from the entire lemon then cut half of the lemon into 4-5 slices and juice the other half.
Place two 12 x 12" piece of baking parchment side by side and put half of the shallots and half of the spinach into each. Season well.
Place the barramundi on top, add the lemon slices and drizzle with olive oil.
Close the parchment paper by folding then place both packages onto a baking sheet.
Pop into the oven for 10-12 minutes.
Meanwhile, place a small skillet over medium heat and add a small amount of oil.
Add the chopped almonds and sauté for 2 minutes.
Add the dates and cook for a further 2 minutes until warmed through.
Remove from the heat then add the lemon zest, lemon juice, and parsley.
Season well then serve and enjoy.

Nutrition:
Calories: 477 | Net carbs: 45g | Fat: 25g | Protein: 24g

192. Sardine Fish Cakes

Preparation Time: 5 minutes | **Cooking time:** 20 minutes | **Servings:** 6

Ingredients:
6 fresh cleaned sardines
2 garlic cloves, minced
1 medium onion, finely chopped
2 tablespoons fresh dill, chopped
1 cup breadcrumbs
1 free-range egg
2 tablespoons lemon juice
Pinch of salt & pepper, to taste
5 tablespoons extra virgin olive oil

Wedges of lemon, to serve

Directions:
Find a medium bowl and add the sardines, mashing well with a fork.
Add the remaining ingredients (except the olive oil and lemon) and stir well to combine.
Shape into six cakes.
Place a skillet over medium heat and add the oil.
Fry the cakes for a few minutes on each side until brown then serve and enjoy.

Nutrition:
Calories: 197 | Net carbs: 9g | Fat: 14g | Protein: 8g

193. Baked Salmon Tacos

Preparation Time: 5 minutes | **Cooking time:** 25 minutes | **Servings:** 8

Ingredients:
8-10 corn tortillas
½ lb. fresh salmon
1 teaspoon olive oil
Garlic powder, to taste
Ground cumin, to taste
Chili powder (optional), to taste
Salt & pepper, to taste
For the sauce...
1 cup plain Greek yogurt
Juice of 1/2 lime
1 clove garlic, minced
Handful fresh cilantro, chopped
For the toppings...
1 avocado, diced
Shredded iceberg lettuce, to taste
Lime wedges, to taste

Directions:
Preheat your oven to 375°F and line a baking sheet with foil.
Wrap the tortillas in foil and place them into the oven.
Place the salmon onto the baking sheet and drizzle with oil.
Sprinkle it with garlic, cumin, chili, and salt and pepper.
Pop into the oven for 10 minutes until cooked through.
Meanwhile, find a medium bowl and add the ingredients for the sauce. Stir well then pop to one side.
When the salmon is cooked, remove it from the oven and cut it into bite-sized pieces.
Remove the tortillas from the oven and fill with the salmon, toppings, and sauce.
Serve and enjoy.

Nutrition:
Calories: 92 | Net carbs: 13g | Fat: 2g | Protein: 7g

194. No-Drain Pasta alla Norma

Preparation Time: 5 minutes | **Cooking time:** 15 minutes | **Servings:** 6

Ingredients:
1 medium globe eggplant (about 1 pound), cut into ¾-inch cubes
1 tablespoon extra-virgin olive oil
1 cup chopped onion (about ½ medium onion)
8 ounces uncooked thin spaghetti
1 (15-ounce) container part-skim ricotta cheese
3 Roma tomatoes, chopped (about 2 cups)
2 garlic cloves, minced (about 1 teaspoon)
¼ teaspoon kosher or sea salt
½ cup loosely packed fresh basil leaves
Grated Parmesan cheese, for serving (optional)

Directions:
Lay three paper towels on a large plate, and pile the cubed eggplant on top. (Don't cover the eggplant.) Microwave the eggplant on high for 5 minutes to dry and partially cook it.
In a large stockpot over medium-high heat, heat the oil. Add the eggplant and the onion and cook for 5 minutes, stirring occasionally.
Add the spaghetti, ricotta, tomatoes, garlic, and salt. Cover with water by a ½ inch (about 4 cups of water). Cook uncovered for 12 to 15 minutes, or until the pasta is just al dente (tender with a bite), stirring occasionally to prevent the pasta from sticking together or sticking to the bottom of the pot.
Remove the pot from the heat and let the pasta stand for 3 more minutes to absorb more liquid while you tear the basil into pieces. Sprinkle the basil over the pasta and gently stir. Serve with Parmesan cheese, if desired.
Prep tip: We use the microwave in this recipe to partially cook and moisten the eggplant, making it less spongy and less likely to sop up oil. We use a similar moistening trick in the Israeli

Eggplant, Chickpea, and Mint Sauté by broiling the eggplant to make it silky smooth.

Nutrition:
Per serving | Calories: 389 | Total fat: 9g | Saturated fat: 4g | Cholesterol: 22mg | Sodium: 177mg | Total Carbohydrates: 62g | Fiber: 4g | Protein: 19g

195. Zucchini with Bow Ties

Preparation Time: 5 minutes | **Cooking time:** 15 minutes | **Servings:** 4

Ingredients:
3 tablespoons extra-virgin olive oil
2 garlic cloves, minced (about 1 teaspoon)
3 large or 4 medium zucchinis, diced (about 4 cups)
½ teaspoon freshly ground black pepper
¼ teaspoon kosher or sea salt
½ cup 2% milk
¼ teaspoon ground nutmeg
8 ounces uncooked farfalle (bow ties) or other small pasta shape
½ cup grated Parmesan or Romano cheese (about 2 ounces)
1 tablespoon freshly squeezed lemon juice (from ½ medium lemon)

Directions:
In a large skillet over medium heat, heat the oil. Add the garlic and cook for 1 minute, stirring frequently. Add the zucchini, pepper, and salt. Stir well, cover, and cook for 15 minutes, stirring once or twice.
In a small, microwave-safe bowl, warm the milk in the microwave on high for 30 seconds. Stir the milk and nutmeg into the skillet and cook uncovered for another 5 minutes, stirring occasionally.
While the zucchini is cooking, in a large stockpot, cook the pasta according to the package directions.
Drain the pasta in a colander, saving about 2 tablespoons of pasta water. Add the pasta and pasta water to the skillet. Mix everything and remove it from the heat. Stir in the cheese and lemon juice and serve.

Nutrition:
Per serving | Calories: 410 | Total fat: 17g | Saturated fat: 4g | Cholesterol: 13mg | Sodium: 382mg | Total Carbohydrates: 45g | Fiber: 4g | Protein: 15g

196. Roasted Asparagus Caprese Pasta

Preparation Time: 10 minutes | **Cooking time:** 15 minutes | **Servings:** 6

Ingredients:
8 ounces uncooked small pasta, like orecchiette (little ears) or farfalle (bow ties)
1½ pounds fresh asparagus, ends trimmed, and stalks chopped into 1-inch pieces (about 3 cups)
1-pint grape tomatoes, halved (about 1½ cups)
2 tablespoons extra-virgin olive oil
¼ teaspoon freshly ground black pepper
¼ teaspoon kosher or sea salt
2 cups fresh mozzarella, drained and cut into bite-size pieces (about 8 ounces)
⅓ cup torn fresh basil leaves
2 tablespoons balsamic vinegar

Directions:
Preheat the oven to 400°F.
In a large stockpot, cook the pasta according to the package directions. Drain, reserving about ¼ cup of the pasta water.
While the pasta is cooking, in a large bowl, toss the asparagus, tomatoes, oil, pepper, and salt together. Spread the mixture onto a large, rimmed baking sheet and bake for 15 minutes, stirring twice as it cooks.
Remove the vegetables from the oven, and add the cooked pasta to the baking sheet. Mix with a few tablespoons of pasta water to help the sauce become smoother and the saucy vegetables stick to the pasta.
Gently mix in the mozzarella and basil. Drizzle with the balsamic vinegar. Serve from the baking sheet or pour the pasta into a large bowl. If you want to make this dish ahead of time or to serve it cold, follow the recipe up to step 4, then refrigerate the pasta and vegetables. When you are ready to serve, follow step 5 either with the cold pasta or with warm pasta that's been gently reheated in a pot on the stove.

Nutrition:
Per serving | Calories: 307 | Total fat: 14g | Saturated fat: 6g | Cholesterol: 29mg | Sodium:

318mg | Total Carbohydrates: 33g | Fiber: 9g | Protein: 18g

197. Speedy Tilapia with Red Onion and Avocado

Preparation Time: 10 minutes | **Cooking time:** 5 minutes | **Servings:** 4

Ingredients:
1 tablespoon extra-virgin olive oil
1 tablespoon freshly squeezed orange juice
¼ teaspoon kosher or sea salt
4 (4-ounce) tilapia fillets, more oblong than square, skin-on or skinned
¼ cup chopped red onion (about ⅛ onion)
1 avocado, pitted, skinned, and sliced

Directions:
In a 9-inch glass pie dish, use a fork to mix the oil, orange juice, and salt. Working with one fillet at a time, place each in the pie dish and turn to coat on all sides. Arrange the fillets in a wagon-wheel formation, so that one end of each fillet is in the center of the dish and the other end is temporarily draped over the edge of the dish. Top each fillet with 1 tablespoon of onion, then fold the end of the fillet that's hanging over the edge in half over the onion. When finished, you should have 4 folded-over fillets with the fold against the outer edge of the dish and the ends all in the center.
Cover the dish with plastic wrap, leaving a small part open at the edge to vent the steam. Microwave on high for about 3 minutes. The fish is done when it just begins to separate into flakes (chunks) when pressed gently with a fork.
Top the fillets with the avocado and serve.
Prep tip: Because most fish skin is relatively thin, it cooks at about the same rate as fish flesh, which is why you can use this microwave method for both skin-on and skinless fish.

Nutrition:
Per serving | Calories: 200 | Total fat: 11g | Saturated fat: 2g | Cholesterol: 55mg | Sodium: 161mg | Total Carbohydrates: 4g | Fiber: 3g | Protein: 22g

198. Grilled Fish on Lemons

Preparation Time: 10 minutes | **Cooking time:** 10 minutes | **Servings:** 4

Ingredients:
4 (4-ounce) fish fillets, such as tilapia, salmon, catfish, cod, or your favorite fish
Nonstick cooking spray
3 to 4 medium lemons
1 tablespoon extra-virgin olive oil
¼ teaspoon freshly ground black pepper
¼ teaspoon kosher or sea salt

Directions:
Using paper towels, pat the fillets dry and let stand at room temperature for 10 minutes. Meanwhile, coat the cold cooking grate of the grill with nonstick cooking spray, and preheat the grill to 400°F, or medium-high heat. Or preheat a grill pan over medium-high heat on the stovetop.
Cut one lemon in half and set half aside. Slice the remaining half of that lemon and the remaining lemons into ¼-inch-thick slices. (You should have about 12 to 16 lemon slices.) Into a small bowl, squeeze 1 tablespoon of juice out of the reserved lemon half.
Add the oil to the bowl with the lemon juice, and mix well. Brush both sides of the fish with the oil mixture, and sprinkle evenly with pepper and salt.
Carefully place the lemon slices on the grill (or the grill pan), arranging 3 to 4 slices together in the shape of a fish fillet, and repeat with the remaining slices. Place the fish fillets directly on top of the lemon slices, and grill with the lid closed. (If you're grilling on the stovetop, cover with a large pot lid or aluminum foil.) Turn the fish halfway through the cooking time only if the fillets are more than half an inch thick. (See tip for cooking time.) The fish is done and ready to serve when it just begins to separate into flakes (chunks) when pressed gently with a fork.

Nutrition:
Per serving | Calories: 147 | Total fat: 5g | Saturated fat: 1g | Cholesterol: 55mg | Sodium: 158mg | Total Carbohydrates: 4g | Fiber: 1g | Protein: 22g

199. Weeknight Sheet Pan Fish Dinner

Preparation Time: 10 minutes | **Cooking time:** 10 minutes | **Servings:** 4

Ingredients:
Nonstick cooking spray
2 tablespoons extra-virgin olive oil
1 tablespoon balsamic vinegar
4 (4-ounce) fish fillets, such as cod or tilapia (½ inch thick)
2½ cups green beans (about 12 ounces)
1-pint cherry or grape tomatoes (about 2 cups

Directions:
Preheat the oven to 400°F. Coat two large, rimmed baking sheets with nonstick cooking spray.
In a small bowl, whisk together the oil and vinegar. Set aside.
Place two pieces of fish on each baking sheet.
In a large bowl, combine the beans and tomatoes. Pour in the oil and vinegar, and toss gently to coat. Pour half of the green bean mixture over the fish on one baking sheet, and the remaining half over the fish on the other. Turn the fish over, and rub it in the oil mixture to coat. Spread the vegetables evenly on the baking sheets so hot air can circulate them.
Bake for 5 to 8 minutes, until the fish is just opaque and not translucent. The fish is done and ready to serve when it just begins to separate into flakes (chunks) when pressed gently with a fork.

Nutrition:
Per serving | Calories: 193 | Total fat: 8g | Saturated fat: 2g | Cholesterol: 55mg | Sodium: 49mg | Total Carbohydrates: 8g | Fiber: 3g | Protein: 23g

200. Crispy Polenta Fish Sticks

Preparation Time: 15 minutes | **Cooking time:** 10 minutes | **Servings:** 4

Ingredients:
2 large eggs, lightly beaten 1 tablespoon 2% milk
1-pound skinned fish fillets (cod, tilapia, or other white fish) about ½ inch thick, sliced into 20 (1-inch-wide) strips
½ cup yellow cornmeal
½ cup whole-wheat panko bread crumbs or whole-wheat bread crumbs
¼ teaspoon smoked paprika
¼ teaspoon kosher or sea salt
¼ teaspoon freshly ground black pepper
Nonstick cooking spray

Directions:
Place a large, rimmed baking sheet in the oven. Preheat the oven to 400°F with the pan inside.
In a large bowl, mix the eggs and milk. Using a fork, add the fish strips to the egg mixture and stir gently to coat.
Put the cornmeal, bread crumbs, smoked paprika, salt, and pepper in a quart-size zip-top plastic bag. Using a fork or tongs, transfer the fish to the bag, letting the excess egg wash drip off into the bowl before transferring. Seal the bag and shake gently to completely coat each fish stick.
With oven mitts, carefully remove the hot baking sheet from the oven and spray it with nonstick cooking spray. Using a fork or tongs, remove the fish sticks from the bag and arrange them on the hot baking sheet, with space between them so the hot air can circulate and crisp them up.
Bake for 5 to 8 minutes, until gentle pressure with a fork causes the fish to flake, and serve.

Nutrition:
Calories: 256 | Total fat: 6g | Saturated fat: 1g | Cholesterol: 148mg | Sodium: 321mg | Total Carbohydrates: 22g | Fiber: 2g | Protein: 29g

201. Salmon Skillet Supper

Preparation Time: 5 minutes | **Cooking time:** 15 minutes | **Servings:** 4

Ingredients:
1 tablespoon extra-virgin olive oil
2 garlic cloves, minced (about 1 teaspoon)
1 teaspoon smoked paprika
1 pint grape or cherry tomatoes, quartered (about 1½ cups)
1 (12-ounce) jar roasted red peppers, drained, and chopped
1 tablespoon water
¼ teaspoon freshly ground black pepper
¼ teaspoon kosher or sea salt

1 pound salmon fillets, skin removed, cut into 8 pieces
1 tablespoon freshly squeezed lemon juice (from ½ medium lemon)

Directions:
In a large skillet over medium heat, heat the oil. Add the garlic and smoked paprika and cook for 1 minute, stirring often. Add the tomatoes, roasted peppers, water, black pepper, and salt. Turn up the heat to medium-high, bring to a simmer, and cook for 3 minutes, stirring occasionally and smashing the tomatoes with a wooden spoon toward the end of the cooking time.

Add the salmon to the skillet, and spoon some of the sauce over the top. Cover and cook for 10 to 12 minutes, or until the salmon is cooked through (145°F using a meat thermometer) and just starts to flake.

Remove the skillet from the heat, and drizzle lemon juice over the top of the fish. Stir the sauce, then break up the salmon into chunks with a fork. You can serve it straight from the skillet.

Nutrition:
Per serving
Calories: 289 | Total fat: 13g | Saturated fat: 2g | Cholesterol: 68mg | Sodium: 393mg | Total Carbohydrates: 10g | Fiber: 2g | Protein: 31g

202. Orange and Garlic Shrimp

Preparation Time: 20 minutes | **Cooking time:** 10 minutes | **Servings:** 6

Ingredients:
1 large orange
3 tablespoons extra-virgin olive oil, divided
1 tablespoon chopped fresh rosemary (about 3 sprigs) or 1 teaspoon dried rosemary
1 tablespoon chopped fresh thyme (about 6 sprigs) or 1 teaspoon dried thyme
3 garlic cloves, minced (about 1½ teaspoons)
¼ teaspoon freshly ground black pepper
¼ teaspoon kosher or sea salt
1½ pounds fresh raw shrimp, (or frozen and thawed raw shrimp) shells and tails removed

Directions:
Zest the entire orange using a Microplane or citrus grater.

In a large zip-top plastic bag, combine the orange zest and 2 tablespoons of oil with the rosemary, thyme, garlic, pepper, and salt. Add the shrimp, seal the bag, and gently massage the shrimp until all the ingredients are combined and the shrimp is completely covered with the seasonings. Set aside.

Heat a grill, grill pan, or a large skillet over medium heat. Brush on or swirl in the remaining 1 tablespoon of oil. Add half the shrimp, and cook for 4 to 6 minutes, or until the shrimp turn pink and white, flipping halfway through if on the grill or stirring every minute if in a pan. Transfer the shrimp to a large serving bowl. Repeat with the remaining shrimp, and add them to the bowl.

While the shrimp cook, peel the orange and cut the flesh into bite-size pieces. Add to the serving bowl, and toss with the cooked shrimp. Serve immediately or refrigerate and serve cold.

Nutrition:
Per serving | Calories: 190 | Total fat: 8g | Saturated fat: 1g | Cholesterol: 221mg | Sodium: 215mg | Total Carbohydrates: 4g | Fiber: 1g | Protein: 24g

203. Lamb Chops with Herb Butter

Preparation Time: 10 minutes | **Cooking time:** 10 minutes | **Servings:** 4

Ingredients:
8 lamb chops
1 tbsp butter
1 tbsp olive oil
Salt
Pepper
4oz herb butter (shop-bought)
1 lemon, cut into wedges

Directions:
Season the lamb chops with a little salt and pepper
Add the butter to the pan and wait to melt
Fry the lamb chops on each side for around 4 minutes, depending on the thickness
Arrange on a serving plate with a chunk of herb butter and a lemon wedge

Nutrition:
Carbs - 0.3g | Fat: - 62g | Protein - 43g | Calories - 729

204. Healthy Lasagna

Preparation Time: 5 minutes | **Cooking time:** 10 minutes | **Servings:** 4

Ingredients:
2 tbsp olive oil
1 onion
1 clove of garlic
20oz beef, ground
3 tbsp tomato paste
0.5 tsp basil, dried
2 tsp salt
0.5 cup of water
0.25 tsp black pepper
8 eggs
10oz cream cheese
5 tbsp psyllium husk powder
2 cups sour cream
5oz cheese, shredded
2oz parmesan cheese, grated
0.5 cup chopped parsley, fresh
Baking tray lined with parchment paper
Large ovenproof dish

Directions:
Chop the onion finely, and the garlic
Cook in the olive oil until it has gone soft
Add the ground beef and break up with a spoon as it cooks
Add the garlic, pepper, tomato paste and combine
Add the water and allow to boil, before turning the heat down to a simmer, for around 10 minutes
Meanwhile, you can make the lasagna pasta from scratch - preheat your oven to 150°C
Into a bowl, add the eggs, cream cheese, half the salt, and combine well
Add the ground psyllium husk and combine once more, allowing it to rest for a few minutes
Take a baking tray and line it with parchment paper
Spread the mixture over the tray in a thin layer, with a second piece of parchment over the top
Place in the oven for 12 minutes
Once cool, remove the paper and slice up the lasagna sheets to pieces which will fit into your ovenproof dish
Preheat your oven to 200°C
In a bowl, mix the sour cream and parmesan, leaving just a little of the parmesan for the topping
Season and add the parsley, combining once more
Take your baking dish and add the lasagna sheets
Add the cheese mixture on top of the sheets
Add the meat sauce on top
Sprinkle some cheese on top and place in the oven
Bake until the cheese has melted

Nutrition:
Carbs - 9g | Fat: - 76g | Protein - 42g | Calories - 901

205. Chicken Alfredo

Preparation Time: 5 minutes | **Cooking time:** 20 minutes | **Servings:** 4

Ingredients:
4 eggs
6 extra egg yolks
2 tbsp olive oil
2.5 tsp salt
30oz chicken breasts, cut into half pieces
10oz bacon, fried
1.25 cup of heavy cream for whipping
0.75 cup of milk, whole
0.75 cup of parmesan cheese
4 cloves of garlic
Pepper
A little butter for cooking
1 cup of water
4 tbsp pesto
6.5 tbsp psyllium husk powder
4 tbsp coconut flour
4 cloves of garlic
8 mushrooms
1 sliced red bell pepper
Baking tray lined with parchment paper

Directions:
Preheat the oven to 150°C
In a separate bowl, mix the eggs, and combine with the olive oil and water
Combine with the psyllium husk powder and coconut flour in a separate bowl
Whisk the dry ingredients into the wet batter and allow to rest for a few minutes

Take a baking tray and line it with parchment paper
Add the batter to the paper and spread out evenly
Place into the oven and cook for 10 minutes
Allow to cool before removing the paper and creating a roll
Cut into strips
Preheat the oven to 200°C
Season the chicken with salt and pepper and cook over medium heat with the butter
Once cooked, place the chicken into a baking dish and cook for 10 minutes
Meanwhile, fry the bacon
Shred the cheese and add to the bacon, with the cream and milk, bring everything to the boil, and stir regularly
Add the garlic and pesto and combine
Add salt and pepper and stir well
Add the mushroom and sliced peppers to a separate frying pan and cook with the butter
Once ready, mix the mushroom sauce and pasta, tossing well
Serve with the vegetables and the rest of the sauce over the top

Nutrition:
Carbs - 12g | Fat: - 114g | Protein - 85g | Calories - 1460

206. Fried Halloumi & Avocados

Preparation Time: 5 minutes | **Cooking time:** 5 minutes | **Servings:** 2

Ingredients:
10oz halloumi cheese
2 tbsp butter
2 avocados
0.5 cup sour cream
0.25 cucumber
2 tbsp olive oil
2 tbsp pistachio nuts
Salt
Pepper

Directions:
Cut the cheese into slices and add to a frying pan, with the butter for cooking
Cook for a few minutes on each side, until the cheese, turns golden and a little gooey
Place the cheese onto a plate
Slice up the cucumber and arrange it on the plate
Remove the skin and seed from the avocado and cut them into slices
Add the cheese on top of the avocado, drizzle with olive oil, and season

Nutrition:
Carbs - 12g | Fat: - 100g | Protein - 36g| Calories - 1112

207. Chicken Korma

Preparation Time: 5 minutes | **Cooking time:** 10 minutes | **Servings:** 4

Ingredients:
1 sliced red onion
4oz yogurt (Greek yogurt works best)
4 tbsp ghee
3 cloves
1 bay leaf
1 star anise
1 cinnamon stick
3 cardamom pods
8 black peppercorns
15oz chicken thighs, skinless
1 tsp garlic paste
0.5 tsp turmeric
1 tsp red chili powder
1 tsp coriander seeds, ground
0.5 tsp garam masala
1 tsp cumin, ground
Salt

Directions:
Take a large saucepan and melt the ghee
Once melted, add the onions, and cook until they turn golden
Take the onions out and mix in a bowl with the yogurt, blending if necessary
Warm up the ghee once more and add the bay leaf, cloves, star anise, cardamom pods, black peppercorns, and the cinnamon stick
Cook for half a minute
Add the chicken and season with salt
Add the garlic paste and cook for two minutes, stirring often
Add the coriander, garam masala, turmeric, red chili powder, and cumin, combine well and cook for two more minute
Add the onion and yogurt mixture and combine everything once more

Add a little water and combine
the lid on the pot and cook for 15 minutes
Serve whilst still warm

Nutrition:
Carbs - 6g | Fat: - 48g | Protein - 27g | Calories - 568

208. Mediterranean Tuna Noodle Casserole

Preparation Time: 15 minutes | **Cooking time:** 40 minutes | **Servings:** 5

Ingredients:
10 oz dried egg noodles
9 oz halved frozen artichoke hearts
6 oz drained olive oil-packed tuna
4 sliced scallions
1-pound sliced ¼ inch thick small red potatoes
2 cup milk
¾ cup finely grated Parmesan cheese
¾ cup drained capers
½ cup finely chopped flat-leaf parsley
½ cup sliced black olives
¼ cup flour
4 tbsp unsalted butter
2 tsp Kosher salt, divided

Directions:
Place a grill in the middle of the oven and heat to 400° F. Lightly coat a 2-quart baking tray with oil. Set aside.
Bring a large pan of salted water to a boil. Add the noodles and cook for 2 min less than recommended in the package directions. Strain noodles. Season immediately with olive oil so that they don't pile up. Set aside.
Fill the pan with water again and bring to a boil. Add the potato slices and cook for 4 minutes Drain well, then bring them back to the pan.
Cook butter in a small saucepan over medium heat, while the noodles and potatoes are cooking. When it melts and expands, add the flour, and cook for about 5 min mixing constantly, until the sauce thickens slightly, about 5 minutes Add 1 tsp salt and pepper to taste.
Add the egg noodles to the potato pan, then pour the sauce over it. Add and mix the remaining 1 tsp of salt, capers, olive oil, tuna, artichoke hearts, shallots, parsley, and ½ cup of Parmesan. Taste and season with more salt as needed.

Transfer to the baking tray and distribute it in a uniform layer. Season with the remaining ¼ cup of Parmesan and bake, uncovered, about 25 minutes

Nutrition:
457 Calories | 37g Protein | 21g Fat

209. Acquapazza Snapper

Preparation Time: 10 minutes | **Cooking time:** 35 minutes | **Servings:** 4

Ingredients:
1 ½ pounds cut into 4 pieces red snapper fillets
1 ½ coarsely chopped ripe tomatoes
3 cups water
2 tbsp olive oil
1 tbsp chopped thyme leaves
1 tbsp chopped oregano leaves
¼ tsp red pepper flakes
3 cloves minced garlic

Directions:
Cook oil in a casserole large enough to hold all 4 pieces of snapper fillets in a single layer over medium heat. Cook garlic and red pepper flakes Add the water, tomatoes, thyme, oregano, and simmer. Cover, reduce over medium-low heat and simmer for 15 minutes Remove the lid and continue to simmer for another 10 min so that the liquid decreases slightly, pressing occasionally on the tomatoes. Taste and season with salt as needed.
Put the snapper fillets in the casserole with the skin facing down, if there is skin. Season with salt, and cook for 8 to 10 minutes
Place the snapper fillets on 4 large, shallow bowls and put the broth around it. Serve immediately.

Nutrition:
501 Calories | 52g Protein | 26g Fat

210. Eggplant Brown Rice Bowl

Preparation Time: 20 minutes | **Cooking time:** 40 minutes | **Servings:** 4

Ingredients:
2 pounds cut into ½ inch-thick rounds eggplants
15 oz drained and rinsed garbanzo beans

4 cup cooked brown rice
½ cup tahini
½ cup coarsely chopped cilantro
¼ cup coarsely chopped mint leaves
¼ cup pomegranate arils
4 tbsp olive oil
1 tbsp zaatar
1 ½ tsp maple syrup
1 tsp squeezed lemon juice
½ tsp ground turmeric
1 clove minced garlic

Directions:
Situate the rack in the middle of the oven and preheat to 400° F.
Place the eggplant on a rimmed baking sheet. Season with 3 tbsp of olive oil, then sprinkle with zaatar and a large pinch of salt. Using your hands, mix until the eggplant is well coated. Place the eggplants in a single layer. Cook for 15 minutes Flip the eggplants and cook for another 10 minutes Remove from the oven and season with a pinch of salt and black pepper. Set aside.
Put the tahini and 1/3 cup of water in a small bowl and blend until smooth and thick. Add 1 tbsp of olive oil, maple syrup, turmeric, squeezed lemon juice, garlic, and season with salt.
Divide the rice into 4 bowls. Complete with the garbanzo beans and eggplants. Sprinkle with mint, pomegranate arils, and cilantro. Season generously the turmeric tahini on top.

Nutrition:
307 Calories | 31g Protein | 18g Fat

211. Extra-Crispy Veggie-Packed Pizza

Preparation Time: 15 minutes | **Cooking time:** 18 minutes | **Servings:** 4

Ingredients:
1 (5 oz) thin whole-wheat pizza crust
2 ½ oz crumbled feta cheese
2 oz baby spring mix
2 thinly sliced tomatoes
1 cup shaved zucchini strips
½ cup thinly sliced red onion
¼ cup chopped basil
¼ cup basil pesto
1 tbsp canola oil
1 tbsp white wine vinegar
½ tsp kosher salt, divided
¼ tsp black pepper
1/8 tsp crushed red pepper

Directions:
Set the oven to 400°F with the rack in the upper position. Combine the oil, vinegar, black pepper, and ¼ tsp of salt in a bowl. Mix the zucchini in the mixture and let stand at room temperature for 10 minutes
Meantime, place pizza crust on a baking tray, spread the basil pesto on the crust. Season the cheese over the pesto and garnish with tomatoes and red pepper. Cook on the grill above 400°F for 6 minutes Raise the grill and continue to cook for about 2 minutes Pull out from the oven and leave to cool for 2 minutes
Add the spring mixture, basil, and onion to the zucchini mixture. Put the prepared mixture evenly on the pizza and season with the remaining ¼ tsp of salt.

Nutrition:
399 Calories | 31g Protein | 19g Fat

212. Greek Turkey Burgers

Preparation Time: 15 minutes | **Cooking time:** 10 minutes | **Servings:** 4

Ingredients:
4 Whole-Wheat hamburger buns
1 pound 93% lean ground turkey
2 cups arugula
½ cup sliced cucumber
½ cup thinly sliced red onion
1/3 cup chopped kalamata olives
1/3 cup plain whole-milk Greek yogurt
¼ cup canola mayonnaise
1 tbsp lemon juice
2 tsp dried oregano
1 tsp ground cumin
¼ tsp kosher salt
¼ tsp black pepper, divided

Directions:
Combine turkey, oregano, cumin, mayonnaise, salt, and 1/8 tsp of pepper. Form the mixture into 4 patties.
Heat a big cast-iron pan at high heat. Slightly coat the pan with cooking spray and add the turkey patties. Cook for about 4 to 5 min per side.

Combine the yogurt, lemon juice, olives, and the remaining 1/8 tsp of pepper in a small bowl. Sprinkle the yogurt mixture on the cut sides of the top and bottom buns. Divide the arugula between the lower halves of the sandwiches, garnish with cooked patties, cucumber, and red onion. Wrap with the top halves of the rolls and serve.

Nutrition:
459 Calories | 48g Protein | 19g Fat

213. Beef and Lamb Kofta Lettuce Wraps

Preparation Time: 20 minutes | **Cooking time:** 40 minutes | **Servings:** 4

Ingredients:
12 Boston lettuce leaves
1 slice torn into pieces whole-grain bread
1 large egg
1 package (about 8.8 oz) precooked brown rice
8 oz ground sirloin
6 oz lean ground lamb
¾ cup 2% reduced-fat Greek yogurt
5 tbsp grated red onion divided
3 tbsp diced English cucumber
2 tbsp chopped parsley
1 tbsp olive oil, divided
1 tbsp chopped mint
1 tsp paprika
¾ tsp kosher salt, divided
½ tsp ground allspice
½ tsp ground cinnamon
½ tsp ground black pepper, divided

Directions:
Put the bread in a mini kitchen robot and blend until large crumbs are formed. Combine bread, sirloin, lamb, egg, allspice, mint, parsley, cinnamon, 2 tbsp of onion, ½ tsp of salt, and ¼ tsp of black pepper. Form the mixture into 12 patties. Preheat a non-stick pan over medium-high heat and add 1 tsp of oil. Place the patties on the pan, cook for 2 to 3 min on each side.
Combine the yogurt, the remaining ¼ tsp of pepper, ¼ tsp of salt, the cucumber, and the 3 tbsp of onion in a medium bowl and mix.
Cook the rice according to package directions. Season with paprika and the remaining 2 tsp of oil.
Place the lettuce leaves on a large serving plate and put the rice, patties, and yogurt mixture.

Nutrition:
471 Calories | 47g Protein | 16g Fat

214. Chicken Souvlaki

Preparation Time: 25 minutes | **Cooking time:** 10 minutes | **Servings:** 4

Ingredients:
4 pocketless pitas
2 cut into thin wedges tomatoes
1 cut into thin wedges small onion
1 halved cucumber
1 1/3 pound chicken breasts
2 cups plain yogurt
1/3 cup black olives
6 tbsp butter
2 tbsp olive oil
1 tbsp dried oregano
1 ½ tsp lemon juice
1 ¼ tsp salt
¼ tsp dried dill
1 clove minced garlic

Directions:
Put the yogurt in a colander lined with a paper towel and place it on a bowl, leave to drain in the refrigerator for 15 minutes. In a medium glass bowl combine the cucumber with 1 tsp of salt, let it rest for about 15 minutes Squeeze the cucumber to remove the liquid. Return the cucumber to the bowl and add the drained yogurt, garlic, dill, and 1/8 tsp of pepper.
Preheat the grill or the broiler. In a small glass bowl combine the oil oregano, lemon juice, the remaining ¼ tsp of salt, and the remaining ¼ tsp of pepper. Dip the chicken cubes into the oil mixture and thread them onto the skewers. Grill the chicken over high heat, flipping once until cooked, about 5 min in total. Transfer the chicken to a plate.
Spread both sides of the pitas with butter and grill, flipping once for about 4 min in total. Cut into quarters.
Place the pitas on plates and garnish with the onion, tomatoes, and chicken skewers with any sauce accumulated. Serve with the tzatziki and olives.

Nutrition:
460 Calories | 40g Protein | 18g Fat

215. Spicy Chicken Shawarma

Preparation Time: 15 minutes | **Cooking time:** 6 minutes | **Servings:** 4

Ingredients:
1-pound chicken breast
4 (6-inch) halved pitas
½ cup chopped plum tomato
½ cup chopped cucumber
¼ cup chopped red onion
5 tbsp plain low-fat Greek-style yogurt, divided
2 tbsp lemon juice, divided
2 tbsp finely chopped parsley
2 tbsp extra-virgin olive oil
1 tbsp tahini
½ tsp salt
½ tsp crushed red pepper
¼ tsp ground cumin
¼ tsp ground ginger
1/8 tsp ground coriander

Directions:
Combine the parsley, salt, red pepper, ginger, cumin, coriander, 1 tbsp of yogurt, 1 tbsp of juice, and 2 cloves of garlic. Add the chicken, stir to coat. Preheat oil in a nonstick pan over medium-high heat. Add the chicken mixture to the pan and cook for 6 min
In the meantime, combine the remaining 1 tbsp of lemon juice, the remaining ¼ cup of yogurt, and the remaining 1 clove of garlic and the tahini, mixing well. Put 1 ½ tsp of the tahini mixture inside each half of the pita, divide the chicken between the halves of the pita. Fill each half of the pita with 1 tbsp of cucumber, 1 tbsp of tomato, and 1 ½ tsp of onion.

Nutrition:
440 Calories | 37g Protein | 19g Fat

216. Lemon Chicken Pita Burgers with Spiced Yogurt Sauce

Preparation Time: 15 minutes | **Cooking time:** 6 minutes | **Servings:** 4

Ingredients:
4 (6-inch) cut in half pitas
2 lightly beaten large egg whites
1-pound ground chicken
2 cups shredded lettuce
½ cup diced tomato
½ cup chopped green onions
½ cup plain low-fat yogurt
1/3 cup Italian-seasoned breadcrumbs
1 tbsp olive oil
1 tbsp Greek seasoning blend
2 tsp grated lemon zest, divided
1 ½ tsp chopped oregano
½ tsp coarsely ground black pepper

Directions:
Combine the chicken, eggs, onion, black pepper, breadcrumbs, Greek seasoning blend, and 1 tsp of zest, mixing well. Split the mixture into 8 equal portions and make patties ¼-inch thick.
Heat the oil in a large nonstick pan over medium-high heat. Put on the patties and cook for 2 min per side. Cover, lower the heat to medium, and cook for 4 minutes
Combine oregano, yogurt, and the remaining zest. Fill each half of the pita with 1 patty, 1 tbsp of yogurt mix, 1 tbsp of tomato, and ¼ cup of lettuce.

Nutrition:
391 Calories | 40g Protein | 20g Fat

217. Lamb Chop with Pistachio Gremolata

Preparation Time: 10 minutes | **Cooking time:** 8 minutes | **Servings:** 4

Ingredients:
8 trimmed lamb loin chops
2 tbsp chopped flat-leaf parsley
2 tbsp finely chopped pistachios
1 tbsp chopped cilantro
2 tsp grated lemon zest
½ tsp salt
½ tsp ground cumin
¼ tsp ground coriander
¼ tsp black pepper
1/8 tsp salt
1/8 ground cinnamon
1 clove minced garlic

Directions:
Heat a nonstick pan at medium-high heat. Combine the cumin, coriander, cinnamon, salt, and black pepper, and season evenly on both

sides of the lamb. Coat the pan with cooking spray and add the lamb, cook for 4 min per side. In the meantime, combine the pistachios, cilantro, parsley, lemon zest, salt, and garlic, season over the lamb.

Nutrition:
409 Calories | 41g Protein | 22g Fat

218. Pita Salad with Cucumber, Fennel, and Chicken

Preparation Time: 10 minutes | **Cooking time:** 12 minutes | **Servings:** 4

Ingredients:
2 (6-inch) pitas
½ halved lengthwise and thinly sliced English cucumber
2 cups thinly sliced fennel bulb
1 cup shredded skinless, boneless rotisserie chicken breast
½ cup chopped flat-leaf parsley
¼ cup vertically sliced red onion
¼ cup lemon juice
3 tbsp extra-virgin olive oil
1 tbsp white wine vinegar
½ tsp chopped oregano
½ tsp salt, divided
¼ tsp black pepper, divided

Directions:
Preheat the oven to 350°F.
Situate pitas on a baking tray and bake for 12 min, cool down for 1 minute. Cut into small pieces, and combine with fennel, chicken, parsley, and red onion. Season with ¼ tsp of salt and 1/8 tsp of pepper.
Add the juice, oregano, vinegar, the remaining ¼ tsp of salt, and 1/8 tsp of pepper. Gradually add the oil, mixing with a whisk. Season with dressing over the pita mixture to coat and serve.

Nutrition:
413 Calories | 38g Protein | 17g Fat

219. Halibut with Lemon-Fennel Salad

Preparation Time: 15 minutes | **Cooking time:** 5 minutes | **Servings:** 4

Ingredients:
4 halibut fillets
2 cups thinly sliced fennel bulb
¼ cup thinly vertically sliced red onion
2 tbsp lemon juice
1 tbsp thyme leaves
1 tbsp chopped flat-leaf parsley
5 tsp extra-virgin olive oil, divided
1 tsp coriander
½ tsp salt
½ tsp cumin
¼ tsp ground black pepper
2 cloves minced garlic

Directions:
Combine the coriander, cumin, salt, and black pepper in a small bowl. Combine 2 tsp of olive oil, garlic, and 1 ½ tsp of spice mixture in another small bowl, evenly rub the garlic mixture on the halibut. Heat 1 tsp of oil in a large nonstick pan over medium-high heat. Cook the halibut to the pan for 5 minutes
Combine the remaining 2 tsp of oil, ¾ tsp of the spice mixture, the fennel bulb, onion, lemon juice, thyme leaves, and parsley in a bowl, mix well to coat, and serve salad with halibut.

Nutrition:
427 Calories | 39g Protein | 20g Fat

220. Cabbage Roll Casserole with Veal

Preparation Time: 5 minutes | **Cooking time:** 4–8 hours | **Servings:** 6

Ingredients:
1-pound raw ground veal
1 head of cabbage
1 medium green pepper
1 medium onion, chopped
1 (15-ounce) can tomatoes
2 (15-ounce) cans tomato sauce
1 teaspoon minced garlic
1 tablespoon Worcestershire sauce
1 tablespoon beef bouillon

½ teaspoon salt
½ teaspoon pepper
1 cup uncooked brown rice

Directions:
Situate all the ingredients to your slow cooker
Stir well to combine.
Set your slow cooker to high and cook for 4 hours, or cook for 8 hours on low.

Nutrition:
335 Calories | 18g Fat | 22.9g protein

221. Slow-Cooked Daube Provencal

Preparation Time: 15 minutes | **Cooking time:** 4–8 hours | **Servings:** 8–10

Ingredients:
1 tablespoon olive oil
10 garlic cloves, minced
2 pounds boneless chuck roast
1½ teaspoons salt
½ teaspoon black pepper
1 cup dry red wine
2 cups carrots, chopped
1½ cups onion, chopped
½ cup beef broth
1 (14-ounce) can diced tomatoes
1 tablespoon tomato paste
1 teaspoon fresh rosemary, chopped
1 teaspoon fresh thyme, chopped
½ teaspoon orange zest, grated
½ teaspoon ground cinnamon
¼ teaspoon ground cloves
1 bay leaf

Directions:
Preheat the skillet and then add the olive oil. Cook minced garlic and onions
Add the cubed meat, salt, and pepper and cook until the meat has browned.
Transfer the meat to the slow cooker.
Put beef broth to the skillet and let simmer for about 3 minutes to deglaze the pan, then pour into the slow cooker over the meat.
Add the rest of the ingredients to the slow cooker and stir well to combine.
Set your slow cooker to low and cook for 8 hours, or set it to high and cook for 4 hours.
Serve with a side of egg noodles, rice, or some crusty Italian bread.

Nutrition:
547 Calories | 30.5g Fat | 45.2g protein

222. Osso Bucco

Preparation Time: 30 minutes | **Cooking time:** 8 hours | **Servings:** 2–4

Ingredients:
4 beef shanks or veal shanks
1 teaspoon sea salt
½ teaspoon ground black pepper
3 tablespoons whole wheat flour
1–2 tablespoons olive oil
2 medium onions, diced
2 medium carrots, diced
2 celery stalks, diced
4 garlic cloves, minced
1 (14-ounce) can diced tomatoes
2 teaspoons dried thyme leaves
½ cup beef or vegetable stock

Directions:
Season the shanks on both sides, then dip in the flour to coat.
Heat a large skillet over high heat. Add the olive oil. When the oil is hot, add the shanks and brown evenly on both sides. When browned, transfer to the slow cooker.
Pour the stock into the skillet and let simmer for 3–5 minutes while stirring to deglaze the pan.
Add the rest of the ingredients to the slow cooker and pour the stock from the skillet over the top.
Click the slow cooker to low and cook for 8 hours.
Serve the Osso Bucco over quinoa, brown rice, or even cauliflower rice.

Nutrition:
589 Calories | 21.3g Fat | 74.7g protein

223. Slow Cooker Beef Bourguignon

Preparation Time: 5 minutes | **Cooking time:** 6–8 hours | **Servings:** 6–8

Ingredients:
1 tablespoon extra-virgin olive oil
6 ounces bacon
3 pounds beef brisket
1 large carrot
1 large white onion

6 cloves garlic
½ teaspoon coarse salt
½ teaspoon pepper
2 tablespoons whole wheat
12 small pearl onions
3 cups red wine
2 cups beef stock
2 tablespoons tomato paste
1 beef bouillon cube
1 teaspoon fresh thyme
2 tablespoons fresh parsley
2 bay leaves
2 tablespoons butter
1-pound mushrooms

Directions:
Preheat skillet over medium-high heat, pour olive oil. When the oil has heated, cook the bacon until it is crisp, then place it in your slow cooker. Save the bacon fat in the skillet.
Dry the beef with a paper towel and cook it in the same skillet with the bacon fat until all sides have the same brown coloring.
Transfer to the slow cooker.
Add the onions and carrots to the slow cooker and season with salt and pepper. Stir to combine the ingredients and make sure everything is seasoned.
Pour the red wine into the skillet and simmer for 4–5 minutes to deglaze the pan, then whisk in the flour, stirring until smooth.
When the liquid has thickened, pour it into the slow cooker and stir to coat everything with the wine mixture. Add the tomato paste, bouillon cube, thyme, parsley, 4 cloves of garlic, and bay leaf.
Set your slow cooker to high and cook for 6 hours, or set it to low and cook for 8 hours.
Before serving, melt the butter in a skillet over medium heat. When the oil is hot, add the remaining 2 cloves of garlic and cook for about 1 minute before adding the mushrooms.
Cook the mushrooms until soft, then add to the slow cooker and mix to combine.
Serve with mashed potatoes, rice, or noodles.

Nutrition:
672 Calories | 32g Fat | 56g protein

224. Balsamic Beef

Preparation Time: 5 minutes | **Cooking time:** 8 hours | **Servings:** 8–10

Ingredients:
2 pounds boneless chuck roast
1 tablespoon olive oil
Rub
1 teaspoon garlic powder
½ teaspoon onion powder
1 teaspoon sea salt
½ teaspoon black pepper
Sauce
½ cup balsamic vinegar
2 tablespoons honey
1 tablespoon honey mustard
1 cup beef broth
1 tablespoon tapioca

Directions:
Incorporate all the ingredients for the rub.
In a separate bowl, mix the balsamic vinegar, honey, honey mustard, and beef broth.
Coat the roast in olive oil, then rub in the spices from the rub mix.
Place the roast in the slow cooker and then pour the sauce over the top.
Select the slow cooker to low and cook for 8 hours.
If you want to thicken, pour the liquid into a saucepan and heat to boiling on the stovetop. Stir in the flour until smooth and let simmer until the sauce thickens.

Nutrition:
306 Calories | 19g Fat | 25g protein

225. Veal Pot Roast

Preparation Time: 20 minutes | **Cooking time:** 5 hours | **Servings:** 6–8

Ingredients:
2 tablespoons olive oil
Salt and pepper
3-pound boneless veal roast
4 medium carrots, peeled
2 parsnips, peeled and halved
2 white turnips, peeled and quartered
10 garlic cloves, peeled
2 sprigs fresh thyme
1 orange, scrubbed and zested

1 cup chicken or veal stock

Directions:
Heat a large skillet over medium-high heat.
Coat veal roast all over with olive oil, then season with salt and pepper.
When the skillet is hot, add the veal roast and sear on all sides.
Once the roast is cooked on all sides, transfer it to the slow cooker.
Toss the carrots, parsnips, turnips, and garlic into the skillet. Stir and cook for about 5 minutes—not all the way through, just to get some of the brown bits from the veal and give them a bit of color.
Transfer the vegetables to the slow cooker, placing them all around the meat.
Top the roast with the thyme and the zest from the orange. Slice the orange in half and squeeze the juice over the top of the meat.
Add the chicken stock, then cook the roast on low for 5 hours.

Nutrition:
426 Calories | 12.8g Fat | 48.8g protein

226. Mediterranean Rice and Sausage

Preparation Time: 15 minutes | **Cooking time:** 8 hours | **Servings:** 6

Ingredients:
1½ pounds Italian sausage, crumbled
1 medium onion, chopped
2 tablespoons steak sauce
2 cups long-grain rice, uncooked
1 (14-ounce) can diced tomatoes with juice
½ cup water
1 medium green pepper, diced

Directions:
Spray your slow cooker with olive oil or nonstick cooking spray.
Add the sausage, onion, and steak sauce to the slow cooker.
Cook on low for 8 to 10 hours.
After 8 hours, add rice, tomatoes, water, and green pepper. Stir to combine thoroughly.
Cook for 20 to 25 minutes.

Nutrition:
650 Calories | 36g Fat | 22g protein

227. Spanish Meatballs

Preparation Time: 20 minutes | **Cooking time:** 5 hours | **Servings:** 6

Ingredients:
1-pound ground turkey
1-pound ground pork
2 eggs
1 (20-ounce) can diced tomatoes
¾ cup sweet onion, minced, divided
¼ cup plus 1 tablespoon breadcrumbs
3 tablespoons fresh parsley, chopped
1½ teaspoons cumin
1½ teaspoons paprika (sweet or hot)

Directions:
Spray the slow cooker with olive oil.
In a mixing bowl, mix ground meat, eggs, about half of the onions, the breadcrumbs, and the spices.
Wash your hands and mix until everything is well combined. Shape into meatballs.
Mix 2 tablespoons of olive oil over medium heat. When the skillet and oil are hot, add the meatballs and brown on all sides. When they are done, transfer them to the slow cooker.
Add the rest of the onions and the tomatoes to the skillet and allow them to cook for a few minutes, scraping the brown bits from the meatballs up to add flavor.
Pour the tomatoes over the meatballs in the slow cooker and cook on low for 5 hours.

Nutrition:
372 Calories | 21.7g Fat | 28.5g protein

228. Lamb Shanks with Red Wine

Preparation Time: 20 minutes | **Cooking time:** 5 hours | **Servings:** 4

Ingredients:
2 tablespoons olive oil
2 tablespoons flour
4 lamb shanks, trimmed
1 onion, chopped
2 garlic cloves, crushed
2/3 cup red wine
3 cups tomato sauce

Directions:
Heat a skillet over high heat. Add the olive oil.

Season the lamb shanks then roll in the flour. Shake off excess flour and place the shanks in the skillet to brown on all sides.
Spray the slow cooker with olive oil and place the browned shanks in the slow cooker.
Add the crushed garlic to the red wine. Mix with the tomato sauce and then pour the mixture over the lamb shanks and cook on low for 5–6 hours

Nutrition:
354 Calories | 12g Fat | 42g protein

229. Leg of Lamb with Rosemary and Garlic

Preparation Time: 15 minutes | **Cooking time:** 8 hours | **Servings:** 4–6

Ingredients:
3–4-pound leg of lamb
4 garlic cloves, sliced thin
5–8 sprigs of fresh rosemary (more if desired)
2 tablespoons olive oil
1 lemon, halved
¼ cup flour

Directions:
Put the skillet over high heat and pour olive oil. When the olive oil is hot, add the leg of lamb and sear on both sides until brown.
Spray the slow cooker with olive oil and then transfer the lamb to the slow cooker.
Squeeze the lemon over the meat and then place it in the pot next to the lamb.
Take a sharp knife and make small incisions in the meat, then stuff the holes you created with rosemary and garlic.
Place any remaining rosemary and garlic on top of the roast.
Cook on low for 8 hours.

Nutrition:
557 Calories | 39g Fat | 46g protein

230. Lemon Honey Lamb Shoulder

Preparation Time: 10 minutes | **Cooking time:** 8 hours | **Servings:** 4

Ingredients:
3 cloves garlic, thinly sliced
1 tablespoon fresh rosemary, chopped
1 teaspoon lemon zest, grated
½ teaspoon each salt and pepper
4–5-pound boneless lamb shoulder roast
3 tablespoons lemon juice
1 tablespoon honey
6 shallots, quartered
2 teaspoons cornstarch

Directions:
Stir garlic, rosemary, lemon zest, salt, and pepper.
Rub the spice mixture into the lamb shoulder. Make sure to coat the whole roast.
Spray the slow cooker with olive oil and add the lamb.
Mix the honey and lemon juice and then pour over the meat.
Arrange the shallots beside the meat in the slow cooker.
Cook on low for 8 hours.
Serve. You can make a gravy by transferring the juice from the slow cooker to a medium saucepan. Thoroughly mix the cornstarch into a little water until smooth. Then mix into the juice and bring to a simmer. Simmer until the mixture thickens.

Nutrition:
240 Calories | 11g Fat | 31g protein

231. Italian Shredded Pork Stew

Preparation Time: 20 minutes | **Cooking time:** 8 hours | **Servings:** 8

Ingredients:
2 medium sweet potatoes
2 cups fresh kale, chopped
1 large onion, chopped
4 cloves garlic, minced
1 2½–3½ pound boneless pork shoulder butt roast
1 (14-ounce) can cannellini beans
1½ teaspoons Italian seasoning
½ teaspoon salt
½ teaspoon pepper
3 (14½-ounce) cans chicken broth
Sour cream (optional)

Directions:
Coat slow cooker with nonstick cooking spray or olive oil.

Place the cubed sweet potatoes, kale, garlic, and onion into the slow cooker.
Add the pork shoulder on top of the potatoes.
Add the beans, Italian seasoning salt, and pepper.
Pour the chicken broth over the meat.
Cook on low for 8 hours.
Serve with sour cream, if desired.

Nutrition:
283 Calories | 13g Fat | 24g protein

232. Rosemary-Lemon Snapper Baked in Parchment

Preparation Time: 15 minutes | **Cooking time:** 15 minutes | **Servings:** 4

Ingredients:
1¼ pounds fresh red snapper fillet, cut into two equal pieces
2 lemons, thinly sliced
6 to 8 sprigs fresh rosemary, stems removed or
1 to 2 tablespoons dried rosemary
½ cup extra-virgin olive oil
6 garlic cloves, thinly sliced
1 teaspoon salt
½ teaspoon freshly ground black pepper

Directions:
Preheat the oven to 425°F.
Place two large sheets of parchment (about twice the size of each piece of fish) on the counter. Place 1 piece of fish in the center of each sheet.
Top the fish pieces with lemon slices and rosemary leaves.
In a small bowl, combine the olive oil, garlic, salt, and pepper. Drizzle the oil over each piece of fish.
Top each piece of fish with a second large sheet of parchment and starting on a long side, fold the paper up to about 1 inch from the fish. Repeat on the remaining sides, going in a clockwise direction. Fold in each corner once to secure.
Place both parchment pouches on a baking sheet and bake until the fish is cooked for 10 to 12 minutes.

Nutrition:
Calories: 390 | Total Fat: 29g | Total Carbohydrates: 3g | Net Carbohydrates: 3g, | Fiber: 0g, | Protein: 29g | Sodium: 674mg

233. Shrimp in Creamy Pesto over Zoodles

Preparation Time: 10 minutes | **Cooking time:** 10 minutes | **Servings:** 4

Ingredients:
1 pound peeled and deveined fresh shrimp
Salt
Freshly ground black pepper
2 tablespoons extra-virgin olive oil
½ small onion, slivered
8 ounces store-bought jarred pesto
¾ cup crumbled goat or feta cheese, plus more for serving
6 cups Zucchini Noodles (from about 2 large zucchini), for serving
¼ cup chopped flat-leaf Italian parsley, for garnish

Directions:
In a bowl, season the shrimp with salt and pepper and set aside.
In a large skillet, heat the olive oil over medium-high heat. Sauté the onion until just golden, 5 to 6 minutes.
Reduce the heat to low and add the pesto and cheese, whisking to combine and melt the cheese. Bring to a low simmer and add the shrimp. Reduce the heat back to low and cover. Cook until the shrimp is cooked through and pink, another 3 to 4 minutes.
Serve warm over Zucchini Noodles, garnishing with chopped parsley and additional crumbled cheese, if desired.

Nutrition:
Calories: 491 | Total Fat: 35g | Total Carbohydrates: 15g | Net Carbohydrates: 11g, | Fiber: 4g, | Protein: 29g | Sodium: 870mg

234. Nut-Crusted Baked Fish

Preparation Time: 10 minutes | **Cooking time:** 20 minutes | **Servings:** 4

Ingredients:
½ cup extra-virgin olive oil, divided
1-pound flaky white fish (such as cod, haddock, or halibut), skin removed
½ cup shelled finely chopped pistachios
½ cup ground flaxseed
Zest and juice of 1 lemon, divided

1 teaspoon ground cumin
1 teaspoon ground allspice
½ teaspoon salt (use 1 teaspoon if pistachios are unsalted)
¼ teaspoon freshly ground black pepper

Directions:
Preheat the oven to 400°F.
Line a baking sheet with parchment paper or aluminum foil and drizzle 2 tablespoons olive oil over the sheet, spreading to evenly coat the bottom.
Cut the fish into 4 equal pieces and place them on the prepared baking sheet.
In a small bowl, combine the pistachios, flaxseed, lemon zest, cumin, allspice, salt, and pepper. Drizzle in ¼ cup olive oil and stir well.
Divide the nut mixture evenly atop the fish pieces. Drizzle the lemon juice and the remaining 2 tablespoons oil over the fish and bake until cooked through, 15 to 20 minutes, depending on the thickness of the fish.

Nutrition:
Calories: 509 | Total Fat: 41g | Total Carbohydrates: 9g | Net Carbohydrates: 3g, | Fiber: 6g, | Protein: 26g | Sodium: 331mg

235. Pesto Walnut Noodles

Preparation Time: 10 minutes | **Cooking time:** 15 minutes | **Servings:** 4

Ingredients:
4 Zucchini, Made into Zoodles
¼ Cup Olive Oil, Divided
½ Teaspoon Crushed Red Pepper
2 Cloves Garlic, Minced & Divided
¼ Teaspoon Black Pepper
¼ Teaspoon sea salt
2 Tablespoons Parmesan Cheese, Grated & Divided
1 Cup Basil, Fresh & Packed
¾ Cup Walnut Pieces, Divided

Directions:
Start by making your zucchini noodles by using a spiralizer to get ribbons. Combine your zoodles with a minced garlic clove and a tablespoon of oil. Season with salt and pepper and crushed red pepper. Set it to the side.
Get out a large skillet and heat a ½ a tablespoon of oil over medium-high heat. Add in half of your zoodles, cooking for five minutes. You will need to stir every minute or so. Repeat with another ½ a tablespoon of oil and your remaining zoodles.
Make your pesto while your zoodles cook. Put your garlic clove, a tablespoon of parmesan, basil leaves, and ¼ cup of walnuts in your food processor. Season with salt and pepper if desired, and drizzle the remaining two tablespoons of oil in until completely blended.
Add the pesto to your zoodles, topping with remaining walnuts and parmesan to serve.

Nutrition:
Calories: 301 | Protein: 7 Grams | Fat: 28 Grams | Carbohydrates: 11 Grams | Sodium: 160 mg

236. Tomato Tabbouleh

Preparation Time: 10 minutes | **Cooking time:** 20 minutes | **Servings:** 4

Ingredients:
8 Beefsteak Tomatoes
½ Cup Water
3 Tablespoons Olive Oil, Divided
½ Cup Whole Wheat Couscous, Uncooked
1 ½ Cups Parsley, Fresh & Minced
2 Scallions Chopped
1/3 Cup Mint, Fresh & Minced
Sea Salt & Black Pepper to Taste
1 Lemon
4 Teaspoons Honey, Raw
1/3 Cup Almonds, Chopped

Directions:
Start by heating your oven to 400 degrees. Take your tomato and slice the top off of each one before scooping the flesh out. Put the top flesh and seeds in a mixing bowl.
Get out a baking dish before adding in a tablespoon of oil to grease it. Place your tomatoes in the dish, and then cover your dish with foil.
Now you will make your couscous while your tomatoes cook. Bring the water to a boil using a saucepan and then add the couscous in and cover. Remove it from heat, and allow it to sit for five minutes. Fluff it with a fork.
Chop your tomato flesh and tops up, and then drain the excess water using a colander. Measure a cup of your chopped tomatoes and

place them back in the mixing bowl. Mix with mint scallions, pepper, salt, and parsley.
Zest your lemon into the bowl, and then half the lemon. Squeeze the lemon juice in, and mix well.
Add your tomato mix to the couscous.
Carefully remove your tomatoes from the oven and then divide your tabbouleh among your tomatoes. Cover the pan with foil and then put it in the oven. Cook for another eight to ten minutes. Your tomatoes should be firm but still tender.
Drizzle with honey and top with almonds before serving.

Nutrition:
Calories: 314 | Protein: 8 Grams | Fat: 15 Grams | Carbohydrates: 41 Grams | Sodium: 141

237. Lemon Faro Bowl

Preparation Time: 10 minutes | **Cooking time:** 15 minutes | **Servings:** 6

Ingredients:
1 Tablespoon + 2 Teaspoons Olive Oil, Divided
1 Cup Onion, Chopped
2 Cloves Garlic, Minced
1 Carrot, Shredded
2 Cups Vegetable Broth, Low Sodium
1 Cup Pearled Faro
2 Avocados, Peeled, Pitted & Sliced
1 Lemon, Small
Sea Salt to Taste

Directions:
Start by placing a saucepan over medium-high heat. Add in a tablespoon of oil and then throw in your onion once the oil is hot. Cook for about five minutes, stirring frequently to keep it from burning.
Add in your carrot and garlic. Allow it to cook for about another minute while you continue to stir. Add in your broth and faro. Allow it to come to a boil and adjust your heat to high to help. Once it boils, lower it to medium-low and cover your saucepan. Let it simmer for twenty minutes. The faro should be al dente and plump.
Pour the faro into a bowl and add in your avocado and zest. Drizzle with your remaining oil and add in your lemon wedges.

Nutrition:
Calories: 279 | Protein: 7 Grams | Fat: 14 Grams | Carbohydrates: 36 Grams | Sodium: 118 mg

238. Chickpea & Red Pepper Delight

Preparation Time: 15 minutes | **Cooking time:** 15 minutes | **Servings:** 3

Ingredients:
1 Red Bell Pepper, Diced
2 Cups Water
4 Sun-Dried Tomatoes
¼ Cup Red Wine Vinegar
2 Tablespoon Olive Oil
2 Cloves Garlic, Chopped
29 Ounces Chickpeas, Canned, Drained & Rinsed
½ Cup Parsley, Chopped / Sea Salt to Taste

Directions:
Get a baking sheet and put your red bell pepper on it with the skin side up.
Bake for eight minutes. Your skin should bubble, and then place it in a bag to seal it.
Remove your bell peppers in about ten minutes, and then slice them into thin slices.
Get out two cups of water and pour it into a bowl. Microwave for four minutes and add in your sundried tomatoes, letting them sit for ten minutes. Drain them before slicing them into thin strips. Mix your red wine vinegar and garlic with your olive oil. Ross your roasted red bell pepper with parsley, sun-dried tomatoes, and chickpeas. Season with salt before serving.

Nutrition:
Calories: 195 | Protein: 9.3 Grams | Fat: 8.5 Grams | Carbohydrates: 25.5 Grams | Sodium: 142 mg

239. Eggplant Rolls

Preparation Time: 10 minutes | **Cooking time:** 6 minutes | **Servings:** 6

Ingredients:
1 eggplant, ½ inch sliced lengthwise
Sea salt & black pepper to taste
1 tablespoon olive oil
1/3 cup cream cheese
½ cup tomatoes, chopped
1 clove garlic, minced

2 tablespoons dill, chopped

Directions:
Slice your eggplant before brushing it down with olive oil. Season your eggplant slices with salt and pepper.
Grill the eggplants for three minutes per side.
Get out a bowl and combine cream cheese, garlic, dill, and tomatoes in a different bowl.
Allow your eggplant slices to cool and then spread the mixture over each one. Roll them and pin them with a toothpick to serve.

Nutrition:
Calories: 91 | Protein: 2.1 Grams | Fat: 7 Grams | Carbohydrates: 6.3 Grams | Sodium: 140 mg

240. Heavenly Quinoa

Preparation Time: 15 minutes | **Cooking time:** 5 minutes | **Servings:** 5

Ingredients:
1 cup almonds
1 cup quinoa
1 teaspoon cinnamon
1 pinch sea salt
1 teaspoon vanilla extract, pure
2 cups milk
2 tablespoons honey, raw
3 dates, dried, pitted & chopped fine
5 apricots, dried & chopped fine

Directions:
Get out a skillet to toast your almonds in for about five minutes. They should be golden and aromatic.
Place your quinoa and cinnamon in a saucepan using medium heat. Add in your vanilla, salt, and milk. Stir and then bring it to a boil. Reduce your heat, and allow it to simmer for fifteen minutes.
Add in your dates, honey, apricots, and half of your almonds.
Serve topped with almonds and parsley if desired.

Nutrition:
Calories: 344 | Protein: 12.6 Grams | Fat: 13.8 Grams | Carbohydrates: 45.7 Grams | Sodium: 96 mg

241. Mediterranean Lettuce Wraps

Preparation Time: 10 minutes | **Cooking time:** 10 minutes | **Servings:** 4

Ingredients:
One-fourth cup of tahini
One-fourth cup of olive oil, extra-virgin
One teaspoon of lemon zest
One-fourth cup of lemon juice
One and a half tsp. of pure maple syrup
Three fourth tsp. of kosher salt
Half tsp. of paprika
Two cans (15 ounces) of rinsed chickpeas, no-salt-added
Half cup of sliced and roasted red pepper - drained and jarred
Half cup of thinly sliced shallots
Twelve leaves of Bibb lettuce, large
One-fourth cup of almonds, roasted and chopped
Two tsp. of fresh parsley, chopped

Directions:
Whisk lemon zest, tahini, oil, maple syrup, lemon juice, paprika, and all in a bowl.
After which, add peppers, chickpeas, and shallots.
Now, toss for coating.
After this, divide this mixture among the lettuce leaves (say about one-third cup for every portion).
Top with parsley and almonds.
Before serving, wrap lettuce leaves around this filling for proper garnishing.

Nutrition:
Carbohydrate - 44 g | Protein - 16 g | Fat: - 28 g | Calories: 498

242. Greek Salad Nachos

Preparation Time: 15 minutes | **Cooking time:** 15 minutes | **Servings:** 6

Ingredients:
A ⅓ cup of hummus
2 tablespoons of extra-virgin olive oil
1 tablespoon of lemon juice
¼ teaspoon of ground pepper
3 cups of whole-grain pita chips
1 cup of chopped lettuce

A ½ cup of quartered grape tomatoes
A ¼ cup of crumbled feta cheese
2 tablespoons of chopped olives
2 tablespoons of minced red onion
1 tablespoon of minced fresh oregano

Directions:
Whisk pepper, lemon juice, oil, and hummus in a bowl.
Spread the pita chips on a plate in one layer. Cover the chips with about ¾ of that hummus mix and top it with tomatoes, red onion, olives, feta, and lettuce. Cover it with the rest of the hummus. Sprinkle oregano on top before serving it.

Nutrition:
Carbohydrate – 13 g | Protein: – 4 g | Fat: – 10 g | Calories: 159

243. Sirloin with Sweet Bell Peppers

Preparation Time: 20 minutes | **Cooking time:** 8 minutes | **Servings:** 4

Ingredients:
12 ounces boneless top sirloin steak, about 1-inch thick, trimmed of visible Fat | 1 tablespoon olive oil, divided
Sea salt
Freshly ground black pepper
1 yellow bell pepper, thinly sliced
1 red bell pepper, thinly sliced
1 orange bell pepper, thinly sliced
1 small red onion, thinly sliced
4 garlic cloves, crushed
Juice of 1 lemon

Directions:
Preheat the oven to broil.
Lightly oil the steak on both sides with 1 teaspoon of olive oil and season with salt and pepper. Place the steak on a baking sheet.
In a large bowl, toss together the bell peppers, onion, garlic, and remaining 2 teaspoons of olive oil. Season lightly with salt and pepper. Spread the vegetables on the baking sheet around the steak.
Broil the steak and vegetables until the steak is browned and the desired doneness, turning once, about 4 minutes per side.
Remove from the oven and let the steak rest for 10 minutes. Slice thinly on the bias against the grain. Drizzle the vegetables with lemon juice and serve.

Nutrition:
Calories: 170 | Total fat: 7g | Saturated fat: 2g | Carbohydrates: 11g | Sugar: 2g | Fiber: 2g | Protein: 18g

244. Quinoa and Spinach Salad with Figs and Balsamic Dressing

Preparation Time: 10 minutes, plus cooling time | **Cooking time:** 15 minutes | **Servings:** 4

Ingredients:
½ cup quinoa
1 cup water
6 cups chopped spinach
8 ripe figs, quartered
¼ cup sunflower seeds
½ cup store-bought balsamic dressing
½ cup crumbled goat cheese

Directions:
Rinse the quinoa under cold running water to remove its bitter flavor. In a small saucepan, combine the quinoa and water and bring to a boil over medium heat. Reduce the heat to low and simmer, uncovered until the liquid is absorbed, 10 to 15 minutes. Transfer to a dish and refrigerate until cool.
In a large bowl, toss the spinach, cooked quinoa, figs, and sunflower seeds until well mixed. Add the dressing, toss to coat, and transfer the salad to serving plates. Top with goat cheese and serve.

Nutrition:
Calories: 348 | Total fat: 12g | Saturated fat: 3g | Carbohydrates: 54g | Sugar: 21g | Fiber: 7g | Protein: 11g

245. Greek-Style Tuna Salad in Pita

Preparation Time: 25 minutes | **Cooking time:** 0 minutes | **Servings:** 4

Ingredients:
2 (5-ounce) cans water-packed tuna, drained
½ English cucumber, chopped
1 yellow bell pepper, chopped

¼ cup chopped oil-packed sun-dried tomatoes
2 tablespoons pitted, chopped Kalamata olives
2 tablespoons chopped fresh parsley
1 tablespoon freshly squeezed lemon juice
Sea salt
Freshly ground black pepper
4 whole-wheat pita bread rounds, halved
½ cup crumbled feta cheese
1 cup shredded Boston lettuce

Directions:
In a large bowl, stir together the tuna, cucumber, bell pepper, sun-dried tomatoes, olives, parsley, and lemon juice. Season with salt and pepper. Scoop the tuna salad into the pita halves and top them with feta cheese and lettuce. Serve.

Nutrition:
Calories: 192 | Total fat: 6g | Saturated fat: 3g | Carbohydrates: 23g | Sugar: 5g | Fiber: 3g | Protein: 14g

246. Delicious Broccoli Tortellini Salad

Preparation Time: 10 minutes | **Cooking time:** 20 to 25 minutes | **Servings:** 12

Ingredients:
1 cup sunflower seeds, or any of your favorite seeds
3 heads of broccoli, fresh is best!
½ cup sugar
20 ounces cheese-filled tortellini
1 onion
2 teaspoons cider vinegar
½ cup mayonnaise
1 cup raisins-optional

Directions:
Cut your broccoli into florets and chop the onion. Follow the directions to make the cheese-filled tortellini. Once they are cooked, drain, and rinse them with cold water.
In a bowl, combine your mayonnaise, sugar, and vinegar. Whisk well to give the ingredients a dressing consistency.
In a separate large bowl, toss in your seeds, onion, tortellini, raisins, and broccoli.
Pour the salad dressing into the large bowl and toss the ingredients together. You will want to ensure everything is thoroughly mixed as you'll want a taste of the salad dressing with every bite!

Nutrition:
Calories: 272 | Fats: 8.1 Grams | Carbohydrates: 38.6 Grams | Protein: 5 Grams

247. Tuna and Cheese Bake

Preparation Time: 5 minutes | **Cooking time:** 15 minutes | **Servings:** 4

Ingredients:
10 ounces canned tuna, drained and flaked
4 eggs, whisked
½ cup feta cheese, shredded
1 tablespoon chives, chopped
1 tablespoon parsley, chopped
Salt and black pepper to the taste
3 teaspoons olive oil

Directions:
Grease a baking dish with the oil, add the tuna and the rest of the ingredients except the cheese, toss and bake at 370 degrees F for 15 minutes. Sprinkle the cheese on top, leave the mix aside for 5 minutes, slice, and serve for breakfast.

Nutrition:
Calories 283 | Fat: 14.2 | Fiber 5.6 | Carbs 12.1 | Protein: 6.4

248. Instant Pot Potato Salad

Preparation Time: 5 minutes, | **Cooking time:** 10 minutes | **Servings:** 2

Ingredients:
6 potatoes, peeled and cubed
4 eggs
1 cup mayonnaise
1 tablespoon dill pickle juice
Salt and pepper for taste
2 cups water
¼ cup chopped onion
2 tablespoons chopped parsley
1 tablespoon muster

Directions:
Take your steamer basket and put it in a pressure cooker pot.
Add the water, potatoes, and eggs, and then cook on high pressure for 4 minutes.

When finished, pull the eggs out and let them cool in cold water.

Add the other ingredients together, and then the cooled potatoes and mix it in. you can then dice the eggs and put them in the salad, and then add salt and pepper for taste. Let it chill for an hour if you want that.

Nutrition:
Calories: 230, | Fat: 9 g | Carbs: 22g | Net Carbs: 15 g | Protein: 12 g | Fiber: 7 g. | Sodium: 117mg

249. Veggie Hummus Sandwich

Preparation Time: 10 minutes | **Cooking time:** 10 minutes | **Servings:** 2

Ingredients:
4 slices of whole-grain bread
6 tbsp of hummus
1 cup of salad greens or spinach
½ cup of shredded carrot
½ medium bell pepper halved
½ cup of cucumber, sliced
½ avocado, mashed

Directions:
Combine all the ingredients in a small mixing bowl. Spread hummus over a piece of toast or pita bread. Pour the mixture of cucumber, carrot, bell pepper, and greens into the sandwich. Then, cut the sandwich in half or quarters and serve or put it in a plastic bag ready for your lunch at work or school.

Nutrition:
Calories: 320 | Fat: 14g | Carbs: 40g

250. Spicy Potato Salad

Preparation Time: 10 minutes | **Cooking time:** 15 minutes | **Servings:** 4

Ingredients:
1 and ½ pounds baby potatoes, peeled and halved
A pinch of salt and black pepper
2 tablespoons harissa paste
6 ounces Greek yogurt
Juice of 1 lemon
¼ cup red onion, chopped
¼ cup parsley, chopped

Directions:
Put the potatoes in a pot, add water to cover, add salt, bring to a boil over medium-high heat, cook for 12 minutes, drain, and transfer them to a bowl.
Add the harissa and the rest of the ingredients, toss, and serve for lunch.

Nutrition:
Calories 354 | Fat: 19.2 | Fiber 4.5 | Carbs 24.7 | Protein: 11.2

251. Tomato and Halloumi Platter

Preparation Time: 5 minutes | **Cooking time:** 4 minutes | **Servings:** 4

Ingredients:
1-pound tomatoes, sliced
½ pound halloumi, cut into 4 slices
2 tablespoons parsley, chopped
1 tablespoon basil, chopped
2 tablespoons olive oil
A pinch of salt and black pepper
Juice of 1 lemon

Directions:
Brush the halloumi slices with half of the oil, put them on your preheated grill and cook over medium-high heat and cook for 2 minutes on each side.
Arrange the tomato slices on a platter, season with salt and pepper, drizzle the lemon juice and the rest of the oil all over, top with the halloumi slices, sprinkle the herbs on top, and serve for lunch.

Nutrition:
Calories 181 | Fat: 7.3 | Fiber 1.4 | Carbs 4.6 | Protein: 1.1

252. Bean Lettuce Wraps

Preparation Time: 5 minutes | **Cooking time:** 20 minutes | **Servings:** 4

Ingredients:
8 Romaine lettuce leaves
½ cup Garlic hummus or any prepared hummus
¾ cup chopped tomatoes
15 ounce can great northern beans, drained and rinsed
½ cup diced onion

1 tablespoon extra-virgin olive oil
¼ cup chopped parsley
¼ teaspoon black pepper

Directions:
Set a skillet on top of the stove range over medium heat.
In the skillet, warm the oil for a couple of minutes.
Add the onion into the oil. Stir frequently as the onion cooks for a few minutes.
Combine the pepper and tomatoes and cook for another couple of minutes. Remember to stir occasionally.
Add the beans and continue to stir and cook for 2 to 3 minutes.
Turn the burner off, remove the skillet from heat, and add the parsley.
Set the lettuce leaves on a flat surface and spread 1 tablespoon of hummus on each leaf.
Divide the bean mixture onto the 8 leaves.
Spread the bean mixture down the center of the leaves.
Fold the leaves by starting lengthwise on one side.
Fold over the other side so the leaf is completely wrapped.
Serve and enjoy!

Nutrition:
Calories: 211 | Fats: 8 Grams | Carbohydrates: 28 Grams | Protein: 10 Grams

253. Red Bean & Green Salad

Preparation Time: 10 minutes | **Cooking time:** 0 minutes | **Servings:** 6

Ingredients:
1 cup red beans, cooked & drained
1 cup lettuce, shredded & chopped
2 cups spinach leaves
1 cup red onions, sliced into thin rings
½ cup walnuts, halved
3 tablespoon olive oil
3 tablespoons lemon juice, fresh
1 clove garlic, minced
1 teaspoon dijon mustard
¼ teaspoon sea salt, fine / ¼ teaspoon black pepper

Directions:
Combine your lettuce, spinach, walnut, red beans, and red onion.
In a different bowl mix your olive oil, garlic, Dijon mustard, and lemon juice to form your dressing.
Drizzle the dressing over the salad and adjust salt and pepper as necessary.
Serve immediately.

Nutrition:
Calories: 242 | Protein: 10.1 Grams | Fat: 13.7 Grams | Carbohydrates: 22.7 Grams | Sodium: 121 mg

254. Chickpea Patties

Preparation Time: 10 minutes | **Cooking time:** 15 minutes | **Servings:** 8

Ingredients:
1 Cup Flour
¾ Cup hot water
1 egg, whisked
½ teaspoon cumin
½ teaspoon sea salt, fine
1 cup spinach, fresh & chopped
3 cloves garlic, minced
1/8 teaspoon baking soda
¾ cup chickpeas, cooked
2 scallions, small & chopped
1 cup olive oil

Directions:
Get a bowl and mix your salt, cumin, and flour. Add in your water and egg to form a batter. Whisk well. It should thicken.
Stir in your baking soda, garlic, spinach, chickpeas, and scallions, blending well.
Get a pan and place it over high heat. Add in your oil. Once your oil begins to simmer, pour in a tablespoon of your batter, frying on both sides. Repeat until all your batter is used.
Garnish with lime and greens before serving.

Nutrition:
Calories: 352 | Protein: 6.1 Grams | Fat: 27.1 Grams | Carbohydrates: 24 Grams | Sodium: 160 mg

255. Red Onion Tilapia

Preparation Time: 10 minutes | **Cooking time:** 5 minutes | **Servings:** 4

Ingredients:
1 tablespoon olive oil
1 tablespoon orange juice, fresh
¼ teaspoon sea salt, fine
1 avocado, pitted, skinned & sliced
¼ cup red onion, chopped
4 tilapia fillets, 4 ounces each

Directions:
Start by getting out a pie dish that is nine inches. Glass is best. Use a fork to mix your slat, orange juice, and oil. Dip one filet at a time and then put them in your dish. They should be coated on both sides. Put them in a wheel formation so that each fillet is in the center of the dish and draped over the edge. Top each fillet with a tablespoon of onion. Fold the fillet that's hanging over your pie dish in half so that it's over the onion.
Cover it with plastic wrap but don't close it all the way. They should be able to vent the steam. Microwave for three minutes.
Tip with avocado to serve.

Nutrition:
Calories: 200 | Protein: 22 Grams | Fat: 11 Grams | Carbohydrates: 4 Grams | Sodium: 151

256. Chicken & Asparagus

Preparation Time: 10 minutes | **Cooking time:** 10 minutes | **Servings:** 4

Ingredients:
1 lb. Chicken breast, boneless & skinless
¼ cup flour
4 tablespoons butter
½ teaspoon sea salt, fine
½ teaspoon black pepper
1 teaspoon lemon pepper seasoning
2 slices lemon
1-2 cups asparagus, chopped
2 tablespoons honey, raw
Parsley to garnish

Directions:
Cover your chicken using plastic wrap and beat it until it's ¾ of an inch thick.
Get out a bowl and mix your salt, flour, and pepper. Coat your chicken in your flour mixture.
Get out a pan to melt two tablespoons of butter over medium-high heat.
Place the chicken breast in the pan to cook for three to five minutes. It should turn golden brown on each side.
While your chicken is cooking sprinkle the lemon on each side. Once it's cooked, transfer it to a plate. In the same pan add in your asparagus, cooking until it's crisp but tender. It should turn a bright green. Set it to the side.
You'll use the same pan to add your lemon slices to caramelize.

Nutrition:
Calories: 530 | Protein: 36.8 Grams | Fat: 33.3 Grams | Carbohydrates: 28.8 Grams | Sodium: 130 mg

257. Beef Kofta

Preparation Time: 15 minutes | **Cooking time:** 15 minutes | **Servings:** 4

Ingredients:
1 lb. Ground beef, 93% lean or more
½ cup onions, minced
1 tablespoon olive oil
½ teaspoon sea salt, fine
½ teaspoon coriander, ground
½ teaspoon cumin, ground
¼ teaspoon cinnamon
¼ teaspoon mint leaves, dried
¼ teaspoon allspice

Directions:
Mix your beef, salt, cumin, coriander, cinnamon, oil, onion, mint, and allspice in a large bowl.
Get out wooden skewers and shape beef kebabs from the mixture.
Refrigerate for ten minutes before grilling them. You will need to preheat your grill and cook them for fourteen minutes. Remember to turn them constantly to avoid burning.
Serve warm.

Nutrition:
Calories: 216 | Protein: 26.1 Grams | Fat: 12.2 Grams | Carbohydrates: 1.3 Grams | Sodium: 152 mg

258. Raisin Rice Pilaf

Preparation Time: 5 minutes | **Cooking time:** 15 minutes | **Servings:** 4

Ingredients:
1 tablespoon olive oil
1 teaspoon cumin
1 cup onion, chopped
½ cup carrot, shredded
½ teaspoon cinnamon
2 cups instant brown rice
1 ¾ cup orange juice
1 cup golden raisins
¼ cup water
½ cup pistachios, shelled
Fresh Chives, Chopped for Garnish

Directions:
Place a medium saucepan over medium-high heat before adding in your oil. Add in your onion, and stir often so it doesn't burn. Cook for about five minutes and then add in your cumin, cinnamon, and carrot. Cook for about another minute.
Add in your orange juice, water, and rice. Bring it all to a boil before covering your saucepan. Turn the heat down to medium-low and then allow it to simmer for six to seven minutes. Your rice should be cooked all the way through, and all the liquid should be absorbed.
Stir in your pistachios, chives, and raisins. Serve warm.

Nutrition:
Calories: 320 | Protein: 6 Grams | Fat: 7 Grams | Carbohydrates: 61 Grams | Sodium: 37 mg

259. Lebanese Delight

Preparation Time: 5 minutes | **Cooking time:** 25 minutes | **Servings:** 5

Ingredients:
1 tablespoon olive oil
1 cup vermicelli (can be substituted for thin spaghetti) broken into 1 to 1 ½ inch pieces
3 cups cabbage, shredded
3 cups vegetable broth, low sodium
½ cup water
1 cup instant brown rice
¼ teaspoon sea salt, fine
2 cloves garlic
¼ teaspoon crushed red pepper
½ cup cilantro fresh & chopped
Lemon slices to garnish

Directions:
Get a saucepan and then place it over medium-high heat. Add in your oil and once it's hot you will need to add in your pasta. Cook for three minutes or until your pasta is toasted. You will have to stir often to keep it from burning.
Add in your cabbage, cooking for another four minutes. Continue to stir often.
Add in your water and rice. Season with salt, red pepper, and garlic before bringing it all to a boil over high heat. Stir, and then cover. Once it's covered turn the heat down to medium-low. Allow it all to simmer for ten minutes.
Remove the pan from the burner and then allow it to sit without lifting the lid for five minutes. Take the garlic cloves out and then mash them using a fork. Place them back in, and stir them into the rice. Stir in your cilantro as well and serve warm. Garnish with lemon wedges if desired.

Nutrition:
Calories: 259 | Protein: 7 Grams | Fat: 4 Grams | Carbohydrates: 49 Grams | Sodium: 123 mg

260. Flavorful Braised Kale

Preparation Time: 15 minutes | **Cooking time:** 15 minutes | **Servings:** 4

Ingredients:
1 lb. Kale, stems removed & chopped roughly
1 cup cherry tomatoes, halved
2 teaspoons olive oil
4 cloves garlic, sliced thin
½ cup vegetable stock
¼ teaspoon sea salt, fine
1 tablespoon lemon juice, fresh
1/8 teaspoon black pepper

Directions:
Start by heating your olive oil in a frying pan using medium heat, and add in your garlic. Sauté for a minute or two until lightly golden.
Mix your kale and vegetable stock with your garlic, adding it to your pan.
Cover the pan and then turn the heat down to medium-low.

Allow it to cook until your kale wilts and part of your vegetable stock should be dissolved. It should take roughly five minutes.

Stir in your tomatoes and cook without a lid until your kale is tender, and then remove it from heat.

Mix in your salt, pepper, and lemon juice before serving warm.

Nutrition:
Calories: 70 | Protein: 4 Grams | Fat: 0.5 Grams | Carbohydrates: 9 Grams | Sodium: 133 mg

261. Tomato and Wine-Steamed Mussels

Preparation Time: 10 minutes | **Cooking time:** 15 minutes | **Servings:** 4

Ingredients:
1 tablespoon olive oil
1 sweet onion, chopped
1 tablespoon minced garlic
⅛ teaspoon red pepper flakes
4 tomatoes, chopped
¼ cup low-sodium fish or chicken stock
¼ cup dry white wine
3 pounds mussels, cleaned and rinsed
Juice and zest of 1 lemon
¼ cup pitted, sliced Kalamata olives
3 tablespoons chopped fresh parsley
Sea salt
Freshly ground black pepper

Directions:
In a large saucepan, heat the olive oil over medium-high heat. Sauté the onion, garlic, and red pepper flakes until softened, about 3 minutes. Stir in the tomatoes, stock, and wine and bring to a boil.

Add the mussels to the saucepan and cover. Steam until the mussels are opened, 6 to 7 minutes. Remove from the heat and discard any unopened shells.

Stir in the lemon juice, lemon zest, olives, and parsley. Season with salt and pepper and serve.

Nutrition:
Calories: 162 | Total fat: 7g | Saturated fat: 1g | Carbohydrates: 12g | Sugar: 5g | Fiber: 3g | Protein: 12g

262. Tangy Tilapia Fish Fillets with Crusty Coating

Preparation Time: 5 minutes | **Cooking time:** 10 minutes | **Servings:** 4

Ingredients:
¼-cup ground flaxseed
1-cup almonds, finely chopped (divided)
4-6 oz. tilapia fillets
½-tsp salt
2-tbsp olive oil

Directions:
Combine the flaxseed with half of the almonds in a shallow mixing bowl to serve as a crusty coating, instead of a flour mixture.

Sprinkle the tilapia fillets evenly with salt. Dredge the fillet in the flaxseed-almond mixture. Set aside.

Heat the olive oil in a heavy, thick-bottomed skillet placed over medium heat. Add the coated fillets, and cook for 4 minutes on each side until golden brown, flipping once. Remove the fillets, and transfer them to a serving plate.

In the same skillet, add the remaining almonds. Toast for a minute until turning golden brown, stirring frequently.

To serve, sprinkle the toasted almonds over the fish fillets.

Nutrition:
Calories: 258 | Total Fats: 21.3g | Fiber: 4.9g | Carbohydrates: 7.1g | Protein: 11.6g

263. Feta-Fused Mussels Marmite

Preparation Time: 10 minutes | **Cooking time:** 20 minutes | **Servings:** 6

Ingredients:
2-tbsp olive oil
1-pc medium onion, chopped
1-cup white wine
½-tsp salt
2-lbs mussels (without the shell)
1-dash of cayenne pepper
2-cloves of garlic, chopped
1-tbsp tomato paste
2-oz of feta cheese grated
Bunch of parsley, chopped

Directions:
Preheat your oven to 400 °F.
Heat the oil in a large pot placed over medium-high heat and sauté the onion for 3 minutes until tender. Pour the white wine, and add the tomato, salt, and mussels. Bring to a boil until all the mussels break open and the wine evaporates. Add the cayenne and garlic. Simmer for 5 minutes.
Take out the top shell of the mussels. Sprinkle the opened mussels with feta cheese and parsley. Place the pot in the preheated oven. Grill for 8 minutes until the cheese begins to melt and appear with a golden color.
 TIP: Remove any closed mussel; a closed one is an indication that it is bad!

Nutrition:
Calories: 227 | Total Fats: 10.1g | Fiber: 0.6g | Carbohydrates: 9.8g | Protein: 19.8g

264. Sauced Shellfish in White Wine

Preparation Time: 10 minutes | **Cooking time:** 10 minutes | **Servings:** 6

Ingredients:
2-lbs fresh cuttlefish
½-cup olive oil
1-pc large onion, finely chopped
1-cup of Robola white wine
¼-cup lukewarm water
1-pc bay leaf
½-bunch parsley, chopped
4-pcs tomatoes, grated
Salt and pepper

Directions:
Take out the hard centerpiece of cartilage (cuttlebone), the bag of ink, and the intestines from the cuttlefish. Wash the cleaned cuttlefish with running water. Slice it into small pieces, and drain excess water.
Heat the oil in a saucepan placed over medium-high heat and sauté the onion for 3 minutes until tender. Add the sliced cuttlefish and pour in the white wine. Cook for 5 minutes until it simmers.
Pour in the water, and add the tomatoes, bay leaf, parsley, tomatoes, salt, and pepper. Simmer the mixture over low heat until the cuttlefish slices are tender and left with their thick sauce. Serve them warm with rice.
TIP: Be careful not to overcook the cuttlefish as its texture becomes very hard. A safe rule of thumb is grilling the cuttlefish over a raging fire for 3 minutes before using it in any recipe.

Nutrition:
Calories: 308 | Total Fats: 18.1g | Fiber: 1.5g | Carbohydrates: 8g | Protein: 25.6g

265. Couscous with Tuna and Pepperoncini

Preparation Time: 10 minutes | **Cooking time:** 15 minutes | **Servings:** 4

Ingredients:
1 cup chicken broth or water
¾ teaspoon salt
1¼ cups couscous
⅓ cup fresh parsley, chopped
1 lemon, quartered
2 cans (5 Oz each) oil-packed tuna
1 pint cherry tomatoes, halved
Extra-virgin olive oil (for serving)
½ cup pepperoncini, sliced
¼ cup capers
Salt, pepper, to taste

Directions:
Add 1 cup chicken broth or water to a small pot and boil it. Turn the heat off, stir in 1¼ cups of couscous, and cover it. Let it boil for 10 minutes. In the meantime, take another bowl and add 1 pint of halved cherry tomatoes, ½ cup of sliced pepperoncini, ¼ cup capers, ⅓ cup fresh chopped parsley, and oil-packed tuna; toss well. Fluff the couscous with a fork. Season with pepper and salt; drizzle with olive oil.
Top with the mixture of tuna and serve your meal with lemon wedges.

Nutrition:
226 calories | 10 g fat | 44 g total carbohydrates | 22 g protein

266. Lemon Chicken with Asparagus

Preparation Time: 10 minutes | **Cooking time:** 10 minutes | **Servings:** 3-4

Ingredients:
1 lb. boneless skinless chicken breasts
2 tablespoons honey + 2 tablespoons butter
1/4 cup flour
2 lemons, sliced
1/2 teaspoon salt, pepper to taste
1 teaspoon lemon pepper seasoning
1-2 cups asparagus, chopped
2 tablespoons butter

Directions:
Cut the chicken breast in half horizontally. In a shallow dish, mix 1/4 cup flour and salt and pepper to taste; toss the chicken breast until coated.
To a skillet, add 2 tablespoons of butter and melt over medium heat. Then add the coated chicken breast and cook each side for about 4-5 minutes, sprinkling both sides with lemon pepper.
Once the chicken is completely cooked through and is golden brown, transfer it to a plate.
For Asparagus and Lemons:
To the pan, add 1-2 cups chopped asparagus; sauté until bright green for a few minutes.
Remove from the pan and keep it aside. Place the slices of lemon to the bottom of the pan and cook each side until caramelized, for a few minutes without stirring.
Add a bit of butter along with the lemon slices. Take the lemons out of the pan and put them aside.
Serve the chicken with the asparagus and enjoy!

Nutrition:
232 calories | 9 g fat | 10.4 g total carbs | 27.5 g protein

267. Cilantro Lime Chicken

Preparation Time: 10 minutes | **Cooking time:** 12 minutes | **Servings:** 4

Ingredients:
2 tablespoons olive oil
1/4 teaspoon salt
1.5 lb. boneless chicken breast
1/2 teaspoon ground cumin
1/4 cup lime juice
1/4 cup fresh cilantro
For Avocado Salsa:
1/2 tablespoon red wine vinegar
Salt, to taste
4 avocados, diced
1 garlic clove, minced
1/2 cup fresh cilantro, diced
1/2 teaspoon red pepper flakes
3 tablespoons lime juice

Directions:
Add cilantro, lime juice, 1/2 teaspoon ground cumin, 2 tablespoons olive oil, and salt to a bowl; whisk well.
Add the marinade and chicken breast to a large Ziploc bag; marinate for about 15 minutes.
Preheat the grill to 400°F. Grill the chicken until it's no longer pink, for about 5-7 minutes per side. Remove from the grill.
For avocado salsa: add lime juice, cilantro, 1/2 tablespoon red wine vinegar, 1/2 teaspoon red pepper flakes, 1 minced clove of garlic, salt, and 4 diced avocados to a blender; process well until smooth.
Serve and enjoy!

Nutrition:
317 calories | 22 g fat | 11 g total Carbohydrates | 24 g protein

268. Shrimp and Leek Spaghetti

Preparation Time: 10 minutes | **Cooking time:** 20 minutes | **Servings:** 4

Ingredients:
1 lb. peeled, deveined raw shrimp
8 oz. uncooked whole-grain spaghetti
1 tablespoon garlic, chopped
2 cups leek, chopped
1 ½ tablespoons olive oil
¼ cup heavy cream
2 cups frozen baby sweet peas
2 tablespoons dill, chopped
2 teaspoons lemon zest
2 tablespoons lemon juice
½ teaspoon black pepper
¾ teaspoon kosher salt

Directions:
Cook the pasta according to the package instructions. Drain and reserve ½ cup cooking liquid. Cover the pasta.
Pat dry the shrimp and season with pepper and ¼ teaspoon salt.
Heat half of the oil in a skillet over high heat. Add shrimp and cook for 4 minutes, stirring often. Transfer to a plate and cover.
Reduce the heat to medium-high. Add garlic, leek, ½ teaspoon salt, and the remaining oil. Cook for 3 minutes, stirring often.
Add cream, peas, lemon zest, lemon juice, and the reserved liquid. Reduce the heat to medium and cook for 3 minutes. Add the shrimp to the skillet and toss well.
Add the pasta evenly to 4 bowls. Add the sauce and the shrimp on top.
Add dill and serve.

Nutrition:
446 calories | 13 g fat | 59 g total carbs | 28 g protein

269. Lamb and Beet Meatballs

Preparation Time: 5 minutes | **Cooking time:** 20 minutes | **Servings:** 4

Ingredients:
1 tablespoon olive oil
1 (8 oz.) package beets, cooked
6 oz. ground lamb
1/2 cup bulgur, uncooked
1 teaspoon ground cumin
1/2 cup cucumber, grated
1/2 cup sour cream, reduced-Fat | 2 tablespoons fresh mint, thinly sliced
2 tablespoons fresh lemon juice
1 oz. almond flour
4 cups mixed baby greens
3/4 teaspoon kosher salt
3/4 teaspoon freshly ground black pepper

Directions:
Preheat the oven to 425F.
Add the beets to a food processor and pulse until finely chopped, then combine the chopped beets with bulgur, lamb, cumin, ½ teaspoon of salt, pepper, and almond flour in a bowl.
Divide the lamb mixture and shape it into 12 meatballs.
Heat the oil in a skillet over medium-high heat, then add it into prepared meatballs. Cook until nicely browned on all sides, for about 4 minutes. Transfer the browned meatballs to the preheated oven and bake until well cooked, about 8 minutes.
Combine the remaining ¼ teaspoon of salt with cucumber, juice, mint, and sour cream in a bowl, then divide the greens among the serving plates. Top the greens with the meatballs evenly and serve with the cucumber mixture. Enjoy!

Nutrition:
338 calories | 21 g fat | 25 g total carbs | 14 g protein

270. Chicken Wings Platter

Preparation Time: 10 minutes | **Cooking time:** 20 minutes | **Servings:** 4

Ingredients:
2 pounds chicken wings
½ cup tomato sauce
A pinch of salt and black pepper
1 teaspoon smoked paprika
1 tablespoon cilantro, chopped
1 tablespoon chives, chopped

Directions:
In your instant pot, combine the chicken wings with the sauce and the rest of the ingredients, stir, put the lid on and cook on High for 20 minutes.
Release the pressure naturally for 10 minutes, arrange the chicken wings on a platter, and serve as an appetizer.

Nutrition:
Calories 203, | Fat: 13g | Fiber 3g, | Carbohydrates: 5g, | Protein: 8g

271. Spicy Sweet Red Hummus

Preparation Time: 10 minutes | **Cooking time:** 0 minutes | **Servings:** 8

Ingredients:
1 (15 ounces) can garbanzo beans, drained
1 (4 ounces) jar roasted red peppers
1 1/2 tablespoons tahini
1 clove garlic, minced
1 tablespoon chopped fresh parsley

1/2 teaspoon cayenne pepper
1/2 teaspoon ground cumin
1/4 teaspoon salt
3 tablespoons lemon juice

Directions:
In a blender, add all ingredients and process until smooth and creamy.
Adjust seasoning to taste if needed.
Can be stored in an airtight container for up to 5 days.

Nutrition:
Calories: 64 | Carbohydrates: 9.6g | Protein: 2.5g | Fat: 2.2g

272. Dill Relish on White Sea Bass

Preparation Time: 15 minutes | **Cooking time:** 12 minutes | **Servings:** 4

Ingredients:
1 ½ tbsp chopped white onion
1 ½ tsp chopped fresh dill
1 lemon, quartered
1 tsp Dijon mustard
1 tsp lemon juice
1 tsp pickled baby capers, drained
4 pieces of 4-oz white sea bass fillets

Directions:
Preheat the oven to 375oF.
Mix lemon juice, mustard, dill, capers, and onions in a small bowl.
Prepare four aluminum foil squares and place 1 fillet per foil.
Squeeze a lemon wedge per fish.
Evenly divide into 4 the dill spread and drizzle over the fillet.
Close the foil over the fish securely and pop it in the oven.
Bake for 10 to 12 minutes or until fish is cooked through.
Remove from foil and transfer to a serving platter, serve and enjoy.

Nutrition:
Calories: 115 | Carbohydrates: 12g | Protein: 7g | Fat: 1g

273. Mustard Chops with Apricot-basil Relish

Preparation Time: 18 minutes | **Cooking time:** 12 minutes | **Servings:** 4

Ingredients:
¼ cup basil, finely shredded
¼ cup olive oil
½ cup mustard
¾ lb. fresh apricots, stone removed, and fruit diced
1 shallot, diced small
1 tsp ground cardamom
3 tbsp raspberry vinegar
4 pork chops
Pepper and salt

Directions:
Make sure that pork chops are defrosted well. Season with pepper and salt. Slather both sides of each pork chop with mustard. Preheat the grill to medium-high fire.
In a medium bowl, mix cardamom, olive oil, vinegar, basil, shallot, and apricots. Toss to combine and season with pepper and salt, mixing once again.
Grill chops for 5 to 6 minutes per side. As you flip, baste with mustard.
Serve pork chops with the Apricot-Basil relish and enjoy.

Nutrition:
Calories: 486.5 | Carbohydrates: 7.3g | Protein: 42.1g | Fat: 32.1g

274. Seafood and Veggie Pasta

Preparation Time: 10 minutes | **Cooking time:** 20 minutes | **Servings:** 4

Ingredients:
¼ tsp pepper
¼ tsp salt
1 lb raw shelled shrimp
1 lemon, cut into wedges
1 tbsp butter
1 tbsp olive oil
2 5-oz cans chopped clams, drained (reserve 2 tbsp clam juice)
2 tbsp dry white wine
4 cloves garlic, minced
4 cups zucchini, spiraled (use a veggie spiralizer)

4 tbsp Parmesan Cheese
Chopped fresh parsley to garnish

Directions:
Ready the zucchini and spiralize with a veggie spiralizer. Arrange 1 cup of zucchini noodle per bowl. Total of 4 bowls.
On medium fire, place a large nonstick saucepan and heat oil and butter.
For a minute, sauté garlic. Add shrimp and cook for 3 minutes until opaque or cooked.
Add white wine, reserved clam juice, and clams. Bring to a simmer and continue simmering for 2 minutes or until half of the liquid has evaporated. Stir constantly.
Season with pepper and salt. And if needed add more to taste.
Remove from fire and evenly distribute seafood sauce to 4 bowls.
Top with a tablespoonful of Parmesan cheese per bowl, serve and enjoy.

Nutrition:
Calories: 324.9 | Carbohydrates: 12g | Protein: 43.8g | Fat: 11.3g

275. Creamy Alfredo Fettuccine

Preparation Time: 5 minutes | **Cooking time:** 25 minutes | **Servings:** 4

Ingredients:
Grated parmesan cheese
½ cup freshly grated parmesan cheese
1/8 tsp freshly ground black pepper
½ tsp salt
1 cup whipping cream
2 tbsp butter
8 oz dried fettuccine, cooked and drained

Directions:
On medium-high fire, place a big fry pan and heat butter.
Add pepper, salt, and cream, and gently boil for three to five minutes.
Once thickened, turn off the fire and quickly stir in ½ cup of parmesan cheese. Toss in pasta, mix well.
Top with another batch of parmesan cheese and serve.

Nutrition:
Calories: 202 | Carbohydrates: 21.1g | Protein: 7.9g | Fat: 10.2g

276. Walnut-Rosemary Crusted Salmon

Preparation Time: 10 minutes | **Cooking time:** 20 minutes | **Servings:** 4

Ingredients:
1 lb. or 450 g. frozen skinless salmon fillet
2 tsps. Dijon mustard
1 clove garlic, minced
¼ tsp. lemon zest
½ tsp. honey
½ tsp. kosher salt
1 tsp. freshly chopped rosemary
3 tbsps. panko breadcrumbs
¼ tsp. crushed red pepper
3 tbsps. chopped walnuts
2 tsp. extra-virgin olive oil

Directions:
Preheat the oven to 420 F/215 C and use parchment paper to line a rimmed baking sheet.
In a bowl combine mustard, lemon zest, garlic, lemon juice, honey, rosemary, crushed red pepper, and salt
In another bowl mix walnut, panko, and 1 tsp oil
Place parchments paper on the baking sheet and put the salmon on it
Spread mustard mixture on the fish, and top with the panko mixture.
Spray the rest of the olive oil lightly on the salmon.
Bake for about 10 -12 minutes or until the salmon is being separated by a fork
Serve hot

Nutrition:
Calories 222 | Fat: 12 g | Sat. fat 2 g | Fiber 0.8 g | Carbohydrates: 4 g | Sugars 1 g | Protein: 24 g | Sodium: 256 mg

277. Quick Tomato Spaghetti

Preparation Time: 10 minutes | **Cooking time:** 20 minutes | **Servings:** 4

Ingredients:
8 oz. or 226.7g spaghetti
3 tbsps. olive oil

4 garlic cloves, sliced
1 jalapeno, sliced
2 c. cherry tomatoes
Salt and pepper
1 tsp. balsamic vinegar
½ c. Parmesan, grated

Directions:
Heat a large pot of water on medium flame. Add a pinch of salt and bring to a boil then add the spaghetti.
Allow cooking for 8 minutes.
While the pasta cooks, heat the oil in a skillet and add the garlic and jalapeno. Cook for an extra 1 minute then stir in the tomatoes, pepper, and salt.
Cook for 5-7 minutes until the tomatoes' skins burst.
Add the vinegar and remove off heat.
Drain spaghetti well and mix it with the tomato sauce. Sprinkle with cheese and serve right away.

Nutrition:
Calories 298 | Fat: 13.5 g | Sat. fat 2.7 g | Fiber 10.5 g | Carbohydrates: 36 g | Sugar: 8 g | Protein: 9.7 g | Sodium: 223 mg

278. Crispy Italian Chicken

Preparation Time: 10 minutes | **Cooking time:** 20 minutes | **Servings:** 4

Ingredients:
4 chicken legs
1 tsp. dried basil
1 tsp. dried oregano
Salt and pepper
3 tbsps. olive oil
1 tbsp. balsamic vinegar

Directions:
Season the chicken with salt, pepper, basil, and oregano.
Using a skillet, add oil and heat. Add the chicken to the hot oil.
Let each side cook for 5 minutes until golden then cover the skillet with a lid.
Adjust your heat to medium and cook for 10 minutes on one side then flip the chicken repeatedly, cooking for another 10 minutes until crispy.
Serve the chicken and enjoy.

Nutrition:
Calories: 262 | Fat: 13.9 g | Sat. fat: 4 g | Fiber: 0 g | Carbohydrates: 0.3 g | Sugar: 0 g | Protein: 32.6 g | Sodium: 405 mg

279. Chili Oregano Baked Cheese

Preparation Time: 5 minutes | **Cooking time:** 25 minutes | **Servings:** 4

Ingredients:
8 oz. or 226.7g feta cheese
4 oz. or 113g mozzarella, crumbled
1 sliced chili pepper
1 tsp. dried oregano
2 tbsps. olive oil

Directions:
Place the feta cheese in a small deep-dish baking pan.
Top with the mozzarella then season with pepper slices and oregano.
cover your pan with a lid. Cook in the preheated oven at 350 F/176 C for 20 minutes.
Serve the cheese and enjoy it.

Nutrition:
Calories 292 | Fat: 24.2 g | Sat. fat 7 g | Fiber 2 g | Carbohydrates: 5.7 g | Sugar: 3 g | Protein: 16.2 g | Sodium: 287 mg

280. Sea Bass in a Pocket

Preparation Time: 5 minutes | **Cooking time:** 25 minutes | **Servings:** 4

Ingredients:
4 sea bass fillets
4 sliced garlic cloves
1 sliced celery stalk
1 sliced zucchini
1 c. halved cherry tomatoes halved
1 shallot, sliced
1 tsp. dried oregano
Salt and pepper

Directions:
Mix the garlic, celery, zucchini, tomatoes, shallot, and oregano in a bowl. Add salt and pepper to taste.
Take 4 sheets of baking paper and arrange them on your working surface.

Spoon the vegetable mixture in the center of each sheet.
Top with a fish fillet then wrap the paper so it resembles a pocket.
Place the wrapped fish in a baking tray and cook in the preheated oven at 350 F/176 C for 15 minutes. Serve the fish warm and fresh.

Nutrition:
Calories 149 | Fat: 2.8 g | Sat. fat 0.7 g | Fiber 0 g | Carbohydrates: 5.2 g | Sugar: 0 g | Protein: 25.2 g | Sodium: 87 mg

281. Shrimp, Avocado and Feta Wrap

Preparation Time: 15 minutes | **Cooking time:** 10 minutes | **Servings:** 2

Ingredients:
3 oz. or 85g chopped shrimps, cooked
1 tbsp. lime juice
2 tbsps. crumbled feta cheese
¼ c. diced avocado
1 whole-wheat tortilla
¼ c. diced tomato
1 sliced scallion

Directions:
On a non-stick skillet add shrimps and cook for 5 minutes or until nice pink color
Add feta cheese on the tortilla's one side
Top cheese with the rest of the ingredients. Add the shrimp on the top so they will be in the middle of the wrap when you roll it.
Add lime juice to give it the tangy zing to the wrap.
Then roll the wrap tightly, but make sure that the ingredients don't fall off.
Then cut the wrap into two halves and serve it.

Nutrition:
Calories 371 | Fat: 14 g | Sat fat 4 g | Fiber 6 g | Carbohydrates: 34 g | Sugars 6 g | Protein: 29 g | Sodium: 34 mg

282. Broiled Tilapia Parmesan

Preparation Time: 15 minutes | **Cooking time:** 15 minutes | **Servings:** 8

Ingredients:
½ c. Parmesan cheese
¼ c. butter, soft
3 tbsps. mayonnaise
2 tbsps. fresh lemon juice
¼ tsp. dried basil
¼ tsp. ground black pepper
1/8 tsp. onion powder
1/8 tsp. celery salt
2 lbs. or 900 g Tilapia fillets

Directions:
Preheat the grill on your oven. Cover a drip tray or grill pan with aluminum foil.
Combine parmesan, butter, mayonnaise, and lemon juice in a small bowl. Apply a seasoning of onion powder, pepper, dried basil, and celery salt mix well and set aside.
Set the fillets in a single layer on the prepared dish. Grill a few centimeters from the heat for 2 to 3 minutes, turn the fillets and grill for a few minutes.
Remove from the oven and cover with Parmesan cheese mixture on top.
Grill for another 2 minutes or until the garnish is golden brown and fish flakes easily with a fork. Be careful not to overcook the fish.
Serve and enjoy!

Nutrition:
Calories 224 | Fat: 12.8 g | Sat fat 3 g | Fiber 0.2 g | Carbohydrates: 0.8 g | Sugars 0 g | Protein: 25.4 g | Sodium: 220mg

283. Italian Herb Grilled Chicken

Preparation Time: 10 minutes | **Cooking time:** 20 minutes | **Servings:** 4

Ingredients:
½ c. lemon juice
½ c. extra-virgin olive oil
3 tbsps. minced garlic
2 tsps. dried oregano
1 tsp. red pepper flakes
1 tsp. salt
2 lbs. or 900 g boneless chicken breasts, skinless

Directions:
In a medium bowl, combine garlic, lemon juice, olive oil, oregano, red pepper flakes, and salt.
Divide chicken breast horizontally to get 2 thin pieces. Repeat this process with the rest of the chicken breasts.

Set the chicken in the bowl with the marinade and let sit for at least 10 minutes before cooking.
Place the skillet on high heat and add oil.
Cook each side of the breasts for 4 minutes.
Serve warm.

Nutrition:
Calories 479 | Fat: 32 g | Sat fat 5 g | Fiber 1 g | Carbohydrates: 5 g | Sugars 1 g | Protein: 47 g | Sodium: 943 mg

284. Mediterranean Grilled Shrimp

Preparation Time: 20 minutes | **Cooking time:** 5 minutes | **Servings:** 4-7

Ingredients:
2 tablespoons garlic, minced
½ cup lemon juice
3 tablespoons fresh Italian parsley, finely chopped
¼ cup extra-virgin olive oil
1 teaspoon salt
2 pounds jumbo shrimp (21-25), peeled and deveined

Directions:
In a large bowl, mix the garlic, lemon juice, parsley, olive oil, and salt.
Add the shrimp to the bowl and toss to make sure all the pieces are coated with the marinade. Let the shrimp sit for 15 minutes.
Preheat a grill, grill pan, or lightly oiled skillet to high heat. While heating, thread about 5 to 6 pieces of shrimp onto each skewer.
Place the skewers on the grill, grill pan, or skillet and cook for 2 to 3 minutes on each side until cooked through. Serve warm.

Nutrition:
Calories: 402; | Protein: 57g | Total Carbohydrates: 4g | Sugars: 1g; | Fiber: 0g | Total Fat: 18g;

285. Italian Breaded Shrimp

Preparation Time: 10 minutes | **Cooking time:** 5 minutes | **Servings:** 4

Ingredients:
2 large eggs
2 cups seasoned Italian breadcrumbs
1 teaspoon salt
1 cup flour
1-pound large shrimp (21-25), peeled and deveined
Extra-virgin olive oil

Directions:
In a small bowl, beat the eggs with 1 tablespoon water, then transfer to a shallow dish.
Add the breadcrumbs and salt to a separate shallow dish; mix well.
Place the flour into a third shallow dish.
Coat the shrimp in the flour, then egg, and finally the breadcrumbs. Place on a plate and repeat with all the shrimp.
Preheat a skillet over high heat. Pour in enough olive oil to coat the bottom of the skillet. Cook the shrimp in the hot skillet for 2 to 3 minutes on each side. Take the shrimp out and drain it on a paper towel. Serve warm.

Nutrition:
Calories: 714; | Protein: 37g | Total Carbohydrates: 63g | Sugars: 4g; | Fiber: 3g | Total Fat: 34g

286. Fried Fresh Sardines

Preparation Time: 5 minutes | **Cooking time:** 5 minutes | **Servings:** 4

Ingredients:
Avocado oil
1½ pounds whole fresh sardines, scales removed
1 teaspoon salt
1 teaspoon freshly ground black pepper
2 cups flour

Directions:
Preheat a deep skillet over medium heat. Pour in enough oil so there is about 1 inch of it in the pan. Season the fish with salt and pepper.
Dredge the fish in the flour so it is completely covered.
Slowly drop in 1 fish at a time, making sure not to overcrowd the pan.
Cook for about 3 minutes on each side or just until the fish is golden brown on all sides. Serve warm.

Nutrition:
Calories: 794; | Protein: 48g | Total Carbohydrates: 44g; | Fiber: 2g | Total Fat: 47g

287. White Wine–Sautéed Mussels

Preparation Time: 10 minutes | **Cooking time:** 10 minutes | **Servings:** 4

Ingredients:
3 pounds live mussels, cleaned
4 tablespoons (½ stick) salted butter
2 shallots, finely chopped
2 tablespoons garlic, minced
2 cups dry white wine

Directions:
Scrub the mussel shells to make sure they are clean; trim off any that have a beard (hanging string). Put the mussels in a large bowl of water, discarding any that are not tightly closed.
In a large pot over medium heat, cook the butter, shallots, and garlic for 2 minutes.
Add the wine to the pot, and cook for 1 minute.
Add the mussels to the pot, toss with the sauce, and cover with a lid. Let cook for 7 minutes.
Discard any mussels that have not opened.
Serve in bowls with the wine broth.

Nutrition:
Calories: 777; | Protein: 82g | Total Carbohydrates: 29g | Sugars: 1g | Total Fat: 27g | Saturated Fat: 10g

288. Paprika-Spiced Fish

Preparation Time: 5 minutes | **Cooking time:** 10 minutes | **Servings:** 4

Ingredients:
4 (5-ounce) sea bass fillets
½ teaspoon salt
1 tablespoon smoked paprika
3 tablespoons unsalted butter
Lemon wedges

Directions:
Season the fish on both sides with salt. Repeat with the paprika.
Preheat a skillet over high heat. Melt the butter. Once the butter is melted, add the fish, and cook for 4 minutes on each side.
Once the fish is done, move to a serving dish and squeeze lemon over the top.

Nutrition:
Calories: 257; | Protein: 34 | Total Carbohydrates: 1g; | Fiber: 1g | Total Fat: 13g

289. Citrus-Herb Scallops

Preparation Time: 10 minutes | **Cooking time:** 4 minutes | **Servings:** 4

Ingredients:
1 pound sea scallops
Sea salt
Freshly ground black pepper
2 tablespoons olive oil
Juice of 1 lime
Pinch red pepper flakes
1 tablespoon chopped fresh cilantro

Directions:
Season the scallops lightly with salt and pepper. In a large skillet, heat the olive oil over medium-high heat. Add the scallops to the skillet, making sure they do not touch one another.
Sear on both sides, turning once, for a total of about 3 minutes. Add the lime juice and red pepper flakes to the skillet and toss the scallops in the juice. Serve topped with cilantro.

Nutrition:
Calories: 160 | Total fat: 8g | Saturated fat: 1g | Carbohydrates: 3g | Sugar: 0g | Fiber: 0g | Protein: 19g

290. Whole Trout Baked with Lemon and Herbs

Preparation Time: 10 minutes | **Cooking time:** 20 minutes | **Servings:** 4

Ingredients:
1 tablespoon olive oil, divided
2 (8-ounce) whole trout, cleaned
Sea salt
Freshly ground black pepper
1 lemon, thinly sliced into about 6 pieces
1 tablespoon finely chopped fresh dill
1 tablespoon chopped fresh parsley
½ cup low-sodium fish stock or chicken stock

Directions:
Preheat the oven to 400°F.

Lightly grease a 9-by-13-inch baking dish with 1 teaspoon of olive oil.
Rinse the trout, pat dry with paper towels, and coat with the remaining 2 teaspoons of olive oil. Season with salt and pepper.
Stuff the interior of the trout with the lemon slices, dill, and parsley and place into the prepared baking dish. Bake the fish for 10 minutes, then add the fish stock to the dish. Continue to bake until the fish flakes easily with a fork, about 10 minutes. Serve.

Nutrition:
Calories: 194 | Total fat: 10g | Saturated fat: 2g | Carbohydrates: 1g | Sugar: 0g | Fiber: 0g | Protein: 25g

291. Skillet Cod with Fresh Tomato Salsa

Preparation Time: 20 minutes | **Cooking time:** 8 minutes | **Servings:** 4

Ingredients:
3 tomatoes, finely chopped
1 green bell pepper, finely chopped
¼ red onion, finely chopped
¼ cup pitted, chopped green olives
2 tablespoons white wine vinegar
1 tablespoon chopped fresh basil
½ teaspoon minced garlic
4 (4-ounce) cod fillets
Sea salt
Freshly ground black pepper
1 tablespoon olive oil

Directions:
In a small bowl, stir together the tomatoes, bell pepper, onion, olives, vinegar, basil, and garlic until well mixed. Set aside.
Season the fish with salt and pepper.
In a large skillet, heat the olive oil over medium-high heat. Pan-fry the fish, turning once, until it is just cooked through, about 4 minutes per side. Transfer to serving plates and top with a generous scoop of tomato salsa.

Nutrition:
Calories: 181 | Total fat: 7g | Saturated fat: 1g; | Carbohydrates: 9g | Sugar: 4g | Fiber: 3g | Protein: 22g

292. Broiled Flounder with Nectarine and White Bean Salsa

Preparation Time: 20 minutes | **Cooking time:** 8 minutes | **Servings:** 4

Ingredients:
2 nectarines, pitted and chopped
1 (15-ounce) can low-sodium cannellini beans, rinsed and drained
1 red bell pepper, chopped
1 scallion, both white and green parts, chopped
2 tablespoons chopped fresh cilantro
2 tablespoons freshly squeezed lime juice
4 (4-ounce) flounder fillets
1 teaspoon smoked paprika
Sea salt
Freshly ground black pepper

Directions:
Preheat the oven to broil.
In a medium bowl, combine the nectarines, beans, bell pepper, scallion, cilantro, and lime juice.
Season the fish with paprika, salt, and pepper.
Place the fish on a baking sheet and broil, turning once, until just cooked through, about 8 minutes total. Serve the fish topped with the salsa.

Nutrition:
Calories: 259 | Total fat: 8g | Saturated fat: 1g | Carbohydrates: 23g | Sugar: 8g | Fiber: 7g | Protein: 26g

293. Trout with Ruby Red Grapefruit Relish

Preparation Time: 15 minutes | **Cooking time:** 15 minutes | **Servings:** 4

Ingredients:
1 ruby red grapefruit, peeled, sectioned, and chopped
1 large navel orange, peeled, sectioned, and chopped
¼ English cucumber, chopped
2 tablespoons chopped red onion
1 tablespoon minced or grated lime zest
1 teaspoon minced fresh or canned peperoncino
1 teaspoon chopped fresh thyme
4 (4-ounce) trout fillets

Sea salt
Freshly ground black pepper
1 tablespoon olive oil

Directions:
Preheat the oven to 400°F.
In a medium bowl, stir together the grapefruit, orange, cucumber, onion, lime zest, peperoncino, and thyme. Cover the relish with plastic wrap and set it aside in the refrigerator.
Season the trout lightly with salt and pepper and place on a baking sheet.
Brush the fish with olive oil and roast in the oven until it flakes easily with a fork, about 15 minutes. Serve topped with the chilled relish.

Nutrition:
Calories: 178 | Total fat: 6g | Saturated fat: 1g | Carbohydrates: 10g | Sugar: 7g | Fiber: 2g | Protein: 25g

294. Classic Pork Tenderloin Marsala

Preparation Time: 10 minutes | **Cooking time:** 20 minutes | **Servings:** 4

Ingredients:
4 (3-ounce) boneless pork loin chops, trimmed
Sea salt
Freshly ground black pepper
¼ cup whole-wheat flour
1 tablespoon olive oil
2 cups sliced button mushrooms
½ sweet onion, chopped
1 teaspoon minced garlic
½ cup Marsala wine
½ cup low-sodium chicken stock
1 tablespoon cornstarch
1 tablespoon chopped fresh parsley

Directions:
Lightly season the pork chops with salt and pepper.
Pour the flour onto a plate and dredge the pork chops to coat both sides, shaking off the excess.
In a large skillet, heat the olive oil over medium-high heat and pan-fry the pork chops until cooked through and browned, turning once, about 10 minutes total. Transfer the chops to a plate and set aside.
In the skillet, combine the mushrooms, onion, and garlic and sauté until the vegetables are softened, about 5 minutes.
Stir in the wine, scraping up any bits from the skillet, and bring the liquid to a simmer.
In a small bowl, stir together the stock and cornstarch until smooth. Add the stock mixture to the skillet and bring to a boil; cook, stirring, until slightly thickened, about 4 minutes. Serve the chops with the sauce, garnished with parsley.

Nutrition:
Calories: 200 | Total fat: 6g | Saturated fat: 1g | Carbohydrates: 11g | Sugar: 1g | Fiber: 1g | Protein: 20g

295. Chili-Spiced Lamb Chops

Preparation Time: 2 minutes | **Cooking time:** 10 minutes | **Servings:** 4

Ingredients:
4 (4-ounce) loin lamb chops with bones, trimmed
Sea salt
Freshly ground black pepper
1 tablespoon olive oil
2 tablespoons Sriracha sauce
1 tablespoon chopped fresh cilantro

Directions:
Preheat the oven to 450°F.
Lightly season the lamb chops with salt and pepper.
In a large ovenproof skillet, heat the olive oil over medium-high heat. Brown the chops on both sides, about 2 minutes per side, and spread the chops with sriracha.
Place the skillet in the oven and roast until the desired doneness, 4 to 5 minutes for medium. Serve topped with cilantro.

Nutrition:
Calories: 223 | Total fat: 14g | Saturated fat: 4g | Carbohydrates: 1g | Sugar: 1g | Fiber: 0g | Protein: 23g

296. Greek Herbed Beef Meatballs

Preparation Time: 10 minutes | **Cooking time:** 20 minutes | **Servings:** 4

Ingredients:
1-pound extra-lean ground beef
½ cup panko breadcrumbs
¼ cup grated Parmesan cheese
¼ cup low-fat milk
2 large eggs
1 tablespoon chopped fresh parsley
1 teaspoon chopped fresh oregano
1 teaspoon minced garlic
¼ teaspoon freshly ground black pepper
Sea salt

Directions:
Preheat the oven to 400°F.
In a large bowl, combine the ground beef, breadcrumbs, Parmesan cheese, milk, eggs, parsley, oregano, garlic, and pepper. Season lightly with salt.
Roll the beef mixture into 1-inch meatballs and arrange it on a baking sheet.
Bake the meatballs until they are cooked through and browned, turning them several times, about 20 minutes. Serve with a sauce such as Marinara Sauce or stuffed into a pita.

Nutrition:
Calories: 243 | Total fat: 8g | Saturated fat: 3g | Carbohydrates: 13g | Sugar: 1g | Fiber: 2g | Protein: 24g

297. Chicken in Tomato-Balsamic Pan Sauce

Preparation Time: 10 minutes | **Cooking time:** 20 minutes | **Servings:** 4

Ingredients:
2 (8 oz. or 226.7 g each) boneless chicken breasts, skinless
½ tsp. salt
½ tsp. ground pepper
3 tbsps. extra-virgin olive oil
½ c. halved cherry tomatoes
2 tbsps. sliced shallot
¼ c. balsamic vinegar
1 tbsp. minced garlic
1 tbsp. toasted fennel seeds, crushed
1 tbsp. butter

Directions:
Slice the chicken breasts into 4 pieces and beat them with a mallet till it reaches a thickness of a ¼ inch. Use ¼ teaspoons of pepper and salt to coat the chicken.
Heat two tablespoons of oil in a skillet and keep the heat to a medium. Cook the chicken breasts for three minutes on each side. Transfer it to a serving plate and cover it with foil to keep it warm.
Add one tablespoon oil, shallot, and tomatoes in a pan and cook till it softens. Add vinegar and boil the mix till the vinegar gets reduced by half. Put fennel seeds, garlic, salt, and pepper and cook for about four minutes.
Remove it from the heat and stir it with butter. Pour this sauce over chicken and serve.

Nutrition:
Calories 294 | Fat: 17 g | Sat. fat 4 g | Fiber 2 g | Carbohydrates: 10 g | Sugar: 3 g | Protein: 25 g | Sodium: 371 mg

298. Seasoned Buttered Chicken

Preparation Time: 10 minutes | **Cooking time:** 20 minutes | **Servings:** 4

Ingredients:
½ c. heavy whipping cream
1 tbsp. salt
½ c. bone broth
1 tbsp. pepper
4 tbsps. butter
4 chicken breast halves

Directions:
Place the cooking pan on your oven over medium heat and add in one tablespoon of butter. Once the butter is warm and melted, place the chicken in and cook for five minutes on either side. At the end of this time, the chicken should be cooked through and golden; if it is, go ahead and place it on a plate.
Next, you are going to add the bone broth into the warm pan. Add heavy whipping cream, salt, and pepper. Then, leave the pan alone until your sauce begins to simmer. Allow this process to happen for five minutes to let the sauce thicken up.
Finally, you are going to add the rest of your butter and the chicken back into the pan. Be sure

to use a spoon to place the sauce over your chicken and smother it completely. After a few minutes, your dish will be complete and ready to serve!

Nutrition:
Calories 350 | Fat: 25 g | Sat. fat 13 g | Fiber 10 g | Carbohydrates: 17 g | Sugars 2 g | Protein: 25 g | Sodium: 394 mg

299. Shrimps with Lemon and Pepper

Preparation Time: 15 minutes | **Cooking time:** 10 minutes | **Servings:** 4

Ingredients:
40 deveined shrimps, peeled
6 minced garlic cloves
Salt and black pepper
3 tbsps. olive oil
¼ tsp. sweet paprika
A pinch of crushed red pepper flakes
¼ tsp. grated lemon zest
3 tbsps. Sherry or another wine
1½ tbsps. sliced chives
Juice of 1 lemon

Directions:
Adjust your heat to medium-high and set a pan in place.
Add oil and shrimp, sprinkle with pepper and salt, and cook for 1 minute
Add paprika, garlic, and pepper flakes, stir and cook for 1 minute.
Gently stir in sherry and allow to cook for an extra minute
Take shrimp off the heat, add chives and lemon zest, stir and transfer shrimp to plates.
Add lemon juice all over and serve

Nutrition:
Calories 140 | Fat: 1 g | Sat. fat 0.3 g | Fiber 0 g | Carbohydrates: 1 g | Sugars 0 g | Protein: 18 g | Sodium: 200 mg

300. Breaded and Spiced Halibut

Preparation Time: 5 minutes | **Cooking time:** 25 minutes | **Servings:** 4

Ingredients:
¼ c. chopped fresh chives
¼ c. chopped fresh dill
¼ tsp. ground black pepper
¾ c. panko breadcrumbs
1 tbsp. extra-virgin olive oil
1 tsp. finely grated lemon zest
1 tsp. sea salt
1/3 c. chopped fresh parsley
4 (6 oz. or 170 g. each) halibut fillets

Directions:
In a medium bowl, mix olive oil and the rest ingredients except halibut fillets and breadcrumbs
Place halibut fillets into the mixture and marinate for 30 minutes
Preheat your oven to 400 F/204 C
Set a foil to a baking sheet, grease with cooking spray
Dip the fillets to the breadcrumbs and put them on the baking sheet
Cook in the oven for 20 minutes
Serve hot.

Nutrition:
Calories 667 | Fat: 24.5 g | Sat. fat 6.5 g | Fiber 2 g | Carbohydrates: 30.6 g | Sugars 0.9 g | Protein: 54.8 g | Sodium: 152 mg

301. Curry Salmon with Mustard

Preparation Time: 10 minutes | **Cooking time:** 20 minutes | **Servings:** 4

Ingredients:
¼ tsp. ground red pepper or chili powder
¼ tsp. turmeric, ground
¼ tsp. salt
1 tsp. honey
¼ tsp. garlic powder
2 tsps. whole grain mustard
4 (6 oz. or 170 g. each) salmon fillets

Directions:
In a bowl mix mustard and the rest ingredients except salmon
Preheat the oven to 350 F/176 C
Grease a baking dish with cooking spray.
Place salmon on a baking dish with skin side down and spread evenly mustard mixture on top of fillets
Place into the oven and cook for 10-15 minutes or until flaky.

Nutrition:
Calories 324 | Fat: 18.9 g | Sat. fat 2 g | Fiber 1.3 g | Carbohydrates: 2.9 g | Sugars 1 g | Protein: 34 g | Sodium: 110 mg

302. Mediterranean Lamb Chops

Preparation Time: 10 minutes | **Cooking time:** 10 minutes | **Servings:** 4

Ingredients:
4 lamb shoulder chops, 8 ounces each
2 tablespoons Dijon mustard
2 tablespoons Balsamic vinegar
1 tablespoon garlic, chopped
½ cup olive oil
2 tablespoons shredded fresh basil

Directions:
Pat your lamb chop dry using a kitchen towel and arrange them on a shallow glass baking dish.
Take a bowl and whisk in Dijon mustard, balsamic vinegar, garlic, pepper and mix well.
Whisk in the oil very slowly into the marinade until the mixture is smooth.
Stir in basil.
Pour the marinade over the lamb chops and stir to coat both sides well.
Cover the chops and allow them to marinate for 1-4 hours (chilled).
Take the chops out and leave them for 30 minutes to allow the temperature to reach a normal level.
Preheat your grill to medium heat and add oil to the grate.
Grill the lamb chops for 5-10 minutes per side until both sides are browned.
Once the center of the chop reads 145 degrees Fahrenheit, the chops are ready, serve and enjoy!

Nutrition: (Per Serving)
Calories: 521 | Fat: 45g | Carbohydrates: 3.5g | Protein: 22g

303. Pasta Salad with Chicken Club

Preparation Time: 20 minutes | **Cooking time:** 10 minutes | **Servings:** 6

Ingredients:
8 oz corkscrew pasta
3/4 cup Italian dressing
1/4 cup mayonnaise
2 cups roasted chicken cooked and minced
12 slices of crispy cooked bacon, crumbled
1 cup diced Münster cheese
1 cup chopped celery
1 cup chopped green pepper
8 oz. Cherry tomatoes halved
1 avocado - peeled, seeded, and chopped

Directions:
Bring a large pan of lightly salted water to a boil. Boil the pasta, occasionally stirring until well-cooked but firm, 10 to 12 minutes. Drain and rinse with cold water.
Beat the Italian dressing and mayonnaise in a large bowl. Stir the pasta, chicken, bacon, Münster cheese, celery, green pepper, cherry tomatoes, and avocado through the vinaigrette until everything is well mixed.

Nutrition: (Per Serving)
485 calories | 30.1 g fat | 37.1 g carbohydrates | 19.2 g of protein | 48 mg cholesterol | 723 mg of sodium.

304. Alfredo Peppered Shrimp

Preparation Time: 5 minutes | **Cooking time:** 20 minutes | **Servings:** 6

Ingredients:
12 kg penne
1/4 cup butter
2 tablespoons extra virgin olive oil
1 onion, diced
2 cloves of chopped garlic
1 red pepper, diced
1/2 kg Portobello mushrooms, cubed
1 pound shrimp, peeled and thawed
1 jar of Alfredo sauce
1/2 cup of grated Romano cheese
1/2 cup of cream
1/4 cup chopped parsley
1 teaspoon cayenne pepper
salt and pepper to taste

Directions:
Bring a large pot of lightly salted water to a boil. Put the pasta and cook for 8 to 10 minutes or until al dente; drain.
Meanwhile, melt the butter and olive oil in a pan over medium heat. Stir in the onion and cook until soft and translucent, about 2 minutes. Stir

in garlic, red pepper, and mushrooms; cook over medium heat until soft, about 2 minutes longer. Stir in the shrimp and fry until firm and pink, then add Alfredo sauce, Romano cheese, and cream; bring to a boil, constantly stirring until thick, about 5 minutes. Season with cayenne pepper, salt, and pepper to taste. Add the drained pasta to the sauce and sprinkle with chopped parsley.

Nutrition: (Per Serving)
707 Calories | 45 g Fat | 50.6 g Carbohydrates | 28.4 g of Protein | 201 mg of Cholesterol | 1034 mg of sodium.

305. Blackened Salmon Fillets

Preparation Time: 15 minutes | **Cooking time:** 5 minutes | **Servings:** 4

Ingredients:
2 tablespoons paprika powder
1 tablespoon cayenne pepper powder
1 tablespoon onion powder
2 teaspoons salt
1/2 teaspoon ground white pepper
1/2 teaspoon ground black pepper
1/4 teaspoon dried thyme
1/4 teaspoon dried basil
1/4 teaspoon dried oregano
4 salmon fillets, skin, and bones removed
1/2 cup unsalted butter, melted

Directions:
Combine bell pepper, cayenne pepper, onion powder, salt, white pepper, black pepper, thyme, basil, and oregano in a small bowl.
Brush salmon fillets with 1/4 cup butter and sprinkle evenly with the cayenne pepper mixture. Sprinkle each fillet with ½ of the remaining butter.
Cook the salmon in a large heavy-bottomed pan, until dark, 2 to 5 minutes. Turn the fillets, sprinkle with the remaining butter, and continue to cook until the fish easily peels with a fork.

Nutrition: (Per Serving)
511 Calories | 38.3 grams of Fat | 4.5 grams of Carbohydrates | 37.4 g of Protein | 166 mg Cholesterol | 1248 mg of sodium

306. Cajun Seafood Pasta

Preparation Time: 15 minutes | **Cooking time:** 8 minutes | **Servings:** 6

Ingredients:
2 cups thick whipped cream
1 tablespoon chopped fresh basil
1 tablespoon chopped fresh thyme
2 teaspoons salt
2 teaspoons ground black pepper
1 1/2 teaspoon ground red pepper flakes
1 teaspoon ground white pepper
1 cup chopped green onions
1 cup chopped parsley
1/2 shrimp, peeled
1/2 cup scallops
1/2 cup of grated Swiss cheese
1/2 cup grated Parmesan cheese
1-pound dry fettuccine pasta

Directions:
Cook the pasta in a large pot with boiling salted water until al dente.
Meanwhile, pour the cream into a large skillet. Cook over medium heat, constantly stirring until it boils. Reduce heat and add spices, salt, pepper, onions, and parsley. Let simmer for 7 to 8 minutes or until thick.
Stir seafood and cook until shrimp are no longer transparent. Stir in the cheese and mix well.
Drain the pasta. Serve the sauce over the noodles.

Nutrition: (Per Serving)
695 Calories | 36.7 grams of Fat | 62.2 g Carbohydrates | 31.5 g of Protein | 193 mg Cholesterol | 1054 mg of sodium

307. Scrumptious Salmon Cakes

Preparation Time: 15 minutes | **Cooking time:** 10 minutes | **Servings:** 8

Ingredients:
2 cans of salmon, drained and crumbled
3/4 cup Italian breadcrumbs
1/2 cup chopped fresh parsley
2 eggs, beaten
2 green onions, minced
2 teaspoons seafood herbs
1 1/2 teaspoon ground black pepper
1 1/2 teaspoons garlic powder

3 tablespoons Worcestershire sauce
2 tablespoons Dijon mustard
3 tablespoons grated Parmesan
2 tablespoons creamy vinaigrette
1 tablespoon olive oil

Directions:
Combine salmon, breadcrumbs, parsley, eggs, green onions, seafood herbs, black pepper, garlic powder, Worcestershire sauce, parmesan cheese, Dijon mustard, and creamy vinaigrette; divide and shape into eight patties.
Heat olive oil in a large frying pan over medium heat. Bake the salmon patties in portions until golden brown, 5 to 7 minutes per side. Repeat if necessary with more olive oil.

Nutrition: (Per Serving)
263 Calories | 12.3 g Fat | 10.8 g of Carbohydrates | 27.8 g of Protein | 95 mg Cholesterol | 782 mg of sodium

308. Easy Tuna Patties

Preparation Time: 15 minutes | **Cooking time:** 10 minutes | **Servings:** 4

Ingredients:
2 teaspoons lemon juice
3 tablespoons grated Parmesan
2 eggs
10 tablespoons Italian breadcrumbs
3 tuna cans, drained
3 tablespoons diced onion
1 pinch of ground black pepper
3 tablespoons vegetable oil

Directions:
Beat the eggs and lemon juice in a bowl. Stir in the Parmesan cheese and breadcrumbs to obtain a paste. Add tuna and onion until everything is well mixed. Season with black pepper. Form the tuna mixture into eight 1-inch-thick patties.
Heat the vegetable oil in a frying pan over medium heat; fry the patties until golden brown, about 5 minutes on each side.

Nutrition: (Per Serving)
325 Calories | 15.5 grams of Fat | 13.9 g of Carbohydrates | 31.3 g of Protein | 125 mg Cholesterol | 409 mg of sodium.

309. Brown Butter Perch

Preparation Time: 15 minutes | **Cooking time:** 5 minutes | **Servings:** 4

Ingredients:
1 cup flour
1 teaspoon salt
1/2 teaspoon finely ground black pepper
1/2 teaspoon cayenne pepper
8 oz fresh perch fillets
2 tablespoons butter
1 lemon cut in half

Directions:
In a bowl, beat flour, salt, black pepper, and cayenne pepper. Gently squeeze the perch fillets into the flour mixture to coat well and remove excess flour.
Heat the butter in a frying pan over medium heat until it is foamy and brown hazel. Place the fillets in portions in the pan and cook them light brown, about 2 minutes on each side. Place the cooked fillets on a plate, squeeze the lemon juice, and serve.

Nutrition: (Per Serving)
271 Calories | 11.5 g of Fat | 30.9 g of Carbohydrates | 12.6 g of Protein | 43 mg of Cholesterol | 703 mg of sodium.

310. Fish in Foil

Preparation Time: 10 minutes | **Cooking time:** 15-20 minutes | **Servings:** 2

Ingredients:
2 fillets of rainbow trout
1 tablespoon of olive oil
2 teaspoons of salt with garlic
1 teaspoon ground black pepper
1 fresh jalapeño pepper, sliced
1 lemon cut into slices

Directions:
Preheat the oven to 200 degrees C (400 degrees F). Rinse and dry the fish.
Rub the fillets with olive oil and season with garlic salt and black pepper. Lay each on a large sheet of aluminum foil. Garnish with jalapeño slices and squeeze the juice from the lemon onto the fish. Place the lemon slices on the fillets.

Carefully seal all edges of the foil to form closed bags. Place the packages on a baking sheet.
Bake in the preheated oven for 15 to 20 minutes, depending on the size of the fish. The fish is cooked when it easily breaks with a fork.

Nutrition: (Per Serving)
213 Calories | 10.9 g Fat | 7.5 grams of Carbohydrates | 24.3 g of Protein | 67 mg of Cholesterol | 1850 mg of sodium.

311. Herby Juicy Chicken Fillets

Preparation Time: 5 minutes | **Cooking time:** 20 minutes | **Servings:** 4

Ingredients:
2 tablespoons olive oil
4 chicken fillets
1/4 cup red wine
3/4 cup chicken broth
Sea salt and freshly ground black pepper, to taste
1/2 teaspoon dried marjoram
1 teaspoon dried sage
1/2 teaspoon dried parsley flakes
1/2 teaspoon dried basil

Directions:
Press the "Sauté" button and adjust to the highest setting. Heat the oil and sear the chicken fillets for about 8 minutes, turning them over once or twice to ensure even cooking.
Pour in the red wine and scrape up the browned bits. Add the rest of the above ingredients.
Secure the lid. Choose the "Poultry" mode and cook for 5 minutes at high pressure. Once cooking is complete, use a natural pressure release; carefully remove the lid. Bon appétit!

Nutrition:
357 Calories | 18.4g Fat | 0.6g Carbs | 43.2g Protein | 0.3g Sugars | 0g Fiber

312. Wild Rice Pilaf with Beans

Preparation Time: 5 minutes | **Cooking time:** 30 minutes | **Servings:** 4

Ingredients:
1 tablespoon olive oil
1/2 cup shallots, chopped
1/2 cup artichoke hearts, chopped
2 garlic cloves, minced
1 ½ cups wild rice
1/2 cup red kidney beans
3 cups vegetable broth
1 chili pepper, minced
1 teaspoon sage
1 teaspoon thyme
Sea salt and ground black pepper, to taste
2 ripe tomatoes, pureed

Directions:
Press the "Sauté" button to preheat your Instant Pot. Then, sauté the shallots, artichoke, and garlic for 2 to 3 minutes.
Add the remaining ingredients to the inner pot of your Instant Pot.
Secure the lid. Choose the "Manual" mode and cook for 20 minutes at high pressure. Once cooking is complete, use a quick pressure release; carefully remove the lid.
Ladle into individual bowls and serve warm. Bon appétit!

Nutrition:
384 Calories | 5.6g Fat | 67g Carbs | 19.4g Protein | 5.2g Sugars | 9.6g Fiber

313. Arroz con Pollo with a Twist

Preparation Time: 5 minutes | **Cooking time:** 15 minutes | **Servings:** 5

Ingredients:
2 tablespoons olive oil
1 Spanish onion, chopped
1 teaspoon garlic, minced
2 sweet peppers, diced
5 chicken drumsticks, boneless and chopped
2 cups water
1 cup cream of onion soup
2 Roma tomatoes, pureed
1 teaspoon Mojo Picante
1 teaspoon Spanish paprika
2 thyme sprigs, chopped
1 rosemary sprig, chopped
Sea salt and ground black pepper, to taste
1 ½ cups orzo, rinsed

Directions:
Press the "Sauté" button to preheat your Instant Pot; heat 1 tablespoon of olive oil until it just starts smoking. Sauté the Spanish onion, garlic, and sweet peppers until they are tender and fragrant; reserve.

Heat the remaining tablespoon of olive oil and adjust your Instant Pot to the highest setting. Sear the chicken until golden-brown and crispy. Add in the water, cream of onion soup, tomatoes, Mojo Picante, Spanish paprika, thyme, rosemary, salt, and black pepper.

Lastly, stir in the orzo and bring to a rolling boil. Secure the lid. Choose the "Manual" mode and cook for 6 minutes at high pressure. Once cooking is complete, use a natural pressure release; carefully remove the lid.

Taste, adjust the seasonings, and serve warm.

Nutrition:
435 Calories | 19.4g Fat | 37.6g Carbs | 28.7g Protein | 2.8g Sugars | 5.6g Fiber

314. Mackerel Fillets with Authentic Skordalia Sauce

Preparation Time: 5 minutes | **Cooking time:** 15 minutes | **Servings:** 3

Ingredients:
3 mackerel fillets
Sea salt and ground black pepper, to taste
1/2 teaspoon paprika
1 lemon, sliced
Skordalia Sauce:
4 cloves garlic
1/2 teaspoon sea salt
2 mashed potatoes
4 tablespoons olive oil
2 tablespoons wine vinegar

Directions:
Place 1/2 lemon and 1 cup of water in the inner pot. Place the rack on top. Arrange the mackerel fillets on the rack.
Sprinkle salt, black pepper, and paprika over the mackerel fillets.
Secure the lid. Choose the "Manual" mode and cook for 4 minutes at high pressure. Once cooking is complete, use a quick pressure release; carefully remove the lid.
Meanwhile, make the sauce by blending all the ingredients in your food processor.
Garnish the mackerel fillets with the remaining lemon slices and serve with the Skordalia sauce on the side. Enjoy!

Nutrition:
517 Calories | 33.6g Fat | 28g Carbohydrates | 24.3g Protein | 2.4g Sugars | 3.6g Fiber

315. Spanish Repollo Guisado

Preparation Time: 5 minutes | **Cooking time:** 10 minutes | **Servings:** 5

Ingredients:
2 tablespoons olive oil
1 large-sized Spanish onion, chopped
2 garlic cloves, minced
1/2 teaspoon cumin seeds
1 cup tomato sauce
1 cup water
2 tablespoons vegetable bouillon granules
1 tablespoon white wine vinegar
1/4 teaspoon ground bay leaf
1 teaspoon Spanish paprika
1/4 teaspoon ground black pepper, to taste
Sea salt, to taste
2 pounds purple cabbage, slice into wedges

Directions:
Press the "Sauté" button to preheat your Instant Pot; heat the olive oil. Once hot, sauté the Spanish onion until it is tender and translucent. Add in the garlic and cumin seeds; continue to sauté an additional minute, stirring frequently. Stir the remaining ingredients, minus the vinegar, into the inner pot of your Instant Pot. Secure the lid. Choose the "Manual" mode and cook for 5 minutes at high pressure. Once cooking is complete, use a quick pressure release; carefully remove the lid.

Nutrition:
191 Calories | 6.4g Fat | 29.8g Carbohydrates | 5.1g Protein | 14.4g Sugars | 7.8g Fiber

316. Spring Wax Beans with New Potatoes

Preparation Time: 5 minutes | **Cooking time:** 20 minutes | **Servings:** 3

Ingredients:
1 tablespoon olive oil
2 scallion stalks, chopped
5 new potatoes, scrubbed and halved
1 sweet pepper, seeded and sliced
2 green garlic stalks, chopped

1/2 cup tomato sauce
2 tablespoons tomato paste
1/2 teaspoon brown sugar
1/2 cup roasted vegetable broth
1 pound wax beans, trimmed
Sea salt and ground black pepper, to taste

Directions:
Press the "Sauté" button to preheat your Instant Pot; heat the olive oil until sizzling. Now, sauté the scallions and new potatoes until just tender and fragrant.
Stir in the sweet pepper and green garlic and continue to sauté for an additional 30 seconds.
Add in the tomato sauce, tomato paste, brown sugar, vegetable broth, and wax beans. Season with salt and black pepper.
Secure the lid. Choose the "Manual" mode and cook for 3 minutes at high pressure. Once cooking is complete, use a natural pressure release for 10 minutes; carefully remove the lid.
Taste, adjust seasonings, and serve. Bon appétit!

Nutrition:
399 Calories | 5.6g Fat | 80g Carbs | 11.4g Protein | 15.8g Sugars | 13.5g Fiber

317. Sweet Sausage Marsala

Preparation & Cooking time: 25-30 minutes | **Servings:** 6

Ingredients:
Italian sausage links (1 lb.)
Green and red bell pepper (1 medium of each color)
Tomatoes (14.5 oz. can)
Large onion (half of 1)
Garlic (.5 tsp.)
Dried oregano (.125 tsp.)
Black pepper (.125 tsp.)
Marsala wine (1 tbsp.)
Water (.33 cup)
Uncooked bow-tie pasta (16 oz.)

Directions:
Slice the onion and green peppers. Dice the garlic.
Prepare a large soup pot or other pot of boiling water - about half full. Toss in the pasta and simmer for about eight to ten minutes.
Meanwhile, add the sausage to a medium skillet and pour in the water. Set the temperature using the med-high heat temperature. Put a top on the pot and simmer for eight minutes.
When the pasta is done, drain it into a colander and set it to the side for now.
Drain the sausage and return to the skillet. Stir in the wine, garlic, onion, and peppers. Simmer it for about five minutes using the med-high temperature setting or until done.
Empty in the tomatoes, oregano, and black pepper.
Add the pasta and continue stirring. Serve and enjoy it anytime.

Nutrition:
Calories: 509 | Protein: 21.9 grams | Fat: 16.1 grams

318. Feta Chicken Burgers

Preparation & Cooking time: 30 minutes | **Servings:** 6

Ingredients:
Reduced-fat mayonnaise (.25 cup)
Finely chopped cucumber (.25 cup)
Black pepper (.25 tsp.)
Garlic powder (1 tsp.)
Chopped roasted sweet red pepper (.5 cup)
Greek seasoning (.5 tsp.)
Lean ground chicken (1.5 lb.)
Crumbled feta cheese (1 cup)
Whole wheat burger buns (6 toasted)

Directions:
Heat the broiler to the oven ahead of time.
Combine the mayo and cucumber. Set aside.
Whisk each of the seasonings and the red pepper for the burgers. Work in the chicken and the cheese. Shape the mixture into six ½-inch thick patties.
Broil the burgers approximately four inches from the heat source. It should take about three to four minutes per side until the thermometer reaches 165° Fahrenheit.
Serve on the buns with the cucumber sauce. Top it off with tomato and lettuce if desired and serve.

Nutrition:
Calories: 356 | Protein: 31 grams | Fat: 14 grams

319. Baked Salmon with Dill

Preparation & Cooking time: 15 minutes | **Servings:** 4

Ingredients:
Salmon fillets (4- 6 oz. portions - 1-inch thickness)
Kosher salt (.5 tsp.)
Finely chopped fresh dill (1.5 tbsp.)
Black pepper (.125 tsp.)
Lemon wedges (4)

Directions:
Warm the oven in advance to reach 350° Fahrenheit.
Lightly grease a baking sheet with a misting of cooking oil spray and add the fish. Lightly spritz the fish with the spray along with a shake of salt, pepper, and dill.
Bake it until the fish is easily flaked (10 minutes). Serve with lemon wedges.

Nutrition:
Calories: 251 | Protein: 28 grams | Fat: 16 grams

320. Herb-Crusted Halibut

Preparation & Cooking time: 25 minutes | **Servings:** 4

Ingredients:
Fresh parsley (.33 cup)
Fresh dill (.25 cup)
Fresh chives (.25 cup)
Lemon zest (1 tsp.)
Panko breadcrumbs (.75 cup)
Olive oil (1 tbsp.)
Freshly cracked black pepper (.25 tsp.)
Sea salt (1 tsp.)
Halibut fillets (4 - 6 oz.)

Directions:
Chop the fresh dill, chives, and parsley. Prepare a baking tray using a sheet of foil. Set the oven to reach 400° Fahrenheit.
Combine the salt, pepper, lemon zest, olive oil, chives, dill, parsley, and breadcrumbs in a mixing bowl.
Rinse the halibut thoroughly. Use paper towels to dry it before baking.
Arrange the fish on the baking sheet. Spoon the crumbs over the fish and press them into each of the fillets.
Bake it until the top is browned and easily flaked for about 10 to 15 minutes.

Nutrition:
Calories: 273 | Protein: 38 grams | Fat: 7 grams

321. Marinated Tuna Steak

Preparation & Cooking time: 15-20 minutes | **Servings:** 4

Ingredients:
Olive oil (2 tbsp.)
Orange juice (.25 cup)
Soy sauce (.25 cup)
Lemon juice (1 tbsp.)
Fresh parsley (2 tbsp.)
Garlic clove (1)
Ground black pepper (.5 tsp.)
Fresh oregano (.5 tsp.)
Tuna steaks (4 - 4 oz. steaks)

Directions:
Mince the garlic and chop the oregano and parsley.
In a glass container, mix the pepper, oregano, garlic, parsley, lemon juice, soy sauce, olive oil, and orange juice.
Warm the grill using the high heat setting. Grease the grate with oil.
Add to tuna steaks and cook for five to six minutes. Turn and baste with the marinated sauce.
Cook another five minutes or until it's the way you like it. Discard the remaining marinade.

Nutrition:
Calories: 200 | Protein: 27.4 grams | Fat: 7.9 grams

322. Niçoise-Style Tuna Salad with Olives & White Beans

Preparation & Cooking time: 20-30 minutes | **Servings:** 4

Ingredients: Needed:
Green beans (.75 lb.)
Solid white albacore tuna (12 oz. can)
Great Northern beans (16 oz. can)

Sliced black olives (2.25 oz.)
Thinly sliced medium red onion (¼ of 1)
Hard-cooked eggs (4 large)
Dried oregano (1 tsp.)
Olive oil (6 tbsp.)
Black pepper and salt (as desired)
Finely grated lemon zest (.5 tsp.)
Water (.33 cup)
Lemon juice (3 tbsp.)

Directions:
Drain the can of tuna, Great Northern beans, and black olives. Trim and snap the green beans into halves. Thinly slice the red onion. Cook and peel the eggs until hard-boiled.
Pour the water and salt into a skillet and add the beans. Place a top on the pot and switch the temperature setting to high. Wait for it to boil.
Once the beans are cooking, set a timer for five minutes. Immediately, drain and add the beans to a cookie sheet with a raised edge on paper towels to cool.
Combine the onion, olives, white beans, and drained tuna. Mix them with the zest, lemon juice, oil, and oregano.
Dump the mixture over the salad and gently toss. Adjust the seasonings to your liking. Portion the tuna-bean salad with the green beans and eggs to serve.

Nutrition:
Calories: 548 | Protein: 36.3 grams | Fat: 30.3 grams

323. Tilapia with Avocado & Red Onion

Preparation & Cooking time: 15 minutes | **Servings:** 4

Ingredients:
Olive oil (1 tbsp.)
Sea salt (.25 tsp.)
Fresh orange juice (1 tbsp.)
Tilapia fillets (four 4 oz. - more rectangular than square)
Red onion (.25 cup)
Sliced avocado (1)
Also Needed: 9-inch pie plate

Directions:
Combine the salt, juice, and oil to add to the pie dish. Work with one fillet at a time. Place it in the dish and turn to coat all sides.
Arrange the fillets in a wagon wheel-shaped formation. (Each of the fillets should be in the center of the dish with the other end draped over the edge.)
Place a tablespoon of the onion on top of each of the fillets and fold the end into the center. Cover the dish with plastic wrap, leaving one corner open to vent the steam.
Place in the microwave using the high heat setting for three minutes. It's done when the center can be easily flaked.
Top the fillets off with avocado and serve.

Nutrition:
Calories: 200 | Protein: 22 grams | Fat: 11 grams

324. Mixed Spice Burgers

Preparation & Cooking time: 25-30 minutes | **Servings:** 6/2 chops each

Ingredients:
Medium onion (1)
Fresh parsley (3 tbsp.)
Clove of garlic (1)
Ground allspice (.75 tsp.)
Pepper (.75 tsp.)
Ground nutmeg (.25 tsp.)
Cinnamon (.5 tsp.)
Salt (.5 tsp.)
Fresh mint (2 tbsp.)
90% lean ground beef (1.5 lb.)
Optional: Cold Tzatziki sauce

Directions:
Finely chop/mince the parsley, mint, garlic, and onions.
Whisk the nutmeg, salt, cinnamon, pepper, allspice, garlic, mint, parsley, and onion.
Add the beef and prepare six (6) 2x4-inch oblong patties.
Use the medium temperature setting to grill the patties or broil them four inches from the heat source for four to six minutes per side.
When they're done, the meat thermometer will register 160° Fahrenheit. Serve with the sauce if desired.

Nutrition:
Calories: 231 | Protein: 32 grams | Fat: 9 grams

325. Delicious Pork & Orzo

Preparation & Cooking time: 30 minutes | **Servings:** 6

Ingredients:
Pork tenderloin (1.5 lb.)
Olive oil (2 tbsp.)
Water (3 quarts)
Uncooked orzo pasta (1.25 cups)
Salt (.25 tsp.)
Coarsely ground pepper (1 tsp.)
Fresh baby spinach (6 oz. pkg.)
Grape tomatoes (1 cup)
Feta cheese (.75 cup)

Directions:
Rub the pork in pepper and slice the pepper into one-inch cubes.
Prepare a large skillet with oil and warm using the medium temperature setting.
Toss in the pork and cook for eight to ten minutes. Pour water and salt into a Dutch oven and wait for it to boil. Add the orzo to simmer (lid off) for eight minutes. Stir in the spinach and cook until it's wilted and tender (45-60 sec.). Drain it in a colander.
Cut the tomatoes into halves and add in with the pork and heat, adding in the orzo mixture and crumbled feta cheese.

Nutrition:
Calories: 372 | Protein: 31 grams | Fat: 11 grams

326. Mezze Platter with Toasted Za'atar Pita Bread

Preparation & Cooking time: 10 minutes | **Servings:** 4

Ingredients: Needed:
Whole-wheat pita rounds (4)
Olive oil (4 tbsp.)
Za'atar (4 tsp.)
Greek yogurt (1 cup)
Black pepper & Kosher salt (to your liking)
Hummus (1 cup)
Marinated artichoke hearts (1 cup)
Assorted olives (2 cups)
Sliced roasted red peppers (1 cup)
Cherry tomatoes (2 cups)
Salami (4 oz.)

Directions:
Use the medium-high heat setting to heat a large skillet.
Lightly brush the pita bread with the oil on each side and add the za'atar for seasoning.
Prepare in batches by adding the pita into a skillet and toasting until browned. It should take about two minutes on each side. Slice each of the pitas into quarters.
Season the yogurt with pepper and salt.
To assemble, divide the potatoes and add the hummus, yogurt, artichoke hearts, olives, red peppers, tomatoes, and salami.

Nutrition:
Calories: 731 | Protein: 26 grams | Fat: 48 grams

327. Mediterranean Whole Wheat Pizza

Preparation & Cooking time: 25 minutes | **Servings:** 4

Ingredients:
Whole-wheat pizza crust (1)
Basil pesto (4 oz. jar)
Artichoke hearts (.5 cup)
Kalamata olives (2 tbsp.)
Pepperoncini (2 tbsp. drained)
Feta cheese (.25 cup)

Directions:
Program the oven to 450° Fahrenheit.
Drain and pull the artichokes to pieces. Slice/chop the pepperoncini and olives.
Arrange the pizza crust onto a floured work surface and cover it using pesto. Arrange the artichoke, pepperoncini slices, and olives over the pizza. Lastly, crumble and add the feta.
Bake in the hot oven until the cheese has melted, and it has a crispy crust for 10-12 minutes.

Nutrition:
Calories: 277 | Protein: 9.7 grams | Fat: 18.6 grams

328. Lamb & Vegetable Bake

Preparation Time: 20 minutes | **Cooking time:** 1 hour and 10 minutes | **Servings:** 8

Ingredients:
1/4 cup olive oil
1 lb. lean lamb, boneless & chopped into ½ inch pieces
2 red potatoes, large, scrubbed & diced
1 onion, chopped roughly
2 cloves garlic, minced
28 ounces diced tomatoes with liquid, canned & no salt
2 zucchinis, cut into ½ inch slices
1 red bell pepper, seeded & cut into 1-inch cubes
2 tablespoons flat-leaf parsley, chopped
1 tablespoon paprika
1 teaspoon thyme
1/2 teaspoon cinnamon
1/2 cup red wine
sea salt & black pepper to taste

Directions:
Start by turning the oven to 325, and then get out a large stew pot. Place it over medium-high heat to heat your olive oil. Once your oil is hot stir in your lamb, browning the meat. Stir frequently to keep it from running, and then place your lamb in a baking dish. Cook your garlic, onion, and potatoes in the skillet until they're tender, which should take five to six minutes more. Add them to the baking dish as well. Pour the zucchini, pepper, and tomatoes into the pan with your herbs and spices. Allow it to simmer for ten minutes more before pouring it into your baking dish. Pour in the wine and pepper sauce. Add in your tomato, and then cover with foil. Bake for an hour. Take the cover off for the last fifteen minutes of baking, and adjust seasoning as needed.

Nutrition:
240 Calories | 14g Fats | 36g protein

329. Southwest Chipotle Chili

Preparation Time: 15 minutes | **Cooking time:** 30 minutes | **Servings:** 4

Ingredients:
1 (3 ounces) link chorizo sausage, quartered lengthwise and sliced
12 ounces lean ground beef
1 medium onion, chopped
1/2 teaspoon chipotle chili powder
2 1/2 cups water
1 (15.5 ounces) can no-salt-added black beans, rinsed, and drained
1 cup frozen corn kernels
1 (5.6 ounces) package Knorr® Fiesta Sides™ - Spanish Rice
2 plum tomatoes, chopped

Directions:
In a big deep nonstick skillet, brown chorizo over medium-high heat. If wished, put pepper and salt to season ground beef. In the same skillet, put the onion and ground beef and allow to cook over medium-high heat for 5 minutes, mixing from time to time, till onions are soft and beef is browned.
Mix in chili powder and let cook for 30 seconds, mixing, till aromatic. Put corn, beans, and water, and boil over medium-high heat.
Mix in Knorr(R) Fiesta Sides (TM) - Spanish Rice; lower the heat and allow to simmer with cover for 7 minutes till rice is soft. Mix in tomatoes and allow to sit for 2 minutes before serving. Serve, if wished, with corn tortillas, lime wedges, and chopped cilantro, avocado, and scallions.

Nutrition:
481 Calories | 25.2g Protein | 21.9g Total Fat

330. Mediterranean Chicken and Tomato Dish

Preparation Time: 10 minutes | **Cooking time:** 20 minutes | **Servings:** 4

Ingredients:
Chicken thighs
1 Tablespoon thyme, chopped
Garlic cloves, minced
1 Teaspoon red pepper flakes, crushed
½ cup heavy cream
¾ cup chicken stock
½ cup sun-dried tomatoes in olive oil
¼ cup parmesan cheese, grated
Basil leaves, chopped for serving

Directions:
Preheat the pan with the oil over medium-high heat, add chicken, salt and pepper to taste, cook

for 3 minutes on each side, transfer to a plate, and leave aside for now.
Return pan to heat, add thyme, garlic, and pepper flakes, stir, and cook for 1 minute.
Add stock, tomatoes, salt and pepper, heavy cream, and parmesan, stir and bring to a simmer.
Add chicken pieces, stir, place in the oven at 350 degrees F and bake for 15 minutes.
Take the pan out of the oven, leave chicken aside for 2-3 minutes, divide between plates and serve with basil sprinkled on top.

Nutrition:
212 Calories | 4g Fat | 3g Protein

331. Beef Tartar

Preparation Time: 10 minutes | **Cooking time:** 0 minutes | **Servings:** 1

Ingredients:
1 shallot, chopped
4 ounces beef fillet
5 small cucumbers
1 egg yolk
2 teaspoons mustard
1 tablespoon parsley
1 parsley sprig

Directions:
Incorporate meat with shallot, egg yolk, salt, pepper, mustard, cucumbers, and parsley.
Stir well and arrange on a platter.
Garnish with the chopped parsley spring and serve.

Nutrition:
210 Calories | 3g Fat | 8g Protein

332. Cabbage and Beef Stir Fry

Preparation Time: 5 minutes | **Cooking time:** 5 minutes | **Servings:** 2

Ingredients:
5oz butter
20oz ground beef
25oz cabbage (green)
1 tsp salt
1 tsp onion powder
0.25 tsp pepper
1 tbsp white wine vinegar
2 cloves of garlic
3 sliced scallions
1 tsp chili flakes
1 tbsp chopped ginger, fresh
1 tbsp sesame oil

Directions:
Shred up the cabbage with a food processor
Add the butter to the frying pan and cook the cabbage for a few minutes
Add the vinegar and the spices and combine
Transfer to a bowl
Add the remaining butter to the pan and add the chili flakes, garlic, and ginger, cooking for a few minutes
Add the meat and wait for the juices to disappear, before turning the heat down a little
Add the cabbage and scallions to the pot and stir well
Season and serve with sesame oil

Nutrition:
Carbs - 10g | Fat: - 93g | Protein - 33g | Calories - 1023

333. Simple Pork Stir Fry

Preparation Time: 10 minutes | **Cooking time:** 15 minutes | **Servings:** 4

Ingredients:
4 ounces bacon, chopped
4 ounces snow peas
2 tablespoons butter
1-pound pork loin, cut into thin strips
2 cups mushrooms, sliced
¾ cup white wine
½ cup yellow onion, chopped
3 tablespoons sour cream

Directions:
Put snow peas in a saucepan, add water to cover, add a pinch of salt, bring to a boil over medium heat, cook until they are soft, drain and leave aside.
Preheat the pan over medium-high heat, add bacon, cook for a few minutes, drain grease, transfer to a bowl, and leave aside.
Heat a pan with 1 tablespoon butter over medium heat, add pork strips, season with salt and pepper to taste, brown for a few minutes and transfer to a plate as well.
Return pan to medium heat, add remaining butter, and melt it. Add onions and mushrooms, stir, and cook for 4 minutes.

Add wine, and simmer until it's reduced. Add cream, peas, and pork, season with salt and pepper to taste, stir, heat up, divide between plates, top with bacon and serve.

Nutrition:
310 Calories | 4g Fat | 10g Protein

Chapter 4: Vegetarian Recipes

334. Roasted Portobello Mushrooms with Kale and Red Onion

Preparation Time: 15 minutes, plus 15 minutes to marinate | **Cooking time:** 30 minutes | **Servings:** 4

Ingredients:
¼ cup white wine vinegar
3 tablespoons extra-virgin olive oil, divided
½ teaspoon honey
¾ teaspoon kosher salt, divided
¼ teaspoon freshly ground black pepper
4 large portobello mushrooms, stems removed
1 red onion, julienned
2 garlic cloves, minced
1 (8-ounce) bunch kale, stemmed and chopped small
¼ teaspoon red pepper flakes
¼ cup grated Parmesan or Romano cheese

Directions:
Line a baking sheet with parchment paper or foil. In a medium bowl, whisk together the vinegar, 1½ tablespoons of the olive oil, honey, ¼ teaspoon of the salt, and the black pepper. Arrange the mushrooms on the baking sheet and pour the marinade over them. Marinate for 15 to 30 minutes.

Meanwhile, preheat the oven to 400°F. Bake the mushrooms for 20 minutes, turning over halfway through. Heat the remaining 1½ tablespoons olive oil in a large skillet or ovenproof sauté pan over medium-high heat. Add the onion and the remaining ½ teaspoon salt and sauté until golden brown, 5 to 6 minutes. Add the garlic and sauté for 30 seconds. Add the kale and red pepper flakes and sauté until the kale cooks down for about 5 minutes.

Remove the mushrooms from the oven and increase the temperature to broil. Carefully pour the liquid from the baking sheet into the pan with the kale mixture; mix well. Turn the mushrooms over so that the stem side is facing up. Spoon some of the kale mixture on top of each mushroom. Sprinkle 1 tablespoon Parmesan cheese on top of each. Broil until golden brown, 3 to 4 minutes.

Nutrition:
200 Calories | 13g Total Fat | 4g Fiber | 8g Protein

335. Balsamic Marinated Tofu with Basil and Oregano

Preparation Time: 10 minutes, plus 30 minutes to marinate | **Cooking time:** 30 minutes | **Servings:** 4

Ingredients:
¼ cup extra-virgin olive oil
¼ cup balsamic vinegar
2 tablespoons low-sodium soy sauce
3 garlic cloves, grated
2 teaspoons pure maple syrup
Zest of 1 lemon
1 teaspoon dried basil
1 teaspoon dried oregano
½ teaspoon dried thyme
½ teaspoon dried sage
¼ teaspoon kosher salt
¼ teaspoon freshly ground black pepper
¼ teaspoon red pepper flakes (optional)
1 (16-ounce) block extra-firm tofu, cut into ½-inch or 1-inch cubes

Directions:
In a bowl or gallon zip-top bag, mix the olive oil, vinegar, soy sauce, garlic, maple syrup, lemon zest, basil, oregano, thyme, sage, salt, black pepper, and red pepper flakes, if desired. Add the tofu and mix gently. Put in the refrigerator and marinate for 30 minutes, or up to overnight if you desire.
Preheat the oven to 425°F. Line a baking sheet with parchment paper or foil. Arrange the marinated tofu in a single layer on the prepared baking sheet. Bake for 20 to 30 minutes, turning over halfway through, until slightly crispy on the outside and tender on the inside.

Nutrition:
225 Calories | 16g Total Fat | 2g Fiber | 13g Protein

336. Ricotta, Basil, and Pistachio–Stuffed Zucchini

Preparation Time: 15 minutes | **Cooking time:** 25 minutes | **Servings:** 4

Ingredients:
2 medium zucchinis, halved lengthwise
1 tablespoon extra-virgin olive oil
1 onion, diced
1 teaspoon kosher salt
2 garlic cloves, minced
¾ cup ricotta cheese
¼ cup unsalted pistachios, shelled and chopped
¼ cup fresh basil, chopped
1 large egg, beaten
¼ teaspoon freshly ground black pepper

Directions:
Preheat the oven to 425°F. Line a baking sheet with parchment paper or foil. Scoop out the seeds/pulp from the zucchini, leaving ¼-inch flesh around the edges. Transfer the pulp to a cutting board and chop the pulp.
Heat the olive oil in a large skillet or sauté pan over medium heat. Add the onion, pulp, and salt and sauté for about 5 minutes. Add the garlic and sauté for 30 seconds. In a medium bowl, combine the ricotta cheese, pistachios, basil, egg, and black pepper. Add the onion mixture and mix well.
Place the 4 zucchini halves on the prepared baking sheet. Fill the zucchini halves with the ricotta mixture. Bake for 20 minutes, or until golden brown.

Nutrition:
200 Calories | 12g Total Fat | 3g Fiber | 11g Protein

337. Farro with Roasted Tomatoes and Mushrooms

Preparation Time: 20 minutes | **Cooking time:** 1 hour | **Servings:** 4

Ingredients:
For the Tomatoes
2 pints cherry tomatoes
1 teaspoon extra-virgin olive oil
¼ teaspoon kosher salt
For the Farro
3 to 4 cups water
½ cup farro
¼ teaspoon kosher salt
For the Mushrooms
2 tablespoons extra-virgin olive oil
1 onion, julienned
½ teaspoon kosher salt
¼ teaspoon freshly ground black pepper

10 ounces baby bell mushrooms, stemmed and sliced thin
½ cup no-salt-added vegetable stock
1 (15-ounce) can low-sodium cannellini beans, drained and rinsed
1 cup baby spinach
2 tablespoons fresh basil, cut into ribbons
¼ cup pine nuts, toasted
Aged balsamic vinegar (optional)

Directions:
To Make the Tomatoes
Preheat the oven to 400°F. Line a baking sheet with parchment paper or foil. Toss the tomatoes, olive oil, and salt together on the baking sheet and roast for 30 minutes.
To Make the Farro
Bring the water, farro, and salt to a boil in a medium saucepan or pot over high heat. Cover, reduce the heat to low, and simmer, and cook for 30 minutes, or until the farro is al dente. Drain and set aside.
To Make the Mushrooms
Heat the olive oil in a large skillet or sauté pan over medium-low heat. Add the onions, salt, and black pepper and sauté until golden brown and starting to caramelize, about 15 minutes. Add the mushrooms, increase the heat to medium, and sauté until the liquid has evaporated and the mushrooms brown, about 10 minutes. Add the vegetable stock and deglaze the pan, scraping up any brown bits, and reduce the liquid for about 5 minutes. Add the beans and warm through, about 3 minutes.
Remove from the heat and mix in the spinach, basil, pine nuts, roasted tomatoes, and farro. Garnish with a drizzle of balsamic vinegar, if desired.

Nutrition:
375 Calories | 15g Total Fat | 10g Fiber | 14g Protein

338. Baked Orzo with Eggplant, Swiss Chard, and Mozzarella

Preparation Time: 20 minutes | **Cooking time:** 1 hour | **Servings:** 4

Ingredients:
2 tablespoons extra-virgin olive oil
1 large (1-pound) eggplant, diced small
2 carrots, peeled and diced small
2 celery stalks, diced small
1 onion, diced small
½ teaspoon kosher salt
3 garlic cloves, minced
¼ teaspoon freshly ground black pepper
1 cup whole-wheat orzo
1 teaspoon no-salt-added tomato paste
1½ cups no-salt-added vegetable stock
1 cup Swiss chard, stemmed and chopped small
2 tablespoons fresh oregano, chopped
Zest of 1 lemon
4 ounces mozzarella cheese, diced small
¼ cup grated Parmesan cheese
2 tomatoes, sliced ½-inch-thick

Directions:
Preheat the oven to 400°F. Heat the olive oil in a large oven-safe sauté pan over medium heat. Add the eggplant, carrots, celery, onion, and salt and sauté for about 10 minutes. Add the garlic and black pepper and sauté for about 30 seconds. Add the orzo and tomato paste and sauté for 1 minute. Add the vegetable stock and deglaze the pan, scraping up the brown bits. Add the Swiss chard, oregano, and lemon zest and stir until the chard wilts.
Remove from the heat and mix in the mozzarella cheese. Smooth the top of the orzo mixture flat. Sprinkle the Parmesan cheese over the top. Arrange the tomatoes in a single layer on top of the Parmesan cheese. Bake for 45 minutes.

Nutrition:
470 Calories | 17g Total Fat | 7g Fiber | 18g Protein

339. Barley Risotto with Tomatoes

Preparation Time: 20 minutes | **Cooking time:** 45 minutes | **Servings:** 4

Ingredients:
2 tablespoons extra-virgin olive oil
2 celery stalks, diced
½ cup shallots, diced
4 garlic cloves, minced
3 cups no-salt-added vegetable stock
1 (14.5-ounce) can no-salt-added diced tomatoes
1 (14.5-ounce) can no-salt-added crushed tomatoes

1 cup pearl barley
Zest of 1 lemon
1 teaspoon kosher salt
½ teaspoon smoked paprika
¼ teaspoon red pepper flakes
¼ teaspoon freshly ground black pepper
4 thyme sprigs
1 dried bay leaf
2 cups baby spinach
½ cup crumbled feta cheese
1 tablespoon fresh oregano, chopped
1 tablespoon fennel seeds, toasted (optional)

Directions:

Heat the olive oil in a large saucepan over medium heat. Add the celery and shallots and sauté for about 4 to 5 minutes. Add the garlic and sauté for 30 seconds. Add the vegetable stock, diced tomatoes, crushed tomatoes, barley, lemon zest, salt, paprika, red pepper flakes, black pepper, thyme, and the bay leaf, and mix well. Bring to a boil, then lower to low, and simmer. Cook, stirring occasionally, for 40 minutes.
Remove the bay leaf and thyme sprigs. Stir in the spinach. In a small bowl, combine the feta, oregano, and fennel seeds. Serve the barley risotto in bowls topped with the feta mixture.

Nutrition:
375 Calories | 12g Total Fat | 13g Fiber | 11g Protein

340. Chickpeas and Kale with Spicy Pomodoro Sauce

Preparation Time: 10 minutes | **Cooking time:** 35 minutes | **Servings:** 4

Ingredients:

2 tablespoons extra-virgin olive oil
4 garlic cloves, sliced
1 teaspoon red pepper flakes
1 (28-ounce) can no-salt-added crushed tomatoes
1 teaspoon kosher salt
½ teaspoon honey
1 bunch kale, stemmed and chopped
2 (15-ounce) cans low-sodium chickpeas, drained and rinsed
¼ cup fresh basil, chopped
¼ cup grated pecorino Romano cheese

Directions:

Heat the olive oil in a large skillet or sauté pan over medium heat. Add the garlic and red pepper flakes and sauté until the garlic is a light golden brown, about 2 minutes. Add the tomatoes, salt, and honey and mix well. Reduce the heat to low and simmer for 20 minutes.
Add the kale and mix in well. Cook for about 5 minutes. Add the chickpeas and simmer for about 5 minutes. Remove from heat and stir in the basil. Serve topped with pecorino cheese.

Nutrition:
420 Calories | 13g Total Fat | 12g Fiber | 20g Protein

341. Roasted Feta with Kale and Lemon Yogurt

Preparation Time: 15 minutes | **Cooking time:** 20 minutes | **Servings:** 4

Ingredients:

1 tablespoon extra-virgin olive oil
1 onion, julienned
¼ teaspoon kosher salt
1 teaspoon ground turmeric
½ teaspoon ground cumin
½ teaspoon ground coriander
¼ teaspoon freshly ground black pepper
1 bunch kale, stemmed and chopped
7-ounce block feta cheese, cut into ¼-inch-thick slices
½ cup plain Greek yogurt
1 tablespoon lemon juice

Directions:

Preheat the oven to 400°F. Heat the olive oil in a large ovenproof skillet or sauté pan over medium heat. Add the onion and salt; sauté until lightly golden brown, about 5 minutes. Add the turmeric, cumin, coriander, and black pepper; sauté for 30 seconds. Add the kale and sauté for about 2 minutes. Add ½ cup water and continue to cook down the kale, about 3 minutes. Remove from the heat and place the feta cheese slices on top of the kale mixture. Place in the oven and bake until the feta softens, 10 to 12 minutes. In a small bowl, combine the yogurt and lemon juice. Serve the kale and feta cheese topped with lemon yogurt.

Nutrition:
210 Calories | 14g Total Fat | 2g Fiber | 11g Protein

342. Roasted Eggplant and Chickpeas with Tomato Sauce

Preparation Time: 15 minutes | **Cooking time:** 1 hour | **Servings:** 4

Ingredients:
Olive oil cooking spray
1 large (about 1 pound) eggplant, sliced into ¼-inch-thick rounds
1 teaspoon kosher salt, divided
1 tablespoon extra-virgin olive oil
3 garlic cloves, minced
1 (28-ounce) can no-salt-added crushed tomatoes
½ teaspoon honey
¼ teaspoon freshly ground black pepper
2 tablespoons fresh basil, chopped
1 (15-ounce) can no-salt-added or low-sodium chickpeas, drained and rinsed
¾ cup crumbled feta cheese
1 tablespoon fresh oregano, chopped

Directions:
Preheat the oven to 425°F. Line two baking sheets with foil and lightly spray with olive oil cooking spray. Arrange the eggplant in a single layer and sprinkle with ½ teaspoon of the salt. Bake for 20 minutes, turning once halfway, until lightly golden brown.
Meanwhile, heat the olive oil in a large saucepan over medium heat. Add the garlic and sauté for 30 seconds. Add the crushed tomatoes, honey, the remaining ½ teaspoon salt, and black pepper. Simmer for about 20 minutes, until the sauce reduces a bit and thickens. Stir in the basil.
After removing the eggplant from the oven, reduce the oven temperature to 375°F. In a large rectangular or oval baking dish, ladle in the chickpeas and 1 cup sauce. Layer the eggplant slices on top, overlapping as necessary to cover the chickpeas. Spread the remaining sauce on top of the eggplant. Sprinkle the feta cheese and oregano on top.
Cover the baking dish with foil and bake for 15 minutes. Remove the foil and bake for an additional 15 minutes.

Nutrition:
320 Calories | 11g Total Fat | 12g Fiber | 14g Protein

343. Baked Falafel Sliders

Preparation Time: 10 minutes | **Cooking time:** 30 minutes | **Servings:** 6

Ingredients:
Olive oil cooking spray
1 (15-ounce) can low-sodium chickpeas, drained and rinsed
1 onion, roughly chopped
2 garlic cloves, peeled
2 tablespoons fresh parsley, chopped
2 tablespoons whole-wheat flour
½ teaspoon ground coriander
½ teaspoon ground cumin
½ teaspoon baking powder
½ teaspoon kosher salt
¼ teaspoon freshly ground black pepper

Directions:
Preheat the oven to 350°F. Line a baking sheet with parchment paper or foil and lightly spray with olive oil cooking spray. In a food processor, add the chickpeas, onion, garlic, parsley, flour, coriander, cumin, baking powder, salt, and black pepper. Process until smooth, stopping to scrape down the sides of the bowl.
Make 6 slider patties, each with a heaping ¼ cup of mixture, and arrange on the prepared baking sheet. Bake for 30 minutes, turning over halfway through.

Nutrition:
90 Calories | 1g Total Fat | 3g Fiber | 4g Protein

344. Portobello Caprese

Preparation Time: 15 minutes | **Cooking time:** 30 minutes | **Servings:** 2

Ingredients:
1 tablespoon olive oil, plus more for greasing the baking pan
1 cup cherry tomatoes
Salt and freshly ground black pepper, to taste
4 large fresh basil leaves, thinly sliced, divided
3 medium garlic cloves, minced
2 large portobello mushrooms, stems removed
4 pieces mini Mozzarella balls

1 tablespoon Parmesan cheese, grated

Directions:

Preheat the oven to 350°F (180ºC). Grease a baking pan with olive oil. Drizzle 1 tablespoon olive oil in a nonstick skillet, and heat over medium-high heat. Add the tomatoes to the skillet, and sprinkle salt and black pepper to season. Prick some holes on the tomatoes for juice during the cooking. Put the lid on and cook the tomatoes for 10 minutes or until tender.

Reserve 2 teaspoons of basil and add the remaining basil and garlic to the skillet. Crush the tomatoes with a spatula, then cook for half a minute. Stir constantly during the cooking. Set aside. Arrange the mushrooms in the baking pan, cap side down, and sprinkle with salt and black pepper to taste.

Spoon the tomato mixture and Mozzarella balls on the gill of the mushrooms, then scatter with Parmesan cheese to coat well. Bake in the preheated oven for 20 minutes or until the mushrooms are fork-tender and the cheeses are browned. Remove the stuffed mushrooms from the oven and serve with basil on top.

Nutrition:

285 Calories | 21.8g total Fat | 2.1g Fiber | 14.3g protein

345. Mushroom and Cheese Stuffed Tomatoes

Preparation Time: 15 minutes | **Cooking time:** 20 minutes | **Servings:** 4

Ingredients:

4 large ripe tomatoes
1 tablespoon olive oil
½ pound (454 g) white or cremini mushrooms, sliced
1 tablespoon fresh basil, chopped
½ cup yellow onion, diced
1 tablespoon fresh oregano, chopped
2 garlic cloves, minced
½ teaspoon salt
¼ teaspoon freshly ground black pepper
1 cup part-skim Mozzarella cheese, shredded
1 tablespoon Parmesan cheese, grated

Directions:

Preheat the oven to 375°F (190ºC). Cut a ½-inch slice off the top of each tomato. Scoop the pulp into a bowl and leave ½-inch tomato shells. Arrange the tomatoes on a baking sheet lined with aluminum foil. Heat the olive oil in a nonstick skillet over medium heat.

Add the mushrooms, basil, onion, oregano, garlic, salt, and black pepper to the skillet and sauté for 5 minutes or until the mushrooms are soft.

Pour the mixture into the bowl of tomato pulp, then add the Mozzarella cheese and stir to combine well. Spoon the mixture into each tomato shell, then top with a layer of Parmesan. Bake in the preheated oven for 15 minutes or until the cheese is frothy and the tomatoes are soft. Remove the stuffed tomatoes from the oven and serve warm.

Nutrition:

254 Calories | 14.7g total Fat | 5.2g Fiber | 17.5g protein

346. Tabbouleh

Preparation Time: 15 minutes | **Cooking time:** 5 minutes | **Servings:** 6

Ingredients:

4 tablespoons olive oil, divided
4 cups riced cauliflower
3 garlic cloves, finely minced
Salt and freshly ground black pepper, to taste
½ large cucumber, peeled, seeded, and chopped
½ cup Italian parsley, chopped
Juice of 1 lemon
2 tablespoons minced red onion
½ cup mint leaves, chopped
½ cup pitted Kalamata olives, chopped
1 cup cherry tomatoes, quartered
2 cups baby arugula or spinach leaves
2 medium avocados, peeled, pitted, and diced

Directions:

Warm 2 tablespoons olive oil in a nonstick skillet over medium-high heat. Add the riced cauliflower, garlic, salt, and black pepper to the skillet and sauté for 3 minutes or until fragrant. Transfer them to a large bowl.

Add the cucumber, parsley, lemon juice, red onion, mint, olives, and remaining olive oil to the bowl. Toss to combine well. Reserve the bowl in the refrigerator for at least 30 minutes.

Remove the bowl from the refrigerator. Add the cherry tomatoes, arugula, and avocado to the bowl. Sprinkle with salt and black pepper, and toss to combine well. Serve chilled.

Nutrition:
198 Calories | 17.5g total Fat | 6.2g Fiber | 4.2g protein

347. Spicy Broccoli Rabe And Artichoke Hearts

Preparation Time: 5 minutes | **Cooking time:** 15 minutes | **Servings:** 4

Ingredients:
3 tablespoons olive oil, divided
2 pounds (907 g) fresh broccoli rabe
3 garlic cloves, finely minced
1 teaspoon red pepper flakes
1 teaspoon salt, plus more to taste
13.5 ounces (383 g) artichoke hearts
1 tablespoon water
2 tablespoons red wine vinegar
Freshly ground black pepper, to taste

Directions:
Warm 2 tablespoons of olive oil in a nonstick skillet over medium-high heat. Add the broccoli, garlic, red pepper flakes, and salt to the skillet and sauté for 5 minutes or until the broccoli is soft.
Add the artichoke hearts to the skillet and sauté for 2 more minutes or until tender. Add water to the skillet and turn down the heat to low. Put the lid on and simmer for 5 minutes. Meanwhile, combine the vinegar and 1 tablespoon of olive oil in a bowl.
Drizzle the simmered broccoli and artichokes with oiled vinegar, and sprinkle with salt and black pepper. Toss to combine well before serving.

Nutrition:
272 Calories | 21.5g total Fat | 9.8g Fiber | 11.2g protein

348. Cauliflower Steaks with Olive Citrus Sauce

Preparation Time: 15 minutes | **Cooking time:** 30 minutes | **Servings:** 4

Ingredients:
1 or 2 large heads cauliflower
1/3 cup extra-virgin olive oil
¼ teaspoon kosher salt
1/8 teaspoon ground black pepper
Juice of 1 orange
Zest of 1 orange
¼ cup black olives, pitted and chopped
1 tablespoon Dijon or grainy mustard
1 tablespoon red wine vinegar
½ teaspoon ground coriander

Directions:
Preheat the oven to 400°F. Line a baking sheet with parchment paper or foil. Cut off the stem of the cauliflower so it will sit upright. Slice it vertically into four thick slabs. Place the cauliflower on the prepared baking sheet. Drizzle with olive oil, salt, and black pepper. Bake for about 30 minutes, turning over once, until tender and golden brown.
In a medium bowl, combine the orange juice, orange zest, olives, mustard, vinegar, and coriander; mix well. Serve the cauliflower warm or at room temperature with the sauce.

Nutrition:
265 Calories | 21g Total Fat | 4g Fiber | 5g Protein

349. Pistachio Mint Pesto Pasta

Preparation Time: 10 minutes | **Cooking time:** 10 minutes | **Servings:** 4

Ingredients:
8 ounces whole-wheat pasta
1 cup fresh mint
½ cup fresh basil
1/3 cup unsalted pistachios, shelled
1 garlic clove, peeled
½ teaspoon kosher salt
Juice of ½ lime
1/3 cup extra-virgin olive oil

Directions:
Cook the pasta according to the package directions. Drain, reserving ½ cup of the pasta

water, and set aside. In a food processor, add the mint, basil, pistachios, garlic, salt, and lime juice. Process until the pistachios are coarsely ground. Add the olive oil in a slow, steady stream and process until incorporated.

In a large bowl, mix the pasta with the pistachio pesto; toss well to incorporate. If a thinner, more saucy consistency is desired, add some of the reserved pasta water and toss well.

Nutrition:
420 Calories | 3g Total Fat | 2g Fiber | 11g Protein

350. Burst Cherry Tomato Sauce with Angel Hair Pasta

Preparation Time: 10 minutes | **Cooking time:** 20 minutes | **Servings:** 4

Ingredients:
8 ounces angel hair pasta
2 tablespoons extra-virgin olive oil
3 garlic cloves, minced
3 pints cherry tomatoes
½ teaspoon kosher salt
¼ teaspoon red pepper flakes
¾ cup fresh basil, chopped
1 tablespoon white balsamic vinegar (optional)
¼ cup grated Parmesan cheese (optional)

Directions:
Cook the pasta according to the package directions. Drain and set aside.
Heat the olive oil in a skillet or large sauté pan over medium-high heat. Add the garlic and sauté for 30 seconds. Add the tomatoes, salt, and red pepper flakes and cook, stirring occasionally, until the tomatoes burst, about 15 minutes.
Remove from the heat and add the pasta and basil. Toss together well. (For out-of-season tomatoes, add the vinegar, if desired, and mix well.) Serve with the grated Parmesan cheese, if desired.

Nutrition:
305 Calories | 8g Total Fat | 3g Fiber | 11g Protein

351. Baked Tofu with Sun-Dried Tomatoes and Artichokes

Preparation Time: 15 minutes, plus 15 minutes to marinate | **Cooking time:** 30 minutes | **Servings:** 4

Ingredients:
1 (16-ounce) package extra-firm tofu, cut into 1-inch cubes
2 tablespoons extra-virgin olive oil, divided
2 tablespoons lemon juice, divided
1 tablespoon low-sodium soy sauce or gluten-free tamari
1 onion, diced
½ teaspoon kosher salt
2 garlic cloves, minced
1 (14-ounce) can artichoke hearts, drained
8 sun-dried tomato halves packed in oil, drained, and chopped
¼ teaspoon freshly ground black pepper
1 tablespoon white wine vinegar
Zest of 1 lemon
¼ cup fresh parsley, chopped

Directions:
Preheat the oven to 400°F. Line a baking sheet with foil or parchment paper. In a bowl, combine the tofu, 1 tablespoon of olive oil, 1 tablespoon of lemon juice, and the soy sauce. Allow to sit and marinate for 15 to 30 minutes. Arrange the tofu in a single layer on the prepared baking sheet and bake for 20 minutes, turning once, until light golden brown.
Heat the remaining 1 tablespoon olive oil in a large skillet or sauté pan over medium heat. Add the onion and salt; sauté until translucent, 5 to 6 minutes. Add the garlic and sauté for 30 seconds. Add the artichoke hearts, sun-dried tomatoes, and black pepper and sauté for 5 minutes. Add the white wine vinegar and the remaining 1 tablespoon lemon juice and deglaze the pan, scraping up any brown bits. Remove the pan from the heat and stir in the lemon zest and parsley. Gently mix in the baked tofu.

Nutrition:
230 Calories | 14g Total Fat | 5g Fiber | 14g Protein

352. Baked Mediterranean Tempeh with Tomatoes and Garlic

Preparation Time: 25 minutes, plus 4 hours to marinate | **Cooking time:** 35 minutes | **Servings:** 4

Ingredients:
For the Tempeh
12 ounces tempeh
¼ cup white wine
2 tablespoons extra-virgin olive oil
2 tablespoons lemon juice
Zest of 1 lemon
¼ teaspoon kosher salt
¼ teaspoon freshly ground black pepper
For the Tomatoes and Garlic Sauce
1 tablespoon extra-virgin olive oil
1 onion, diced
3 garlic cloves, minced
1 (14.5-ounce) can no-salt-added crushed tomatoes
1 beefsteak tomato, diced
1 dried bay leaf
1 teaspoon white wine vinegar
1 teaspoon lemon juice
1 teaspoon dried oregano
1 teaspoon dried thyme
¾ teaspoon kosher salt
¼ cup basil, cut into ribbons

Directions:
To Make the Tempeh
Place the tempeh in a medium saucepan. Add enough water to cover it by 1 to 2 inches. Bring to a boil over medium-high heat, cover, and lower heat to a simmer. Cook for 10 to 15 minutes. Remove the tempeh, pat dry, cool, and cut into 1-inch cubes.
In a large bowl, combine the white wine, olive oil, lemon juice, lemon zest, salt, and black pepper. Add the tempeh, cover the bowl, and put in the refrigerator for 4 hours, or up to overnight. Preheat the oven to 375°F. Place the marinated tempeh and the marinade in a baking dish and cook for 15 minutes.
To Make the Tomatoes and Garlic Sauce
Heat the olive oil in a large skillet over medium heat. Add the onion and sauté until transparent, 3 to 5 minutes. Add the garlic and sauté for 30 seconds. Add the crushed tomatoes, beefsteak tomato, bay leaf, vinegar, lemon juice, oregano, thyme, and salt. Mix well. Simmer for 15 minutes.
Add the baked tempeh to the tomato mixture and gently mix. Garnish with basil.
SUBSTITUTION TIP: If you're out of tempeh or simply want to speed up the cooking process, you can swap in a 14.5-ounce can of white beans for the tempeh. Drain and rinse the beans and add them to the sauce with the crushed tomatoes. It still makes a great vegan entrée in half the time!

Nutrition:
330 Calories | 20g Total Fat | 4g Fiber | 18g Protein

353. Shakshuka

Preparation Time: 10 minutes | **Cooking time:** 25 minutes | **Servings:** 4

Ingredients:
5 tablespoons olive oil, divided
1 red bell pepper, finely diced
½ small yellow onion, finely diced
14 ounces (397 g) crushed tomatoes, with juices
6 ounces (170 g) frozen spinach, thawed and drained of excess liquid
1 teaspoon smoked paprika
2 garlic cloves, finely minced
2 teaspoons red pepper flakes
1 tablespoon capers, roughly chopped
1 tablespoon water
6 large eggs
¼ teaspoon freshly ground black pepper
¾ cup feta or goat cheese, crumbled
¼ cup fresh flat-leaf parsley or cilantro, chopped

Directions:
Preheat the oven to 300ºF (150ºC). Heat 2 tablespoons olive oil in an oven-safe skillet over medium-high heat. Add the bell pepper and onion to the skillet and sauté for 6 minutes or until the onion is translucent and the bell pepper is soft.
Add the tomatoes and juices, spinach, paprika, garlic, red pepper flakes, capers, water, and 2 tablespoons olive oil to the skillet. Stir to combine well and bring to a boil. Turn down the

heat to low, then put the lid on and simmer for 5 minutes.

Crack the eggs over the sauce, and keep a little space between each egg, leave the egg intact and sprinkle with freshly ground black pepper. Cook for another 8 minutes or until the eggs reach the right doneness.

Scatter the cheese over the eggs and sauce, and bake in the preheated oven for 5 minutes or until the cheese is frothy and golden brown. Drizzle with the remaining 1 tablespoon olive oil and spread the parsley on top before serving warm.

Nutrition:
335 Calories | 26.5g total Fat | 5g Fiber | 16.8g protein

354. Spanakopita

Preparation Time: 15 minutes | **Cooking time:** 50 minutes | **Servings:** 6

Ingredients:
6 tablespoons olive oil, divided
1 small yellow onion, diced
4 cups frozen chopped spinach
4 garlic cloves, minced
½ teaspoon salt
½ teaspoon freshly ground black pepper
4 large eggs, beaten
1 cup ricotta cheese
¾ cup feta cheese, crumbled
¼ cup pine nuts

Directions:
Preheat the oven to 375°F (190ºC). Coat a baking dish with 2 tablespoons olive oil. Heat 2 tablespoons olive oil in a nonstick skillet over medium-high heat. Add the onion to the skillet and sauté for 6 minutes or until translucent and tender.

Add the spinach, garlic, salt, and black pepper to the skillet and sauté for 5 minutes more. Transfer them to a bowl and set them aside. Combine the beaten eggs and ricotta cheese in a separate bowl, then pour them into the bowl of spinach mixture. Stir to mix well.

Pour the mixture into the baking dish, and tilt the dish so the mixture coats the bottom evenly. Bake in the preheated oven for 20 minutes or until it begins to set. Remove the baking dish from the oven, and spread the feta cheese and pine nuts on top, then drizzle with the remaining 2 tablespoons olive oil.

Return the baking dish to the oven and bake for another 15 minutes or until the top is golden brown. Remove the dish from the oven. Allow the spanakopita to cool for a few minutes and slice to serve.

Nutrition:
340 Calories | 27.3g total Fat | 10.1g total Carbs | 4.8g Fiber | 18.2g protein

355. Tagine

Preparation Time: 20 minutes | **Cooking time:** 1 hour | **Servings:** 6

Ingredients:
½ cup olive oil
6 celery stalks, sliced into ¼-inch crescents
2 medium yellow onions, sliced
1 teaspoon ground cumin
½ teaspoon ground cinnamon
1 teaspoon ginger powder
6 garlic cloves, minced
½ teaspoon paprika
1 teaspoon salt
¼ teaspoon freshly ground black pepper
2 cups low-sodium vegetable stock
2 medium zucchinis, cut into ½-inch-thick semicircles
2 cups cauliflower, cut into florets
1 medium eggplant, cut into 1-inch cubes
1 cup green olives, halved and pitted
13.5 ounces (383 g) artichoke hearts, drained and quartered
½ cup chopped fresh cilantro leaves, for garnish
½ cup plain Greek yogurt, for garnish
½ cup chopped fresh flat-leaf parsley, for garnish

Directions:
Heat the olive oil in a stockpot over medium-high heat. Add the celery and onion to the pot and sauté for 6 minutes or until the celery is tender and the onion is translucent. Add the cumin, cinnamon, ginger, garlic, paprika, salt, and black pepper to the pot and sauté for 2 minutes more until aromatic.

Pour the vegetable stock into the pot and bring to a boil. Turn down the heat to low, and add the zucchini, cauliflower, and eggplant to the pot. Put the lid on and simmer for 30 minutes or until the vegetables are soft. Then add the olives and artichoke hearts to the pot and simmer for 15 minutes more. Pour them into a large serving bowl or a Tagine, then serve with cilantro, Greek yogurt, and parsley on top.

Nutrition:
312 Calories | 21.2g total Fat | 9.2g Fiber | 6.1g protein

356. Citrus Pistachios and Asparagus

Preparation Time: 10 minutes | **Cooking time:** 10 minutes | **Servings:** 4

Ingredients:
Zest and juice of 2 clementines or 1 orange
Zest and juice of 1 lemon
1 tablespoon red wine vinegar
3 tablespoons extra-virgin olive oil, divided
1 teaspoon salt, divided
¼ teaspoon freshly ground black pepper
½ cup pistachios, shelled
1 pound (454 g) fresh asparagus, trimmed
1 tablespoon water

Directions:
Combine the zest and juice of clementine and lemon, vinegar, 2 tablespoons of olive oil, ½ teaspoon of salt, and black pepper in a bowl. Stir to mix well. Set aside.
Toast the pistachios in a nonstick skillet over medium-high heat for 2 minutes or until golden brown. Transfer the roasted pistachios to a clean work surface, then chop roughly. Mix the pistachios with the citrus mixture. Set aside.
Heat the remaining olive oil in the nonstick skillet over medium-high heat. Add the asparagus to the skillet and sauté for 2 minutes, then season with remaining salt. Add the water to the skillet. Turn down the heat to low, and put the lid on. Simmer for 4 minutes until the asparagus is tender.
Remove the asparagus from the skillet to a large dish. Pour the citrus and pistachios mixture over the asparagus. Toss to coat well before serving.

Nutrition:
211 Calories | 17.5g total Fat | 3.8g Fiber | 5.9g protein

357. Tomato and Parsley Stuffed Eggplant

Preparation Time: 15 minutes | **Cooking time:** 2 hours and 10 minutes | **Servings:** 6

Ingredients:
¼ cup extra-virgin olive oil
3 small eggplants, cut in half lengthwise
1 teaspoon sea salt
½ teaspoon freshly ground black pepper
1 large yellow onion, finely chopped
4 garlic cloves, minced
15 ounces (425 g) diced tomatoes, with the juice
¼ cup fresh flat-leaf parsley, finely chopped

Directions:
Coat the insert of the slow cooker with 2 tablespoons of olive oil. Cut some slits on the cut side of each eggplant half, keep a ¼-inch space between each slit. Place the eggplant halves in the slow cooker, skin side down. Sprinkle it with salt and black pepper.
Heat the remaining olive oil in a nonstick skillet over medium-high heat. Add the onion and garlic to the skillet and sauté for 3 minutes or until the onion is translucent.
Add the parsley and tomatoes with the juice to the skillet, and sprinkle with salt and black pepper. Sauté for 5 more minutes or until they are tender. Divide and spoon the mixture in the skillet on the eggplant halves.
Put the slow cooker lid on and cook on HIGH for 2 hours until the eggplant is soft. Transfer the eggplant to a plate, and allow to cool for a few minutes before serving.

Nutrition:
455 Calories | 13g total Fat | 14g Fiber | 14g protein

358. Ratatouille

Preparation Time: 15 minutes | **Cooking time:** 7 hours | **Servings:** 6

Ingredients:
3 tablespoons extra-virgin olive oil
1 large eggplant, unpeeled, sliced

2 large onions, sliced
4 small zucchinis, sliced
2 green bell peppers, cut into thin strips
6 large tomatoes, cut in ½-inch wedges
2 tablespoons fresh flat-leaf parsley, chopped
1 teaspoon dried basil
2 garlic cloves, minced
2 teaspoons sea salt
¼ teaspoon freshly ground black pepper

Directions:
Coat the insert of the slow cooker with 2 tablespoons of olive oil. Arrange the vegetable slices, strips, and wedges alternately in the insert of the slow cooker. Spread the parsley on top of the vegetables, and season with basil, garlic, salt, and black pepper. Drizzle with the remaining olive oil. Put the slow cooker lid on and cook on LOW for 7 hours until the vegetables are tender. Transfer the vegetables to a plate and serve warm.

Nutrition:
265 Calories | 1.7g total Fat | 13.7g Fiber | 8.3g protein

359. Gemista

Preparation Time: 15 minutes | **Cooking time:** 4 hours | **Servings:** 4

Ingredients:
2 tablespoons extra-virgin olive oil
4 large bell peppers, any color
½ cup uncooked couscous
1 teaspoon oregano
1 garlic clove, minced
1 cup crumbled feta cheese
1 (15-ounce / 425-g) can cannellini beans, rinsed and drained
Salt and freshly ground black pepper, to taste
4 green onions, white and green parts separated, thinly sliced
1 lemon cut into 4 wedges, for serving

Directions:
Coat the insert of the slow cooker with 2 tablespoons of olive oil. Cut a ½-inch slice below the stem from the top of the bell pepper. Discard the stem only and chop the sliced top portion under the stem, and reserve in a bowl. Hollow the bell pepper with a spoon.

Add the remaining ingredients, except for the green parts of the green onion and lemon wedges, to the bowl of chopped bell pepper top. Stir to mix well. Spoon the mixture in the hollowed bell pepper, and arrange the stuffed bell peppers in the slow cooker, then drizzle with more olive oil.
Put the slow cooker lid on and cook on HIGH for 4 hours or until the bell peppers are soft.
Remove the bell peppers from the slow cooker and serve on a plate. Sprinkle with green parts of the green onions, and squeeze the lemon wedges on top before serving.

Nutrition:
246 Calories | 9g total Fat | 6.5g Fiber | 11.1g protein

360. Stuffed Cabbage Rolls

Preparation Time: 15 minutes | **Cooking time:** 2 hours | **Servings:** 4

Ingredients:
4 tablespoons olive oil, divided
1 large head green cabbage, cored
1 large yellow onion, chopped
3 ounces (85 g) feta cheese, crumbled
½ cup dried currants
3 cups cooked pearl barley
2 tablespoons fresh flat-leaf parsley, chopped
2 tablespoons pine nuts, toasted
½ teaspoon sea salt
½ teaspoon black pepper
15 ounces (425 g) crushed tomatoes, with the juice
½ cup apple juice
1 tablespoon apple cider vinegar

Directions:
Coat the insert of the slow cooker with 2 tablespoons of olive oil. Blanch the cabbage in a pot of water for 8 minutes. Remove it from the water, and allow it to cool, then separate 16 leaves from the cabbage. Set aside.
Drizzle the remaining olive oil in a nonstick skillet, and heat over medium heat. Add the onion to the skillet and sauté for 6 minutes or until the onion is translucent and soft. Transfer the onion to a bowl.
Add the feta cheese, currants, barley, parsley, and pine nuts to the bowl of cooked onion, then

sprinkle with ¼ teaspoon of salt and ¼ teaspoon of black pepper.
Arrange the cabbage leaves on a clean work surface. Spoon 1/3 cup of the mixture on the center of each leaf, then fold the edge of the leaf over the mixture and roll it up. Place the cabbage rolls in the slow cooker, seam side down.
Combine the remaining ingredients in a separate bowl, then pour the mixture over the cabbage rolls. Put the slow cooker lid on and cook on HIGH for 2 hours. Remove the cabbage rolls from the slow cooker and serve warm.

Nutrition:
383 Calories | 14.7g total Fat | 12.9g Fiber | 10.7g protein

361. Brussels Sprouts with Balsamic Glaze

Preparation Time: 15 minutes | **Cooking time:** 2 hours | **Servings:** 6

Ingredients:
Balsamic Glaze:
1 cup balsamic vinegar
¼ cup honey
2 tablespoons extra-virgin olive oil
2 pounds (907 g) Brussels sprouts, trimmed and halved
2 cups low-sodium vegetable soup
1 teaspoon sea salt
Freshly ground black pepper, to taste
¼ cup Parmesan cheese, grated
¼ cup pine nuts, toasted

Directions:
Coat the insert of the slow cooker with olive oil.
Make the balsamic glaze: Combine the balsamic vinegar and honey in a saucepan. Stir to mix well. Over medium-high heat, bring to a boil. Turn down the heat to low, then simmer for 20 minutes or until the glaze reduces in half and has a thick consistency.
Put the Brussels sprouts, vegetable soup, and ½ teaspoon of salt in the slow cooker, stir to combine. Put the slow cooker lid on and cook on HIGH for 2 hours until the Brussels sprouts are soft.
Transfer the Brussels sprouts to a plate, and sprinkle the remaining salt and black pepper to season. Drizzle the balsamic glaze over the Brussels sprouts, then serve with Parmesan and pine nuts.

Nutrition:
270 Calories | 10.6g total Fat | 6.9g Fiber | 8.7g protein

362. Spinach Salad with Citrus Vinaigrette

Preparation Time: 10 minutes | **Cooking time:** 0 minute | **Servings:** 4

Ingredients:
Citrus Vinaigrette:
¼ cup extra-virgin olive oil
3 tablespoons balsamic vinegar
½ teaspoon fresh lemon zest
½ teaspoon salt
Salad:
1-pound (454 g) baby spinach, washed, stems removed
1 large ripe tomato, cut into ¼-inch pieces
1 medium red onion, thinly sliced

Directions:
Make the citrus vinaigrette: Stir together the olive oil, balsamic vinegar, lemon zest, and salt in a bowl until mixed well.
Make the salad: Place the baby spinach, tomato, and onions in a separate salad bowl. Pour the citrus vinaigrette over the salad and gently toss until the vegetables are coated thoroughly.

Nutrition:
173 Calories | 14.2g total Fat | 4.2g Fiber | 4.1g protein

363. Simple Celery and Orange Salad

Preparation Time: 15 minutes | **Cooking time:** 0 minute | **Servings:** 6

Ingredients:
Salad:
3 celery stalks, including leaves, sliced diagonally into ½-inch slices
½ cup green olives
¼ cup sliced red onion
2 large peeled oranges, cut into rounds
Dressing:
1 tablespoon extra-virgin olive oil

1 tablespoon freshly squeezed lemon or orange juice
1 tablespoon olive brine
¼ teaspoon kosher or sea salt
¼ teaspoon freshly ground black pepper

Directions:
Make the salad: Put the celery stalks, green olives, onion, and oranges in a shallow bowl. Mix well and set aside.
Make the dressing: In a separate bowl, combine the olive oil, lemon juice, olive brine, salt, and pepper. Stir with a fork to combine well.
Pour the dressing into the bowl of salad and lightly toss until coated thoroughly.
Serve chilled or at room temperature.

Nutrition:
24 Calories | 1.2g total Fat | 1.2g Fiber | 1.1g protein

364. Rice with Vermicelli

Preparation Time: 5 minutes | **Cooking time:** 45 minutes | **Servings:** 6

Ingredients:
2 cups short-grain rice
3½ cups water, plus more for rinsing and soaking the rice
¼ cup olive oil
1 cup broken vermicelli pasta
Salt

Directions:
Rinse the rice under cold water until the water runs clear. Place the rice in a bowl, cover with water, and let soak for 10 minutes. Drain and set aside. In a medium pot over medium heat, heat the olive oil.
Stir in the vermicelli and cook for 2 to 3 minutes, stirring continuously, until golden. (Watch it! It happens fast.)
Add the rice and cook for 1 minute, stirring, so the rice is well coated in the oil. Add the water and a pinch of salt and bring the liquid to a boil. Reduce the heat to low, cover the pot, and simmer for 20 minutes. Remove from the heat and let rest, covered, for 10 minutes. Fluff with a fork and serve.

Nutrition:
346 Calories | 9g total Fat | 60g Carbohydrates | 2g fiber

365. Fava Beans and Rice

Preparation Time: 10 minutes | **Cooking time:** 35 minutes | **Servings:** 4

Ingredients:
¼ cup olive oil
4 cups fresh fava beans, shelled
4½ cups water, plus more for drizzling
2 cups basmati rice
1/8 teaspoon salt
1/8 teaspoon freshly ground black pepper
2 tablespoons pine nuts, toasted
½ cup chopped fresh garlic chives, or fresh onion chives

Directions:
In a large saucepan over medium heat, heat the olive oil. Add the fava beans and drizzle them with a bit of water to avoid burning or sticking. Cook for 10 minutes.
Gently stir in the rice. Add the water, salt, and pepper. Increase the heat and bring the mixture to a boil. Cover the pan, reduce the heat to low, and simmer for 15 minutes.
Turn off the heat and let the mixture rest for 10 minutes before serving. Spoon onto a serving platter and sprinkle with the toasted pine nuts and chives.

Nutrition:
587 Calories | 17g total Fat | 97g Carbohydrates | 2g fiber

366. Buttered Fava Beans

Preparation Time: 30 minutes | **Cooking time:** 15 minutes | **Servings:** 4

Ingredients:
½ cup vegetable broth
4 pounds fava beans, shelled
¼ cup fresh tarragon, divided
1 teaspoon chopped fresh thyme
¼ teaspoon freshly ground black pepper
1/8 teaspoon salt
2 tablespoons butter
1 garlic clove, minced
2 tablespoons chopped fresh parsley

Directions:
In a shallow pan over medium heat, bring the vegetable broth to a boil. Add the fava beans, 2 tablespoons of tarragon, thyme, pepper, and salt. Cook for about 10 minutes until the broth is almost absorbed and the beans are tender.
Stir in the butter, garlic, and remaining 2 tablespoons of tarragon. Cook for 2 to 3 minutes. Sprinkle with the parsley and serve hot.

Nutrition:
458 Calories | 9g total Fat | 81g Carbohydrates | 37g protein

367. Freekeh

Preparation Time: 10 minutes | **Cooking time:** 40 minutes | **Servings:** 4

Ingredients:
4 tablespoons Ghee
1 onion, chopped
3½ cups vegetable broth
1 teaspoon ground allspice
2 cups freekeh
2 tablespoons pine nuts, toasted

Directions:
In a heavy-bottomed saucepan over medium heat, melt the ghee. Stir in the onion and cook for about 5 minutes, stirring constantly, until the onion is golden. Pour in the vegetable broth, add the allspice, and bring to a boil. Stir in the freekeh and return the mixture to a boil. Reduce the heat to low, cover the pan, and simmer for 30 minutes, stirring occasionally. Spoon the freekeh into a serving dish and top with the toasted pine nuts.

Nutrition:
459 Calories | 18g total Fat | 64g Carbohydrates | 10g fiber

368. Fried Rice Balls with Tomato Sauce

Preparation Time: 15 minutes | **Cooking time:** 20 minutes | **Servings:** 8

Ingredients:
1 cup bread crumbs
2 cups cooked risotto
2 large eggs, divided
¼ cup freshly grated Parmesan cheese
8 fresh baby mozzarella balls, or 1 (4-inch) log fresh mozzarella, cut into 8 pieces
2 tablespoons water
1 cup corn oil
1 cup Basic Tomato Basil Sauce, or store-bought

Directions:
Pour the bread crumbs into a small bowl and set aside. In a medium bowl, stir together the risotto, 1 egg, and the Parmesan cheese until well combined. Moisten your hands with a little water to prevent sticking and divide the risotto mixture into 8 pieces. Place them on a clean work surface and flatten each piece.
Place 1 mozzarella ball on each flattened rice disk. Close the rice around the mozzarella to form a ball. Repeat until you finish all the balls. In the same medium, now-empty bowl, whisk the remaining egg and the water. Dip each prepared risotto ball into the egg wash and roll it in the bread crumbs. Set aside.
In a large sauté pan or skillet over high heat, heat the corn oil for about 3 minutes. Gently lower the risotto balls into the hot oil and fry for 5 to 8 minutes until golden brown. Stir them, as needed, to ensure the entire surface is fried. Using a slotted spoon, transfer the fried balls to paper towels to drain.
In a medium saucepan over medium heat, heat the tomato sauce for 5 minutes, stirring occasionally, and serve the warm sauce alongside the rice balls.

Nutrition:
255 Calories | 15g total Fat | 16g Carbohydrates | 2g fiber

369. Spanish-Style Rice

Preparation Time: 10 minutes | **Cooking time:** 35 minutes | **Servings:** 4

Ingredients:
¼ cup olive oil
1 small onion, finely chopped
1 red bell pepper, seeded and diced
1½ cups white rice
1 teaspoon sweet paprika
½ teaspoon ground cumin
½ teaspoon ground coriander
1 garlic clove, minced

3 tablespoons tomato paste
3 cups vegetable broth
1/8 teaspoon salt, plus more as needed

Directions:
In a large heavy-bottomed skillet over medium heat, heat the olive oil. Stir in the onion and red bell pepper. Cook for 5 minutes or until softened. Add the rice, paprika, cumin, and coriander and cook for 2 minutes, stirring often.
Add the garlic, tomato paste, vegetable broth, and salt. Stir to combine, taste, and season with more salt, as needed. Increase the heat to bring the mixture to a boil. Reduce the heat to low, cover the skillet, and simmer for 20 minutes.
Let the rice rest, covered, for 5 minutes before serving.

Nutrition:
414 Calories | 14g total Fat | 63g Carbohydrates | 2g fiber

370. Zucchini with Rice and Tzatziki

Preparation Time: 20 minutes | **Cooking time:** 35 minutes | **Servings:** 4

Ingredients:
¼ cup olive oil
1 onion, chopped
3 zucchinis, diced
1 cup vegetable broth
½ cup chopped fresh dill
Salt
Freshly ground black pepper
1 cup short-grain rice
2 tablespoons pine nuts, or slivered almonds, toasted
1 cup Tzatziki Sauce, Plain Yogurt, or store-bought

Directions:
In a heavy-bottomed pot over medium heat, heat the olive oil. Add the onion, turn the heat to medium-low, and sauté for 5 minutes. Add the zucchini and cook for 2 minutes more.
Stir in the vegetable broth and dill and season with salt and pepper. Increase the heat to medium and bring the mixture to a boil.
Stir in the rice and return the mixture to a boil. Reduce the heat to very low, cover the pot, and cook for 15 minutes. Remove from the heat and let the rice rest, covered, for 10 minutes. Spoon the rice onto a serving platter, sprinkle with the pine nuts, and serve with tzatziki sauce.

Nutrition:
414 Calories | 17g total Fat | 57g Carbohydrates | 5g fiber:

371. Cannellini Beans with Rosemary and Garlic Aioli

Preparation Time: 10 minutes | **Cooking time:** 10 minutes | **Servings:** 4

Ingredients:
4 cups cooked cannellini beans
4 cups water
½ teaspoon salt
3 tablespoons olive oil
2 tablespoons chopped fresh rosemary
½ cup Garlic Aioli
¼ teaspoon freshly ground black pepper

Directions:
In a medium saucepan over medium heat, combine the cannellini beans, water, and salt. Bring to a boil. Cook for 5 minutes. Drain. In a skillet over medium heat, heat the olive oil.
Add the beans. Stir in the rosemary and aioli. Reduce the heat to medium-low and cook, stirring, just to heat through. Season with pepper and serve.

Nutrition:
545 Calories | 36g total Fat | 42g Carbohydrates | 14g fiber

372. Jeweled Rice

Preparation Time: 15 minutes | **Cooking time:** 30 minutes | **Servings:** 6

Ingredients:
½ cup olive oil, divided
1 onion, finely chopped
1 garlic clove, minced
½ teaspoon chopped peeled fresh ginger
4½ cups water
1 teaspoon salt, divided, plus more as needed
1 teaspoon ground turmeric
2 cups basmati rice
1 cup fresh sweet peas
2 carrots, peeled and cut into ½-inch dice

½ cup dried cranberries
Grated zest of 1 orange
1/8 teaspoon cayenne pepper
¼ cup slivered almonds, toasted

Directions:
In a large heavy-bottomed pot over medium heat, heat ¼ cup of olive oil. Add the onion and cook for 4 minutes. Add the garlic and ginger and cook for 1 minute more.

Stir in the water, ¾ teaspoon of salt, and the turmeric. Bring the mixture to a boil. Stir in the rice and return the mixture to a boil. Taste the broth and season with more salt, as needed. Reduce the heat to low, cover the pot, and cook for 15 minutes. Turn off the heat. Let the rice rest on the burner, covered, for 10 minutes. Meanwhile, in a medium sauté pan or skillet over medium-low heat, heat the remaining ¼ cup of olive oil. Stir in the peas and carrots. Cook for 5 minutes.

Stir in the cranberries and orange zest. Season with the remaining ¼ teaspoon of salt and the cayenne. Cook for 1 to 2 minutes. Spoon the rice onto a serving platter. Top with the peas and carrots and sprinkle with the toasted almonds.

Nutrition:
460 Calories | 19g total Fat | 65g Carbohydrates | 4g fiber

373. Bulgur with Tomatoes and Chickpeas

Preparation Time: 10 minutes | **Cooking time:** 35 minutes | **Servings:** 6

Ingredients:
½ cup olive oil
1 onion, chopped
6 tomatoes, diced, or 1 (16-ounce) can diced tomatoes
2 tablespoons tomato paste
2 cups water
1 tablespoon Harissa, or store-bought
1/8 teaspoon salt
2 cups coarse bulgur
1 (15-ounce) can chickpeas, drained and rinsed

Directions:
In a heavy-bottomed pot over medium heat, heat the olive oil. Add the onion and sauté for 5 minutes. Add the tomatoes with their juice and cook for 5 minutes.

Stir in the tomato paste, water, harissa, and salt. Bring to a boil.

Stir in the bulgur and chickpeas. Return the mixture to a boil. Reduce the heat to low, cover the pot, and cook for 15 minutes. Let rest for 15 minutes before serving.

Nutrition:
413 Calories | 19g total Fat | 55g Carbohydrates | 14g fiber

374. Chickpea Medley

Preparation Time: 5 minutes | **Cooking time:** 0 minutes | **Servings:** 4

Ingredients:
2 tablespoons tahini
2 tablespoons coconut amino
1 (15-ounce) can chickpeas
1 cup finely chopped lightly packed spinach
1 carrot, peeled and grated

Directions:
In a medium bowl, whisk together the tahini and coconut aminos.

Add the chickpeas, spinach, and carrot to the bowl. Stir well and serve at room temperature. Store leftovers in an airtight container in the refrigerator for up to 1 week.

Nutrition:
161 Calories | 6g Total Fat | 7g Protein

375. Moroccan Couscous

Preparation Time: 10 minutes | **Cooking time:** 5 minutes | **Servings:** 4

Ingredients:
1 cup couscous
1½ cups water
1½ teaspoons grated orange or lemon zest
¾ cup freshly squeezed orange juice
4 or 5 garlic cloves, minced or pressed
2 tablespoons raisins
2 tablespoons pure maple syrup or agave nectar
2¼ teaspoons ground cumin
2¼ teaspoons ground cinnamon
¼ teaspoon paprika
2½ tablespoons minced fresh mint

2 teaspoons freshly squeezed lemon juice
½ teaspoon sea salt

Directions:
In a medium pot, combine the couscous and water. Add the orange zest and juice, garlic, raisins, maple syrup, cumin, cinnamon, and paprika, and stir. Bring the mixture to a boil over medium-high heat.
Remove the couscous from the heat and stir well. Cover with a tight-fitting lid and set aside until all the liquids are absorbed and the couscous is tender and fluffy. Gently stir in the mint, lemon juice, and salt. Serve warm or cold. Store leftovers in an airtight container in the refrigerator for up to 5 days.

Nutrition:
242 Calories | 1g Total Fat | 7g Protein

376. Lemony Asparagus Pasta

Preparation Time: 10 minutes | **Cooking time:** 20 minutes | **Servings:** 6

Ingredients:
1-pound spaghetti, linguini, or angel hair pasta
2 crusty bread slices
½ cup plus 1 tablespoon avocado oil, divided
3 cups chopped asparagus (1½-inch pieces)
½ cup vegan "chicken" broth or vegetable broth, divided
6 tablespoons freshly squeezed lemon juice
8 garlic cloves, minced or pressed
3 tablespoons finely chopped fresh curly parsley
1 tablespoon grated lemon zest
1½ teaspoons sea salt

Directions:
Bring a large pot of water to a boil over high heat and cook the pasta until al dente according to the instructions on the package.
Meanwhile, in a medium skillet, crumble the bread into coarse crumbs. Add 1 tablespoon of oil to the pan and stir well to combine over medium heat. Cook for about 5 minutes, stirring often until the crumbs are golden brown. Remove from the skillet and set aside.
Add the chopped asparagus and ¼ cup of broth in the skillet and cook over medium-high heat until the asparagus is bright green and crisp-tender, about 5 minutes. Transfer the asparagus to a very large bowl.

Add the remaining ½ cup of oil, remaining ¼ cup of broth, lemon juice, garlic, parsley, zest, and salt to the asparagus bowl and stir well.
When the noodles are done, drain well, and add them to the bowl. Gently toss with the asparagus mixture. Just before serving, stir in the toasted bread crumbs. Store leftovers in an airtight container in the refrigerator for up to 2 days.

Nutrition:
526 Calories | 23g Total Fat | 13g Protein

377. Moroccan Tempeh

Preparation Time: 20 minutes | **Cooking time:** 20 minutes | **Servings:** 4

Ingredients:
1-pound plain tempeh
1 cup water
¼ cup tamari, shoyu, or soy sauce
1½ cups gluten-free all-purpose flour
½ cup cornmeal
¼ cup sesame seeds
1 teaspoon paprika
1 teaspoon sea salt
1 teaspoon freshly ground black pepper
1 cup plain unsweetened non-dairy milk
½ cup sunflower oil
1 recipe Luscious Moroccan Sauce

Directions:
Gently slice the tempeh into 8 rectangular cutlets that are approximately 2½ by 4 inches in size and ½ inch thick, or half their original thickness. Place them in a single layer in a large skillet. Evenly pour the water and tamari on top. Turn the cutlets over to coat both sides with the liquid. Cover and cook over medium heat for 5 minutes. Flip the cutlets, cover, and cook for another 5 minutes, or until all the liquid has been absorbed. Transfer the tempeh to a plate and wipe out the skillet. Set aside.
In a shallow bowl, mix the flour, cornmeal, sesame seeds, paprika, salt, and pepper. Pour the milk into another shallow bowl.
In the now-empty skillet, heat the oil over medium-high heat. While it is heating, dip a tempeh cutlet in the milk, and then in the flour coating. Then dip the tempeh in the milk again, then in the flour coating a second time to form

an even, thick layer of coating on all sides. Repeat with all the tempeh cutlets.

Working in batches, pan-fry the cutlets for about 2 minutes on each side until golden brown. Remove and drain on paper towels. Place each tempeh cutlet on a plate, drizzle with the sauce, and serve immediately.

Nutrition:
968 Calories | 54g Total Fat | 30g Protein

378. Pasta with Lemon and Artichokes

Preparation Time: 10 minutes | **Cooking time:** 15 minutes | **Servings:** 4

Ingredients:
16 ounces linguine or angel hair pasta
¼ cup extra-virgin olive oil
8 garlic cloves, finely minced or pressed
2 (15-ounce) jars water-packed artichoke hearts, drained and quartered
2 tablespoons freshly squeezed lemon juice
¼ cup thinly sliced fresh basil
1 teaspoon sea salt
Freshly ground black pepper

Directions:
Bring a large pot of water to a boil over high heat and cook the pasta until al dente according to the directions on the package.
While the pasta is cooking, heat the oil in a skillet over medium heat and cook the garlic, stirring often, for 1 to 2 minutes until it just begins to brown. Toss the garlic with the artichokes in a large bowl.
When the pasta is done, drain it and add it to the artichoke mixture, then add the lemon juice, basil, salt, and pepper. Gently stir and serve.

Nutrition:
423 Calories | 14g Total Fat | 15g Protein

379. Roasted Pine Nut Orzo

Preparation Time: 10 minutes | **Cooking time:** 15 minutes | **Servings:** 4

Ingredients:
16 ounces orzo
1 cup diced roasted red peppers
¼ cup pitted, chopped Kalamata olives
4 garlic cloves, minced or pressed
3 tablespoons olive oil
1½ tablespoons freshly squeezed lemon juice
2 teaspoons balsamic vinegar
1 teaspoon sea salt
¼ cup pine nuts
¼ cup packed thinly sliced or torn fresh basil

Directions:
Bring a large pot of water to a boil over medium-high heat and add the orzo. Cook, stirring often, for 10 minutes, or until the orzo has a chewy and firm texture. Drain well.
While the orzo is cooking, in a large bowl, combine the peppers, olives, garlic, olive oil, lemon juice, vinegar, and salt. Stir well.
In a dry skillet, toast the pine nuts over medium-low heat until aromatic and lightly browned, shaking the pan often so that they cook evenly. Watch them closely, as this process will take only about 2 minutes. When lightly browned, immediately remove the pine nuts from the pan and set them aside.
Stir the orzo into the pepper-olive mixture and mix well. Serve topped with pine nuts and basil.

Nutrition:
424 Calories | 22g Total Fat | 9g Protein

380. Greek Flatbreads

Preparation Time: 15 minutes | **Cooking time:** 10 minutes | **Servings:** 4

Ingredients:
4 Pita Bread rounds or store-bought pita rounds
1 recipe Happy Hummus
2 cups baby spinach leaves
1 cup sliced grape tomatoes
½ cup pitted, halved Kalamata olives
½ cup thinly sliced red onion
1/3 cup thinly sliced fresh basil
¼ cup sliced Greek pepperoncini (optional)
3 tablespoons extra-virgin olive oil (optional)

Directions:
Preheat the oven to 350°F. Place the pita rounds directly on the oven rack and bake for 5 to 10 minutes until lightly browned and crisp.
Place a pita on each plate. Spread the hummus evenly over each. Evenly distribute the spinach, tomatoes, olives, onion, basil, and pepperoncini

(if using) on top. Drizzle with olive oil (if using), then cut into quarters and serve immediately.

Nutrition:
645 Calories | 32g Total Fat | 23g Protein

381. Mediterranean Macro Plate

Preparation Time: 15 minutes | **Cooking time:** 10 minutes | **Servings:** 6

Ingredients:
6 cups cauliflower florets
8 ounces firm or extra-firm tofu
Olive oil cooking spray
1 tablespoon herbs de Provence
Sea salt
1 recipe Ful Medames
1 recipe Happy Hummus
6 cups sliced cucumber

Directions:
Pour an inch or two of water into a large pot and insert a steamer rack. Bring the water to a boil, add the cauliflower, cover, and cook over medium heat until tender, about 10 minutes.
While the cauliflower is cooking, cut the tofu into 1-inch cubes. Heat a large skillet over medium-high heat. Spray with cooking spray and lay the tofu in a single layer in the skillet. Sprinkle evenly with the herbs de Provence and salt. Cook for 4 minutes, or until the undersides are golden brown. Spray with cooking spray, flip, and cook for an additional 3 to 4 minutes until golden brown on the other side. Remove from the heat.
Divide the ful medames and hummus among 6 plates. Add a scoop of tofu and cauliflower to each plate and divide the cucumber for dipping into the hummus. Serve immediately.

Nutrition:
559 Calories | 23g Total Fat | 27g Protein

382. The Athena Pizza

Preparation Time: 15 minutes | **Cooking time:** 10 minutes | **Servings:** 4

Ingredients:
4 Pita Bread rounds or store-bought pita bread
6 cups lightly packed stemmed and thinly sliced kale
2 tablespoons freshly squeezed lemon juice
1 tablespoon extra-virgin olive oil
4 garlic cloves, finely minced or pressed
¼ teaspoon sea salt
1 recipe Macadamia-Rosemary Cheese
1 cup halved grape or cherry tomatoes
½ cup pitted, chopped Kalamata olives

Directions:
Preheat the oven to 400°F. Arrange the pita bread rounds in a single layer on two large rimmed baking sheets. Bake for 5 to 10 minutes until golden brown and crisp. Remove and set aside.
In a large bowl, mix the kale, lemon juice, and olive oil. Using your hands, work the lemon and oil into the kale, squeezing firmly, so that the kale becomes soft and tenderized, as well as a darker shade of green. Stir in the garlic and salt. Assemble the pizzas by spreading each pita with a generous coating of macadamia cheese and topping evenly with the kale salad, tomatoes, and olives. Cut each pizza into quarters and serve immediately.

Nutrition:
616 Calories | 39g Total Fat | 16g Protein | 57g Carbs

383. Mujadara

Preparation Time: 5 minutes | **Cooking time:** 45 minutes | **Servings:** 4

Ingredients:
¾ cup dried brown lentils
¼ cup long-grain brown rice
3 cups vegetarian "chicken" broth or vegetable broth
5 garlic cloves, minced or pressed
2 tablespoons extra-virgin olive oil, divided
4 cups thinly sliced onion
Sea salt
1 teaspoon balsamic vinegar

Directions:
In a large pot, combine the lentils, rice, broth, and garlic and bring to a boil over high heat. Reduce the heat to low, partially cover the pot, and simmer for 45 minutes, or until the lentils and rice are tender and the water is absorbed.
While the lentils and rice are cooking, heat a large skillet over medium-low heat. Add 1

tablespoon of oil and the onion. Cook, stirring often, for 40 minutes, or until the onions are very well browned and caramelized. If the pan becomes too dry at any point, add water as needed and stir. Once done, remove from the heat and season with salt.

When the lentils and rice are done, stir in the vinegar and remaining 1 tablespoon of oil and season with salt. Serve the lentil-rice mixture topped with the caramelized onions.

Nutrition:
281 Calories | 8g Total Fat | 12g Protein

384. Briam

Preparation Time: 10 minutes | **Cooking time:** 1 hour | **Servings:** 4

Ingredients:
Olive oil cooking spray
2 medium zucchinis, cut into ½-inch-thick rounds
2 gold potatoes, thinly sliced
4 tomatoes, sliced
1¾ cups tomato sauce
10 garlic cloves, cut into large chunks
1½ tablespoons olive oil
4 teaspoons dried basil
2 teaspoons dried oregano
1 teaspoon sea salt

Directions:
Preheat the oven to 400°F. Spray a large baking dish lightly with cooking spray.
In a large bowl, combine the zucchini, potatoes, tomatoes, tomato sauce, garlic, olive oil, basil, oregano, and salt and stir well. Pour the vegetable mixture into the prepared dish.
Bake for 30 minutes, stir well, and bake for another 30 minutes, or until the potatoes are tender. Stir again and serve.

Nutrition:
338 Calories | 20g Total Fat | 7g Protein | 9g Fiber

385. Zucchini Boats with Couscous Stuffing

Preparation Time: 10 minutes | **Cooking time:** 40 minutes | **Servings:** 4

Ingredients:
1 tablespoon olive oil, plus more for greasing pan
2 large zucchinis
1¼ cups vegetarian "chicken" broth or vegetable broth
1 cup Israeli couscous
3 shallots, minced
1 cup canned or fresh diced tomatoes
1 tablespoon capers
2 tablespoons zaatar
2 cups chopped arugula
Sea salt
Freshly ground black pepper

Directions:
Preheat the oven to 400 degrees F. Lightly grease a large baking dish with oil. Cut each zucchini in half lengthwise. Use a spoon to scoop out the seeds and enough interior flesh to make a deep trough. If possible, leave the flesh intact where the stem end was so the stuffing won't fall out. Arrange the zucchini, cut-side up, in the prepared dish.
In a medium saucepan, bring the broth to a simmer. Add the couscous, cover the pan, and cook for 8 minutes, or until just tender. Remove from the heat and let sit for 2 to 3 minutes, then drain excess liquid if needed.
Meanwhile, in a large skillet, heat the oil over medium heat. Add the shallots and sauté for 3 to 4 minutes, stirring frequently. Add the tomatoes and their juices, capers, and za'atar. Cook, stirring frequently, for about 3 minutes. Add the cooked couscous and arugula and sauté for 2 to 4 minutes until the arugula is wilted and the mixture is saucy, but not watery. Remove the filling from the heat and season with salt and pepper.
Spoon the couscous filling into the zucchini boats and bake for 25 minutes, or until the zucchini is tender. Remove and serve warm or hot.

Nutrition:
235 Calories | 4g Total Fat | 8g Protein | 5g Fiber

386. Pasta with Creamy Tomato Sauce

Preparation Time: 10 minutes | **Cooking time:** 10 minutes | **Servings:** 4

Ingredients:
16 ounces linguine
2 cups chopped onion
1 cup chopped carrot
½ cup dry white wine
½ cup raw unsalted cashew pieces
¼ to ½ cup water
2 (14.5-ounce) cans diced tomatoes
4 garlic cloves, peeled
24 large basil leaves, 12 left whole, and 12 cuts into thin ribbons
1 teaspoon sea salt
¼ teaspoon freshly ground black pepper

Directions:
Bring a large pot of water to a boil over high heat and cook the pasta until al dente according to the directions on the package. Drain.
Meanwhile, in a large skillet, combine the onion, carrot, and wine. (If you're not using a high-speed blender, add the cashews now as well.) Sauté the vegetables over medium heat for 5 minutes, stirring often. As you go, add the water, as needed, to prevent sticking.
Add the tomatoes and their juices. Cook, stirring often, for another 5 minutes. Transfer the mixture to a high-speed blender. Add the garlic, whole basil leaves, cashews, salt, and pepper. Blend until very smooth. Serve generous portions of the sauce over the pasta and top with the fresh basil ribbons.

Nutrition:
532 Calories | 11g Total Fat | 17g Protein | 8g Fiber

387. Spicy Eggplant Polenta

Preparation Time: 10 minutes | **Cooking time:** 30 minutes | **Servings:** 4

Ingredients:
For the polenta
1 cup cornmeal
3¼ cups water
2 tablespoons olive oil
3 tablespoons nutritional yeast
½ to ¾ teaspoon sea salt
For the eggplant
2 pounds eggplant, peeled and cut into small cubes (about 12 cups)
3 tablespoons olive oil
2 to 4 cups water, divided
1 cup tomato sauce
5 garlic cloves, minced or pressed
4 teaspoons harissa paste
¼ cup pine nuts
1 teaspoon sea salt
2 tablespoons thinly sliced fresh basil

Directions:
To make the polenta
In a medium-large pot, combine the cornmeal and water and cook over medium heat, whisking constantly, until it begins to thicken. Once it begins to thicken a bit, turn the heat down to the lowest setting possible. Continue to cook, whisking very often, for 10 minutes, or until thick. If you desire a slightly thinner consistency, whisk in a bit more water.
Remove the polenta from the heat and whisk in the oil, nutritional yeast, and salt. Set aside.
To make the eggplant
In a large skillet or wok, combine the eggplant, olive oil, and 2 cups of water. Cook over medium-high heat, stirring often, for 5 minutes. Add the tomato sauce, garlic, and harissa, and reduce the heat to medium-low. Continue to cook, stirring often, for 10 minutes, or until the eggplant is very soft. You will need to add up to 2 more cups of water during this process, depending on your variety of eggplant. I typically use all 4 cups to reach the desired sauciness level. What you're aiming for is a thick (but still saucy and wet) tomato sauce.
While the tomato sauce is cooking, in a dry skillet, toast the pine nuts over low heat, shaking often, for 2 minutes, or until lightly browned and aromatic. Once the eggplant is tender, stir in the salt. Ladle the polenta onto plates and top with the eggplant mixture. Finish with a sprinkle of toasted pine nuts and fresh basil.

Nutrition:
409 Calories | 29g Total Fat | 12g Protein

388. Greek Tostadas

Preparation Time: 15 minutes | **Cooking time:** 10 minutes | **Servings:** 6

Ingredients:
Olive oil cooking spray
6 (6-inch) corn tortillas
7 cups stemmed and finely chopped Lacinato or curly kale
2 tablespoons freshly squeezed lemon juice
1 tablespoon extra-virgin olive oil
2 garlic cloves, minced or pressed
¼ teaspoon sea salt
1 recipe Happy Hummus
2 avocados, peeled, pitted, and chopped
¾ cup finely chopped purple cabbage
2 tomatoes, chopped
2 limes or lemons, quartered (optional)

Directions:
Preheat the oven to 400°F. Spray a rimmed baking sheet with cooking spray. Arrange the tortillas in a single layer on the prepared sheet. Spray the tops generously with oil and bake for 5 to 10 minutes until lightly browned and crisp. Set aside.
In a large bowl, combine the kale, lemon juice, and olive oil. Using your hands, work the lemon and oil into the kale, squeezing firmly, so that the kale becomes soft and tenderized, as well as a darker shade of green. Stir in the garlic and salt. To assemble, top the baked tortillas with a generous layer of hummus. Top evenly with the massaged kale, avocado chunks, cabbage, and tomatoes. If desired, serve with lime or lemon wedges for squeezing over the top.

Nutrition:
474 Calories | 28g Total Fat

389. Asparagus Risotto

Preparation Time: 15 minutes | **Cooking time:** 30 minutes | **Servings:** 4

Ingredients:
5 cups vegetable broth, divided
3 tablespoons unsalted butter, divided
1 tablespoon olive oil
1 small onion, chopped
1½ cups Arborio rice
1-pound fresh asparagus, ends trimmed, cut into 1-inch pieces, tips separated
¼ cup freshly grated Parmesan cheese, plus more for serving

Directions:
In a saucepan over medium heat, bring the vegetable broth to a boil. Turn the heat to low and keep the broth at a steady simmer. In a 4-quart heavy-bottomed saucepan over medium heat, melt 2 tablespoons of butter with the olive oil. Add the onion and cook for 2 to 3 minutes. Add the rice and stir with a wooden spoon while cooking for 1 minute until the grains are well coated in the butter and oil.
Stir in ½ cup of warm broth. Cook, stirring often, for about 5 minutes until the broth is completely absorbed. Add the asparagus stalks and another ½ cup of broth. Cook, stirring often until the liquid is absorbed. Continue adding the broth, ½ cup at a time, and cooking until it is completely absorbed before adding the next ½ cup. Stir frequently to prevent sticking. After about 20 minutes, the rice should be cooked but still firm.
Add the asparagus tips, the remaining 1 tablespoon of butter, and the Parmesan cheese. Stir vigorously to combine. Remove from the heat, top with additional Parmesan cheese, if desired, and serve immediately.

Nutrition:
434 Calories | 14g total Fat | 67g Carbohydrates | 6g fiber

390. Vegetable Paella

Preparation Time: 25 minutes | **Cooking time:** 45 minutes | **Servings:** 6

Ingredients:
¼ cup olive oil
1 large sweet onion, chopped
1 large red bell pepper, seeded and chopped
1 large green bell pepper, seeded and chopped
3 garlic cloves, finely minced
1 teaspoon smoked paprika
5 saffron threads
1 zucchini, cut into ½-inch cubes
4 large ripe tomatoes, peeled, seeded, and chopped
1½ cups short-grain Spanish rice

3 cups vegetable broth, warmed

Directions:
Preheat the oven to 350°F. In a paella pan or large oven-safe skillet over medium heat, heat the olive oil. Add the onion and red and green bell peppers and cook for 10 minutes.
Stir in the garlic, paprika, saffron threads, zucchini, and tomatoes. Turn the heat to medium-low and cook for 10 minutes.
Stir in the rice and vegetable broth. Increase the heat to bring the paella to a boil. Reduce the heat to medium-low and cook for 15 minutes. Cover the pan with aluminum foil and put it in the oven.
Bake for 10 minutes or until the broth is absorbed.

Nutrition:
288 Calories | 10g total Fat | 46g Carbohydrates | 3g fiber

391. Eggplant and Rice Casserole

Preparation Time: 30 minutes | **Cooking time:** 35 minutes | **Servings:** 4

Ingredients:
For the Sauce
½ cup olive oil
1 small onion, chopped
4 garlic cloves, mashed
6 ripe tomatoes, peeled and chopped
2 tablespoons tomato paste
1 teaspoon dried oregano
¼ teaspoon ground nutmeg
¼ teaspoon ground cumin
For the Casserole
4 (6-inch) Japanese eggplants, halved lengthwise
2 tablespoons olive oil
1 cup cooked rice
2 tablespoons pine nuts, toasted
1 cup water

Directions:
To Make the Sauce
In a heavy-bottomed saucepan over medium heat, heat the olive oil. Add the onion and cook for 5 minutes. Stir in the garlic, tomatoes, tomato paste, oregano, nutmeg, and cumin. Bring to a boil. Cover, reduce heat to low and simmer for 10 minutes. Remove and set aside.

To Make the Casserole
Preheat the broiler. While the sauce simmers, drizzle the eggplant with the olive oil and place them on a baking sheet. Broil for about 5 minutes until golden. Remove and let cool. Turn the oven to 375°F. Arrange the cooled eggplant, cut-side up, in a 9-by-13-inch baking dish. Gently scoop out some flesh to make room for the stuffing.
In a bowl, combine half the tomato sauce, the cooked rice, and pine nuts. Fill each eggplant half with the rice mixture. In the same bowl, combine the remaining tomato sauce and water. Pour over the eggplant. Bake, covered, for 20 minutes until the eggplant is soft.

Nutrition:
453 Calories | 39g total Fat | 29g Carbohydrates | 7g fiber

392. Many Vegetable Couscous

Preparation Time: 15 minutes | **Cooking time:** 45 minutes | **Servings:** 8

Ingredients:
¼ cup olive oil
1 onion, chopped
4 garlic cloves, minced
2 jalapeño peppers, pierced with a fork in several places
½ teaspoon ground cumin
½ teaspoon ground coriander
1 (28-ounce) can crushed tomatoes
2 tablespoons tomato paste
1/8 teaspoon salt
2 bay leaves
11 cups water, divided
4 carrots, peeled and cut into 2-inch pieces
2 zucchinis, cut into 2-inch pieces
1 acorn squash, halved, seeded, and cut into 1-inch-thick slices
1 (15-ounce) can chickpeas, drained and rinsed
¼ cup chopped Preserved Lemons (optional)
3 cups couscous

Directions:
In a large heavy-bottomed pot over medium heat, heat the olive oil. Stir in the onion and cook for 4 minutes. Stir in the garlic, jalapeños, cumin, and coriander. Cook for 1 minute. Add the

tomatoes, tomato paste, salt, bay leaves, and 8 cups of water. Bring the mixture to a boil.

Add the carrots, zucchini, and acorn squash and return to a boil. Reduce the heat slightly, cover, and cook for about 20 minutes until the vegetables are tender but not mushy. Remove 2 cups of the cooking liquid and set aside. Season as needed.

Add the chickpeas and preserved lemons (if using). Cook for 2 to 3 minutes, and turn off the heat.

In a medium pan, bring the remaining 3 cups of water to a boil over high heat. Stir in the couscous, cover, and turn off the heat. Let the couscous rest for 10 minutes. Drizzle with 1 cup of the reserved cooking liquid. Using a fork, fluff the couscous.

Mound it on a large platter. Drizzle it with the remaining cooking liquid. Remove the vegetables from the pot and arrange them on top. Serve the remaining stew in a separate bowl.

Nutrition:
415 Calories | 7g total Fat | 75g Carbohydrates | 9g fiber

393. Kushari

Preparation Time: 25 minutes | **Cooking time:** 1 hour and 20 minutes | **Servings:** 8

Ingredients:
For the sauce
2 tablespoons olive oil
2 garlic cloves, minced
1 (16-ounce) can tomato sauce
¼ cup white vinegar
¼ cup Harissa, or store-bought
1/8 teaspoon salt
For the rice
1 cup olive oil
2 onions, thinly sliced
2 cups dried brown lentils, rinsed, and picked over for debris
4 quarts plus ½ cup water, divided
2 cups short-grain rice
1 teaspoon salt, plus more for cooking the pasta
1-pound short elbow pasta
1 (15-ounce) can chickpeas, drained and rinsed

Directions:
To make the sauce

In a saucepan over medium heat, heat the olive oil. Add the garlic and cook for 1 minute. Stir in the tomato sauce, vinegar, harissa, and salt. Increase the heat to bring the sauce to a boil. Reduce the heat to low and cook for 20 minutes or until the sauce has thickened. Remove and set aside.

To make the rice
Line a plate with paper towels and set it aside. In a large pan over medium heat, heat the olive oil. Add the onions and cook for 7 to 10 minutes, stirring often, until crisp and golden. Transfer the onions to the prepared plate and set them aside. Reserve 2 tablespoons of the cooking oil. Reserve the pan.

In a large pot over high heat, combine the lentils and 4 cups of water. Bring to a boil and cook for 20 minutes. Drain, transfer to a bowl, and toss with the reserved 2 tablespoons of cooking oil. Set aside. Reserve the pot.

Place the pan you used to fry the onions over medium-high heat and add the rice, 4½ cups of water, and the salt to it. Bring to a boil. Reduce the heat to low, cover the pot, and cook for 20 minutes. Turn off the heat and let the rice rest for 10 minutes. In the pot used to cook the lentils, bring the remaining 8 cups of water, salted, to a boil over high heat. Drop in the pasta and cook for 6 minutes or according to the package instructions. Drain and set aside.

To assemble
Spoon the rice onto a serving platter. Top it with lentils, chickpeas, and pasta. Drizzle with the hot tomato sauce and sprinkle with the crispy fried onions.

Nutrition:
668 Calories | 13g total Fat | 113g Carbohydrates | 18g fiber

394. Italian Oven Roasted Vegetables

Preparation Time: 5 minutes | **Cooking time:** 30 minutes | **Servings:** 4

Ingredients:
2 sliced medium onions
½ tbs. salt
1 tbs. Italian seasoning
2 sliced yellow squash
1/8 tsp pepper powder

3 minced cloves of garlic
2 sweet and large green and red peppers
2 tbsp. olive oil

Directions:
Take all the cut, chopped, minced, and diced vegetables and put them in a large salad mixing bowl.
After this, you will have to add the required amounts of salt, Italian seasoning, and pepper powder to the vegetables.
Toss the ingredients for some time to ensure that everything has mixed well.
Then pour the olive oil into this mixture and again blend well.
Place the marinated vegetables in a roasting oven and put them inside the microwave oven.
The oven must be preheated at 425-degree temperature. The baking will take no longer than 25 minutes.
After pulling out the tray from the oven, you can sprinkle on some extra cheese. This is optional and can be omitted.

Nutrition:
Carbohydrate – 16g | Protein - 3g | Fat: – 4g | Calories: 100

395. Pesto with Basil and Spinach

Preparation Time: 20 minutes | **Cooking time:** 0 minutes | **Servings:** 24

Ingredients:
1 1/2 cup small spinach leaves
3/4 cup fresh basil leaves
1/2 cup grilled pine nuts
1/2 cup grated Parmesan cheese
4 cloves of garlic, peeled and quartered
3/4 teaspoon of kosher salt
1/2 teaspoon freshly ground black pepper
1 tablespoon fresh lemon juice
1/2 teaspoon lemon zest
1/2 cup extra virgin olive oil

Directions:
Mix spinach, basil, pine nuts, Parmesan, garlic, salt, pepper, lemon juice, lemon zest, and 2 tablespoons of olive oil in a food processor until smooth.
Sprinkle the remaining olive oil into the mixture.

Nutrition: (Per Serving)
67 Calories | 6.6 g Fat | 0.8 g Carbohydrates | 1.5 g of Protein | 1 mg Cholesterol | 87 mg of sodium.

396. Broiled Mushrooms Burgers and Goat Cheese

Preparation Time: 15 minutes | **Cooking time:** 5 minutes | **Servings:** 4

Ingredients:
4 large Portobello mushroom caps
1 red onion, cut into ¼ inch thick slices
2 tablespoons extra virgin olive oil
2 tablespoons balsamic vinegar
Pinch of salt
¼ cup goat cheese
¼ cup sun-dried tomatoes, chopped
4 ciabatta buns
1 cup kale, shredded

Directions:
Preheat your oven to broil.
Take a large bowl and add mushrooms caps, onion slices, olive oil, balsamic vinegar, and salt. Mix well.
Place mushroom caps (bottom side up) and onion slices on your baking sheet.
Take a small bowl and stir in goat cheese and sun-dried tomatoes.
Toast the buns under the broiler for 30 seconds until golden.
Spread the goat cheese mix on top of each bun.
Place mushroom cap and onion slice on each bun bottom and cover with shredded kale.
Put everything together and serve.
Enjoy!

Nutrition: (Per Serving)
Calories: 327 | Fat: 11g | Carbohydrates: 49g | Protein: 11g

397. Whole Grain Pita Bread Stuffed with Olives and Chickpeas

Preparation Time: 10 minutes | **Cooking time:** 20 minutes | **Servings:** 2

Ingredients:
2 wholegrain pita pockets
2 tbsps. olive oil

2 garlic cloves, chopped
1 onion, chopped
½ tsp. cumin
10 black olives, chopped
2 c. cooked chickpeas
Salt and pepper

Directions:
Slice open the pita pockets and set them aside
Adjust your heat to medium and set a pan in place. Add in the olive oil and heat.
Add the garlic, onion, and cumin to the hot pan and stir as the onions soften and the cumin is fragrant
Add the olives, chickpeas, salt, and pepper, and toss everything together until the chickpeas become golden
Set the pan from heat and use your wooden spoon to roughly mash the chickpeas so that some are intact and some are crushed
Heat your pita pockets in the microwave, in the oven, or on a clean pan on the stove
Fill them with your chickpea mixture and enjoy!

Nutrition:
Calories 503 | Fat: 19 g | Sat. fat 8.9 g | Fiber 14 g | Carbohydrates: 54 g | Sugars 9 g | Protein: 15.7 g | Sodium: 276 mg

398. Simple Penne Anti-Pasto

Preparation Time: 15 minutes | **Cooking time:** 15 minutes | **Servings:** 4

Ingredients:
¼ cup pine nuts, toasted
½ cup grated Parmigiano-Reggiano cheese, divided
8oz penne pasta, cooked and drained
1 6oz jar drained, sliced, marinated, and quartered artichoke hearts
1 7 oz jar drained and chopped sun-dried tomato halves packed in oil
3 oz chopped prosciutto
1/3 cup pesto
½ cup pitted and chopped Kalamata olives
1 medium red bell pepper

Directions:
Slice bell pepper, discard membranes, seeds, and stem. On a foiled lined baking sheet, place bell pepper halves, press down by hand, and broil in the oven for eight minutes. Remove from the oven, put in a sealed bag for 5 minutes before peeling and chopping.
Place chopped bell pepper in a bowl and mix in artichokes, tomatoes, prosciutto, pesto, and olives.
Toss in ¼ cup cheese and pasta. Transfer to a serving dish and garnish with ¼ cup cheese and pine nuts. Serve and enjoy!

Nutrition:
Calories: 606 | Carbohydrates: 70.3g | Protein: 27.2g | Fat: 27.6g

399. Broiled Tomatoes with Feta

Preparation Time: 10 minutes | **Cooking time:** 8 minutes | **Servings:** 4

Ingredients:
4 large tomatoes, cut in half horizontally
1 tablespoon olive oil
1 teaspoon minced garlic
½ cup crumbled feta cheese
Sea salt
Freshly ground black pepper

Directions:
Preheat the oven to broil.
Place the tomato halves, cut-side up, in a 9-by-13-inch baking dish and drizzle them with the olive oil. Rub the garlic into the tomatoes.
Broil the tomatoes for about 5 minutes, until softened. Sprinkle with the feta cheese and broil for 3 minutes longer.
Season with salt and pepper. Serve.

Nutrition:
Calories: 113 | Total fat: 8g | Saturated fat: 3g | Carbohydrates: 8g | Sugar: 6g | Fiber: 2g | Protein: 4g

400. Sautéed Dark Leafy Greens

Preparation Time: 10 minutes | **Cooking time:** 10 minutes | **Servings:** 4

Ingredients:
2 tablespoons olive oil
8 cups stemmed and coarsely chopped spinach, kale, collard greens, or Swiss chard
Juice of ½ lemon
Sea salt
Freshly ground black pepper

Directions:
In a large skillet, heat the olive oil over medium-high heat. Add the greens and toss with tongs until wilted and tender, 8 to 10 minutes.
Remove the skillet from the heat and squeeze in the lemon juice, tossing to coat evenly. Season with salt and pepper and serve.

Nutrition:
Calories: 129 | Total fat: 7g | Saturated fat: 1g | Carbohydrates: 14g | Sugar: 0g | Fiber: 2g | Protein: 4g

401. Alethea's Lemony Asparagus Pasta

Preparation Time: 10 minutes | **Cooking time:** 20 minutes | **Servings:** 6

Ingredients:
1 pound spaghetti, linguini, or angel hair pasta
2 crusty bread slices
½ cup plus 1 tablespoon avocado oil, divided
3 cups chopped asparagus (1½-inch pieces)
½ cup vegan "chicken" broth or vegetable broth, divided
6 tablespoons freshly squeezed lemon juice
8 garlic cloves, minced or pressed
3 tablespoons finely chopped fresh curly parsley
1 tablespoon grated lemon zest
1½ teaspoons sea salt

Directions:
Bring a large pot of water to a boil over high heat and cook the pasta until al dente according to the instructions on the package.
Meanwhile, in a medium skillet, crumble the bread into coarse crumbs. Add 1 tablespoon of oil to the pan and stir well to combine over medium heat. Cook for about 5 minutes, stirring often until the crumbs are golden brown. Remove from the skillet and set aside.
Add the chopped asparagus and ¼ cup of broth in the skillet and cook over medium-high heat until the asparagus is bright green and crisp-tender, about 5 minutes. Transfer the asparagus to a very large bowl.
Add the remaining ½ cup of oil, remaining ¼ cup of broth, lemon juice, garlic, parsley, zest, and salt to the asparagus bowl and stir well.
When the noodles are done, drain well, and add them to the bowl. Gently toss with the asparagus mixture. Just before serving, stir in the toasted bread crumbs. Store leftovers in an airtight container in the refrigerator for up to 2 days.

Nutrition:
Calories: 526; | Total fat: 23g; | Saturated fat: 3g; | Protein: 13g; | Carbohydrates: 68g; | Fiber: 10g; | Sodium: 1422mg; | Iron: 6mg

402. Herbed Roasted Tomato with Feta Cheese

Preparation Time: 10 minutes | **Cooking time:** 15 minutes | **Servings:** 4

Ingredients:
8 oz. or 230 g feta cheese
2 peeled tomatoes, diced
2 garlic cloves, chopped
1 c. tomato juice
1 thyme sprig
1 oregano sprig
1 tablespoon chopped fresh basil

Directions:
Mix the tomatoes, garlic, tomato juice, thyme, and oregano in a small deep-dish baking pan.
Place the feta cheese on top and cover with aluminum foil.
Cook in the preheated oven at 350 F/176 C for 10-15 minutes.
Sprinkle with basil and serve hot.

Nutrition:
Calories 173 | Fat: 12.2 g | Sat fat 6 g | Fiber 2 g | Carbohydrates: 7.8 g | Sugars 5 g | Protein: 9.2 g | Sodium: 934 mg

403. Roasted Tomato Pita Pizzas

Preparation Time: 10 minutes | **Cooking time:** 20 minutes | **Servings:** 6

Ingredients:
2 pints grape tomatoes (about 3 cups), halved
1 tablespoon extra-virgin olive oil
2 garlic cloves, minced (about 1 teaspoon)
1 teaspoon chopped fresh thyme leaves (from about 6 sprigs)
¼ teaspoon freshly ground black pepper
¼ teaspoon kosher or sea salt

¾ cup shredded Parmesan cheese (about 3 ounces)
6 whole-wheat pita bread

Directions:
Preheat the oven to 425°F.
In a baking pan, mix the tomatoes, oil, garlic, thyme, pepper, and salt. Roast for 10 minutes. Pull out the rack, stir the tomatoes with a spatula or wooden spoon while still in the oven, and mash down the softened tomatoes to release more of their liquid. Roast for an additional 10 minutes.
While the tomatoes are roasting, sprinkle 2 tablespoons of cheese over each pita bread. Place the pitas on a large, rimmed baking sheet and toast in the oven for the last 5 minutes of the tomato cooking time.
Remove the tomato sauce and pita bread from the oven. Stir the tomatoes, spoon about ⅓ cup of sauce over each pita bread, and serve.

Nutrition:
Per serving
Calories: 259 | Total fat: 7g | Saturated fat: 3g
Cholesterol: 10mg | Sodium: 555mg
Total Carbohydrates: 40g | Fiber: 6g | Protein: 12g

Chapter 5: Salads

404. Olives and Lentils Salad

Preparation Time: 10 minutes | **Cooking time:** 0 minutes | **Servings:** 2

Ingredients:
1/3 cup canned green lentils
1 tablespoon olive oil
2 cups baby spinach
1 cup black olives
2 tablespoons sunflower seeds
1 tablespoon Dijon mustard
2 tablespoons balsamic vinegar
2 tablespoons olive oil

Directions:
Mix the lentils with the spinach, olives, and the rest of the ingredients in a salad bowl, toss and serve cold.

Nutrition:
279 Calories | 6.5g Fat | 12g Protein

405. Lime Spinach and Chickpeas Salad

Preparation Time: 10 minutes | **Cooking time:** 0 minutes | **Servings:** 4

Ingredients:
16 ounces canned chickpeas
2 cups baby spinach leaves
½ tablespoon lime juice
2 tablespoons olive oil
1 teaspoon cumin, ground
½ teaspoon chili flakes

Directions:
Mix the chickpeas with the spinach and the rest of the ingredients in a large bowl, toss and serve cold.

Nutrition:
240 Calories | 8.2g Fat | 12g protein

406. Minty Olives and Tomatoes Salad

Preparation Time: 10 minutes | **Cooking time:** 0 minutes | **Servings:** 4

Ingredients:
1 cup kalamata olives
1 cup black olives
1 cup cherry tomatoes
4 tomatoes
1 red onion, chopped
2 tablespoons oregano, chopped
1 tablespoon mint, chopped
2 tablespoons balsamic vinegar
¼ cup olive oil
2 teaspoons Italian herbs, dried

Directions:
In a salad bowl, mix the olives with the tomatoes and the rest of the ingredients, toss, and serve cold.

Nutrition:
190 Calories | 8.1g Fat | 4.6g Protein

407. Beans and Cucumber Salad

Preparation Time: 10 minutes | **Cooking time:** 0 minutes | **Servings:** 4

Ingredients:
15 oz canned great northern beans
2 tablespoons olive oil
½ cup baby arugula
1 cup cucumber
1 tablespoon parsley
2 tomatoes, cubed
2 tablespoon balsamic vinegar

Directions:
Mix the beans with the cucumber and the rest of the ingredients in a large bowl, toss and serve cold.

Nutrition:
233 Calories | 9g Fat | 8g protein

408. Tomato and Avocado Salad

Preparation Time: 10 minutes | **Cooking time:** 0 minutes | **Servings:** 4

Ingredients:
1-pound cherry tomatoes
2 avocados
1 sweet onion, chopped
2 tablespoons lemon juice
1 and ½ tablespoons olive oil
Handful basil, chopped

Directions:
Mix the tomatoes with the avocados and the rest of the ingredients in a serving bowl, toss and serve right away.

Nutrition:
148 Calories | 7.8g Fat | 5.5g Protein

409. Arugula Salad

Preparation Time: 5 minutes | **Cooking time:** 0 minutes | **Servings:** 4

Ingredients:
Arugula leaves (4 cups)
Cherry tomatoes (1 cup)
Pine nuts (.25 cup)
Rice vinegar (1 tbsp.)
Olive/grapeseed oil (2 tbsp.)
Grated parmesan cheese (.25 cup)
Black pepper & salt (as desired)
Large sliced avocado (1)

Directions:
Peel and slice the avocado. Rinse and dry the arugula leaves, grate the cheese, and slice the cherry tomatoes into halves.
Combine the arugula, pine nuts, tomatoes, oil, vinegar, salt, pepper, and cheese.
Toss the salad to mix and portion it onto plates with the avocado slices to serve.

Nutrition:
257 Calories | 23g Fats | 6.1g Protein

410. Chickpea Salad

Preparation Time: 15 minutes | **Cooking time:** 0 minutes | **Servings:** 4

Ingredients:
Cooked chickpeas (15 oz.)
Diced Roma tomato (1)
Diced green medium bell pepper (half of 1)
Fresh parsley (1 tbsp.)
Small white onion (1)
Minced garlic (.5 tsp.)
Lemon (1 juiced)

Directions:
Chop the tomato, green pepper, and onion. Mince the garlic. Combine each of the fixings into a salad bowl and toss well.
Cover the salad to chill for at least 15 minutes in the fridge. Serve when ready.

Nutrition:
163 Calories | 7g Fats | 4g Protein

411. Chopped Israeli Mediterranean Pasta Salad

Preparation Time: 15 minutes | **Cooking time:** 2 minutes | **Servings:** 8

Ingredients:
Small bow tie or other small pasta (.5 lb.)
1/3 cup Cucumber
1/3 cup Radish
1/3 cup Tomato
1/3 cup Yellow bell pepper
1/3 cup Orange bell pepper
1/3 cup Black olives
1/3 cup Green olives
1/3 cup Red onions
1/3 cup Pepperoncini
1/3 cup Feta cheese
1/3 cup Fresh thyme leaves
Dried oregano (1 tsp.)
Dressing:
0.25 cup + more, olive oil
juice of 1 lemon

Directions:
Slice the green olives into halves. Dice the feta and pepperoncini. Finely dice the remainder of the veggies.
Prepare a pot of water with the salt, and simmer the pasta until it's al dente (checking at two minutes under the listed time). Rinse and drain in cold water.
Combine a small amount of oil with the pasta. Add the salt, pepper, oregano, thyme, and veggies. Pour in the rest of the oil, lemon juice, mix and fold in the grated feta.
Pop it into the fridge within two hours, best if overnight. Taste test and adjust the seasonings to your liking; add fresh thyme.

Nutrition:
65 Calories | 5.6g Fats | 0.8g Protein

412. Feta Tomato Salad

Preparation Time: 5 minutes | **Cooking time:** 0 minutes | **Servings:** 4

Ingredients:
Balsamic vinegar (2 tbsp.)
Freshly minced basil (1.5 tsp.) or Dried (.5 tsp.)
Salt (.5 tsp.)
Coarsely chopped sweet onion (.5 cup)
Olive oil (2 tbsp.)
Cherry or grape tomatoes (1 lb.)
Crumbled feta cheese (.25 cup.)

Directions:
Whisk the salt, basil, and vinegar. Toss the onion into the vinegar mixture for 5 minutes Slice the tomatoes into halves and stir in the tomatoes, feta cheese, and oil to serve.

Nutrition:
121 Calories | 9g Fats | 3g Protein

413. Greek Pasta Salad

Preparation Time: 5 minutes | **Cooking time:** 11 minutes | **Servings:** 4

Ingredients:
Penne pasta (1 cup)
Lemon juice (1.5 tsp.)
Red wine vinegar (2 tbsp.)
Garlic (1 clove)
Dried oregano (1 tsp.)
Black pepper and sea salt (as desired)
Olive oil (.33 cup)
Halved cherry tomatoes (5)
Red onion (half of 1 small)
Green & red bell pepper (half of 1 - each)
Cucumber (¼ of 1)
Black olives (.25 cup)
Crumbled feta cheese (.25 cup)

Directions:
Slice the cucumber and olives. Chop/dice the onion, peppers, and garlic. Slice the tomatoes into halves.
Arrange a large pot with water and salt using the high-temperature setting. Once it's boiling, add the pasta and cook for 11 minutes. Rinse it using cold water and drain in a colander.
Whisk the oil, juice, salt, pepper, vinegar, oregano, and garlic. Combine the cucumber, cheese, olives, peppers, pasta, onions, and tomatoes in a large salad dish.
Add the vinaigrette over the pasta and toss. Chill in the fridge (covered) for about three hours and serve as desired.

Nutrition:
307 Calories | 23.6g Fat | 5.4g Protein

414. Pork and Greens Salad

Preparation Time: 10 minutes | **Cooking time:** 15 minutes | **Servings:** 4

Ingredients:
1-pound pork chops
8 ounces white mushrooms, sliced
½ cup Italian dressing
6 cups mixed salad greens
6 ounces jarred artichoke hearts, drained
Salt and black pepper to the taste
½ cup basil, chopped
1 tablespoon olive oil

Directions:
Heat a pan with the oil over medium-high heat, add the pork, and brown for 5 minutes.
Add the mushrooms, stir, and sauté for 5 minutes more.
Add the dressing, artichokes, salad greens, salt, pepper, and basil, cook for 4-5 minutes, divide everything into bowls and serve.

Nutrition:
235 Calories | 6g Fat | 11g Protein

415. Mediterranean Duck Breast Salad

Preparation Time: 10 minutes | **Cooking time:** 20 minutes | **Servings:** 4

Ingredients:
3 tablespoons white wine vinegar
2 tablespoons sugar
2 oranges, peeled and cut into segments
1 teaspoon orange zest, grated
1 tablespoon lemon juice
1 teaspoon lemon zest, grated
3 tablespoons shallot, minced
2 duck breasts
1 head of frisée, torn
2 small lettuce heads
2 tablespoons chives

Directions:
Heat a small saucepan over medium-high heat, add vinegar and sugar, stir and boil for 5 minutes and take off the heat.
Add orange zest, lemon zest, and lemon juice, stir, and leave aside for a few minutes. Add shallot, salt, and pepper to taste and the oil, whisk well and leave aside for now.
Pat dry the duck pieces, score the skin, trim, and season with salt and pepper. Heat a pan over medium-high heat for 1 minute, arrange duck breast pieces skin side down, brown for 8 minutes, reduce heat to medium and cook for 4 more minutes.
Flip pieces, cook for 3 minutes, transfer to a cutting board, and cover them with foil. Put frisée and lettuce in a bowl, stir and divide between plates.
Slice duck, arrange on top, add orange segments, sprinkle chives, and drizzle the vinaigrette.

Nutrition:
320 Calories | 4g Fat | 14g Protein

416. Creamy Chicken Salad

Preparation Time: 10 minutes | **Cooking time:** 0 minute | **Servings:** 6

Ingredients:
20 ounces chicken meat
½ cup pecans, chopped
1 cup green grapes
½ cup celery, chopped
2 ounces canned mandarin oranges, drained
For the creamy cucumber salad dressing:
1 cup Greek yogurt cucumber, chopped garlic clove
1 teaspoon lemon juice

Directions:
In a bowl, mix cucumber with salt, pepper to taste, lemon juice, garlic, and yogurt, and stir very well.
In a salad bowl, mix chicken meat with grapes, pecans, oranges, and celery.
Add cucumber salad dressing, toss to coat, and keep in the fridge until you serve it.

Nutrition:
200 Calories | 3g Fat | 8g Protein

417. Chicken and Cabbage Salad

Preparation Time: 10 minutes | **Cooking time:** 6 minutes | **Servings:** 4

Ingredients:
3 medium chicken breasts

4 ounces green cabbage
5 tablespoon extra-virgin olive oil
Salt and black pepper to taste
2 tablespoons sherry vinegar tablespoon chives
¼ cup feta cheese, crumbled
¼ cup barbeque sauce
Bacon slices, cooked and crumbled

Directions:
In a bowl, mix 4 tablespoon oil with vinegar, salt and pepper to taste and stir well.
Add the shredded cabbage, toss to coat, and leave aside for now.
Season chicken with salt and pepper, heat a pan with remaining oil over medium-high heat, add chicken, cook for 6 minutes, take off heat, transfer to a bowl and mix well with barbeque sauce.
Arrange salad on serving plates, add chicken strips, sprinkle cheese, chives, and crumbled bacon, and serve right away.

Nutrition:
200 Calories | 15g Fat | 33g Protein

418. Roasted Broccoli Salad

Preparation Time: 9 minutes | **Cooking time:** 17 minutes | **Servings:** 4

Ingredients:
1 lb. broccoli
3 tablespoons olive oil, divided
1-pint cherry tomatoes
1 ½ teaspoons honey
3 cups cubed bread, whole grain
1 tablespoon balsamic vinegar
½ teaspoon black pepper
¼ teaspoon sea salt, fine
grated parmesan for serving

Directions:
Set the oven to 450, and then place a rimmed baking sheet.
Drizzle your broccoli with a tablespoon of oil, and toss to coat.
Take out from the oven, and spoon the broccoli. Leave oil at the bottom of the bowl and add in your tomatoes, toss to coat, then mix tomatoes with a tablespoon of honey. place on the same baking sheet.
Roast for fifteen minutes, and stir halfway through your cooking time.
Add in your bread, and then roast for three more minutes.
Whisk two tablespoons of oil, vinegar, and remaining honey. Season. Pour this over your broccoli mix to serve.

Nutrition:
226 Calories | 7g Protein | 12g Fat

419. Tomato Salad

Preparation Time: 22 minutes | **Cooking time:** 0 minute | **Servings:** 4

Ingredients:
1 cucumber, sliced
¼ cup sun-dried tomatoes, chopped
1 lb. tomatoes, cubed
½ cup black olives
1 red onion, sliced
1 tablespoon balsamic vinegar
¼ cup parsley, fresh & chopped
2 tablespoons olive oil

Directions:
Get out a bowl and combine all your vegetables.
To make your dressing mix all your seasoning, olive oil, and vinegar.
Toss with your salad and serve fresh.

Nutrition:
126 Calories | 2.1g Protein | 9.2g Fat

420. Feta Beet Salad

Preparation Time: 16 minutes | **Cooking time:** 0 minute | **Servings:** 4

Ingredients:
6 Red Beets, Cooked & Peeled
3 Ounces Feta Cheese, Cubed
2 Tablespoons Olive Oil
2 Tablespoons Balsamic Vinegar

Directions:
Combine everything, and then serve.

Nutrition:
230 Calories | 7.3g Protein | 12g Fat

421. Chicken and Quinoa Salad

Preparation Time: 10 minutes | **Cooking time:** 20 minutes | **Servings:** 2

Ingredients:
2 tablespoons olive oil
2 ounces quinoa
2 ounces cherry tomatoes, cut in quarters
3 ounces sweet corn
Lime juice from 1 lime
Lime zest from 1 lime, grated
2 spring onions, chopped
Small red chili pepper, chopped
Avocado
2 ounces chicken meat

Directions:
Fill water in a pan, bring to a boil over medium-high heat, add quinoa, stir, and cook for 12 minutes.
Meanwhile, put corn in a pan, heat over medium-high heat, cook for 5 minutes, and leave aside for now.
Drain quinoa, transfer to a bowl, add tomatoes, corn, coriander, onions, chili, lime zest, olive oil, and salt and black pepper to taste and toss.
In another bowl, mix avocado with lime juice and stir well.
Add this to quinoa salad, and chicken, toss to coat, and serve.

Nutrition:
320 Calories | 4g Fat | 7g Protein

422. Melon Salad

Preparation Time: 20 minutes | **Cooking time:** 0 minutes | **Servings:** 6

Ingredients:
¼ teaspoon sea salt
¼ teaspoon black pepper
1 tablespoon balsamic vinegar
1 cantaloupe
12 watermelons
2 cups mozzarella balls, fresh
1/3 cup basil, fresh & torn
2 tablespoons olive oil

Directions:
Spoon out balls of cantaloupe, then situate them in a colander over the bowl.
Using a melon baller to cut the watermelon as well
Drain fruits for ten minutes, then chill the juice. Wipe the bowl dry, and then place your fruit in it.
Mix in basil, oil, vinegar, mozzarella, and tomatoes before seasoning.
Gently mix and serve.

Nutrition:
218 Calories | 10g Protein | 13g Fat

423. Bean and Toasted Pita Salad

Preparation Time: 15 minutes | **Cooking time:** 10 minutes | **Servings:** 4

Ingredients:
3 tbsp chopped fresh mint
3 tbsp chopped fresh parsley
1 cup crumbled feta cheese
1 cup sliced romaine lettuce
½ cucumber, peeled and sliced
1 cup diced plum tomatoes
2 cups cooked pinto beans, well-drained and slightly warmed
Pepper to taste
3 tbsp extra virgin olive oil
2 tbsp ground toasted cumin seeds
2 tbsp fresh lemon juice
1/8 tsp salt
2 cloves garlic, peeled
2 6-inch whole-wheat pita bread, cut or torn into bite-sized pieces

Directions:
In a large baking sheet, spread torn pita bread and bake in a preheated 400oF oven for 6 minutes.
With the back of a knife, mash garlic and salt until paste-like. Add into a medium bowl.
Whisk in ground cumin and lemon juice. In a steady and slow stream, pour oil as you whisk continuously. Season with pepper.
In a large salad bowl, mix cucumber, tomatoes, and beans. Pour in dressing, toss to coat well.
Add mint, parsley, feta, lettuce, and toasted pita, toss to mix once again, and serve.

Nutrition:
Calories: 427 | Carbohydrates: 47.3g | Protein: 17.7g | Fat: 20.4g

424. Goat Cheese 'n Red Beans Salad

Preparation Time: 15 minutes | **Cooking time:** 0 minutes | **Servings:** 4

Ingredients:
2 cans of Red Kidney Beans, drained and rinsed well
Water or vegetable broth to cover beans
1 bunch parsley, chopped
1 1/2 cups red grape tomatoes, halved
3 cloves garlic, minced
3 tablespoons olive oil
3 tablespoons lemon juice
1/2 teaspoon salt
1/2 teaspoon white pepper
6 ounces goat cheese, crumbled

Directions:
In a large bowl, combine beans, parsley, tomatoes, and garlic.
Add olive oil, lemon juice, salt, and pepper.
Mix well and refrigerate until ready to serve.
Spoon into individual dishes topped with crumbled goat cheese.

Nutrition:
Calories: 385 | Carbohydrates: 44.0g | Protein: 22.5g | Fat: 15.0g

425. Peppers and Lentils Salad

Preparation Time: 10 minutes | **Cooking time:** 0 minutes | **Servings:** 4

Ingredients:
14 ounces canned lentils
2 spring onions
1 red bell pepper
1 green bell pepper
1 tablespoon fresh lime juice
1/3 cup coriander
2 teaspoon balsamic vinegar

Directions:
In a salad bowl, combine the lentils with the onions, bell peppers, and the rest of the ingredients, toss and serve.

Nutrition:
200 Calories | 2.45g Fat | 5.6g Protein

426. Cashews and Red Cabbage Salad

Preparation Time: 10 minutes | **Cooking time:** 0 minutes | **Servings:** 4

Ingredients:
1-pound red cabbage, shredded
2 tablespoons coriander, chopped
½ cup cashews halved
2 tablespoons olive oil
1 tomato, cubed
A pinch of salt and black pepper
1 tablespoon white vinegar

Directions:
Mix the cabbage with the coriander and the rest of the ingredients in a salad bowl, toss and serve cold.

Nutrition:
210 Calories | 6.3g Fat | 8g Protein

427. Apples and Pomegranate Salad

Preparation Time: 10 minutes | **Cooking time:** 0 minutes | **Servings:** 4

Ingredients:
3 big apples, cored and cubed
1 cup pomegranate seeds
3 cups baby arugula
1 cup walnuts, chopped
1 tablespoon olive oil
1 teaspoon white sesame seeds
2 tablespoons apple cider vinegar

Directions:
Mix the apples with the arugula and the rest of the ingredients in a bowl, toss and serve cold.

Nutrition:
160 Calories | 4.3g Fat | 10g Protein

428. Chickpeas, Corn and Black Beans Salad

Preparation Time: 10 minutes | **Cooking time:** 0 minutes | **Servings:** 4

Ingredients:
1 and ½ cups canned black beans

½ teaspoon garlic powder
2 teaspoons chili powder
1 and ½ cups canned chickpeas
1 cup baby spinach
1 avocado, pitted, peeled, and chopped
1 cup corn kernels, chopped
2 tablespoons lemon juice
1 tablespoon olive oil
1 tablespoon apple cider vinegar
1 teaspoon chives, chopped

Directions:
Mix the black beans with the garlic powder, chili powder, and the rest of the ingredients in a bowl, toss and serve cold.

Nutrition:
300 Calories | 13.4g Fat | 13g Protein

429. Celery Citrus Salad

Preparation Time: 15 minutes | **Cooking time:** 0 minutes | **Servings:** 6

Ingredients:
1 tablespoon lemon juice, fresh
¼ teaspoon sea salt, fine
¼ teaspoon black pepper
1 tablespoon olive brine
1 tablespoon olive oil
¼ cup red onion, sliced
½ cup green olives
2 oranges, peeled & sliced
3 celery stalks

Directions:
Put your oranges, olives, onion, and celery in a shallow bowl.
Blend oil, olive brine, and lemon juice, pour this over your salad.
Season with salt and pepper before serving.

Nutrition:
65 Calories | 2g Protein | 0.1g Fat

430. Broccoli Crunch Salad

Preparation Time: 10 minutes | **Cooking time:** 20 minutes | **Servings:** 4

Ingredients:
1 lb. Broccoli
3 tablespoons olive oil, divided
1-pint cherry tomatoes
1 ½ teaspoons honey, raw & divided
3 cups cubed bread, whole grain
1 tablespoon balsamic vinegar
½ teaspoon black pepper
¼ teaspoon sea salt, fine

Directions:
Set the oven to 450, and preheat a rimmed baking sheet.
Drizzle your broccoli with a tablespoon of oil, and toss to coat.
Pull out the baking sheet from the oven, and scoop the broccoli on it. Leave the oil in it, add in your tomatoes, then toss tomatoes with a tablespoon of honey. Put on the same baking sheet.
Roast for fifteen minutes, and stir halfway through your cooking time.
Add in your bread, and then roast for three more minutes.
Whisk two tablespoons of oil, vinegar, and remaining honey. Season. Drizzle over broccoli mix to serve.

Nutrition:
226 Calories | 7g Protein | 12g Fat

431. Summer Tomato Salad

Preparation Time: 20 minutes | **Cooking time:** 0 minutes | **Servings:** 4

Ingredients:
1 cucumber, sliced
¼ cup sun-dried tomatoes
1 lb. Tomatoes, cubed
½ cup black olives
1 red onion, sliced
1 tablespoon balsamic vinegar
¼ cup parsley, fresh & chopped
2 tablespoons olive oil

Directions:
Mix all your vegetables. For the dressing, mix all your seasoning, olive oil, and vinegar. Toss with your salad and serve fresh.

Nutrition:
126 Calories | 2.1g Protein | 9.2g Fat

432. Cheese Beet Salad

Preparation Time: 15 minutes | **Cooking time:** 0 minutes | **Servings:** 4

Ingredients:
6 red beets
3 ounces feta cheese
2 tablespoons olive oil
2 tablespoons balsamic vinegar

Directions:
Combine everything, and then serve.

Nutrition:
230 Calories | 7.3g Protein | 12g Fat

433. Cauliflower and Cherry Tomato Salad

Preparation Time: 15 minutes | **Cooking time:** 0 minutes | **Servings:** 4

Ingredients:
1 head cauliflower
2 tablespoons parsley
2 cups cherry tomatoes, halved
2 tablespoons lemon juice, fresh
2 tablespoons pine nuts

Directions:
Blend lemon juice, cherry tomatoes, cauliflower, and parsley then season. Garnish with pine nuts, and mix well before serving.

Nutrition:
64 Calories | 2.8g Protein | 3.3g Fat

434. Watermelon Salad

Preparation Time: 18 minutes | **Cooking time:** 0 minute | **Servings:** 6

Ingredients:
¼ teaspoon sea salt
¼ teaspoon black pepper
1 tablespoon balsamic vinegar
1 cantaloupe, quartered & seeded
12 watermelon, small & seedless
2 cups mozzarella balls, fresh
1/3 cup basil, fresh & torn
2 tablespoons olive oil

Directions:
Scoop out balls of cantaloupe, and then put them in a colander over the bowl.
With a melon baller slice the watermelon.
Allow your fruit to drain for ten minutes, and then refrigerate the juice.
Wipe the bowl dry, and then place your fruit in it.
Stir in basil, oil, vinegar, mozzarella, and tomatoes before seasoning.
Mix well and serve.

Nutrition:
218 Calories | 10g Protein | 13g Fat

435. Orange Celery Salad

Preparation Time: 16 minutes | **Cooking time:** 0 minute | **Servings:** 6

Ingredients:
1 tablespoon lemon juice, fresh
¼ teaspoon sea salt, fine
¼ teaspoon black pepper
1 tablespoon olive brine
1 tablespoon olive oil
¼ cup red onion, sliced
½ cup green olives
2 oranges, peeled & sliced
3 celery stalks, sliced diagonally in ½ inch slices

Directions:
Put your oranges, olives, onion, and celery in a shallow bowl.
Stir oil, olive brine, and lemon juice, pour this over your salad.
Season with salt and pepper before serving.

Nutrition:
65 Calories | 2g Protein | 0.2g Fat

436. Cauliflower & Tomato Salad

Preparation Time: 17 minutes | **Cooking time:** 0 minute | **Servings:** 4

Ingredients:
1 Head Cauliflower, Chopped
2 Tablespoons Parsley, Fresh & chopped
2 Cups Cherry Tomatoes, Halved
2 Tablespoons Lemon Juice, Fresh
2 Tablespoons Pine Nuts

Directions:
Incorporate lemon juice, cherry tomatoes, cauliflower, and parsley and season well. Sprinkle the pine nuts, and mix.

Nutrition:
64 Calories | 2.8g Protein | 3.3g Fat

437. Quinoa Fruit Salad

Preparation Time: 25 minutes | **Cooking time:** 0 minute | **Servings:** 4

Ingredients:
2 tablespoons honey, raw
1 cup strawberries, fresh & sliced
2 tablespoons lime juice, fresh
1 teaspoon basil, fresh & chopped
1 cup quinoa, cooked
1 mango, peeled, pitted & diced
1 cup blackberries, fresh
1 peach, pitted & diced
2 kiwis, peeled & quartered

Directions:
Start by mixing your lime juice, basil, and honey in a small bowl. In a different bowl mix your strawberries, quinoa, blackberries, peach, kiwis, and mango. Add in your honey mixture, and toss to coat before serving.

Nutrition:
159 Calories | 12g Fats | 29g protein

438. Spinach Salad with Grilled Mediterranean Vegetables

Preparation Time: 5 minutes | **Cooking time:** 10 minutes | **Servings:** 4

Ingredients:
1 small orange bell pepper, seeded and quartered
2 large Portobello mushroom caps, stemmed, sliced
1 small summer squash, cut on the bias
1 (14-ounce) can artichoke hearts, drained, rinsed, and quartered
1/4 cup olive oil, plus more to taste
Salt and freshly ground black pepper
1/2 cup feta cheese, diced
1/4 cup kalamata olives, pitted
3 cups baby spinach
1 cup packed basil leaves

Directions:
Place all vegetables in a large mixing bowl. Add 1/4 cup oil and season with salt and pepper, to taste. Toss well making sure each vegetable gets covered with oil. Place a grill pan over medium heat. Once heated, place your vegetables on the grill and cook accordingly: grill mushrooms about 5 minutes per side; peppers and squash about 3 minutes per side.
Once all the vegetables are grilled place them in a large serving bowl to slightly cool. Dice and add feta cheese, pitted olives, spinach, and basil leaves. Gently toss to mix well and drizzle more oil, to taste, if necessary, and serve.

Nutrition:
200 Calories | 6g Fat | 2g Fiber

439. Fava Bean Salad

Preparation Time: 10 minutes | **Cooking time:** 42 minutes | **Servings:** 4

Ingredients:
4.4 pounds fresh fava beans
1.4oz Pecorino flakes
1 teaspoon table salt
Black pepper to taste
3 tablespoons of extra virgin olive oil

Directions:
Start by washing the pods, shell them, and collect the beans in a container.
Put a pot full of water on the stove and bring it to a boil. Once the water is boiling, add in the shelled beans, letting them cook for no more than 4 minutes, to keep them a little crisp. At the end of cooking, rinse them under running water and strain them.
In the meantime, prepare the sauce, pouring the extra virgin olive oil into a small bowl, adding salt and pepper, and using a potato peeler, remove the lemon peel (only the yellow part, as the white part is bitter) and cut into thin strips, adding them in the bowl as well. Mix everything. Finally, pour the sauce onto the beans and stir. Serve and add the cheese flakes to bring even more flavor to the salad.

Nutrition:
193 Calories | 5.6g Carbs | 11.2g Protein | 14g Fat

440. Salmon & Avocado Salad

Preparation Time: 25-30 minutes | **Cooking time:** 0 minutes | **Servings:** 2

Ingredients:
1 lb. Salmon, Cooked & Chopped
1 lb. Shrimp, Cooked & Chopped
½ cup Avocado, Chopped
4 cups green such as spinach or spring mix
½ cup Mayonnaise
2 Tbsp Lime Juice, Fresh
1 Clove Garlic
½ cup Sour Cream
Sea Salt & Black Pepper to Taste
½ Red Onion, Minced
½ cup Cucumber, Chopped

Directions:
Combine garlic, salt, pepper, onion, mayonnaise, sour cream, and lime juice in the bowl,
In a different bowl, mix salmon, shrimp, cucumber, and avocado.
Add the mayonnaise mixture to shrimp, salmon, and then allow it to sit for twenty minutes in the fridge before serving.

Nutrition:
Calories: 309 | Protein: 28 Grams | Fat: 13 Grams | Carbs: 18 Grams

441. Tuna and Potato Salad

Preparation Time: 10 minutes | **Cooking time:** nil | **Servings:** 4

Ingredients:
1 pound baby potatoes, scrubbed, boiled
1 cup tuna chunks, drained
1 cup cherry tomatoes, halved
1 cup medium onion, thinly sliced
8 pitted black olives
2 medium hard-boiled eggs, sliced
1 head Romaine lettuce
Honey lemon mustard dressing
¼ cup olive oil
2 tablespoons lemon juice
1 tablespoon Dijon mustard
1 teaspoon dill weed, chopped
Salt as needed
Pepper as needed

Directions:
Take a small glass bowl and mix in your olive oil, honey, lemon juice, Dijon mustard, and dill. Season the mix with pepper and salt.
Add in the tuna, baby potatoes, cherry tomatoes, red onion, green beans, black olives, and toss. everything nicely.
Arrange your lettuce leaves on a beautiful serving dish to make the base of your salad.
Top them with your salad mixture and place the egg slices.
Drizzle it with the previously prepared Salad Dressing.
Serve hot.

Nutrition: (Per Serving)
Calories: 406 | Fat: 22g | Carbohydrates: 28g | Protein: 26g

442. Brown Rice, Feta, Fresh Pea, and Mint Salad

Preparation Time: 5 minutes | **Cooking time:** 25 minutes | **Servings:** 4

Ingredients:
2 c. brown rice
3 c. water
Salt
5 oz. or 141.7 g crumbled feta cheese
2 c. cooked peas
½ c. chopped mint, fresh
2 tbsps. olive oil
Salt and pepper

Directions:
Place the brown rice, water, and salt into a saucepan over medium heat, cover, and bring to boiling point.
Turn the lower heat and allow it to cook until the water has dissolved and the rice is soft but chewy. Leave to cool completely
Add the feta, peas, mint, olive oil, salt, and pepper to a salad bowl with the cooled rice and toss to combine
Serve and enjoy!

Nutrition:
Calories 613 | Fat: 18.2 g | Sat. fat 7 g | Fiber 12 g | Carbohydrates: 45 g | Sugars 9.8 g | Protein: 21 g | Sodium: 302 mg

443. Tortellini Salad with Broccoli

Preparation Time: 10 minutes | **Cooking time:** 20 minutes | **Servings:** 12

Ingredients:
1 red onion, chopped finely
1 cup sunflower seeds
1 cup raisins
3 heads fresh broccoli, cut into florets
2 tsp cider vinegar
½ cup white sugar
½ cup mayonnaise
20-oz fresh cheese-filled tortellini

Directions:
In a large pot of boiling water, cook tortellini according to the manufacturer's instructions. Drain and rinse with cold water and set aside.
Whisk vinegar, sugar, and mayonnaise to create your salad dressing.
Mix in a large bowl red onion, sunflower seeds, raisins, tortellini, and broccoli. Pour dressing and toss to coat.
Serve and enjoy.

Nutrition:
Calories: 272 | Carbohydrates: 38.7g | Protein: 5.0g | Fat: 8.1g

Chapter 6: Soups and Stews

444. Mediterranean Beef Stew

Preparation Time: 25 minutes | **Cooking time:** 8 hours | **Servings:** 6

Ingredients:
1 tablespoon olive oil
8 ounces sliced mushrooms
1 onion
2 pounds chuck roast
1 cup beef stock
1 (14½-ounce) can tomatoes with juice
½ cup tomato sauce
¼ cup balsamic vinegar
1 can black olives
½ cup garlic cloves
2 tablespoons fresh rosemary
2 tablespoons fresh parsley
1 tablespoon capers

Directions:
Heat a skillet over high heat. Add 1 tablespoon of olive oil. Once heated, cook the chuck roast. Once cooked, stir in the rest of the olive oil (if needed), then toss in the onions and mushrooms. When they have softened, transfer to the slow cooker.
Add the beef stock to the skillet to deglaze the pan, then pour it over the meat in the slow cooker.
Mix the rest of the ingredients to the slow cooker to coat.
Set the temperature on your slow cooker to low and cook for 8 hours.

Nutrition:
471 Calories | 23.4g Fat | 47.1g protein

445. Italian Meatball Soup

Preparation Time: 10 minutes | **Cooking time:** 45 minutes | **Servings:** 6

Ingredients:
1/4 - 1/2 cup freshly grated parmesan cheese (optional)
1 free-range egg
1 cup breadcrumbs, optional
2 tablespoons fresh parsley, minced
1 teaspoon dried oregano
1/2 teaspoon sea salt
½ teaspoon black pepper
3 tablespoons olive oil
For the soup...
2 quarts chicken broth or beef broth
3 tablespoons tomato paste
1 onion, diced
2 bay leaves
4-5 sprigs fresh thyme
½ teaspoon whole black peppercorns

To serve…
Fresh parmesan cheese, grated
1-2 tablespoons fresh basil leaves, torn
1-2 tablespoons fresh parsley, chopped
Salt and pepper, to taste

Directions:
Place all the meatball ingredients except the oil into a medium bowl. Using your hands, mix well and form into meatballs. Place the oil into a stockpot, place over medium heat and add the meatballs, browning on all sides.
Remove the meatballs from the pan. Add more oil to the pan if needed and then add the onion. Cook for five minutes until soft. Add the remaining soup ingredients, stir well then cook for 10 minutes.
Return the meatballs to the pan and simmer for a few minutes to warm through. Serve and enjoy.

Nutrition:
331 Calories | 14.3g Protein | 14.4g Carbs | 30.3g Fat

446. Tuscan White Bean Soup with Sausage and Kale

Preparation Time: 10 minutes | **Cooking time:** 40 minutes | **Servings:** 6

Ingredients:
¼ cup extra virgin olive oil
1 lb. hot sausage,
1 onion, chopped
1 carrot, chopped
1 stalk celery, chopped
2 cloves garlic, chopped
½ lb. kale, stems removed and chopped
4 cups chicken broth
1 x 28 oz. can cannelloni beans, rinsed and drained
1 teaspoon rosemary, dried
1 bay leaf
¼ teaspoon pepper
Salt, to taste
½ cup shredded parmesan

Directions:
Find a stockpot, pop over medium heat, and add the oil. Cook the sausage until browned on all sides. Throw in the onion, carrot, celery, and garlic then cook for a further five minutes. Add the kale and stir through. Next add the broth, beans, rosemary, and bay leaf. Stir well, bring to the boil then cover with the lid. Turn down the heat then simmer for 30 minutes. Serve and enjoy.

Nutrition:
551 Calories | 36.6g Protein | 33.4g Carbs | 30.3g Fat

447. Vegetable Soup

Preparation Time: 10 minutes | **Cooking time:** 45 minutes | **Servings:** 4

Ingredients:
Extra virgin olive oil, to taste
8 oz. sliced baby Bella mushrooms
2 medium-size zucchinis, sliced
1 bunch flat-leaf parsley, chopped
1 red onion, chopped
2 garlic cloves, chopped
2 celery ribs, chopped
2 carrots, peeled, chopped
2 golden potatoes, peeled, diced
1 teaspoon ground coriander
1/2 teaspoon turmeric powder
1/2 teaspoon sweet paprika
1/2 teaspoon thyme
Salt and pepper
1 x 32 oz. can whole peeled tomatoes
2 bay leaves
6 cups turkey or vegetable broth
1 x 15 oz. can garbanzo beans, rinsed and drained
Juice and zest of 1 lime
1/3 cup toasted pine nuts, optional

Directions:
Grab a large stockpot, add a tablespoon of olive oil, and pop over medium heat. Add the mushrooms and cook for five minutes, stirring often. Remove from the pan and pop to one side. Add the sliced zucchini and cook for another five minutes. Remove from the pan.
Add more oil and add the parsley, onions, garlic, celery, carrots, and potatoes. Stir through the spices, salt, and pepper. Cook for five minutes until the veggies are softening. Add the tomatoes, bay leaves and broth then bring to a boil.

Cover and cook on medium-low for 15 minutes. Remove the lid and add the garbanzo beans, mushrooms, and zucchini. Heat then serve and enjoy.

Nutrition:
123 Calories | 12.3g Protein | 33.4g Carbs | 19.3g Fat

448. Vegetable Lover's Chicken Soup

Preparation Time: 10 minutes | **Cooking time:** 20 minutes | **Servings:** 4

Ingredients:
1 ½ cups baby spinach
2 tbsp orzo (tiny pasta)
¼ cup dry white wine
1 14oz low sodium chicken broth
2 plum tomatoes, chopped
1/8 tsp salt
½ tsp Italian seasoning
1 large shallot, chopped
1 small zucchini, diced
8-oz chicken tenders
1 tbsp extra virgin olive oil

Directions:
In a large saucepan, heat oil over medium heat and add the chicken. Stir occasionally for 8 minutes until browned. Transfer to a plate. Set aside.
In the same saucepan, add the zucchini, Italian seasoning, shallot, and salt and stir often until the vegetables are softened, around 4 minutes.
Add the tomatoes, wine, broth, and orzo and increase the heat to high to bring the mixture to boil. Reduce the heat and simmer.
Add the cooked chicken and stir in the spinach last.
Serve hot.

Nutrition:
Calories: 207 | Carbohydrates: 14.8g | Protein: 12.2g | Fat: 11.4g

449. Spring Faro Plate

Preparation Time: 15 minutes | **Cooking time:** 0 minutes | **Servings:** 6

Ingredients:
1 cup faro, cooked
2 cups baby spinach
2 grapefruits, roughly chopped
2 tablespoons balsamic vinegar
¼ teaspoon white pepper
1 tablespoon olive oil

Directions:
Mix baby spinach and faro in the big bowl. Then add grapefruit and shake the ingredients well. Transfer the mixture to the serving plates and sprinkle with white pepper, olive oil, and balsamic vinegar.

Nutrition:
113 Calories | 12.3g Protein | 33.4g Carbs | 19.3g Fat

450. Greek Style Spring Soup

Preparation Time: 10 minutes | **Cooking time:** 20 minutes | **Servings:** 4

Ingredients:
3 cups chicken stock
½ pound chicken breast, shredded
1 tablespoon chives, chopped
1 egg, whisked
½ white onion, diced
1 bell pepper, chopped
1 tablespoon olive oil
¼ cup arborio rice
½ teaspoon salt
1 tablespoon fresh cilantro, chopped

Directions:
Pour olive oil into the stock pan and preheat it.
Add onion and bell pepper. Roast the vegetables for 3-4 minutes. Stir them from time to time.
After this, add rice and stir well.
Cook the ingredients for 3 minutes over medium heat.
Then add chicken stock and stir the soup well.
Add salt and bring the soup to a boil.
Add shredded chicken breast, cilantro, and chives. Add egg and stir it carefully.

Close the lid and simmer the soup for 5 minutes over medium heat.
Remove the cooked soup from the heat.

Nutrition:
Calories 176 | Fat: 5.6 g | Fiber 7.6g | Carbs 23.6 g | Protein: 4.6 g

451. Healthy Vegetable Soup

Preparation Time: 10 minutes | **Cooking time:** 15 minutes | **Servings:** 4

Ingredients:
1 cup can tomatoes, chopped
1 small zucchini, diced
3 oz kale, sliced
1 tbsp garlic, chopped
5 button mushrooms, sliced
2 carrots, peeled and sliced
2 celery sticks, sliced
1/2 red chili, sliced
1 onion, diced
1 tbsp olive oil
1 bay leaf
4 cups vegetable stock
1/4 tsp salt

Directions:
Add oil into the inner pot of the instant pot and set the pot on sauté mode.
Add carrots, celery, onion, and salt and cook for 2-3 minutes.
Add mushrooms and chili and cook for 2 minutes.
Add the remaining ingredients and stir everything well.
Seal the pot with the lid and cook on high for 10 minutes.
Once done, allow to release pressure naturally for 10 minutes then release remaining using quick release. Remove the lid.
Stir well and serve.

Nutrition:
Calories 100 | Fat: 3.8 g | Carbohydrates: 15.1 g | Sugar: 6.6 g | Protein: 3.5 g | Cholesterol: 0 mg

452. Delicious Okra Chicken Stew

Preparation Time: 10 minutes | **Cooking time:** 20 minutes | **Servings:** 4

Ingredients:
1 lb chicken breasts, skinless, boneless, and cubed
1 lemon juice
1/4 cup fresh parsley, chopped
1 tbsp olive oil
12 oz can tomatoes, crushed
1 tsp allspice
14 oz okra, chopped
2 cups chicken stock
1 tsp garlic, minced
1 onion, chopped
Pepper
Salt

Directions:
Add oil into the inner pot of the instant pot and set the pot on sauté mode.
Add chicken and onion and sauté until the chicken is lightly brown for about 5 minutes.
Add the remaining ingredients except for the parsley and stir well.
Seal the pot with the lid and cook on high pressure 15 for minutes.
Once done, allow to release pressure naturally for 10 minutes then release remaining using quick release. Remove the lid.
Stir well and serve.

Nutrition:
Calories 326 | Fat: 12.6 g | Carbohydrates: 15.8 g | Sugar: 6.2 g | Protein: 36.4 g | Cholesterol: 101 mg

453. Tuscan Beef Stew

Preparation Time: 10 minutes | **Cooking time:** 4 hours | **Servings:** 8

Ingredients:
2 pounds beef stew meat
4 carrots
2 (14½-ounce) cans tomatoes
1 medium onion
1 package McCormick Slow Cookers Hearty Beef Stew Seasoning
½ cup water
½ cup dry red wine

1 teaspoon rosemary leaves
8 slices Italian bread

Directions:
Place the cubed beef in the slow cooker along with the carrots, diced tomatoes, and onion wedges.
Mix the seasoning package in the ½ cup of water and stir well, making sure no lumps are remaining.
Add the red wine to the water and stir slightly.
Add the rosemary leaves to the water-and-wine mixture and then pour over the meat, stirring to ensure the meat is completely covered.
Turn the slow cooker to low and cook for 8 hours, or cook for 4 hours on high.
Serve with toasted Italian bread.

Nutrition:
329 Calories | 15g Fat | 25.6g protein

454. Sorghum Stew

Preparation Time: 10 minutes | **Cooking time:** 25 minutes | **Servings:** 5

Ingredients:
1 cup sorghum
½ cup ground sausages
½ cup tomatoes
1 jalapeno pepper, chopped
½ cup bell pepper, chopped
4 cups chicken stock

Directions:
Roast the sausages for 5 minutes in the saucepan. Then add tomatoes, jalapeno, and bell pepper. Cook the ingredients for 10 minutes. After this, add sorghum and chicken stock and boil the stew for 10 minutes more.

Nutrition:
127 Calories | 12.3g Protein | 13.4g Carbs | 19.3g Fat

455. Moroccan Lentil Soup

Preparation Time: 10 minutes | **Cooking time:** 1 hour | **Servings:** 6

Ingredients:
2 tablespoons extra virgin olive oil
1 large yellow onion, finely chopped
2 stalks celery, finely chopped
1 carrot, peeled and finely chopped
1/3 cup chopped parsley, leaves, and tender stems
1/2 cup chopped cilantro, leaves, and tender stems
5 large garlic cloves, minced
2" piece ginger, minced
1 teaspoon ground turmeric
1 teaspoon ground cinnamon
2 teaspoons sweet paprika
1/2 teaspoon Aleppo pepper (or substitute freshly ground black pepper)
1 1/4 cups dry red lentils, rinsed and picked over
1 x 15 oz. can garbanzo beans, drained
1 x 28 oz. can sieve tomatoes
7–8 cups chicken broth or vegetable broth
Coarse salt

Directions:
Grab a large saucepan, add the olive oil, and place over medium heat. Add the onion, celery, carrots, garlic, and ginger, and cook for 5 minutes until soft. Throw in the turmeric, cinnamon, paprika, and pepper and continue to cook for another 5 minutes.
Add the tomatoes and broth, stir well then bring to a simmer. Add the lentils, garbanzo beans, cilantro, and parsley. Cook uncovered for 35 minutes until the lentils become very soft. Season well then serve and enjoy.

Nutrition:
551 Calories | 36.6g Protein | 33.4g Carbs | 30.3g Fat

456. Roasted Red Pepper and Tomato Soup

Preparation Time: 10 minutes | **Cooking time:** 45 minutes | **Servings:** 4

Ingredients:
2 red bell peppers, seeded and halved
3 tomatoes, cored and halved
1/2 medium onion, quartered
2 cloves garlic, peeled and halved
1-2 tablespoons olive oil
1/4 teaspoon salt
1/4 teaspoon ground black pepper
2 cups vegetable broth
2 tablespoons tomato paste
1/4 cup fresh parsley, chopped

1/4 teaspoon Italian seasoning blend
1/4 teaspoon ground paprika
1/8 teaspoon. ground cayenne pepper, or more to taste

Directions:
Preheat your oven to 375°F. Grab a medium bowl and add the red peppers, tomatoes, onion, garlic, olive oil, and salt and pepper. Toss well to coat. Place onto a baking sheet and pop into the oven for 45 minutes until soft. Next, place the veggie broth over medium heat and add the roasted veggies, tomato paste, parsley, paprika, and cayenne.
Stir to combine then simmer for 10 minutes. Use an immersion blender to puree the soup then return to the pan. Reheat if required, add extra seasoning then serve and enjoy.

Nutrition:
531 Calories | 26.3g Protein | 33.4g Carbs | 30.3g Fat

457. Minestrone Soup

Preparation Time: 10 minutes | **Cooking time:** 1 hour | **Servings:** 4

Ingredients:
1 small white onion, minced
4 cloves garlic, minced
1/2 cup sliced carrots
1 medium zucchini sliced, then cut slices in half
1 medium yellow squash sliced, then cut slices in half
2 tablespoons minced fresh parsley
1/4 cup celery sliced
3 tablespoons olive oil
2 x 15 oz. cans cannellini beans, rinsed & drained
2 x 15 oz. cans red kidney beans, rinsed & drained
1 x 14.5 oz. can fire-roasted diced tomatoes, drained
4 cups vegetable stock
2 cups water
1 1/2 teaspoons oregano
1/2 teaspoon basil
1/4 teaspoon thyme
1 teaspoon salt
1/2 teaspoon pepper
3/4 cup small pasta shells
4 cups fresh baby spinach
1/4 cup Parmesan or Romano cheese

Directions:
Grab a stockpot and place over medium heat. Add the oil then the onions, garlic, carrots, zucchini, squash, parsley, and celery. Cook for five minutes until the veggies are getting soft. Pour in the stock, water, beans, tomatoes, herbs, and salt and pepper. Stir well. Reduce the heat, cover, and simmer for 30 minutes.
Add the pasta and spinach, stir well then cover and cook for a further 20 minutes until the pasta is cooked through. Stir through the cheese then serve and enjoy.

Nutrition:
34 Calories | 26.3g Protein | 33.4g Carbs | 30.3g Fat

458. Chicken Wild Rice Soup

Preparation Time: 10 minutes | **Cooking time:** 15 minutes | **Servings:** 6

Ingredients:
2/3 cup wild rice, uncooked
1 tablespoon onion, chopped finely
1 tablespoon fresh parsley, chopped
1 cup carrots, chopped
8-ounce chicken breast, cooked
2 tablespoon butter
1/4 cup all-purpose white flour
5 cups low-sodium chicken broth
1 tablespoon slivered almonds

Directions:
Start by adding rice and 2 cups of broth along with ½ cup water to a cooking pot. Cook the chicken until the rice is al dente and set it aside. Add butter to a saucepan and melt it.
Stir in onion and sauté until soft then add the flour and the remaining broth.
Stir it and then cook for it 1 minute then add the chicken, cooked rice, and carrots. Cook for 5 minutes on a simmer. Garnish with almonds. Serve fresh.

Nutrition:
287 Calories | 21g Protein | 35g Carbohydrates

459. Chicken Noodle Soup

Preparation Time: 10 minutes | **Cooking time:** 25 minutes | **Servings:** 2

Ingredients:
1 1/2 cups low-sodium vegetable broth
1 cup of water
1/4 teaspoon poultry seasoning
1/4 teaspoon black pepper
1 cup chicken strips
1/4 cup carrot
2-ounce egg noodles, uncooked

Directions:
Gather all the ingredients into a slow cooker and toss it. Cook the soup on high heat for 25 minutes.
Serve warm.

Nutrition:
103 Calories | 8g Protein | 11g Carbohydrates

460. Cucumber Soup

Preparation Time: 10 minutes | **Cooking time:** 0 minute | **Servings:** 4

Ingredients:
2 medium cucumbers, peeled and diced
1/3 cup sweet white onion, diced
1 green onion, diced
1/4 cup fresh mint
2 tablespoon fresh dill
2 tablespoon lemon juice
2/3 cup water
1/2 cup half and half cream
1/3 cup sour cream
1/2 teaspoon pepper
Fresh dill sprigs for garnish

Directions:
Gather all the ingredients into a food processor and toss. Puree the mixture and refrigerate for 2 hours. Garnish with dill sprigs. Serve fresh.

Nutrition:
77 Calories | 2g Protein | 6g Carbohydrates

461. Squash and Turmeric Soup

Preparation Time: 10 minutes | **Cooking time:** 30 minutes | **Servings:** 4

Ingredients:
4 cups low-sodium vegetable broth
2 medium zucchini squash, peeled and diced
2 medium yellow crookneck squash, peeled and diced
1 small onion, diced
1/2 cup frozen green peas
2 tablespoon olive oil
1/2 cup plain nonfat Greek yogurt
2 teaspoon turmeric

Directions:
Warm the broth in a saucepan on medium heat. Toss in onion, squash, and zucchini. Let it simmer for approximately 25 minutes then add oil and green peas. Cook for another 5 minutes then allow it to cool. Puree the soup using a handheld blender then add Greek yogurt and turmeric. Refrigerate it overnight and serve fresh.

Nutrition:
100 Calories | 4g Protein | 10g Carbohydrates

462. Leek, Potato and Carrot Soup

Preparation Time: 15 minutes | **Cooking time:** 25 minutes | **Servings:** 4

Ingredients:
1 - leek
¾ - cup diced and boiled potatoes
¾ - cup diced and boiled carrots
1 - garlic clove
1 - tablespoon oil
crushed pepper to taste
3 - cups low sodium chicken stock
chopped parsley for garnish
1 - bay leaf
¼ - teaspoon ground cumin

Directions:
Trim off and take away a portion of the coarse inexperienced portions of the leek, at that factor reduce daintily and flush altogether in virus water. Channel properly. Warmth the oil in an extensively based pot. Include the leek and

garlic, and sear over low warmth for two-3 minutes, till sensitive.

Include the inventory, inlet leaf, cumin, and pepper. Heat the mixture, mix constantly. Include the bubbled potatoes and carrots and stew for 10-15minutes   Modify the flavoring, eliminate the inlet leaf, and serve sprinkled generously with slashed parsley.

To make a pureed soup, manner the soup in a blender or nourishment processor till smooth Come again to the pan. Include ½ field milk. Bring to bubble and stew for 2-3minutes

Nutrition:
315 Calories | 8g Fat | 15g Carbs

463. Roasted Red Pepper Soup

Preparation Time: 30 minutes | **Cooking time:** 35 minutes | **Servings:** 4

Ingredients:
4 - cups low-sodium chicken broth
3 - red peppers
2 - medium onions
3 - tablespoon lemon juice
1 - tablespoon finely minced lemon zest
A pinch of cayenne peppers
¼ - teaspoon cinnamon
½ - cup finely minced fresh cilantro

Directions:
In a medium stockpot, consolidate each one of the fixings except for the cilantro and warmth to the point of boiling over excessive warm temperature.

Diminish the warmth and stew, ordinarily secured, for around 30 minutes, till thickened. Cool marginally. Utilizing a hand blender or nourishment processor, puree the soup. Include the cilantro and tenderly heat.

Nutrition:
265 Calories | 8g Fat | 5g Carbs

464. Yucatan Soup

Preparation Time: 10 minutes | **Cooking time:** 20 minutes | **Servings:** 4

Ingredients:
½ cup onion, chopped
8 cloves garlic, chopped
2 Serrano chili peppers, chopped
1 medium tomato, chopped
1 ½ cups chicken breast, cooked, shredded
2 six-inch corn tortillas, sliced
Nonstick cooking spray
1 tablespoon olive oil
4 cups chicken broth
1 bay leaf
¼ cup lime juice
¼ cup cilantro, chopped
1 teaspoon black pepper

Directions:
Spread the corn tortillas in a baking sheet and bake them for 3 minutes at 400ºF. Place a suitably-sized saucepan over medium heat and add oil to heat. Toss in chili peppers, garlic, and onion, then sauté until soft. Stir in broth, tomatoes, bay leaf, and chicken. Let this chicken soup cook for 10 minutes on a simmer. Stir in cilantro, lime juice, and black pepper. Garnish with baked corn tortillas. Serve.

Nutrition:
215 Calories | 21g Protein | 32g Carbohydrates

465. Zesty Taco Soup

Preparation Time: 10 minutes | **Cooking time:** 7 hours | **Servings:** 2

Ingredients:
1 ½ pounds boneless skinless chicken breast
15 ½ ounces canned dark red kidney beans
15 ½ ounces canned white corn
1 cup canned tomatoes, diced
½ cup onion
15 ½ ounces canned yellow hominy
½ cup green bell peppers
1 garlic clove
1 medium jalapeno
1 tablespoon package McCormick
2 cups chicken broth

Directions:
Add drained beans, hominy, corn, onion, garlic, jalapeno pepper, chicken, and green peppers to a Crockpot. Cover the beans-corn mixture and cook for 1 hour at High temperature. Reduce the heat to LOW and continue cooking for 6 hours. Shred the slow-cooked chicken and return to the taco soup. Serve warm.

Nutrition:
191 Calories | 21g Protein | 20g Carbohydrates

466. Southwestern Posole

Preparation Time: 10 minutes | **Cooking time:** 53 minutes | **Servings:** 4

Ingredients:
1 tablespoon olive oil
1-pound pork loin, diced
½ cup onion, chopped
1 garlic clove, chopped
28 ounces canned white hominy
4 ounces canned diced green chilis
4 cups chicken broth
¼ teaspoon black pepper

Directions:
Place a suitably-sized cooking pot over medium heat and add oil to heat. Toss in pork pieces and sauté for 4 minutes. Stir in garlic and onion, then stir for 4 minutes, or until onion is soft. Add the remaining ingredients, then cover the pork soup. Cook this for 45 minutes, or until the pork is tender. Serve warm.

Nutrition:
286 Calories | 25g Protein | 15g Carbohydrates

467. Spring Vegetable Soup

Preparation Time: 10 minutes | **Cooking time:** 45 minutes | **Servings:** 4

Ingredients:
1 cup fresh green beans, chopped
¾ cup celery, chopped
½ cup onion, chopped
½ cup carrots, chopped
½ cup mushrooms, chopped
½ cup frozen corn
1 medium Roma tomato, chopped
2 tablespoons olive oil
½ cup frozen corn
4 cups vegetable broth
1 teaspoon dried oregano leaves
1 teaspoon garlic powder

Directions:
Place a suitably-sized cooking pot over medium heat and add olive oil to heat. Toss in onion and celery, then sauté until soft. Stir in the corn and rest of the ingredients and cook the soup to boil. Now reduce its heat to a simmer and cook for 45 minutes. Serve warm.

Nutrition:
115 Calories | 3g Protein | 13g Carbohydrates

468. Seafood Corn Chowder

Preparation Time: 10 minutes | **Cooking time:** 12 minutes | **Servings:** 4

Ingredients:
1 tablespoon butter
1 cup onion, chopped
1/3 cup celery, chopped
½ cup green bell pepper, chopped
½ cup red bell pepper, chopped
1 tablespoon white flour
14 ounces chicken broth
2 cups cream
6 ounces evaporated milk
10 ounces surimi imitation crab chunks
2 cups frozen corn kernels
½ teaspoon black pepper
½ teaspoon paprika

Directions:
Place a suitably-sized saucepan over medium heat and add butter to melt. Toss in onion, green and red peppers, and celery, then sauté for 5 minutes. Stir in flour and whisk well for 2 minutes.
Pour in chicken broth and stir until it boils. Add evaporated milk, corn, surimi crab, paprika, black pepper, and creamer. Cook for 5 minutes then serve warm.

Nutrition:
175 Calories | 8g Protein | 24g Carbohydrates | 7g Fat

469. Beef Sage Soup

Preparation Time: 10 minutes | **Cooking time:** 20 minutes | **Servings:** 4

Ingredients:
½ pound ground beef
½ teaspoon ground sage
½ teaspoon black pepper
½ teaspoon dried basil

½ teaspoon garlic powder
4 slices bread, cubed
2 tablespoons olive oil
1 tablespoon herb seasoning blend
2 garlic cloves, minced
3 cups chicken broth
1 ½ cups water
4 tablespoons fresh parsley
2 tablespoons parmesan cheese, grated

Directions:
Preheat your oven to 375ºF. Mix beef with sage, basil, black pepper, and garlic powder in a bowl, then set it aside. Toss the bread cubes with olive oil on a baking sheet and bake them for 8 minutes.
Meanwhile, sauté the beef mixture in a greased cooking pot until it is browned. Stir in garlic and sauté for 2 minutes, then add parsley, water, and broth. Cover the beef soup and cook for 10 minutes on a simmer. Garnish the soup with parmesan cheese and baked bread. Serve warm.

Nutrition:
336 Calories | 26g Protein | 16g Carbohydrates

470. Cabbage Borscht

Preparation Time: 10 minutes | **Cooking time:** 1 hour and 30 minutes | **Servings:** 6

Ingredients:
2 pounds beef steaks
6 cups cold water
2 tablespoons olive oil
½ cup tomato sauce
1 medium cabbage, chopped
1 cup onion, diced
1 cup carrots, diced
1 cup turnips, peeled and diced
1 teaspoon pepper
6 tablespoons lemon juice
4 tablespoons sugar

Directions:
Start by placing steak in a large cooking pot and pour enough water to cover it. Cover the beef pot and cook it on a simmer until it is tender, then shred it using a fork. Add olive oil, onion, tomato sauce, carrots, turnips, and shredded steak to the cooking liquid in the pot.

Stir in black pepper, sugar, and lemon juice to season the soup. Cover the cabbage soup and cook on low heat for 1 ½ hour. Serve warm.

Nutrition:
212 Calories | 19g Protein | 10g Carbohydrates

471. Ground Beef Soup

Preparation Time: 10 minutes | **Cooking time:** 30 minutes | **Servings:** 4

Ingredients:
1-pound lean ground beef
½ cup onion, chopped
2 teaspoons lemon-pepper seasoning blend
1 cup beef broth
2 cups of water
1/3 cup white rice, uncooked
3 cups of frozen mixed vegetables
1 tablespoon sour cream

Directions:
Spray a saucepan with cooking oil and place it over medium heat. Toss in onion and ground beef, then sauté until brown. Stir in broth and the rest of the ingredients, then boil it. Reduce heat to a simmer, then cover the soup to cook for 30 minutes. Garnish with sour cream. Enjoy.

Nutrition:
223 Calories | 20g Protein | 20g Carbohydrates

472. Slow Cooker BBQ Chicken Pizza Soup

Preparation Time: 10 minutes | **Cooking time:** 5 hours | **Servings:** 4

Ingredients:
8 cups chicken broth
4 skinless, boneless chicken breast halves
1 (24 ounces) package frozen corn
1 red onion, diced
1 1/4 cups barbeque sauce
4 cloves garlic, minced
1 1/2 teaspoons salt
1/2 teaspoon ground black pepper
1/2 teaspoon garlic salt
1/2 cup shredded mozzarella cheese, or to taste
1/2 cup chopped fresh cilantro, or to taste

Directions:
In the slow cooker, whisk garlic salt, black pepper, salt, garlic, barbeque sauce, onion, corn, chicken, and chicken broth.
Cook over low heat for 5 hours. Take the chicken out of the slow cooker and chop it into bite-sized pieces; bring it back to the slow cooker and mix. Pour the soup into the serving bowls and add the cilantro and mozzarella cheese on top of each serving.

Nutrition:
292 Calories | 45.1g Carbohydrate | 21.4g Protein

473. Slow Cooker Beef Round Stew

Preparation Time: 15 minutes | **Cooking time:** 4 hours | **Servings:** 6

Ingredients:
1 cup all-purpose flour
salt, to taste
ground black pepper, to taste
2 pounds beef round steak, cubed
3 tablespoons vegetable oil, or as needed
8 ounces fresh mushrooms, chopped
1 large onion, chopped
1 cup chopped carrot
4 cups beef broth, divided
2 (.87 ounce) packages dry brown gravy mix
1 large potato, cubed
1/4 cup frozen peas
1/4 cup frozen corn
1/4 cup frozen lima beans
1/4 cup frozen cut green beans
1 (10.75 ounces) can condensed cream of mushroom soup (optional)

Directions:
Combine flour, black pepper, and salt in a shallow bowl. Season beef with more black pepper and salt. Add beef cubes into the flour mixture, and tap to remove excess flour. In a large skillet, heat vegetable oil over medium heat, add beef cubes, and cook in batches until all sides are browned. Transfer browned beef to a slow cooker. Add carrot, onion, and mushrooms to the skillet with the final batch of meat; place in the slow cooker. Add about 1 cup beef broth into the skillet, stir to loosen any brown bits in the skillet's bottom, then pour into the slow cooker.
Stir dry gravy mix with the remaining beef broth in a saucepan over medium heat until no lumps remain. Bring to a boil; turn heat to medium-low, and simmer for about 2 minutes until thickened. Whisk gravy into the stew. Sit in green beans, lima beans, corn, frozen peas, and potato. Add some cream of mushroom soup if you want your gravy thicker.
Cover the cooker with the lid, adjust to low heat, and cook for about 4 hours until beef is tender. Cook the stew for up to 8 hours if desired.

Nutrition:
303 Calories | 10.2g Total Fat | 27.1g Total Carbohydrate

474. Slow Cooker Chicken Pot Pie Stew

Preparation Time: 15 minutes | **Cooking time:** 5 hours | **Servings:** 6

Ingredients:
4 large skinless, boneless chicken breast halves, cut into cubes
10 medium red potatoes, quartered
1 (8 ounces) package baby carrots
1 cup chopped celery
2 (26 ounces) cans condensed cream of chicken soup
6 cubes chicken bouillon
2 teaspoons garlic salt
1 teaspoon celery salt
1 tablespoon ground black pepper
1 (16 ounces) bag frozen mixed vegetables

Directions:
In a slow cooker, combine black pepper, celery salt, garlic salt, chicken bouillon, chicken soup, celery, carrots, potatoes, and chicken; cook for 5 hours on high.
Stir in the frozen mixed vegetables and cook for another 1 hour.

Nutrition:
263 Calories | 33.7g Total Carbohydrate | 17.1g Protein

475. Slow Cooker Mediterranean Stew

Preparation Time: 10 minutes | **Cooking time:** 10 hours | **Servings:** 4

Ingredients:
1 butternut squash - peeled, seeded, and cubed
2 cups cubed eggplant, with peel
2 cups cubed zucchini
1 (10 ounces) package frozen okra, thawed
1 (8 ounces) can tomato sauce
1 cup chopped onion
1 ripe tomato, chopped
1 carrot, sliced thin
1/2 cup vegetable broth
1/3 cup raisins
1 clove garlic, chopped
1/2 teaspoon ground cumin
1/2 teaspoon ground turmeric
1/4 teaspoon crushed red pepper
1/4 teaspoon ground cinnamon
1/4 teaspoon paprika

Directions:
Mix garlic, raisins, broth, carrot, tomato, onion, tomato sauce, okra, zucchini, eggplant, and butternut squash together in a slow cooker. Use paprika, cinnamon, red pepper, turmeric, and cumin to season.
Put the cover on and cook on Low until the vegetables are soft, about 8-10 hours.

Nutrition:
122 Calories | 30.5g Total Carbohydrate | 3.4g Protein

476. Easy Lemon Chicken Soup

Preparation Time: 10 minutes | **Cooking time:** 10 minutes | **Servings:** 2

Ingredients:
1 1/2 lbs chicken breasts, boneless
3 cups chicken stock
1 tbsp fresh lemon juice
1/2 tsp garlic powder
1/2 onion, chopped
Pepper
Salt

Directions:
Add all ingredients except lemon juice into the inner pot of the instant pot and stir well.
Seal the pot with the lid and cook on high for 10 minutes.
Once done, allow to release pressure naturally. Remove the lid.
Remove chicken from pot and shred using a fork.
Return shredded chicken to the pot.
Stir in lemon juice and serve.

Nutrition:
Calories 676 | Fat: 26.2 g | Carbohydrates: 4.4 g | Sugar: 2.6 g | Protein: 99.9 g | Cholesterol: 303 mg

477. Basil Zucchini Soup

Preparation Time: 10 minutes | **Cooking time:** 15 minutes | **Servings:** 4

Ingredients:
2 zucchinis, chopped
2 tbsp fresh basil, chopped
30 oz vegetable stock
1 tbsp garlic, minced
2 cups tomatoes, chopped
1 1/2 cup corn
1 onion, chopped
1 celery stalk, chopped
1 tbsp olive oil
Pepper
Salt

Directions:
Add oil into the inner pot of the instant pot and set the pot on sauté mode.
Add onion and garlic and sauté for 5 minutes.
Add remaining ingredients except for basil and stir well.
Seal the pot with the lid and cook on high for 10 minutes.
Once done, allow to release pressure naturally for 10 minutes then release remaining using quick release. Remove the lid.
Stir in basil and serve.

Nutrition:
Calories 139 | Fat: 4.8 g | Carbohydrates: 23 g | Sugar: 8.7 g | Protein: 5.2 g | Cholesterol: 0 mg

478. Roasted Tomatoes Soup

Preparation Time: 10 minutes | **Cooking time:** 5 minutes | **Servings:** 2

Ingredients:
14 oz can fire-roasted tomatoes
1 1/2 cups vegetable stock
1/4 cup zucchini, grated
1/2 tsp dried oregano
1/2 tsp dried basil
1/2 cup heavy cream
1/2 cup parmesan cheese, grated
1 cup cheddar cheese, grated
Pepper
Salt

Directions:
Add tomatoes, stock, zucchini, oregano, basil, pepper, and salt into the instant pot and stir well. Seal the pot with the lid and cook on high for 5 minutes.
Once done, release pressure using quick release. Remove the lid.
Set pot on sauté mode. Add heavy cream, parmesan cheese, and cheddar cheese and stir well and cook until the cheese is melted.
Serve and enjoy.

Nutrition:
Calories 460 | Fat: 34.8 g | Carbohydrates: 13.5 g | Sugar: 6 g | Protein: 24.1 g | Cholesterol: 117 mg

479. Southern Style Beef Stew

Preparation Time: 10 minutes | **Cooking time:** 1 hour | **Servings:** 4

Ingredients:
1 tablespoon butter
1 1/2 pounds beef stew meat, cut into 1/2-inch pieces
1 (10 ounces) can diced tomatoes and green chilis
3 (14.5 ounces) cans stewed, diced tomatoes
1 (10 ounces) package frozen cut okra
1 (10 ounces) package frozen baby lima beans
1 (10 ounces) package frozen corn kernels
4 medium potatoes, peeled and diced

Directions:
In a Dutch oven, melt butter over medium-high heat. Add beef; brown quickly on all sides. Put stewed tomatoes and diced tomatoes with green chilies in; add corn, lima beans, and okra. Boil. Lower heat to medium.
Simmer for an hour. Add potatoes. Simmer for 30 minutes more till the meat is very tender.

Nutrition:
373 Calories | 15.2g Total Fat | 36.8g Total Carbohydrate

480. Spicy Black Bean and Quinoa Soup

Preparation Time: 15 minutes | **Cooking time:** 25 minutes | **Servings:** 4

Ingredients:
1 teaspoon olive oil
1/2 cup chopped onion
2 stalks celery, chopped
1 carrot, chopped
1 clove garlic, minced
1 teaspoon ground paprika
1/2 teaspoon red pepper flakes
2 (15 ounce) cans low-sodium chicken broth
1/2 cup water
1/2 cup quinoa
1 (15 ounces) can diced tomatoes with juice
1 (15 ounces) can black beans, drained
1 cup frozen corn
salt and ground black pepper to taste

Directions:
Heat olive oil in a big saucepan on medium-high heat. Add carrot, celery, and onion; mix and cook for 3-5 minutes till carrots and celery are crisp-tender and onion is translucent. Mix in red pepper flakes, paprika, and garlic; cook for 1 minute till fragrant.
Put quinoa, water, and chicken broth into the saucepan; simmer. Lower the heat to medium-low and cover; cook for 20 minutes till quinoa is tender.
Mix in corn, black beans, and diced tomatoes with juice; return to a simmer. Cook without a cover for 5 minutes till black beans are heated through. Season with pepper and salt.

Nutrition:
284 Calories | 49g Total Carbohydrate | 4g Cholesterol

481. Spicy Chicken Noodle Soup

Preparation Time: 10 minutes | **Cooking time:** 20 minutes | **Servings:** 6

Ingredients:
2 skinless, boneless chicken breast halves, diced
2 cloves garlic, minced
6 cups vegetable broth
3 carrots, sliced
1/2 cup frozen corn
1 (8 ounces) package dried thin rice noodles
1 red bell pepper, diced
1 teaspoon dried basil
1/2 teaspoon chili pepper flakes, or to taste

Directions:
In a big pot, cook and stir the chicken for about 5 minutes on medium heat until it turns light brown, then mix in the garlic and let it cook for around 1 minute until it becomes aromatic.
Stir corn, carrots, and vegetable broth into the chicken mixture, then boil. Stir the chili flakes, basil, red pepper, and rice noodles into the chicken mixture. Lower the heat and let it simmer for about 5 minutes until the noodles become tender.

Nutrition: Information
179 Calories | 8.2g Protein | 1.4g Total Fat

482. Spicy Chicken Vegetable Soup

Preparation Time: 10 minutes | **Cooking time:** 40 minutes | **Servings:** 6

Ingredients:
2 (49.5 fluid ounce) cans chicken broth
1 large white onion, chopped
4 large cloves garlic, sliced, or to taste
2 pounds skinless, boneless chicken thighs, cut into chunks
2 (16 ounces) bags frozen mixed vegetables
1 (28 ounces) can diced tomatoes with juice
1 (16 ounces) package frozen turnip greens with turnip pieces
1 (16 ounces) package frozen sliced okra (optional)
1 tablespoon dried oregano
1 teaspoon red pepper flakes
salt and ground black pepper to taste

Directions:
In a big pot, put garlic, onion, and chicken broth; boil. Decrease to low heat. Add in chicken thighs, allow to simmer for 10 minutes until juices run clear. Add pepper, salt, red pepper flakes, oregano, okra, turnips, tomatoes, and mixed vegetables. Let simmer for about 30 minutes, mixing from time to time, until flavors blend.

Nutrition:
310 Calories | 29.1g Total Carbohydrate | 77g Cholesterol

483. Spicy Chicken and Jicama Stew

Preparation Time: 10 minutes | **Cooking time:** 25 minutes | **Servings:** 4

Ingredients:
2 pounds cooked chicken thighs, cubed or shredded
4 cups chicken broth
1 (14.5 ounces) can diced tomatoes
2 cups diced jicama
2 cups diced onion
1 1/2 cups frozen corn
1 1/2 cups frozen peas
1 cup diced celery
1 medium yellow squash, diced
1 teaspoon salt
3/4 teaspoon ground black pepper
1/2 teaspoon cayenne pepper, or more to taste
1 cup sour cream

Directions:
In a Dutch oven or big pot, combine cayenne pepper, pepper, salt, squash, celery, peas, onion, corn, jicama, diced tomatoes with their juices, chicken broth, and chicken. On medium-high heat, bring to a low boil. Bring heat to low and simmer for 15 minutes. Adjust the spices to suit your tastes.
Add sour cream in the soup then keep simmering for 10 minutes until heated through.

Nutrition:
365 Calories | 17.9g Total Carbohydrate | 32.3g Protein

484. Spring Vegetable Noodle Soup

Preparation Time: 10 minutes | **Cooking time:** 30 minutes | **Servings:** 4

Ingredients:
1 tablespoon vegetable oil
1/2 cup chopped onion
1 clove garlic, minced
1 medium potato, peeled and chopped
1/2 cup chopped broccoli
1/2 cup frozen corn
1/2 cup torn spinach
1/2 cup chopped fresh mushrooms
1/2 cup chopped carrots
1/4 cup chopped cabbage
2 (32 fluid ounce) containers chicken broth
6 ounces egg noodles
1 cup canned white beans

Directions:
In a large pot, heat the oil over medium heat, cook the garlic and onion until they get tender. Blend in cabbage, carrots, mushrooms, spinach, corn, broccoli, and potato. Add chicken broth and boil. Turn the heat down to low. Simmer until the potato becomes tender, about 20 minutes.
Mix white beans and egg noodles into the pot, and keep on cooking until beans are heated through and noodles become tender, about 7 minutes.

Nutrition:
245 Calories | 4.9g Total Fat | 41g Total Carbohydrate

485. Stuffed Pepper Soup

Preparation Time: 10 minutes | **Cooking time:** 2 hours | **Servings:** 4

Ingredients:
1 1/2 pounds 90%-lean ground beef
1 large sweet onion, chopped
salt and ground black pepper to taste
4 bell peppers, stemmed and chopped
6 cups chicken stock
2 cups prepared salsa
2 cups tomato sauce
2 cups chopped canned tomatoes
1 cup canned black beans, drained
2 cups cooked rice
2 cups frozen corn

Directions:
On medium-high heat, heat a Dutch oven. Cook and stir the pepper, salt, beef, and onion for 5-7 minutes in the hot pan, until it turns crumbly and brown. Drain it and get rid of the grease. Put bell peppers then stir and cook for about 5 minutes until it becomes soft.
Into the ground beef mixture, stir in the black beans, canned tomatoes, tomato sauce, salsa, and chicken stock. Let it boil and lower the heat to medium and let it simmer for 45 minutes. Stir in corn and rice then simmer for 30 more minutes. Sprinkle with pepper and salt to season.

Nutrition:
353 Calories | 22.4g Protein | 13.1g Total Fat

486. Tender Pork Stew with Beans

Preparation Time: 10 minutes | **Cooking time:** 30 minutes | **Servings:** 4

Ingredients:
2 1/2 (2 pounds) pork tenderloin, trimmed and sliced 1 1/2-inch thick
salt and ground black pepper to taste
1 tablespoon olive oil, or as needed
2 onions, diced
2 red bell peppers, diced
2 tablespoons minced garlic
3 (14.5 ounces) cans diced tomatoes with green chili peppers
2 (15 ounces) cans kidney beans, rinsed and drained
1 1/2 cups beef broth
1 (4 ounces) can diced green chili peppers
2 teaspoons chili powder
1 teaspoon dried basil
1 teaspoon ground cumin
1 (9 ounces) bag frozen shelled edamame
1 (8 ounces) bag frozen corn (optional)
1 (8 ounces) bag frozen sliced carrots (optional)

Directions:
Use black pepper and salt to season the pork tenderloin.
In a heavy pot or big Dutch oven, warm up the olive oil at a moderately high level of heat. Insert the pork. Cook for 1 to 2 minutes on each side until both are brown. Put in garlic, red bell

peppers, and onion, stirring and cooking for around 10 minutes until the onion turns a little tender.

Add cumin, basil, chili powder, green chili peppers, beef broth, kidney beans, green chili peppers, and tomatoes into the pork mixture, stirring throughout. Lead the mixture to boiling point and adjust the setting to medium-low heat. Leave it simmering, covered up, for 1-1/2 to 2 hours until the pork becomes tender and starts to fall apart. During the process, stir every 15 minutes.

Mix in carrots, corn, and edamame into the stew and leave it cooking for around 5 minutes until thoroughly heated. Use the flat edge of the wooden spoon to start breaking pork up into pieces to create a shredded texture.

Nutrition:
581 Calories | 15.1g Total Fat | 39.6g Total Carbohydrate | 72g Protein

487. Garlic Squash Broccoli Soup

Preparation Time: 10 minutes | **Cooking time:** 15 minutes | **Servings:** 4

Ingredients:
1 lb butternut squash, peeled and diced
1 lb broccoli florets
1 tsp dried basil
1 tsp paprika
2 1/2 cups vegetable stock
1 tsp garlic, minced
1 tbsp olive oil
1 onion, chopped
Salt

Directions:
Add oil into the inner pot of the instant pot and set the pot on sauté mode.
Add onion and garlic and sauté for 3 minutes.
Add remaining ingredients and stir well.
Seal the pot with the lid and cook on high pressure for 12 minutes.
Once done, allow to release pressure naturally for 10 minutes then release remaining using quick release. Remove the lid.
Blend soup using an immersion blender until smooth.
Serve and enjoy.

Nutrition:
Calories 137 | Fat: 4.1 g | Carbohydrates: 24.5 g | Sugar: 6.1 g | Protein: 5 g | Cholesterol: 0 mg

488. Chicken Rice Soup

Preparation Time: 10 minutes | **Cooking time:** 9 minutes | **Servings:** 4

Ingredients:
1 lb chicken breast, boneless
2 thyme sprigs
1 tsp garlic, chopped
1/4 tsp turmeric
1 tbsp olive oil
2 tbsp fresh parsley, chopped
2 tbsp fresh lemon juice
1/4 cup rice
1/2 cup celery, diced
1/2 cup onion, chopped
2 carrots, chopped
5 cups vegetable stock
Pepper
Salt

Directions:
Add oil into the inner pot of the instant pot and set the pot on sauté mode.
Add garlic, onion, carrots, and celery and sauté for 3 minutes.
Add the rest of the ingredients and stir well.
Seal the pot with the lid and cook on high for 6 minutes.
Once done, release pressure using quick release. Remove the lid.
Shred chicken using a fork.
Serve and enjoy.

Nutrition:
Calories 237 | Fat: 6.8 g | Carbohydrates: 16.6 g | Sugar: 3.4 g | Protein: 26.2 g | Cholesterol: 73 mg

489. Mussels Soup

Preparation Time: 10 minutes | **Cooking time:** 3 minutes | **Servings:** 2

Ingredients:
6 oz mussels, cleaned
2 tsp Italian seasoning
2 tbsp olive oil
1 cup grape tomatoes, chopped
4 cups chicken stock

1/4 cup fish sauce

Directions:
Add all ingredients into the inner pot of the instant pot and stir well.
Seal the pot with the lid and cook on high for 3 minutes.
Once done, release pressure using quick release. Remove the lid.
Stir well and serve.

Nutrition:
Calories 256 | Fat: 18.6 g | Carbohydrates: 9.9 g | Sugar: 5.5 g | Protein: 14.1 g | Cholesterol: 27 mg

490. Creamy Chicken Soup

Preparation Time: 10 minutes | **Cooking time:** 10 minutes | **Servings:** 6

Ingredients:
2 lbs chicken breast, boneless and cut into chunks
8 oz cream cheese
2 tbsp taco seasoning
1 cup of salsa
2 cups chicken stock
28 oz can tomatoes, diced
Salt

Directions:
Add all ingredients except cream cheese into the instant pot.
Seal the pot with the lid and cook on high pressure for 10 minutes.
Once done, allow to release pressure naturally. Remove the lid.
Remove chicken from pot and shred using a fork.
Return shredded chicken to the pot.
Add cream cheese and stir well.
Serve and enjoy.

Nutrition:
Calories 471 | Fat: 24.1 g | Carbohydrates: 19.6 g | Sugar: 6.2 g | Protein: 43.9 g | Cholesterol: 157 mg

491. Cheesy Chicken Soup

Preparation Time: 10 minutes | **Cooking time:** 15 minutes | **Servings:** 4

Ingredients:
12 oz chicken thighs, boneless
1 cup heavy cream
2 cups cheddar cheese, shredded
3 cups chicken stock
2 tbsp olive oil
1/2 cup celery, chopped
1/4 cup hot sauce
1 tsp garlic, minced
1/4 cup onion, chopped

Directions:
Add all ingredients except cream and cheese into the instant pot and stir well.
Seal the pot with a lid and cook on high pressure for 15 minutes.
Once done, allow to release pressure naturally. Remove the lid.
Shred the chicken using a fork.
Add cream and cheese and stir until cheese is melted.
Serve and enjoy.

Nutrition:
Calories 568 | Fat: 43.6 g | Carbohydrates: 3.6 g | Sugar: 1.5 g | Protein: 40.1 g | Cholesterol: 176 mg

492. Italian Chicken Stew

Preparation Time: 10 minutes | **Cooking time:** 12 minutes | **Servings:** 6

Ingredients:
1 lb chicken breasts, boneless
2 potatoes, peeled and diced
3 carrots, cut into chunks
2 celery stalks, cut into chunks
1 onion, diced
1 tsp garlic, minced
1 tsp ground sage
1/2 tsp thyme
1/2 tsp dried basil
3 cups chicken stock
Pepper
Salt

Directions:
Add all ingredients into the inner pot of the instant pot and stir well.
Seal the pot with the lid and cook on high for 12 minutes.
Once done, allow to release pressure naturally for 10 minutes then release remaining using quick release. Remove the lid.

Remove chicken from pot and shred using a fork. Return shredded chicken to the pot.
Stir well and serve.

Nutrition:
Calories 220 | Fat: 6 g | Carbohydrates: 16.7 g | Sugar: 3.5 g | Protein: 23.9 g | Cholesterol: 67 mg

493. Creamy Carrot Tomato Soup

Preparation Time: 10 minutes | **Cooking time:** 10 minutes | **Servings:** 6

Ingredients:
4 oz can tomatoes, diced
1/2 cup heavy cream
1 cup vegetable broth
1 tbsp dried basil
1 onion, chopped
4 large carrots, peeled and chopped
1/4 cup olive oil
Pepper
Salt

Directions:
Add oil into the inner pot of the instant pot and set the pot on sauté mode.
Add onion and carrots and sauté for 5 minutes.
Add the rest of the ingredients except heavy cream and stir well.
Seal the pot with the lid and cook on high pressure for 5 minutes.
Once done, allow to release pressure naturally. Remove the lid.
Stir in heavy cream and blend soup using an immersion blender until smooth.
Serve and enjoy.

Nutrition:
Calories 144 | Fat: 12.4 g | Carbohydrates: 7.8 g | Sugar: 3.9 g | Protein: 1.8 g | Cholesterol: 14 mg

494. Basil Broccoli Soup

Preparation Time: 10 minutes | **Cooking time:** 15 minutes | **Servings:** 6

Ingredients:
1 lb broccoli florets
1 tbsp olive oil
1 tsp chili powder
1 tsp dried basil
6 cups vegetable stock
1 onion, chopped
2 leeks, chopped
Pepper
Salt

Directions:
Add oil into the inner pot of the instant pot and set the pot on sauté mode.
Add onion and leek and sauté for 5 minutes.
Add the rest of the ingredients and stir well.
Seal the pot with the lid and cook on high for 10 minutes.
Once done, allow to release pressure naturally for 10 minutes then release remaining using quick release. Remove the lid.
Blend soup using an immersion blender until smooth.
Serve and enjoy.

Nutrition:
Calories 79 | Fat: 2.9 g | Carbohydrates: 12.1 g | Sugar: 4 g | Protein: 3.2 g | Cholesterol: 0 mg

495. Shredded Chicken Soup

Preparation Time: 10 minutes | **Cooking time:** 15 minutes | **Servings:** 4

Ingredients:
3 cups chicken stock
1-pound chicken breast, shredded
½ teaspoon dried mint
½ cup Greek yogurt
½ onion, diced
1 tablespoon butter
½ teaspoon salt
½ teaspoon ground black pepper
1 tablespoon fresh dill, chopped

Directions:
Pour chicken stock in the saucepan and bring it to boil.
Add shredded chicken, dried mint, salt, and ground black pepper.
Simmer the liquid for 5 minutes over low heat.
Meanwhile, toss the butter in the skillet and melt it.
Add onion and roast it until it is light brown.
Add the cooked onion to the soup.
Then add yogurt and stir it well.
Bring the soup to a boil, add dill, and remove from the heat.
The soup is cooked.

Nutrition:
Calories 198 | Fat: 5.6 g | Fiber 7.6g | Carbs 23.6 g | Protein: 4.6 g

496. Mediterranean Rabbit Soup

Preparation Time: 5 minutes | **Cooking time:** 20 minutes | **Servings:** 4

Ingredients:
1 lb. Mussels
1 glass White dry wine
8 oz Cheese
8 oz Cream
1/2 Onions head
2 tbsp Olive oil
1 tbsp Parsley, chopped
2 Garlic, cloves
Pepper black ground, to taste

Directions:
Chop onions and garlic lightly browned in olive oil. Put the thawed mussels in this mixture, hold them a little on the fire and add the wine.
Wait until the alcohol is half evaporated, add the cheese, parsley, and black pepper.
When the cheese melts in the wine, add cream a little bit, bring it to a boil and remove from heat.

Nutrition:
Calories: 115 Kcal | Fat: 7.7 g. | Protein: 6.2 g. | Carbs: 2 g.

497. Mushroom Cream Soup

Preparation Time: 5 minutes | **Cooking time:** 20 minutes | **Servings:** 4

Ingredients:
1 lb. Champignons
1 lb. Cream 20%
2 Onion
1 oz Butter
Pepper black ground, to taste

Directions:
Peel and clean the mushrooms through a meat grinder. Add the finely chopped onion.
Fry the mixture in a pan with olive oil until the water evaporates. Salt and pepper.
Put the fried mushrooms in a saucepan, cover with cream and bring to a boil.
Can be served hot or chilled.

Nutrition:
Calories: 117 Kcal | Fat: 10.3 g. | Protein: 3.1 g | Carbs: 3.6 g.

498. Creamy Salmon Soup

Preparation Time: 5 minutes | **Cooking time:** 20 minutes | **Servings:** 6

Ingredients:
1 lb. Cream of 10%
1 lb. Potato
11 oz Salmon
10 oz Tomato
7 oz Leek
5 oz Carrot
1 Greens, bunch
2 tbsp Olive Oil
Pepper black ground, to taste

Directions:
Cut leek rings, rub carrots with a grater. Peeled potatoes cut into small cubes or cubes. Cut the salmon into cubes.
Peel the tomatoes and cut them into cubes. If the skin is badly removed, dip the tomatoes for a few seconds in boiling water.
In a saucepan, fry onions and carrots in olive oil. Add tomatoes and fry slightly. Pour 1 liter of water, bring to a boil.
When the water boils, add potatoes, salt to taste, cook for 5-7 minutes. Then add the salmon and pour in the cream. Boil until potatoes are ready (3-5 minutes).

Nutrition:
Calories: 115 Kcal | Fat: 7.7 g. | Protein: 6.2 g | Carbs: 2 g.

499. Basil and Tomato Soup

Preparation Time: 10 minutes | **Cooking time:** 25 minutes | **Servings:** 2

Ingredients:
2 tbsps. vegetable broth
1 minced garlic clove
½ c. white onion
1 chopped celery stalk
1 chopped carrot
3 c. tomatoes, chopped
Salt and pepper
2 bay leaves

1 ½ c. unsweetened almond milk
1/3 c. basil leaves

Directions:
Heat the vegetable broth in a large saucepan over medium heat. Add in garlic and onions and cook for 4 minutes. Add in carrots and celery. Cook for 1 more minute.
Mix in the tomatoes and bring to a boil. Simmer for 15 minutes. Add the almond milk, basil, and bay leaves. Season with salt and pepper to taste and serve.

Nutrition:
213 Calories | 3.9g Fat | 9g Fiber

500. Kale Chicken Soup

Preparation Time: 5 minutes | **Cooking time:** 20 minutes | **Servings:** 2

Ingredients:
1½ Tbsp Olive Oil
11½ Cups Kale, chopped
½ cup Carrot, minced
1 Cloves Garlic, minced
4 Cups Chicken Broth, low sodium
¾ cup Patina Pasta, uncooked
1 Cups Chicken, cooked & shredded
1½ Tbsp Parmesan Cheese, grated

Directions:
In a stockpot, preheat olive oil and cook for 30 seconds. Stir often, add carrot and kale. Cook for 5 minutes, continuously stirring.
Add broth, pepper, salt turning the heat to high. Bring it to a boil before adding in pasta.
Cook for ten minutes on medium heat. Pasta should be cooked, stir occasionally so it doesn't stick to the bottom.
Add chicken meat and cook for 2 more minutes. Ladle the soup and serve topped with cheese.

Nutrition:
Calories: 187 | Protein: 15 Grams | Fat: 5 Grams | Carbs: 16 Grams

501. Ajoblanco (Cold Spanish Almond Soup)

Preparation & Cooking time: 25 minutes | **Servings:** 4

Ingredients:
Blanched almonds (1 lb.)
Red wine vinegar (3 tbsp.)
Olive oil (6 tbsp.)
Ice-cold water (3 tbsp.)
Garlic (1 clove)
Salt (as desired)
Green grapes (.25 cup)

Directions:
Mince the garlic and peel the grapes.
Combine the oil, almonds, vinegar, water, salt, and garlic in a blender until it's creamy, adding water as needed to keep it thick, but pourable.
Wait for about 15 minutes and chill the delicious soup before garnishing it with the grapes.

Nutrition:
Calories: 853 | Protein: 25 grams | Fat: 77.8 grams

502. Mixed Seafood Stew

Preparation Time: 5 minutes | **Cooking time:** 25 minutes | **Servings:** 8

Ingredients:
2 tablespoons olive oil
2 teaspoons lemon peel, grated
2/3 cup white wine
2 medium onions, finely chopped
3 teaspoons garlic, minced and divided
1-pound plum tomatoes, seeded and diced
½ teaspoon red pepper flakes, crushed
2 tablespoons tomato paste
2 oz. red snapper fillets, cut into 1-inch cubes
2 pounds shrimps, peeled and deveined
2 cups clam juice
2/3 cup mayonnaise, reduced-Fat | Salt, to taste
1-pound sea scallops
2/3 cup fresh parsley, minced

Directions:
Heat olive oil in a Dutch oven on medium heat and add garlic and onions.
Sauté for about 3 minutes and add tomatoes, lemon peel, and pepper flakes.
Sauté for about 2 minutes and stir in wine, salt, tomato paste, and clam juice.
Boil this mixture and reduce it to a simmer.
Cover the lid and cook for about 10 minutes.

Toss in the shrimps, scallops, parsley, and red snapper fillets.
Cover and cook for 10 more minutes and serve topped with garlic and mayonnaise.

Nutrition:
Calories 390 | Total Fat: 15.3 g | Saturated Fat: 2.6 g | Cholesterol: 261 mg | Total Carbs 20.1 g | Dietary Fiber: 1.9 g | Sugar: 7.3 g | Protein: 39 g

503. Wild Rice Soup & Creamy Chicken

Preparation Time: 5 minutes | **Cooking time:** 15 minutes | **Servings:** 8

Ingredients:
4 cups of chicken broth
2 cups of water
2 half-cooked and boneless chicken breasts, grated
1 pack (4.5 ounces) of long-grain fast-cooking rice with a spice pack
1/2 teaspoon of salt
1/2 teaspoon of ground black pepper
3/4 cup flour
1/2 cup butter
2 cups thick cream

Directions:
Combine broth, water, and chicken in a large saucepan over medium heat. Bring to a boil, stir in the rice, and save the seasoning package. Cover and remove from heat.
Combine salt, pepper, and flour in a small bowl. Melt the butter in a medium-sized pan over medium heat. Stir the contents of the herb bag until the mixture bubbles. Reduce the heat and add the flour mixture to the tablespoon to form a roux. Stir the cream little by little until it is completely absorbed and smooth. Bake until thick, 5 minutes.
Add the cream mixture to the stock and rice — Cook over medium heat for 10 to 15 minutes.

Nutrition: (Per Serving)
Calories 462; | Fat: 36.5 grams; | Carbohydrates: 22.6 g; | Protein: 12 g; | Cholesterol: 135 mg; | Sodium: 997 mg.

Chapter 7: Side Dishes

504. Instant Pot® Salsa

Preparation Time: 9 minutes | **Cooking time:** 22 minutes | **Servings:** 12

Ingredients:
12 cups seeded diced tomatoes
6 ounces tomato paste
2 medium yellow onions
6 small jalapeño peppers
4 cloves garlic
¼ cup white vinegar
¼ cup lime juice
2 tablespoons granulated sugar
2 teaspoons salt
¼ cup chopped fresh cilantro

Directions:
Place tomatoes, tomato paste, onions, jalapeños, garlic, vinegar, lime juice, sugar, and salt in the Instant Pot® and stir well. Close it, situate steam release to Sealing. Click the Manual button and time to 20 minutes.
Once the timer beeps, quick-release the pressure. Open, stir in cilantro, and press the Cancel button.
Let salsa cool to room temperature, about 40 minutes, then transfer to a storage container and refrigerate overnight.

Nutrition:
68 Calories | 0.1g Fat | 2g Protein

505. Garlic Rice

Preparation Time: 5 minutes | **Cooking time:** 3 minutes | **Servings:** 4

Ingredients:
2 tablespoons vegetable oil
1 1/2 tablespoons chopped garlic
2 tablespoons ground pork
4 cups cooked white rice
1 1/2 teaspoons of garlic salt
ground black pepper to taste

Directions:
Heat the oil in a large frying pan over medium heat. When the oil is hot, add the garlic and ground pork. Boil and stir until the garlic is golden brown.
Stir in cooked white rice and season with garlic salt and pepper. Bake and stir until the mixture is hot and well mixed for about 3 minutes.

Nutrition: (Per Serving)
Calories 293; | Fat: 9 g; | Carbohydrates: 45.9 g; | Protein: 5.9 g | Cholesterol: 6 mg; | Sodium: 686 mg

506. Roasted Garlic Hummus

Preparation Time: 9 minutes | **Cooking time:** 33 minutes | **Servings:** 4

Ingredients:
1 cup dried chickpeas
4 cups water
1 tablespoon plus ¼ cup extra-virgin olive oil, divided
1/3 cup tahini
1 teaspoon ground cumin
½ teaspoon onion powder
¾ teaspoon salt
½ teaspoon ground black pepper
1/3 cup lemon juice
3 tablespoons mashed roasted garlic
2 tablespoons chopped fresh parsley

Directions:
Situate chickpeas, water, and 1 tablespoon oil in the Instant Pot®. Cover, press steam release to Sealing, set Manual button, and time to 30 minutes.
When the timer beeps, quick-release the pressure. Select the Cancel button and open it. Strain, reserving the cooking liquid.
Place chickpeas, remaining ¼ cup oil, tahini, cumin, onion powder, salt, pepper, lemon juice, and roasted garlic in a food processor and process until creamy. Top with parsley. Serve at room temperature.

Nutrition:
104 Calories | 6g Fat | 4g Protein

507. Tomato Salsa

Preparation Time: 5 minutes | **Cooking time:** 0 minutes | **Servings:** 6

Ingredients:
1 garlic clove, minced
4 tablespoons olive oil
5 tomatoes, cubed
1 tablespoon balsamic vinegar
¼ cup basil, chopped
1 tablespoon parsley, chopped
1 tablespoon chives, chopped
Salt and black pepper to the taste
Pita chips for serving

Directions:
In a bowl, mix the tomatoes with the garlic and the rest of the ingredients except the pita chips, stir, divide into small cups, and serve with the pita chips on the side.

Nutrition:
Calories 160, | Fat: 13.7 | Fiber 5.5 | Carbs 10.1, | Protein: 2.2

508. Black Bean Dip

Preparation Time: 14 minutes | **Cooking time:** 53 minutes | **Servings:** 16

Ingredients:
1 tablespoon olive oil
2 slices bacon
1 small onion,
3 cloves garlic
1 cup low-sodium chicken broth
1 cup dried black beans
1 (14.5-ounce) can diced tomatoes
1 small jalapeño pepper
1 teaspoon ground cumin
½ teaspoon smoked paprika
1 tablespoon lime juice
½ teaspoon dried oregano
¼ cup minced fresh cilantro
¼ teaspoon sea salt

Directions:
Press the Sauté button on the Instant Pot® and heat the oil. Add bacon and onion. Cook for 5 minutes. Cook garlic for 30 seconds. Add broth and scrape any browned bits from the bottom of the pot. Add beans, tomatoes, jalapeño, cumin, paprika, lime juice, oregano, cilantro, and salt. Press the Cancel button.
Close lid, let steam release to Sealing, set Bean button, and default time of 30 minutes. When the timer rings, let the pressure release naturally for 10 minutes. Press the Cancel button and open the lid.
Use an immersion blender to blend the ingredients. Serve warm.

Nutrition:
60 Calories | 2g Fat | 3g Protein

509. Easy Hummus

Preparation Time: 5 minutes | **Cooking time:** 5 minutes | **Servings:** 6

Ingredients:
3 Cloves Garlic, Crushed
1 Tablespoon Olive Oil
1 Teaspoon Sea Salt, Fine
16 Ounces Canned Garbanzo Beans, Drained
1 ½ Tablespoons Tahini
½ Cup Lemon Juice, Fresh

Directions:
Blend your garbanzo beans, tahini, garlic, olive oil, lemon juice, and sea salt for three to five minutes in a blender. Make sure it's mixed well. It should be fluffy and soft.
Refrigerate for at least an hour before serving with either pita bread or cut vegetables.

Nutrition:
Calories: 187 | Protein: 8 Gram | Fat: 7 Grams | Carbs: 25 Grams

510. Tasty Lasagna Rolls

Preparation Time: 10 minutes | **Cooking time:** 20 minutes | **Servings:** 6

Ingredients:
¼ tsp crushed red pepper
¼ tsp salt
½ cup shredded mozzarella cheese
½ cups parmesan cheese, shredded
1 14-oz package tofu, cubed
1 25-oz can of low-sodium marinara sauce
1 tbsp extra virgin olive oil
12 whole wheat lasagna noodles
2 tbsp Kalamata olives, chopped
3 cloves minced garlic
3 cups spinach, chopped

Directions:
Put enough water on a large pot and cook the lasagna noodles according to package instructions. Drain, rinse, and set aside until ready to use.
In a large skillet, sauté garlic over medium heat for 20 seconds. Add the tofu and spinach and cook until the spinach wilts. Transfer this mixture to a bowl and add parmesan olives, salt, red pepper, and 2/3 cup of the marinara sauce.
In a pan, spread a cup of marinara sauce on the bottom. To make the rolls, place noodles on a surface and spread ¼ cup of the tofu filling. Roll up and place it on the pan with the marinara sauce. Do this procedure until all lasagna noodles are rolled.
Place the pan over high heat and bring to a simmer. Reduce the heat to medium and let it cook for three more minutes. Sprinkle mozzarella cheese and let the cheese melt for two minutes. Serve hot.

Nutrition:
Calories: 304 | Carbohydrates: 39.2g | Protein: 23g | Fat: 19.2g

511. Red Pepper Hummus

Preparation Time: 7 minutes | **Cooking time:** 34 minutes | **Servings:** 4

Ingredients:
1 cup dried chickpeas
4 cups water
1 tablespoon plus ¼ cup extra-virgin olive oil, divided
½ cup chopped roasted red pepper, divided
1/3 cup tahini
1 teaspoon ground cumin
¾ teaspoon salt
½ teaspoon ground black pepper
¼ teaspoon smoked paprika
1/3 cup lemon juice
½ teaspoon minced garlic

Directions:
Put chickpeas, water, and 1 tablespoon oil in the Instant Pot®. Put steam release to Sealing, select Manual, and time to 30 minutes.
When the timer rings, quick-release the pressure. Click the Cancel button and open it. Drain and set aside the cooking liquid.
Process chickpeas, 1/3 cup roasted red pepper, remaining ¼ cup oil, tahini, cumin, salt, black pepper, paprika, lemon juice, and garlic using a food processor. Serve, garnished with reserved roasted red pepper on top.

Nutrition:
96 Calories | 8g Fat | 2g Protein

512. Classic Hummus

Preparation Time: 8 minutes | **Cooking time:** 30 minutes | **Servings:** 6

Ingredients:
1 cup dried chickpeas
4 cups water
1 tablespoon plus ¼ cup extra-virgin olive oil
1/3 cup tahini
1½ teaspoons ground cumin
¾ teaspoon salt
½ teaspoon ground black pepper
½ teaspoon ground coriander
1/3 cup lemon juice
1 teaspoon minced garlic

Directions:
Position chickpeas, water, and 1 tablespoon oil in the Instant Pot®. Close, select steam release to Sealing, click Manual, and time to 30 minutes. When the timer rings, quick-release the pressure and open the lid. Press the Cancel button and open the lid. Drain, reserving the cooking liquid.
Blend chickpeas, remaining ¼ cup oil, tahini, cumin, salt, pepper, coriander, lemon juice, and garlic in a food processor. Serve.

Nutrition:
152 Calories | 12g Fat | 4g Protein

513. Greek Eggplant Dip

Preparation Time: 16 minutes | **Cooking time:** 3 minutes | **Servings:** 8

Ingredients:
1 cup water
1 large eggplant
1 clove garlic
½ teaspoon salt
1 tablespoon red wine vinegar
½ cup extra-virgin olive oil
2 tablespoons minced fresh parsley

Directions:
Add water to the Instant Pot®, add the rack to the pot, and place the steamer basket on the rack. Place eggplant in a steamer basket. Close, set steam release to Sealing, turn on Manual button, and set time to 3 minutes. When the timer stops, quick-release the pressure. Click the Cancel button and open it.
Situate eggplant in a food processor and add garlic, salt, and vinegar. Pulse until smooth, about 20 pulses.
Slowly add oil to the eggplant mixture while the food processor runs continuously until oil is completely incorporated. Stir in parsley. Serve at room temperature.

Nutrition:
134 Calories | 14g Fat | 1g Protein

514. Chickpea, Parsley, and Dill Dip

Preparation Time: 11 minutes | **Cooking time:** 22 minutes | **Servings:** 6

Ingredients:
8 cups water
1 cup dried chickpeas
3 tablespoons olive oil
2 garlic cloves
2 tablespoons fresh parsley
2 tablespoons fresh dill
1 tablespoon lemon juice
¼ teaspoon salt

Directions:
Add 4 cups water and chickpeas to the Instant Pot®. Cover, place steam release to Sealing. Set Manual, and time to 1 minute. When the timer beeps, quick-release the pressure until the float valve drops, press the Cancel button, and open the lid.
Drain water, rinse the chickpeas, and return to the pot with 4 cups of freshwater. Set aside to soak for 1 hour.
Add 1 tablespoon of oil to the pot. Close, adjust steam release to Sealing, click Manual, and the time to 20 minutes. When the alarm beeps, let the pressure release for 20 minutes. Click the Cancel, open, and drain chickpeas.
Place chickpeas in a food processor or blender, and add garlic, parsley, dill, lemon juice, and remaining 2 tablespoons water. Blend for about 30 seconds.
With the processor or blender lid still in place, slowly add the remaining 2 tablespoons oil while still blending, then add salt. Serve warm or at room temperature.

Nutrition:
76 Calories | 4g Fat | 2g Protein

515. Yogurt Dip

Preparation Time: 5 minutes | **Cooking time:** 10 minutes | **Servings:** 4

Ingredients:
½ Lemon, Juiced & Zested
1 cup Greek Yogurt, Plain
1 Tablespoon Chives, Fresh & Chopped Fine
2 Teaspoons Dill, Fresh & Chopped
2 Teaspoons Thyme, Fresh & Chopped
1 Teaspoon Parsley, Fresh & Chopped
½ Teaspoon Garlic, Minced
¼ Teaspoon Sea Salt, Fine

Directions:
Get out a bowl and mix all your ingredients until they're well blended. Season with salt before refrigerating. Serve chilled.

Nutrition:
Calories: 59 | Protein: 2 Grams | Fat: 4 Grams | Carbs: 5 Grams

516. Sage Barley Mix

Preparation Time: 10 minutes | **Cooking time:** 45 minutes | **Servings:** 4

Ingredients:
1 tablespoon olive oil
1 red onion, chopped
1 tablespoon leaves, chopped
1 garlic clove, minced
14 ounces barley
½ tablespoon parmesan, grated
6 cups veggie stock
Salt and black pepper to the taste

Directions:
Heat a pan with the oil over medium heat, add the onion and garlic, stir and sauté for 5 minutes. Add the sage, barley, and the rest of the ingredients except the parmesan, stir, bring to a simmer, and cook for 40 minutes. Add the parmesan, stir, divide between plates.

Nutrition:
210 Calories | 6.5g Fat | 3.4g Fiber | 8.6g Carbs | 3.4g protein

517. Chickpeas and Beets Mix

Preparation Time: 10 minutes | **Cooking time:** 25 minutes | **Servings:** 4

Ingredients:
3 tablespoons capers, drained and chopped
Juice of 1 lemon
Zest of 1 lemon, grated
1 red onion, chopped
3 tablespoons olive oil
14 ounces canned chickpeas, drained
8 ounces beets, peeled and cubed
1 tablespoon parsley, chopped
Salt and pepper to the taste

Directions:
Heat a pan with the oil over medium heat, add the onion, lemon zest, lemon juice, and the capers and sauté for 5 minutes.
Add the rest of the ingredients, stir, and cook over medium-low heat for 20 minutes more. Divide the mix between plates and serve as a side dish.

Nutrition:
199 Calories | 4.5g Fat | 2.3g Fiber | 6.5g Carbs | 3.3g protein

518. Creamy Sweet Potatoes Mix

Preparation Time: 10 minutes | **Cooking time:** 1 hour | **Servings:** 4

Ingredients:
4 tablespoons olive oil
1 garlic clove, minced
4 medium sweet potatoes, pricked with a fork
1 red onion, sliced
3 ounces baby spinach
Zest and juice of 1 lemon
A small bunch of dill, chopped
1 and ½ tablespoons Greek yogurt
2 tablespoons tahini paste
Salt and black pepper to the taste

Directions:
Put the potatoes on a baking sheet lined with parchment paper, introduce them in the oven at 350 degrees and cook them for 1 hour. Peel the potatoes then cut them into wedges and put them in a bowl. Add the garlic, the oil, and the

rest of the ingredients, toss, divide the mix between plates and serve.

Nutrition:
214 Calories | 5.6g Fat | 3.4g Fiber | 6.5g Carbs | 3.1g protein

519. Cabbage and Mushrooms Mix

Preparation Time: 10 minutes | **Cooking time:** 15 minutes | **Servings:** 2

Ingredients:
1 yellow onion, sliced
2 tablespoons olive oil
1 tablespoon balsamic vinegar
½ pound white mushrooms, sliced
1 green cabbage head, shredded
4 spring onions, chopped
Salt and black pepper to the taste

Directions:
Heat a pan with the oil over medium heat, add the yellow onion and the spring onions and cook for 5 minutes.
Add the rest of the ingredients, cook everything for 10 minutes, divide between plates and serve.

Nutrition:
199 Calories | 4.5g Fat | 2.4g Fiber | 5.6g Carbs | 2.2g protein

520. Lemon Mushroom Rice

Preparation Time: 10 minutes | **Cooking time:** 30 minutes | **Servings:** 4

Ingredients:
2 cups chicken stock
1 yellow onion, chopped
½ pound white mushrooms, sliced
2 garlic cloves, minced
8 ounces wild rice
Juice and zest of 1 lemon
1 tablespoon chives, chopped
6 tablespoons goat cheese, crumbled
Salt and black pepper to the taste

Directions:
Heat a pot with the stock over medium heat, add the rice, onion, and the rest of the ingredients except the chives and the cheese, bring to a simmer and cook for 25 minutes. Add the remaining ingredients, cook everything for 5 minutes, divide between plates, and serve as a side dish.

Nutrition:
222 Calories | 5.5g Fat | 5.4g Fiber | 12.3g Carbs | 5.6g protein

521. Paprika and Chives Potatoes

Preparation Time: 10 minutes | **Cooking time:** 1 hour and 8 minutes | **Servings:** 4

Ingredients:
4 potatoes, scrubbed and pricked with a fork
1 tablespoon olive oil
1 celery stalk, chopped
2 tomatoes, chopped
1 teaspoon sweet paprika
Salt and black pepper to the taste
2 tablespoons chives, chopped

Directions:
Arrange the potatoes on a baking sheet lined with parchment paper, introduce them in the oven and bake at 350 degrees F for 1 hour. Cool the potatoes down, peel, and cut them into larger cubes. Heat a pan with the oil over medium heat, add the celery and the tomatoes and sauté for 2 minutes. Add the potatoes and the rest of the ingredients, toss, cook everything for 6 minutes, divide the mix between plates and serve as a side dish.

Nutrition:
233 Calories | 8.7g Fat | 4.5g Fiber | 14.4g Carbs | 6.4g protein

522. Bulgur, Kale and Cheese Mix

Preparation Time: 10 minutes | **Cooking time:** 10 minutes | **Servings:** 6

Ingredients:
4 ounces bulgur
4 ounces kale, chopped
1 tablespoon mint, chopped
3 spring onions, chopped
1 cucumber, chopped
A pinch of allspice, ground
2 tablespoons olive oil
Zest and juice of ½ lemon
4 ounces feta cheese, crumbled

Directions:
Put bulgur in a bowl, cover with hot water, aside for 10 minutes, and fluff with a fork. Heat a pan with the oil over medium heat, add the onions and the allspice and cook for 3 minutes.
Add the bulgur and the rest of the ingredients, cook everything for 5-6 minutes more, divide between plates, and serve.

Nutrition:
200 Calories | 6.7g Fat | 3.4g Fiber | 15.4g Carbs | 4.5g protein

523. Spicy Green Beans Mix

Preparation Time: 5 minutes | **Cooking time:** 15 minutes | **Servings:** 4

Ingredients:
4 teaspoons olive oil
1 garlic clove, minced
½ teaspoon hot paprika
¾ cup veggie stock
1 yellow onion, sliced
1-pound green beans, trimmed and halved
½ cup goat cheese, shredded
2 teaspoon balsamic vinegar

Directions:
Heat a pan with the oil over medium heat, add the garlic, stir, and cook for 1 minute. Add the green beans and the rest of the ingredients, toss, cook everything for 15 minutes more, divide between plates, and serve as a side dish.

Nutrition:
188 Calories | 4g Fat | 3g Fiber | 12.4g Carbs | 4.4g protein

524. Beans and Rice

Preparation Time: 10 minutes | **Cooking time:** 55 minutes | **Servings:** 6

Ingredients:
1 tablespoon olive oil
1 yellow onion, chopped
2 celery stalks, chopped
2 garlic cloves, minced
2 cups brown rice
1 and ½ cup canned black beans, rinsed and drained
4 cups water
Salt and black pepper to the taste

Directions:
Heat a pan with the oil over medium heat, add the celery, garlic, and onion, stir, and cook for 10 minutes. Add the rest of the ingredients, stir, bring to a simmer, and cook over medium heat for 45 minutes. Divide between plates and serve.

Nutrition:
224 Calories | 8.4g Fat | 3.4g Fiber | 15.3g Carbs | 6.2g protein

525. Artichoke ala Romana

Preparation Time: 10 minutes | **Cooking time:** 50 minutes | **Servings:** 3

Ingredients:
3 artichokes (ideal would be the "Mammole" variety),
1 bunch of mint
1 clove of garlic
Salt to taste
Black pepper to taste
7 tablespoons of extra virgin olive oil
1 lemon

Directions:
Start by cutting the lemon in half. Then fill a rather large bowl with water and squeeze half a lemon inside.
Take your artichokes and start removing the outer leaves by tearing them with your hands. Then cut the end of the stem and the tip of the artichoke. Once again, with your hands, spread the artichoke, and use a small knife cut into the central part to eliminate the inner beard.
Peel away the stem as well and round the end using a sharp knife. Place the artichoke in the water from step 1 and repeat this process for the others. Cover the bowl with paper towels which will keep the artichokes immersed in the water, set aside, and take care of the filling in the meantime.
Take the mint and mince it. Switch to the garlic, peel it, and mince it as well, adding it to the mint along with a pinch of salt and black pepper. Mix everything.
Drain the artichokes and beat them lightly to remove excess water, then use the mixture prepared in step 4 to stuff them. Season with salt and pepper and transfer them into a pan upside

down, keeping them rather close together. Then pour in both the oil and the water: the artichokes must be covered up to the beginning of their stems.

Cover with a lid and cook for about 30 minutes on low heat. After that, you can serve your warm artichokes ala Romana!

Nutrition:
515 Calories | 8g Carbs | 5.1g Protein | 10.4g Fiber

526. Balsamic Asparagus

Preparation Time: 10 minutes | **Cooking time:** 15 minutes | **Servings:** 4

Ingredients:
3 tablespoons olive oil
3 garlic cloves, minced
2 tablespoons shallot, chopped
Salt and black pepper to the taste
2 teaspoons balsamic vinegar
1 and ½ pound asparagus, trimmed

Directions:
Heat a pan with the oil over medium-high heat, add the garlic and the shallot and sauté for 3 minutes. Add the rest of the ingredients, cook for 12 minutes more, divide between plates, and serve as a side dish.

Nutrition:
100 Calories | 10.5g Fat | 1.2g Fiber | 2.3g Carbs | 2.1g protein

527. Lime Cucumber Mix

Preparation Time: 10 minutes | **Cooking time:** 0 minute | **Servings:** 8

Ingredients:
4 cucumbers, chopped
½ cup green bell pepper, chopped
1 yellow onion, chopped
1 chili pepper, chopped
1 garlic clove, minced
1 teaspoon parsley, chopped
2 tablespoons lime juice
1 tablespoon dill, chopped
Salt and black pepper to the taste
1 tablespoon olive oil

Directions:
In a large bowl, mix the cucumber with the bell peppers and the rest of the ingredients, toss, and serve as a side dish.

Nutrition:
123 Calories | 4.3g Fat | 2.3g Fiber | 5.6g Carbs | 2g protein

528. Walnuts Cucumber Mix

Preparation Time: 5 minutes | **Cooking time:** 0 minute | **Servings:** 2

Ingredients:
2 cucumbers, chopped
1 tablespoon olive oil
Salt and black pepper to the taste
1 red chili pepper, dried
1 tablespoon lemon juice
3 tablespoons walnuts, chopped
1 tablespoon balsamic vinegar
1 teaspoon chives, chopped

Directions:
In a bowl, mix the cucumbers with the oil and the rest of the ingredients, toss, and serve as a side dish.

Nutrition:
121 Calories | 2.3g Fat | 2g Fiber | 6.7g Carbs | 2.4g protein

529. Rosemary Beets

Preparation Time: 10 minutes | **Cooking time:** 20 minutes | **Servings:** 4

Ingredients:
4 medium beets, peeled and cubed
1/3 cup balsamic vinegar
1 teaspoon rosemary, chopped
1 garlic clove, minced
½ teaspoon Italian seasoning
1 tablespoon olive oil

Directions:
Heat a pan with the oil over medium heat, add the beets and the rest of the ingredients, toss, and cook for 20 minutes. Divide the mix between plates and serve as a side dish.

Nutrition:
165 Calories | 3.4g Fat | 4.5g Fiber | 11.3g Carbs | 2.3g protein

530. Squash and Tomatoes Mix

Preparation Time: 10 minutes | **Cooking time:** 20 minutes | **Servings:** 6

Ingredients:
5 medium squash, cubed
A pinch of salt and black pepper
3 tablespoons olive oil
1 cup pine nuts, toasted
¼ cup goat cheese, crumbled
6 tomatoes, cubed
½ yellow onion, chopped
2 tablespoons cilantro, chopped
2 tablespoons lemon juice

Directions:
Heat a pan with the oil over medium heat, add the onion and pine nuts and cook for 3 minutes. Add the squash and the rest of the ingredients, cook everything for 15 minutes, divide between plates and serve as a side dish.

Nutrition:
200 Calories | 4.5g Fat | 3.4g Fiber | 6.7g Carbs | 4g protein

531. Eggplant Carpaccio

Preparation Time: 10 minutes | **Cooking time:** 6 minutes | **Servings:** 4

Ingredients:
1.5 pounds Eggplant
¾ cup extra virgin olive oil
Lemon juice to taste
6 basil leaves
1 clove of garlic
Salt to taste
Black pepper to taste

Directions:
Start by washing the eggplants under running water and drying them well. Cut them lengthwise into thin slices, using a mandolin to obtain slices of the same thickness.
Heat a stovetop grill, put the slices of eggplants on it, salt, and turn them over to cook on both sides (cook for a couple of minutes or until they are well colored with the typical dark streaks that result from grilling). After cooking, place the eggplants on a plate and let them cool.
Now take care of the marinade: take an ovenproof dish (make sure that the dish allows for the eggplants to always be covered with the marinade so that they absorb the aromatic seasoning) and pour in the oil, the garlic, the salt, the pepper, and the basil. The marinade is ready. Now dip the eggplants in the marinade, cover the dish with plastic wrap and leave to marinate in the refrigerator for a couple of hours. Before serving, season with lemon to taste. Serve the cold eggplant carpaccio as an appetizer or side dish.

Nutrition:
376 Calories | 5.5g Carbs | 2.5g Protein | 4.5g Fiber

532. Beans and Escarole

Preparation Time: 20 minutes | **Cooking time:** 3 hours and 20 minutes | **Servings:** 3

Ingredients:
11oz Escarole
2 cloves of garlic
1 fresh chili pepper
7 teaspoons of extra virgin olive oil
Salt to taste
10.5oz Dried cannellini beans

Directions:
Soak the cannellini beans in a container by covering them with water and letting them sit like this for 12 hours. After this time, rinse the beans under running water, then pour them into a pot with plenty of water and bring to a boil. Cook over low heat for 2 and a half hours, eliminating the foam that forms on the surface with the help of a ladle. Once cooked, drain the beans, and set aside the cooking water.
Chop the chili pepper and peel two cloves of garlic. In a large saucepan, heat the olive oil with the two peeled garlic cloves, and then pour in the previously cooked beans, flavoring with the chili pepper. Add salt. Cook for 5 minutes on medium heat.
Wash and cut the escarole into strips and add them to the beans. Pour in the beans' cooking water or use vegetable broth (about 10.5oz).

Cover with a lid and cook on low heat for 20 minutes. Once the bean and escarole soup are ready, serve it very hot paired with slices of toasted bread.

Nutrition:
515 Calories | 82g Carbs | 24.5g Protein | 16g Fiber

533. Escarole ala Mediterranean

Preparation Time: 10 minutes | **Cooking time:** 25 minutes | **Servings:** 4

Ingredients:
18oz of Escarole (endive)
4 ½ tablespoons(1.8oz) pitted black olives
1 clove of garlic
1 fresh chili pepper
Extra virgin olive oil to taste
Salt to taste

Directions:
Thoroughly wash the leaves that you have detached from the stem (the ones at the base of the escarole), then thinly slice the chili pepper.
Put a saucepan on the stove and pour a little oil inside of it, add a clove of garlic and then the chili pepper. Leave to flavor for a few moments, stir and dip in the escarole leaves. Help yourself with a wooden spoon to soften them. Close with a lid and cook for 10 minutes.
After this time the leaves will have softened, season with salt, and add the pitted olives. Continue cooking for another 10 minutes.
The escarole is ready to be served on a plate and eaten while hot!

Nutrition:
87 Calories | 3.6g Carbs | 2.4g Protein | 2.1g Fiber

534. Puglia Green Beans

Preparation Time: 10 minutes | **Cooking time:** 30 minutes | **Servings:** 4

Ingredients:
2.2 pounds Green beans
2 cloves of garlic
4 tablespoons extra virgin olive oil
1 fresh hot chili pepper
Salt to taste
1-pound Peeled tomatoes

Directions:
Start with the green beans: remove any filaments, wash them with cold water and let them boil for about 15/20 minutes in salted water, then drain them in a colander.
Run the peeled tomatoes through a sieve (or vegetable mill).
Place the oil, the fresh chili pepper (after removing the internal seeds) and the crushed garlic, to brown in a pan; add the tomato sauce and cook over high heat for a few minutes, then add the green beans, season with salt, and cook for another 5 minutes, after which time you will turn off the heat.
Your fantastic Puglia green beans are ready!

Nutrition:
161 Calories | 9.3g Carbs | 9.2g sugars | 10.8g Fat

535. Bean Cream

Preparation Time: 10 minutes | **Cooking time:** 75 minutes | **Servings:** 4

Ingredients:
1 cup (7oz) dried black beans
1 Onion (about 3.5oz)
6 ½ tablespoons Butter
Salt to taste
½ teaspoon cumin powder
½ teaspoon coriander powder
1 Garlic clove

Directions:
First and foremost, soak the beans in abundant cold water for 12 hours (to save time, do it the night before).
After soaking, rinse the beans and strain them. Peel the onion and garlic, mince them, and place them in a pan to simmer with the melted butter; add the beans, a pinch of cumin, and coriander, cover with hot water and simmer again for about an hour until the beans have softened, then add salt to taste.
Take 3/4 of the beans, mash them with a fork or blend them; then mix the bean puree with the whole ones;

Nutrition:
368 Calories | 26g Carbs | 13.4g Protein | 23.4g Fat

536. Tzatziki

Preparation Time: 10 minutes | **Cooking time:** 0 minute | **Servings:** 3

Ingredients:
14 oz Greek yogurt
1 Cucumber
3 cloves of garlic
Mint
2 tablespoon of extra virgin olive oil
Salt to taste

Directions:
Wash and peel the cucumber.
Grate the cucumber and put it in a colander, add a little salt and let it rest for 30 minutes until it has lost its water. Put the grated cucumber in a bowl together with the minced garlic and mint. Then add the yogurt, salt, and oil. Mix the tzatziki with all the ingredients evenly. Decorate the tzatziki with cucumber slices or a little mint and let it rest in the fridge for at least an hour before serving.

Nutrition:
99 Calories | 4.2g Carbs | 12g Protein | 3.9g Fat

537. Mashed Potatoes

Preparation Time: 15 minutes | **Cooking time:** 60 minutes | **Servings:** 4

Ingredients:
2.2 pounds Floury yellow potatoes
6.5 fl. oz whole milk
2 tablespoons butter
2 tablespoons(1oz) Parmesan cheese to be grated
Salt to taste

Directions:
Start by boiling the potatoes: put them into a large pot and cover with plenty of cold water.
Put the pot on the stove and, from the moment the water reaches a boil, cook for 30 to 50 minutes. Remember that cooking times are always indicative and that they depend on the size of the potatoes. Therefore, it is advisable to test them with a fork from time to time: if the prongs enter easily then the potatoes are cooked. Strain them and let them cool for a few minutes, then peel while still hot.
After peeling the potatoes, pour them into the potato masher, (a vegetable mill or fork is also fine, but the consistency won't be as smooth), and subsequently into a pot.
Season with a pinch of salt. In the meantime, put the milk in a small saucepan. Cook the mashed potatoes on low heat and when the milk is hot, pour it onto the potatoes and mix with a whisk until it has been completely absorbed (it will take a few moments)
Turn off the heat and stir in the butter and Parmesan cheese.
Stir again to combine everything well and your mashed potatoes are ready!

Nutrition:
284 Calories | 37.2g Carbs | 8g Protein | 11.4g Fat

538. Genovese Pesto

Preparation Time: 20 minutes | **Cooking time:** 0 minute | **Servings:** 2

Ingredients:
1 cup(0.9oz) Basil leaves
3 ½ tablespoon of extra virgin olive oil
2 tablespoons Parmesan cheese to be grated
8 teaspoons Grated Pecorino
1 ½ tablespoons pine nuts
½ clove of garlic
Pinch of coarse salt

Directions:
Start preparing the pesto by placing the peeled garlic in the mortar together with a few coarse grains of salt. Begin pounding and, when the garlic has been reduced to a paste, add the basil leaves with another pinch of coarse salt, which will help to better break down the fibers and retain a nice bright green color.
Then crush the basil in the mortar by turning the pestle from left to right and simultaneously turning the mortar in the opposite direction. Keep doing this until a bright green liquid comes out of the basil leaves; at this point, add the pine nuts and start again to reduce them to a paste.
Add the cheeses a little at a time, stirring constantly, to make the sauce even creamier, and lastly drizzle in the extra virgin olive oil, continuing to mix with the pestle. Mix the ingredients well until you obtain a smooth sauce.

Nutrition:
303 Calories | 1g Carbs | 9.5g Protein | 29g Fat

539. Sicilian Pesto

Preparation Time: 15 minutes | **Cooking time:** 0 minute | **Servings:** 3

Ingredients:
1.1 pounds vine tomatoes
½ cup Pine nuts
10 tablespoons of extra virgin olive oil
1 clove of garlic
1 bunch of basil
7 tablespoons Parmesan cheese
5.5oz Ricotta
Salt to taste
Black pepper to taste

Directions:
Cut the tomatoes in half, remove the internal part, and squeeze them to eliminate the seeds and the excess juice. Then put the tomatoes in a mixer, add the basil leaves, which you have washed and dried, and the pine nuts.
Peel a clove of garlic, cut it in half and add it to the mixture together with the grated Parmesan and ricotta. Add salt and pepper to taste. Finally, pour in the oil and run the mixer on a low speed to keep an eye on the consistency.
When the pesto has reached the right consistency, taste to see if you need to add more salt and pepper.

Nutrition:
479 Calories | 7g Carbs | 18g Protein | 40.2g Fat

540. Cocktail Sauce

Preparation Time: 10 minutes | **Cooking time:** 0 minute | **Servings:** 3

Ingredients:
1 tablespoon Worcestershire sauce
1 teaspoon Cognac
1 tablespoon Mustard
2 tablespoons Ketchup
7oz mayonnaise

Directions:
In a bowl, mix the mayonnaise and the ketchup. Add a tablespoon of mustard and one of Worcestershire sauce and mix until smooth. Finally, add the cognac to the cocktail sauce, stirring until a smooth cream is obtained.
Put the cocktail sauce in the fridge for half an hour, then serve it to be paired with your dishes.

Nutrition:
676 Calories | 5g Carbs | 2.1g Protein | 10g Fat

541. Baked Potatoes

Preparation Time: 15 minutes | **Cooking time:** 65 minutes | **Servings:** 4

Ingredients:
2.2 pounds Golden potatoes
2 sprigs of rosemary
1 clove of garlic
7 teaspoons of extra virgin olive oil
Salt to taste

Directions:
Wash and peel the potatoes with a vegetable peeler, and after cutting them into quarters, cut them into small cubes.
In a pot, bring some water to a boil and then boil the potato cubes for 5 minutes.
After this time, strain the potatoes with a slotted spoon and transfer them to a bowl. Season with extra virgin olive oil, add salt, and mix.
Preheat the oven in ventilated mode to 400°F, leaving the baking tray that will be used to bake the potatoes inside. When the oven has reached the right temperature, remove the tray, and pour a little oil on its surface, distribute the potatoes on it and add the rosemary twigs and one whole clove of garlic, without peeling it.
Bake the potatoes for 1 hour or until they are crispy and golden. During baking, mix the potatoes at least every 20 minutes. When ready, take your potatoes out of the oven, remove the garlic clove, and let them cool.

Nutrition:
264 Calories | 37g Carbs | 5.5g Protein | 10.4g Fat | 3.5g Fibers

542. Homemade Whole Wheat Pita Bread

Preparation Time: 10 minutes | **Cooking time:** 2 hours 30 minutes | **Servings:** 12

Ingredients:
4 cups whole wheat flour (or gluten-free flour)
3 cups unbleached all-purpose flour (or gluten-free alternative)
2 1/4 cups warm water
2 Tbsp. active dry yeast
2 Tbsp. extra virgin olive oil
1 Tbsp. sea salt

Directions:
Combine the yeast and warm water in a very large mixing bowl until thoroughly combined. Stir in the salt.
Gradually stir the two flours into the mixture until you get a dough.
Lightly flour a clean, dry surface and place the dough on top. Knead until the dough becomes smooth.
Add the olive oil into a large bowl and place the dough on top. Turn the dough several times to coat in the oil. Lightly oil one side of a sheet of plastic wrap, then cover over the bowl. Place a clean kitchen towel over the bowl, then set it aside for about 2 hours to rise.
Punch down on the risen dough, then divide into 12 pieces. Roll up into balls and arrange on a lightly floured surface. Cover with a clean kitchen towel and allow to rise for about 15 minutes.
Set the oven to 475 degrees F. Place a baking sheet on the lowest rack inside.
Roll out each ball of dough until each is approximately 6 inches in diameter. Take the baking sheet out of the oven and arrange the unbaked pita on top; do not overcrowd. Bake in batches, if needed.
Bake for 12 minutes, then place on a platter. Consume within 3 days.

Nutrition:
173 Calories | 10.8g Fat | 17.8g Carbohydrates

543. Crisp Spiced Cauliflower with Feta Cheese

Preparation Time: 5 minutes | **Cooking time:** 10 minutes | **Servings:** 4

Ingredients:
3/4 lb. cauliflower, chopped
1/2 Tbsp. ground toasted cumin seeds
1 garlic clove, grated
2 Tbsp. crumbled feta cheese
1 1/2 Tbsp. freshly squeezed lemon juice
1 Tbsp. chopped fresh flat-leaf parsley
Chili flakes
Sweet smoked paprika
Sea salt
Canola oil

Directions:
Place a skillet over a high flame and heat just enough canola oil to cover the bottom.
Allow the oil to smoke slightly, then add the chopped cauliflower and stir fry for about 2 minutes or until browned and crisp. Season with salt.
Reduce to medium flame as you continue to stir fry the cauliflower. Sprinkle in the cumin, lemon juice, grated garlic, and a dash of chili flakes, then stir well to combine.
Transfer the cauliflower to a platter, then top with feta, parsley, and a dash of paprika. Serve right away.

Nutrition:
300 Calories | 19.3g Fat | 30.6g Carbohydrates

544. Spring Peas and Beans with Zesty Thyme Yogurt Sauce

Preparation Time: 5 minutes | **Cooking time:** 10 minutes | **Servings:** 4

Ingredients:
3/4 lb. fresh shelling beans, shelled
3/4 lb. fresh peas (such as English peas, edamame, etc.), shelled
1 lb. pole beans, preferably assorted (such as purple wax, Romano, and yellow)
6 young pea shoots
1/2 tsp. ground sumac
1 1/2 Tbsp. extra virgin olive oil
Sea salt

For the Zesty Thyme Yogurt Sauce:
1/4 cup Greek yogurt
1 1/2 Tbsp. fresh thyme leaves
1 garlic clove, grated
1/2 lemon, juiced, and zested
Cayenne
Sea salt

Directions:
Combine all the ingredients for the yogurt sauce in a bowl, then season to taste with salt and cayenne. Cover the bowl and refrigerate until ready to serve. Prepare a bowl of ice water and set it aside.
Boil some salted water in a saucepan, then add the fresh beans and peas. Boil for 2 minutes, or until tender, then remove immediately with a metal mesh strainer and plunge into the ice water to prevent them from being soggy.
Blot the peas and beans dry using paper towels, then place in a large bowl and set aside. Refill the bowl of ice water.
Boil the salted water in the saucepan again, then add the pole beans and cook for 2 minutes or until almost tender. Remove immediately with a metal mesh strainer and plunge into the ice water to prevent them from being soggy.
Blot the pole beans dry using paper towels, then add to the bowl of peas and beans. Toss everything to combine. Drizzle the olive oil over the peas and beans, then season with salt and sumac. Toss well to combine, then add the yogurt sauce on top. Garnish with pea shoots and thyme, then serve right away.

Nutrition:
153 Calories | 0.5g Fat | 39.1g Carbohydrates

545. Loaded Mediterranean Cauliflower Fries

Preparation Time: 5 minutes | **Cooking time:** 30 minutes | **Servings:** 4

Ingredients:
Loaded Fries:
One 12-ounce bag of frozen cauliflower fries
1 tablespoon plus 1 1/2 teaspoons za'atar
Kosher salt and freshly cracked black pepper
1/2 cup fresh parsley, leaves torn with your hands
1/4 cup finely diced red onion
1/4 cup chopped kalamata olives
1/4 cup extra-virgin olive oil
3 tablespoons chopped pickled pepperoncini
1 medium cucumber, finely diced
1/3 cup crumbled feta
Yogurt Sauce:
1 cup plain whole-milk Greek yogurt
1/2 cup fresh mint, chopped
3 tablespoons chopped capers
1/2 teaspoon ground coriander
Zest of 1 lemon plus juice of up to 2 lemons
Hot sauce, to taste
Kosher salt and freshly cracked black pepper

Directions:
For the loaded fries: Preheat the oven to 425 degrees F. Put a baking sheet in the oven for 10 minutes to heat up.
Toss the frozen cauliflower fries with 1 tablespoon of the zaatar and season with salt and pepper. Place on the hot baking sheet and bake until crispy and hot, 13 to 15 minutes depending on your oven.
While the fries are cooking, in a medium bowl, combine the parsley, onion, olives, olive oil, pepperoncini, cucumber, and the remaining 1 1/2 teaspoons za'atar. Season with pepper (the olives are salty).
For the yogurt sauce: Combine the yogurt, mint, capers, coriander, lemon zest and juice, and some hot sauce in a small mixing bowl. You may add lemon juice depending on how thick your yogurt is, or how tart you would like your sauce. Season with salt and pepper.
To finish, spread the yogurt sauce on the bottom of a plate. Place the crispy fries on top of the sauce. Top with the cucumber-olive salad and finish with the crumbled feta.

Nutrition:
115 Calories | 8g Fat | 11g Carbohydrates

546. Mediterranean Succotash

Preparation Time: 5 minutes | **Cooking time:** 12 minutes | **Servings:** 5

Ingredients:
2 tablespoons extra-virgin olive oil, 2 turns of the pan
1 red onion, diced
2 cloves garlic, chopped

2 bell peppers, yellow, red, and/or green, seeded and chopped
1 bunch asparagus, sliced on the bias, tips 1 1/2 inches long
2 cups frozen corn kernels
1 can butter beans, drained
Salt and pepper
Handful flat-leaf parsley, chopped

Directions:
Heat a medium skillet over medium-high heat. Add oil, onion, garlic, peppers. Sauté peppers, stirring frequently, 5 minutes. Add asparagus and corn, cook 3 to 5 minutes longer. Add beans and heat them through, 1 or 2 minutes.
Season with salt and pepper, to your taste, then stir in the parsley. Transfer to dinner plates or bowls and serve.

Nutrition:
115 Calories | 8g Fat | 115g Carbohydrates

547. Mediterranean Chicken Samosas with Apple Cumin Chutney

Preparation Time: 10 minutes | **Cooking time:** 33 minutes | **Servings:** 3

Ingredients:
Apple Cumin Chutney:
1/2 white onion, diced
1 green apple, peeled and cored
1 tablespoon gari, chopped
1 tablespoon brown sugar
1 teaspoon ground cumin
Salt and pepper
Plain yogurt
Samosas:
Vegetable oil
1-pound chicken thighs, ground
3/4 cup finely diced white onion (about 1/2 onion)
3/4 tablespoon garlic puree (about 2 cloves)
1 tablespoon ground cumin
1/2 teaspoon chili flakes
1 cup grated Asiago cheese
1/4 bunch fresh sage leaves, julienned
16 to 20 spring roll wrappers
1 egg, beaten

Directions:
For the chutney: In a saucepan over medium heat, sweat the onions until softened, about 4 minutes. Add the green apples and reduce the heat to low and cook until the apples soften, about 5 minutes. Add the gari, sugar, cumin, and salt and pepper to taste. Once completely softened, it only takes a couple of minutes, puree everything in a food processor. Let cool. Once the mixture is cooled, add equal parts yogurt and puree again. The chutney can be refrigerated for up to 4 days.
For the samosas: In a preheated saucepan over medium-high heat, add a little bit of vegetable oil and brown the chicken with the onions, garlic puree, cumin, and chili flakes, about 15 minutes. The chicken will render liquid as will the onions. Once browned and fully cooked through, season with salt and pepper. Let cool. Then, add the Asiago and sage. Set aside. Cut the spring roll wrappers in half, creating two long, rectangle-shaped strips.
Using a pastry brush, place egg wash on the top half of the strip. Add about 1 tablespoon of the chicken filling to the bottom half of the strip (the half that does not have the egg wash).
Starting at the bottom, fold the wrapper at a 45-degree angle, making triangles over and over as you work your way up, like folding spanakopita. Apply egg wash if needed to seal the edges once you are done folding the wrapper.
Heat a deep pot with oil to 350 degrees F. Deep-fry the samosas until lightly browned and crispy, 3 to 4 minutes.
Then drain on paper towels and season with salt and pepper while the samosas are still hot and wet. Serve the apple cumin chutney on the side with the samosas.

Nutrition:
200 Calories | 5g Fat | 2g Fiber

548. Toasted Israeli Couscous with Vegetables and Lemon-Balsamic Vinaigrette

Preparation Time: 5 minutes | **Cooking time:** 40 minutes | **Servings:** 4

Ingredients:
1/2-pound Israeli couscous
Salt

12 spears asparagus, grilled and cut into 1/4-inch pieces
1 zucchini, halved, grilled, and cut into 1-inch pieces
1 yellow squash, halved, grilled, and cut into 1-inch pieces
2 large red peppers, grilled, peeled, and diced into bite-size pieces
1/2 cup kalamata olives, pitted and chopped
2 tablespoons chopped fresh basil leaves
Freshly ground black pepper
Lemon-Balsamic Vinaigrette, recipe follows
Lemon-Balsamic Vinaigrette:
1 small shallot, minced
3 tablespoons fresh lemon juice
1 teaspoon lemon zest
3 tablespoons aged balsamic vinegar
1 tablespoon red wine vinegar
Salt and freshly ground black pepper
3/4 cup extra-virgin olive oil

Directions:
Heat large sauté pan on grates of the grill over medium heat. Add couscous and toast until lightly golden brown.
Bring 6 cups of water to a boil over high heat, add 1 tablespoon salt and toasted couscous and cook until al dente. Drain well and place in a large bowl. Add grilled vegetables, olives, basil, and vinaigrette and toss until combined; season with salt and pepper. Let sit at room temperature for 30 minutes before serving or cover and refrigerate.
Lemon-Balsamic Vinaigrette: Whisk shallot, juice, zest, vinegar, and salt and pepper together in a small bowl. Slowly whisk in oil until emulsified.

Nutrition:
200 Calories | 4g Fat | 2g Fiber

549. Elbow Macaroni with Pine Nuts, Lemon and Fennel

Preparation Time: 5 minutes | **Cooking time:** 30 minutes | **Servings:** 2

Ingredients:
Kosher salt
1/4 cup red wine vinegar
1/2 cup plus 2 tablespoons extra-virgin olive oil
1/2 cup toasted Mediterranean pine nuts
2 tablespoons finely chopped kalamata olives
1 tablespoon minced red cherry peppers
1 tablespoon chopped capers
Finely grated zest and juice of 1 lemon (about 3 tablespoons juice)
1 small fennel bulb, trimmed, cored, and thinly sliced, plus 1/2 cup fennel fronds, coarsely chopped
1/4 cup chopped fresh mint leaves
3 cups elbow macaroni (about 12 ounces)
1/2 cup freshly grated Pecorino-Romano

Directions:
Bring a large pot of salted water to a boil. In a large bowl, add the vinegar and 1/2 cup of the oil. Add the pine nuts, olives, cherry pepper, capers, and lemon zest. Toss the sliced fennel with lemon juice and a pinch of salt in a small bowl. Combine the fennel with the dressing mixture. Add the fennel fronds and mint. Season with pepper. Let it sit while you cook the pasta.
Add the pasta to the boiling water and cook according to package directions until al dente. Drain, rinse and pat dry on a sheet pan lined with a kitchen towel. In a large bowl, toss with the remaining 2 tablespoons of oil.
Add the pasta to the fennel mixture and stir to combine. Season with salt and pepper. Sprinkle the pasta with the cheese. Serve room temperature.

Nutrition:
162 Calories | 3g Fat | 2g Fiber

550. Vegetable Couscous

Preparation Time: 5 minutes | **Cooking time:** 13 minutes | **Servings:** 4

Ingredients:
2 tablespoon extra-virgin olive oil
1 bay leaf, fresh or dried
1 medium onion, chopped
1/4 zucchini, diced
1/4 yellow squash, diced
Salt and pepper
1/2 cup canned pumpkin
4 cups chicken or vegetable broth
1 1/2 teaspoons ground cumin, half a palm full
1 teaspoon coriander seeds, 1/3 palm full
2 1/4 cups couscous

1 vine ripe plum tomato, seeded and finely chopped
2 tablespoons each chopped cilantro and flat-leaf parsley
Mediterranean flatbread, for passing

Directions:
Heat a large saucepan over medium-high heat. Add oil, bay leaf, onion, zucchini, and yellow squash to the pot and season with salt and pepper.
Sauté, stirring frequently, 7 or 8 minutes. Add pumpkin and broth to the pan and stir to combine. Add cumin and coriander. Bring broth to a boil.
Add couscous to the broth, stir, cover, and remove from heat. Let stand for 5 minutes. Remove the lid from the pot and fluff couscous with a fork.
Remove bay from the pan, add finely chopped tomato, cilantro, and parsley, toss again with a fork to combine and transfer to a serving platter. Serve with warm Mediterranean flatbreads.

Nutrition:
128 Calories | 5g Fat | 1g Fiber

551. Eggplant Pesto

Preparation Time: 10 minutes | **Cooking time:** 60 minutes | **Servings:** 3

Ingredients:
2.2 pounds Eggplants
2 oz pine nuts
3 ½ tablespoons Grated Grana Padano
¼ cup of extra virgin olive oil
Mint to taste
Salt to taste
Black pepper to taste

Directions:
Wash and dry the eggplants, then arrange them on a tray lined with parchment paper, pierce them with the ends of a fork and cook in a ventilated oven preheated oven at 425°F for 45-50 minutes.
After that time, take the eggplants out of the oven and let them cool. Then remove the top end, cut them in half, and take the pulp out. Place the pulp in a strainer, place the strainer over a bowl, and press with a fork to rid them of excess water.
At this point, transfer the eggplant pulp to a mixer; add the pine nuts, the grated parmesan, and the extra virgin olive oil, then season with salt and pepper. Blend for about a minute, until you get a thick and creamy puree. Finally, add the chopped mint leaves and mix.

Nutrition:
257 Calories | 8g Carbs | 8g Protein | 21.4g Fat

552. Aioli Sauce

Preparation Time: 10 minutes | **Cooking time:** 15 minutes | **Servings:** 4

Ingredients:
4 large cloves of garlic
1 ½ cups of peanut oil
Salt to taste
1 tablespoon filtered lemon juice
White pepper to taste
3 Yolks

Directions:
Put the chopped garlic cloves in a mortar after having removed the internal germ and crush them together with the salt.
Put everything in a blender, adding the fresh egg yolks: blend and add the oil until a thick cream is formed.
At this point stop the blender and add 1 tablespoon of lemon juice; start blending again for a few seconds, then add salt and pepper and season with salt if necessary.

Nutrition:
529 Calories | 0.8g Carbs | 1.9g Protein

553. Power Pods & Hearty Hazelnuts with Mustard-y Mix

Preparation Time: 15 minutes | **Cooking time:** 15 minutes | **Servings:** 4

Ingredients:
1-lb. green beans, trimmed
3-tbsp extra-virgin olive oil (divided)
2-tsp whole grain mustard
1-tbsp red wine vinegar
1/4-tsp salt
1/4-tsp ground pepper
1/4-cup toasted hazelnuts, chopped

Directions:
Preheat your grill to high heat.
In a large mixing bowl, toss the green beans with a tablespoon of olive oil. Place the beans in a grill basket. Grill for 8 minutes until charring a few spots, stirring occasionally.
Combine and whisk together the remaining oil, mustard, vinegar, salt, and pepper in the same mixing bowl. Add the grilled beans and toss to coat evenly.
To serve, top the side dish with hazelnuts.

Nutrition:
181 Calories | 15g Total Fats | 9g Carbohydrates

554. Peppery Potatoes

Preparation Time: 10 minutes | **Cooking time:** 18 minutes | **Servings:** 4

Ingredients:
4-pcs large potatoes, cubed
4-tbsp extra-virgin olive oil (divided) 3-tbsp garlic, minced
1/2-cup coriander or cilantro, finely chopped 2-tbsp fresh lemon juice
1 3/4-tbsp paprika 2-tbsp parsley, minced Salt to taste

Directions:
Place the potatoes in a microwave-safe dish. Pour over a tablespoon of olive oil. Cover the dish tightly with plastic wrap. Heat the potatoes for seven minutes in your microwave to par-cook them.
Heat 2 tablespoons of olive oil in a pan placed over medium-low heat. Add the garlic and cover. Cook for 3 minutes or just enough not to burn the garlic. Add the coriander, and cook for 2 minutes. Transfer the garlic-coriander sauce to a bowl, and set aside.
In the same pan placed over medium heat, heat 1 tablespoon of olive oil. Add the par-cooked potatoes. Do not stir! Cook for 3 minutes until browned, flipping once with a spatula. Continue cooking until browning all the sides.
Take out the potatoes and place them on a dish. Pour over the garlic- coriander sauce and lemon juice. Add the paprika, parsley, and salt. Toss gently to coat evenly.

Nutrition:
316.2 Calories | 14.2g Total Fats | 45.2g Carbohydrates

555. Greek Guacamole Hybrid Hummus

Preparation Time: 10 minutes | **Cooking time:** 0 minute | **Servings:** 1

Ingredients:
1-15 oz. canned chickpeas, no added salt 1-pc ripe avocado, pitted and halved 1/4-cup tahini paste
1-cup fresh cilantro leaves
1/4-cup lemon juice
1-tsp ground cumin
1/4-cup extra-virgin olive oil
1-clove garlic 1/2 tsp salt

Directions:
Drain the chickpeas and reserve 2-tablespoons of the liquid. Pour the reserved liquid into your food processor and add in the drained chickpeas. Add the avocado, tahini, cilantro, lemon juice, cumin, oil, garlic, and salt. Puree the mixture into a smooth consistency.
Serve with pita chips, veggie chips, or crudités.

Nutrition:
156 Calories | 12g Total Fats | 3g Protein: 3g

556. Minty Melon & Fruity Feta with Cool Cucumber

Preparation Time: 15 minutes | **Cooking time:** 0 minute | **Servings:** 4

Ingredients:
3-cups watermelon cubes
2-pcs tomatoes, diced
1-pc lemon, zested and juiced
1-pc cucumber, peeled, seeded & diced
1/2-cup fresh mint, roughly chopped
1/2-bulb red onion, sliced
1/4-cup olive oil
Salt and pepper
1/3 -cup crumbled feta cheese

Directions:
Combine and mix the watermelon, tomatoes, lemon juice, lemon zest, cucumber, mint, red

onion, and olive oil in a large mixing bowl. Sprinkle
over the salt and pepper. Toss to combine evenly. Serve chilled with a sprinkling of crumbled feta cheese.

Nutrition:
205 Calories | 15.5g Total Fats | 18.5g Carbohydrates

557. Limassolian Lemony Steamed Spears with Cheese Chips

Preparation Time: 2 minutes | **Cooking time:** 6 minutes | **Servings:** 4

Ingredients:
1-bunch asparagus
1-tbsp olive oil
Salt and pepper
2-pcs fresh lemons
2-tbsp Mediterranean herb feta crumbled cheese

Directions:
Place the asparagus spears in your steamer. Cover the steamer, and steam for 6 minutes until tender.
Arrange the steamed spears on a serving platter. Toss with olive oil, salt, and freshly squeezed lemons.
To serve, garnish with lemon wedges and sprinkle with feta cheese.

Nutrition:
45 Calories | 1g Total Fats | 11g Carbohydrates

558. Mediterranean Minestrone

Preparation Time: 20 minutes | **Cooking time:** 15 minutes | **Servings:** 4

Ingredients:
2-tbsp olive oil
1-bulb red onion
2-cloves garlic
8-oz. turnips
3-pcs tomatoes, quartered
5-oz. oz. carrots
2-pcs small zucchini, thinly sliced
4-cups vegetable stock
2-tbsp lemon juice
1- 4-oz. can cannellini beans, rinsed and drained
1-tbsp cilantro, chopped
Lemon wedges, to serve
Crusty whole-wheat bread, to serve

Directions:
Heat 1 tbsp oil in a large pot and sauté onion, garlic, and turnip for 5 minutes.
Add tomatoes, carrots, and zucchini and sauté another 2 minutes. Add stock, lemon juice, beans, and remaining oil. Season to taste, bring to a boil, and simmer for 3-4 minutes.
Sprinkle with cilantro and serve with lemon wedges and crusty bread.

Nutrition:
190 Calories | 7g Total Fats | 29g Carbohydrates

559. Sour Cream Broccoli Casserole

Preparation Time: 15 minutes | **Cooking time:** 1 hour | **Servings:** 4

Ingredients:
2 (10.75 ounces) cans condensed cream of chicken soup
1 1/4 cups water
2 tablespoons sour cream
3 skinless, boneless chicken halves - cooked
1 (16 ounces) package frozen broccoli florets
1 cup dry bread crumbs for topping

Directions:
Set an oven to preheat to 175°C (350°F).
Mix the sour cream, water, and soup, then combine. In a 9x13-inch baking dish, pour the mixture, then add the broccoli and chicken and put in breadcrumbs to fully cover the top.
Let it bake in the preheated oven, without cover, for 30 minutes. Take off the cover and let it bake for another half an hour.

Nutrition:
200 Calories | 7g Total Fat | 18g Total Carbohydrate

560. Salsa Verde

Preparation Time: 9 minutes | **Cooking time:** 21 minutes | **Servings:** 8

Ingredients:
1-pound tomatillos

2 small jalapeño peppers
1 small onion
½ cup chopped fresh cilantro
1 teaspoon ground coriander
1 teaspoon sea salt
1½ cups water

Directions:
Cut tomatillos in half and place in the Instant Pot®. Add enough water to cover.
Close lids, set steam release to Sealing, press the Manual button and set time to 2 minutes. Once the timer beeps, release pressure naturally, for 20 minutes. Press the Cancel and open the lid.
Drain off excess water and transfer tomatillos to a food processor or blender, and add jalapeños, onion, cilantro, coriander, salt, and water. Pulse until well combined, about 20 pulses.
Wrap and cool for 2 hours before serving.

Nutrition:
27 Calories | 1g Fat | 1g Protein

561. Mediterranean Chickpea Bowl

Preparation Time: 12 minutes | **Cooking time:** 13 minutes | **Servings:** 2

Ingredients:
½ tbs. of cumin seeds
1 large julienned carrot
A ¼ cup of tomatoes (chopped)
1 medium julienned zucchini
A ¼ cup of lemon juice
2 sliced green chilies
¼ cup of olive oil
A ½ cup of chopped parsley leaves
1 minced clove of garlic
¼ tbs. salt
¼ tbs. cayenne pepper powder
A ¼ cup of radish (sliced)
3 tbs. walnuts (chopped)
1/3 feta cheese (crumbled)
1 big can of chickpeas
Proportionate salad greens

Directions:
For the salad, you will have to make a special dressing that will make the dish tasty. You need to roast the cumin seeds on a dry pan. Make sure the heat is at medium.
When the seeds begin releasing the aroma, put the seeds in a different mixing bowl.
In this bowl, add the olive oil, garlic, lemon juice, and tomatoes. Also, add the cayenne pepper and salt, and mix well to blend in all the ingredients. Take a big bowl and add the chickpeas into it. Then put in the sliced and chopped veggies, and parsley leaves.
Adding walnut pieces will add an extra crunch to the Mediterranean chickpea bowl.
Put in the seasoning you just prepared and then, mix all the ingredients well.

Nutrition:
Carbohydrate – 30g | Protein - 12g | Fat: – 38g
Calories: 492

562. Carrot Spread

Preparation Time: 10 minutes | **Cooking time:** 10 minutes | **Servings:** 4

Ingredients:
¼ cup veggie stock
A pinch of salt and black pepper
1 teaspoon onion powder
½ teaspoon garlic powder
½ teaspoon oregano, dried
1-pound carrots, sliced
½ cup coconut cream

Directions:
In your instant pot, combine all the ingredients except the cream, put the lid on, and cook on High for 10 minutes.
Release the pressure naturally for 10 minutes, transfer the carrots mix to the food processor, add the cream, pulse well, divide into bowls, and serve cold.

Nutrition:
Calories 124, | Fat: 1g | Fiber 2g, | Carbohydrates: 5g, | Protein: 8g

563. Carrot Rice

Preparation Time: 5 minutes | **Cooking time:** 25 minutes | **Servings:** 6

Ingredients:
2 cups of water
1 cube chicken broth
1 grated carrot

1 cup uncooked long-grain rice

Directions:
Bring the water to a boil in a medium-sized saucepan over medium heat. Place in the bouillon cube and let it dissolve.
Stir in the carrots and rice and bring to a boil again.
Lower the heat, cover, and simmer for 20 minutes.
Remove from heat and leave under cover for 5 minutes.

Nutrition: (Per Serving)
Calories 125; | Fat: 0.3 g; | Carbohydrates: 27.1 g; | Protein: 2.7 g; | Cholesterol: <1 mg; | Sodium: 199 mg.

564. Tomato Cream Sauce

Preparation Time: 5 minutes | **Cooking time:** 10 minutes | **Servings:** 5

Ingredients:
2 tablespoons olive oil
1 onion, diced, 1 clove of garlic
1 can diced Italian tomatoes, not drained
1 tablespoon dried basil leaves
3/4 teaspoon white sugar
1/4 teaspoon dried oregano
1/4 teaspoon salt
1/8 teaspoon ground black pepper
1/2 cup heavy cream
1 tablespoon butter

Directions:
Fry onion and garlic in olive oil over medium heat.
Add tomatoes, basil, sugar, oregano, salt, and pepper. Bring to a boil and cook for another 5 minutes or until most of the liquid has evaporated.
Remove from the heat; Stir in whipped cream and butter. Reduce the heat and simmer for another 5 minutes.

Nutrition: (Per Serving)
182 calories | 16.6 g fat | 6.7 grams of carbohydrates | 1.7 g of protein | 39 mg cholesterol | 270 mg of sodium.

565. Butternut Squash Hummus

Preparation Time: 15 minutes | **Cooking time:** 15 minutes | **Servings:** 8

Ingredients:
2 pounds butternut squash, seeded and peeled
1 tablespoon olive oil
¼ cup tahini
2 tablespoons lemon juice
2 cloves of garlic, minced
Salt and pepper to taste

Directions:
Heat the oven to 3000F.
Coat the butternut squash with olive oil.
Place in a baking dish and bake for 15 minutes in the oven.
Once the squash is cooked, place it in a food processor together with the rest of the ingredients.
Pulse until smooth.
Place in individual containers.
Put a label and store it in the fridge.
Allow to warm at room temperature before heating in the microwave oven.
Serve with carrots or celery sticks.

Nutrition:
Calories: 115 | Carbohydrates: 15.8g | Protein: 2.5g | Fat: 5.8g | Fiber: 6.7g

Chapter 8: Drinks

566. Sweet Kale Smoothie

Preparation Time: 10 minutes | **Cooking time:** 15 minutes | **Servings:** 2

Ingredients:
1 cup low-fat plain Greek yogurt
½ cup apple juice
1 apple, cored and quartered
4 Medjool dates
3 cups packed coarsely chopped kale
Juice of ½ lemon
4 ice cubes

Directions:
In a blender, combine the yogurt, apple juice, apple, and dates and pulse until smooth.
Add the kale and lemon juice and pulse until blended. Add the ice cubes and blend until smooth and thick. Pour into glasses and serve.

Nutrition:
Calories: 355 | Total fat: 2g | Saturated fat: 1g; | Carbohydrates: 77g; | Sugar: 58g | Fiber: 8g; | Protein: 11g

567. Gingerbread & Pumpkin Smoothie

Preparation Time: 15 minutes | **Cooking time:** 50 minutes | **Servings:** 1

Ingredients:
1 cup almond milk, unsweetened
2 teaspoons chia seeds
1 banana
½ cup pumpkin puree, canned
¼ teaspoon ginger, ground
¼ teaspoon cinnamon, ground
1/8 teaspoon nutmeg, ground

Directions:
Start by getting out a bowl and mix your chia seeds and almond milk. Allow them to soak for at least an hour, but you can soak them overnight. Transfer them to a blender.
Add in your remaining ingredients, and then blend until smooth. Serve chilled.

Nutrition:
250 Calories | 13g Fats | 26g protein

568. Walnut & Date Smoothie

Preparation Time: 10 minutes | **Cooking time:** 0 minute | **Servings:** 2

Ingredients:
4 dates, pitted
½ cup milk
2 cups Greek yogurt, plain
1/2 cup walnuts
½ teaspoon cinnamon, ground
½ teaspoon vanilla extract, pure
2-3 ice cubes

Directions:
Blend everything until smooth, and then serve chilled.

Nutrition:
109 Calories | 11g Fats | 29g protein

569. Avocado-Blueberry Smoothie

Preparation Time: 5 minutes | **Cooking time:** 0 minutes | **Servings:** 2

Ingredients:
½ cup unsweetened vanilla almond milk
½ cup low-fat plain Greek yogurt
1 ripe avocado, peeled, pitted, and coarsely chopped
1 cup blueberries
¼ cup gluten-free rolled oats
½ teaspoon vanilla extract
4 ice cubes

Directions:
In a blender, combine the almond milk, yogurt, avocado, blueberries, oats, and vanilla and pulse until well blended.
Add the ice cubes and blend until thick and smooth. Serve.

Nutrition:
Calories: 273 | Total fat: 15g | Saturated fat: 2g; | Carbohydrates: 28g; | Sugar: 10g; | Fiber: 9g; | Protein: 10g

570. Cranberry-Pumpkin Smoothie

Preparation Time: 5 minutes | **Cooking time:** 0 minutes | **Servings:** 2

Ingredients:
2 cups unsweetened almond milk
1 cup pure pumpkin purée
¼ cup gluten-free rolled oats
¼ cup pure cranberry juice (no sugar added)
1 tablespoon honey
¼ teaspoon ground cinnamon
Pinch ground nutmeg

Directions:
In a blender, combine the almond milk, pumpkin, oats, cranberry juice, honey, cinnamon, and nutmeg and blend until smooth. Pour into glasses and serve immediately.

Nutrition:
Calories: 190 | Total fat: 7g | Saturated fat: 0g; | Carbohydrates: 26g; | Sugar: 12g | Fiber: 5g; | Protein: 4g

571. Avocado and Apple Smoothie

Preparation Time: 5 minutes | **Cooking time:** 0 minute | **Servings:** 2

Ingredients:
3 c. spinach
1 cored green apple, chopped
1 pitted avocado, peeled and chopped
3 tbsps. chia seeds
1 tsp. honey
1 frozen banana, peeled
2 c. coconut water

Directions:
Using your blender, add in all the ingredients. Process well for 5 minutes to obtain a smooth consistency and serve in glasses.

Nutrition:
208 Calories | 10.1g Fat | 6g Fiber

572. Green Juice

Preparation Time: 5 minutes | **Cooking time:** 0 minute | **Servings:** 1

Ingredients:
3 cups dark leafy greens
1 cucumber
¼ cup fresh Italian parsley leaves
¼ pineapple, cut into wedges
½ green apple
½ orange
½ lemon
Pinch grated fresh ginger

Directions:
Using a juicer, run the greens, cucumber, parsley, pineapple, apple, orange, lemon, and ginger through it, pour into a large cup, and serve.

Nutrition:
200 Calories | 14g Fats | 27g protein

573. Sweet Cranberry Nectar

Preparation Time: 8 minutes | **Cooking time:** 5 minutes | **Servings:** 4

Ingredients:
4 cups fresh cranberries
1 fresh lemon juice
½ cup agave nectar
1 piece of cinnamon stick
1-gallon water, filtered

Directions:
Add cranberries, ½ gallon water, and cinnamon into your pot
Close the lid
Cook on HIGH pressure for 8 minutes
Release the pressure naturally
Firstly, strain the liquid, then add the remaining water
Cool, add agave nectar and lemon
Served chill and enjoy!

Nutrition: (Per Serving)
Calories: 184 | Fat: 0g | Carbohydrates: 49g | Protein: 1g

574. Hearty Pear and Mango Smoothie

Preparation Time: 10 minutes | **Cooking time:** 0 minute | **Servings:** 1

Ingredients:
1 ripe mango, cored and chopped
½ mango, peeled, pitted, and chopped
1 cup kale, chopped
½ cup plain Greek yogurt
2 ice cubes

Directions:
Add pear, mango, yogurt, kale, and mango to a blender and puree.
Add ice and blend until you have a smooth texture.
Serve and enjoy!

Nutrition: (Per Serving)
Calories: 293 | Fat: 8g | Carbohydrates: 53g | Protein: 8g

575. Strawberry Rhubarb Smoothie

Preparation Time: 8 minutes | **Cooking time:** 0 minute | **Servings:** 1

Ingredients:
1 cup strawberries, fresh & sliced
1 rhubarb stalk, chopped
2 tablespoons honey, raw
3 ice cubes
1/8 teaspoon ground cinnamon
½ cup Greek yogurt, plain

Directions:
Start by getting out a small saucepan and fill it with water. Place it over high heat to bring it to a boil, and then add in your rhubarb. Boil for three minutes before draining and transferring it to a blender.
In your blender add in your yogurt, honey, cinnamon, and strawberries. Blend until smooth, and then add in your ice. Blend until there are no lumps and it's thick. Serve cold.

Nutrition:
201 Calories | 11g Fats | 39g protein

576. Breakfast Almond Milk Shake

Preparation Time: 4 minutes | **Cooking time:** 0 minute | **Servings:** 2

Ingredients:
3 cups almond milk
4 tbsp heavy cream
½ tsp vanilla extract
4 tbsp flax meal
2 tbsp protein powder
4 drops of liquid stevia
Ice cubes to serve

Directions:
In the bowl of your food processor, add almond milk, heavy cream, flax meal, vanilla extract, collagen peptides, and stevia.
Blitz until uniform and smooth, for about 30 seconds.
Add a bit more almond milk if it's very thick.
Pour in a smoothie glass, add the ice cubes and sprinkle with cinnamon.

Nutrition:
Calories 326, | Fat: 27g; | Net Carbs: 6g; | Protein: 19g

577. Raspberry Vanilla Smoothie

Preparation Time: 5 minutes | **Cooking time:** 5 minutes | **Servings:** over 2 cups

Ingredients:
1 cup frozen raspberries
A 6-ounce container of vanilla Greek yogurt
½ cup of unsweetened vanilla almond milk

Directions:
Take all your ingredients and place them in an instant pot Ace blender.
Process until smooth and liquified.

Nutrition:
Calories: 155 | Protein: 7 grams | Total Fat: 2 grams | Carbohydrates: 30 grams

578. Mango Pear Smoothie

Preparation Time: 5 minutes | **Cooking time:** 0 minute | **Servings:** 1

Ingredients:
2 ice cubes
½ cup Greek yogurt, plain
½ mango, peeled, pitted & chopped
1 cup kale, chopped
1 pear, ripe, cored & chopped

Directions:
Blend until thick and smooth. Serve chilled.

Nutrition:
350 Calories | 40g Protein | 12g Fats

579. Blueberry Banana Protein Smoothie

Preparation Time: 5 minutes | **Cooking time:** 5 minutes | **Servings:** 1

Ingredients:
½ cup frozen and unsweetened blueberries
½ banana slices up
¾ cup plain nonfat Greek yogurt
¾ cup unsweetened vanilla almond milk
2 cups of ice cubes

Directions:
Add all the ingredients into an instant pot ace blender.
Blend until smooth.

Nutrition:
Calories: 230 | Protein: 19.1 grams | Total Fat: 2.6 grams | Carbohydrates: 32.9 grams

580. Chocolate Banana Smoothie

Preparation Time: 5 minutes | **Cooking time:** 0 minutes | **Servings:** 2

Ingredients:
2 bananas, peeled
1 cup unsweetened almond milk, or skim milk
1 cup crushed ice
3 tablespoons unsweetened cocoa powder
3 tablespoons honey

Directions:
In a blender, combine the bananas, almond milk, ice, cocoa powder, and honey. Blend until smooth.

Nutrition:
Calories: 219; | Protein: 2g | Total Carbohydrates: 57g | Sugars: 40g | Fiber: 6g | Total Fat: 2g |

Saturated Fat: <1g | Cholesterol: 0mg | Sodium: 4mg

581. Fruit Smoothie

Preparation Time: 5 minutes | **Cooking time:** 0 minutes | **Servings:** 2

Ingredients:
2 cups blueberries (or any fresh or frozen fruit, cut into pieces if the fruit is large)
2 cups unsweetened almond milk
1 cup crushed ice
½ teaspoon ground ginger (or other dried ground spice such as turmeric, cinnamon, or nutmeg)

Directions:
In a blender, combine the blueberries, almond milk, ice, and ginger. Blend until smooth.

Nutrition:
Calories: 125; | Protein: 2g | Total Carbohydrates: 23g | Sugars: 14g | Fiber: 5g | Total Fat: 4g; | Fat: <1g | Cholesterol: 0mg | Sodium: 181mg

582. Mango-Pear Smoothie

Preparation Time: 10 minutes | **Cooking time:** 0 minutes | **Servings:** 1

Ingredients:
1 ripe pear, cored and chopped
½ mango, peeled, pitted, and chopped
1 cup chopped kale
½ cup plain Greek yogurt
2 ice cubes

Directions:
In a blender, purée the pear, mango, kale, and yogurt.
Add the ice and blend until thick and smooth. Pour the smoothie into a glass and serve cold.

Nutrition:
Calories: 293 | Total Fat: 8g | Saturated Fat: 5g; | Carbohydrates: 53g | Fiber: 7g; | Protein: 8g

583. Strawberry-Rhubarb Smoothie

Preparation Time: 5 minutes | **Cooking time:** 3 minutes | **Servings:** 1

Ingredients:
1 rhubarb stalk, chopped
1 cup sliced fresh strawberries
½ cup plain Greek yogurt
2 tablespoons honey
Pinch ground cinnamon
3 ice cubes

Directions:
Place a small saucepan filled with water over high heat and bring to a boil. Add the rhubarb and boil for 3 minutes. Drain and transfer the rhubarb to a blender.
Add the strawberries, yogurt, honey, and cinnamon, and pulse the mixture until it is smooth.
Add the ice and blend until thick, with no ice lumps remaining. Pour the smoothie into a glass and serve cold.

Nutrition:
Calories: 295 | Total Fat: 8g | Saturated Fat: 5g; | Carbohydrates: 56g | Fiber: 4g; | Protein: 6g

584. Chia-Pomegranate Smoothie

Preparation Time: 5 minutes | **Cooking time:** 0 minutes | **Servings:** 1

Ingredients:
1 cup pure pomegranate juice (no sugar added)
1 cup frozen berries
1 cup coarsely chopped kale
2 tablespoons chia seeds
3 Medjool dates, pitted and coarsely chopped
Pinch ground cinnamon

Directions:
In a blender, combine the pomegranate juice, berries, kale, chia seeds, dates, and cinnamon and pulse until smooth. Pour into glasses and serve.

Nutrition:
Calories: 275 | Total fat: 5g | Saturated fat: 1g; | Carbohydrates: 59g; | Sugar: 10g | Fiber: 42g; | Protein: 5g

585. Honey and Wild Blueberry Smoothie

Preparation Time: 5 minutes | **Cooking time:** 10 minutes | **Servings:** 2

Ingredients:
1 whole banana
1 cup of mango chunks
½ cup wild blueberries
½ plain, nonfat Greek yogurt
½ cup milk (for blending)
1 tablespoon raw honey
½ cup of kale

Directions:
Add all the above ingredients into an instant pot Ace blender. Add extra ice cubes if needed. Process until smooth.

Nutrition:
Calories: 223 | Protein: 9.4 grams | Total Fat: 1.4 grams | Carbohydrates: 46.8 grams

586. Oats Berry Smoothie

Preparation Time: 5 minutes | **Cooking time:** 5 minutes | **Servings:** 2

Ingredients:
1 cup of frozen berries
1 cup Greek yogurt
¼ cup of milk
¼ cup of oats
2 teaspoon honey

Directions:
Place all ingredients in an instant pot Ace blender and blend until smooth.

Nutrition:
Calories: 295 | Protein: 18 grams | Total Fat: 5 grams | Carbohydrates: 44 grams

587. Kale-Pineapple Smoothie

Preparation Time: 5 minutes | **Cooking time:** 5 minutes | **Servings:** 2

Ingredients:
1 Persian cucumber
fresh mint
1 cup of coconut milk
1 tablespoon honey
1 ½ cups of pineapple pieces
¼ pound baby kale

Directions:
Cut the ends off of the cucumbers and then cut the whole cucumber into small cubes. Strip the mint leaves from the stems.
Add all the ingredients to your instant pot Ace blender and blend until smooth.

Nutrition:
Calories: 140 | Protein: 4 grams | Total Fat: 2.5 grams | Carbohydrates: 30 grams

588. Moroccan Avocado Smoothie

Preparation Time: 5 minutes | **Cooking time:** 0 minutes | **Servings:** 4

Ingredients:
1 ripe avocado, peeled and pitted
1 overripe banana
1 cup almond milk, unsweetened
1 cup of ice

Directions:
Place the avocado, banana, milk, and ice into your instant pot Ace blender.
Blend until smooth with no pieces of avocado remaining.

Nutrition:
Calories: 100 | Protein: 1 gram | Total Fat: 6 grams | Carbohydrates: 11 grams

589. Mediterranean Smoothie

Preparation Time: 5 minutes | **Cooking time:** 5 minutes | **Servings:** 2

Ingredients:
2 cups of baby spinach
1 teaspoon fresh ginger root
1 frozen banana, pre-sliced
1 small mango
½ cup beet juice
½ cup of skim milk
4-6 ice cubes

Directions:
Take all ingredients and place them in your instant pot Ace blender.

Nutrition:
Calories: 168 | Protein: 4 grams | Total Fat: 1 gram | Carbohydrates: 39 grams

590. Anti-Inflammatory Blueberry Smoothie

Preparation Time: 5 minutes | **Cooking time:** 5 minutes | **Servings:** 1

Ingredients:
1 cup of almond milk
1 frozen banana
1 cup frozen blueberries
2 handfuls of spinach
1 tablespoon almond butter
¼ teaspoon cinnamon
¼ teaspoon cayenne
1 teaspoon maca powder

Directions:
Combine all these ingredients into your instant pot Ace blender and blend until smooth.

Nutrition:
Calories: 340 | Protein: 9 grams | Total Fat: 13 grams | Carbohydrates: 55 grams

591. Pina Colada Smoothie

Preparation Time: 10 minutes | **Cooking time:** 0 minutes | **Servings:** 4

Ingredients:
4 bananas
2 cups pineapple, peeled and sliced
2 cups mangoes, cored and diced
1 cup ice
4 tablespoons flaxseed
1¼ cups coconut milk

Directions:
Put all the ingredients in a blender and blend until smooth.
Pour into 4 glasses and immediately serve.

Nutrition:
Calories 417 | Total Fat: 22.1 g | Saturated Fat: 17.4 g | Cholesterol: 0 mg | Total Carbs 56.6 g | Dietary Fiber: 9.2 g | Sugar: 36.6 g | Protein: 5.5 g

592. Avocado & Honey Smoothie

Preparation Time: 5 minutes | **Cooking time:** 0 minute | **Servings:** 2

Ingredients:
1 1/2 cups soy milk
1 avocado, large
2 tablespoons honey, raw

Directions:
Blend all ingredients until smooth, and serve immediately.

Nutrition:
280 Calories | 19g Fats | 30g protein

593. Kiwi Smoothie

Preparation Time: 10 minutes | **Cooking time:** 0 minutes | **Servings:** 2

Ingredients:
1 cup basil leaves
2 bananas
1 cup fresh pineapple
10 kiwis

Directions:
Put all the ingredients in a blender and blend until smooth.
Pour into 2 glasses and immediately serve.

Nutrition:
Calories 378 | Total Fat: 2.5 g | Saturated Fat: 0.3 g | Cholesterol: 0 mg | Total Carbs 93.5 g | Dietary Fiber: 15.6 g | Sugar: 56.7 g | Protein: 6.1 g

594. Summer Smoothie

Preparation Time: 8 minutes | **Cooking time:** 0 minute | **Servings:** 2

Ingredients:
1/2 Banana, Peeled
2 Cups Strawberries, Halved
3 Tablespoons Mint, Chopped
1 1/2 Cups Coconut Water
1/2 Avocado, Pitted & Peeled
1 Date, Chopped
Ice Cubes as Needed

Directions:
Place everything in a blender, and blend until smooth. Add ice cubes to thicken, and serve chilled.

Nutrition:
360 Calories | 12g Fats | 31g protein

Chapter 9: Desserts

595. Orange Butterscotch Pudding

Preparation Time: 10 minutes | **Cooking time:** 15 minutes | **Servings:** 4

Ingredients:
4 caramels
2 eggs, well-beaten
1/4 cup freshly squeezed orange juice
1/3 cup sugar
1 cup cake flour
1/2 teaspoon baking powder
1/4 cup milk
1 stick butter, melted
1/2 teaspoon vanilla essence
Sauce:
1/2 cup golden syrup
2 teaspoons corn flour
1 cup boiling water

Directions:
Melt the butter and milk in the microwave. Whisk in the eggs, vanilla, and sugar. After that, stir in the flour, baking powder, and orange juice. Lastly, add the caramels and stir until everything is well combined and melted.
Divide between the four jars. Add 1 ½ cups of water and a metal trivet to the bottom of the Instant Pot. Lower the jars onto the trivet.
To make the sauce, whisk the boiling water, corn flour, and golden syrup until everything is well combined. Pour the sauce into each jar.
Secure the lid. Choose the "Steam" mode and cook for 15 minutes under high pressure. Once cooking is complete, use a natural pressure release; carefully remove the lid. Enjoy!

Nutrition:
Calories 565; | Fat: 25.9g; | Carbohydrates: 79.6g; | Protein: 6.4g | Sugars 51.5g

596. Mixed Berry and Orange Compote

Preparation Time: 15 minutes | **Cooking time:** 15 minutes | **Servings:** 4

Ingredients:
1/2-pound strawberries
1 tablespoon orange juice
1/4 teaspoon ground cloves
1/2 cup brown sugar
1 vanilla bean
1-pound blueberries
1/2-pound blackberries

Directions:
Place your berries in the inner pot. Add the sugar and let sit for 15 minutes. Add in the orange juice, ground cloves, and vanilla bean.
Secure the lid. Choose the "Manual" mode and cook for 2 minutes at high pressure. Once cooking is complete, use a natural pressure release for 10 minutes; carefully remove the lid. As your compote cools, it will thicken. Bon appétit!

Nutrition:
Calories 224; | Fat: 0.8g; | Carbohydrates: 56.3g; | Protein: 2.1g | Sugars 46.5g

597. Streuselkuchen with Peaches

Preparation Time: 10 minutes | **Cooking time:** 20 minutes | **Servings:** 6

Ingredients:
1 cup rolled oats
1 teaspoon vanilla extract
1/3 cup orange juice
4 tablespoons raisins
2 tablespoons honey
4 tablespoons butter
4 tablespoons all-purpose flour
A pinch of grated nutmeg
1/2 teaspoon ground cardamom
A pinch of salt
1 teaspoon ground cinnamon
6 peaches, pitted and chopped
1/3 cup brown sugar

Directions:
Place the peaches on the bottom of the inner pot. Sprinkle with cardamom, cinnamon, and vanilla. Top with orange juice, honey, and raisins.
In a mixing bowl, whisk together the butter, oats, flour, brown sugar, nutmeg, and salt. Drop by a spoonful on top of the peaches.
Secure the lid. Choose the "Manual" mode and cook for 8 minutes at high pressure. Once cooking is complete, use a natural pressure release for 10 minutes; carefully remove the lid. Bon appétit!

Nutrition:
329 Calories | 10g Fat | 56g Carbohydrates | 6.9g Protein | 31g Sugars

598. Fig and Honey Buckwheat Pudding

Preparation Time: 10 minutes | **Cooking time:** 10 minutes | **Servings:** 4

Ingredients:
1/2 teaspoon ground cinnamon
1/2 cup dried figs, chopped
1/3 cup honey
1 teaspoon pure vanilla extract
3 ½ cups milk
1/2 teaspoon pure almond extract
1 ½ cups buckwheat

Directions:
Add all the above ingredients to your Instant Pot. Secure the lid. Choose the "Multigrain" mode and cook for 10 minutes under high pressure. Once cooking is complete, use a natural pressure release; carefully remove the lid.
Serve topped with fresh fruits, nuts, or whipped topping. Bon appétit!

Nutrition:
Calories 320; | Fat: 7.5g; | Carbohydrates: 57.7g; | Protein: 9.5g | Sugars 43.2g

599. Zingy Blueberry Sauce

Preparation Time: 5 minutes | **Cooking time:** 20 minutes | **Servings:** 10

Ingredients:
1/4 cup fresh lemon juice
1-pound granulated sugar
1 tablespoon freshly grated lemon zest
1/2 teaspoon vanilla extract
2 pounds fresh blueberries

Directions:
Place the blueberries, sugar, and vanilla in the inner pot of your Instant Pot.
Secure the lid. Choose the "Manual" mode and cook for 2 minutes at high pressure. Once cooking is complete, use a natural pressure release for 15 minutes; carefully remove the lid. Stir in the lemon zest and juice. Puree in a food processor; then, strain and push the mixture through a sieve before storing. Enjoy!

Nutrition:
Calories 230; | Fat: 0.3g; | Carbohydrates: 59g; | Protein: 0.7g | Sugars 53.6g

600. Chocolate Almond Custard

Preparation Time: 10 minutes | **Cooking time:** 15 minutes | **Servings:** 3

Ingredients:
3 chocolate cookies, chunks
A pinch of salt
1/4 teaspoon ground cardamom
3 tablespoons honey
1/4 teaspoon freshly grated nutmeg
2 tablespoons butter
3 tablespoons whole milk
1 cup almond flour
3 eggs
1 teaspoon pure vanilla extract

Directions:
In a mixing bowl, beat the eggs with butter. Now, add the milk and continue mixing until well combined.
Add the remaining ingredients in the order listed above. Divide the batter among 3 ramekins.
Add 1 cup of water and a metal trivet to the Instant Pot. Cover ramekins with foil and lower them onto the trivet.
Secure the lid and select "Manual" mode. Cook at High Pressure for 12 minutes. Once cooking is complete, use a quick release; carefully remove the lid.
Transfer the ramekins to a wire rack and allow them to cool slightly before serving. Enjoy!

Nutrition:
Calories 304; | Fat: 18.9g; | Carbohydrates: 23.8g; | Protein: 10g | Sugars 21.1g

601. Honey Stewed Apples

Preparation Time: 5 minutes | **Cooking time:** 5 minutes | **Servings:** 4

Ingredients:
2 tablespoons honey
1 teaspoon ground cinnamon
1/2 teaspoon ground cloves
4 apples

Directions:
Add all ingredients to the inner pot. Now, pour in 1/3 cup of water.
Secure the lid. Choose the "Manual" mode and cook for 2 minutes at high pressure. Once cooking is complete, use a quick pressure release; carefully remove the lid.
Serve in individual bowls. Bon appétit!

Nutrition:
Calories 128; | Fat: 0.3g; | Carbohydrates: 34.3g; | Protein: 0.5g | Sugars 27.5g

602. Greek-Style Compote with Yogurt

Preparation Time: 5 minutes | **Cooking time:** 15 minutes | **Servings:** 4

Ingredients:
1 cup Greek yogurt
1 cup pears
4 tablespoons honey
1 cup apples
1 vanilla bean
1 cinnamon stick
1/2 cup caster sugar
1 cup rhubarb
1 teaspoon ground ginger
1 cup plums

Directions:
Place the fruits, ginger, vanilla, cinnamon, and caster sugar in the inner pot of your Instant Pot.
Secure the lid. Choose the "Manual" mode and cook for 2 minutes at high pressure. Once cooking is complete, use a natural pressure release for 10 minutes; carefully remove the lid.
Meanwhile, whisk the yogurt with the honey. Serve your compote in individual bowls with a dollop of honeyed Greek yogurt. Enjoy!

Nutrition:
Calories 304; | Fat: 0.3g; | Carbohydrates: 75.4g; | Protein: 5.1g | Sugars 69.2g

603. Butterscotch Lava Cakes

Preparation Time: 5 minutes | **Cooking time:** 15 minutes | **Servings:** 6

Ingredients:
7 tablespoons all-purpose flour

A pinch of coarse salt
6 ounces butterscotch morsels
3/4 cup powdered sugar
1/2 teaspoon vanilla extract
3 eggs, whisked
1 stick butter

Directions:
Add 1 ½ cups of water and a metal rack to the Instant Pot. Line a standard-size muffin tin with muffin papers.
In a microwave-safe bowl, microwave butter and butterscotch morsels for about 40 seconds. Stir in the powdered sugar.
Add the remaining ingredients Spoon the batter into the prepared muffin tin.
Secure the lid. Choose the "Manual" and cook at High pressure for 10 minutes. Once cooking is complete, use a quick release; carefully remove the lid.
To remove, let it cool for 5 to 6 minutes. Run a small knife around the sides of each cake and serve. Enjoy!

Nutrition:
Calories 393; | Fat: 21.1g; | Carbohydrates: 45.6g; | Protein: 5.6g | Sugars 35.4g

604. Vanilla Bread Pudding with Apricots

Preparation Time: 5 minutes | **Cooking time:** 15 minutes | **Servings:** 6

Ingredients:
2 tablespoons coconut oil
1 1/3 cups heavy cream
4 eggs, whisked
1/2 cup dried apricots, soaked and chopped
1 teaspoon cinnamon, ground
1/2 teaspoon star anise, ground
A pinch of grated nutmeg
A pinch of salt
1/2 cup granulated sugar
2 tablespoons molasses
2 cups milk
4 cups Italian bread, cubed
1 teaspoon vanilla paste

Directions:
Add 1 ½ cups of water and a metal rack to the Instant Pot.
Grease a baking dish with a nonstick cooking spray. Throw the bread cubes into the prepared baking dish.
In a mixing bowl, thoroughly combine the remaining ingredients Pour the mixture over the bread cubes. Cover with a piece of foil, making a foil sling.
Secure the lid. Choose the "Porridge" mode and High pressure; cook for 15 minutes. Once cooking is complete, use a quick pressure release; carefully remove the lid. Enjoy!

Nutrition:
Calories 410; | Fat: 24.3g; | Carbohydrates: 37.4g; | Protein: 11.5g | Sugars 25.6g

605. Mediterranean-Style Carrot Pudding

Preparation Time: 15 minutes | **Cooking time:** 15 minutes | **Servings:** 4

Ingredients:
1/3 cup almonds, ground
1/4 cup dried figs, chopped
2 large-sized carrots, shredded
1/2 cup water
1 ½ cups milk
1/2 teaspoon ground star anise
1/3 teaspoon ground cardamom
1/4 teaspoon kosher salt
1/3 cup granulated sugar
2 eggs, beaten
1/2 teaspoon pure almond extract
1/2 teaspoon vanilla extract
1 ½ cups jasmine rice

Directions:
Place the jasmine rice, milk, water, carrots, and salt in your Instant Pot.
Stir to combine and secure the lid. Choose "Manual" and cook at High pressure for 10 minutes. Once cooking is complete, use a natural release for 15 minutes; carefully remove the lid.
Now, press the "Sauté" button and add the sugar, eggs, and almonds; stir to combine well. Bring to a boil; press the "Keep Warm/Cancel" button.
Add the remaining ingredients and stir; the pudding will thicken as it sits. Bon appétit!

Nutrition:
331 Calories | 17.2g Fat | 44.5g Carbohydrates | 13.9g Protein | 19.5g Sugars

606. Oatmeal Cakes with Mango

Preparation Time: 5 minutes | **Cooking time:** 17 minutes | **Servings:** 2

Ingredients:
Hotcakes:
2 cups of oatmeal
3 eggs
1 tablespoon baking powder
1¼ cups of natural yogurt
1 teaspoon vanilla extract
1 cup chopped apple in small cubes
Oil spray
Mango honey (syrup):
2 cups diced mango
Orange juice
1 tablespoon maple honey
1 tablespoon vanilla extract
1 cinnamon stick

Directions:
In the pot, place all the ingredients of mango honey. Cover with the valve open and cook at medium-high temperature until it whistles (in about 5 minutes). Reduce the temperature to low, remove the lid, and continue cooking for 4 more minutes. Let cool a little and blend for a few seconds until you get a homogeneous mixture.
Also, blend all the ingredients of the hotcakes (except apple and oil spray) at speed 6, for 1 minute (until you get a homogeneous consistency). Pour into the Mixing Bowl and stir with the apple pieces, using the Balloon Whisk. Preheat at medium-high temperature for 2 minutes. Reduce the temperature to low and sprinkle some oil spray.
Cook 6 to 8 hotcakes, for 2 minutes per side. Repeat with the remaining mixture.

Nutrition:
Calories: 245 | Carbohydrates: 51.6g | Fat: 4.3g | Protein: 8.4g | Sugar: 8g | Cholesterol: 2mg

607. Rice Pudding

Preparation Time: 5 minutes | **Cooking time:** 10 minutes | **Servings:** 10

Ingredients:
6 cups of white rice, previously cooked
2 cups of double cream (heavy whipping cream)
1 cup coconut milk
3 cups of skim milk
2 cinnamon sticks (cinnamon stick)
1 teaspoon allspice
1 teaspoon nutmeg
½ cup brown sugar
Cinnamon powder to taste

Directions:
In the pot, add all the ingredients.
Cook at medium-high temperature for 10 minutes; Stir frequently.
Garnish with a pinch of cinnamon.

Nutrition:
Calories: 344 | Carbohydrates: 46g | Fat: 9.3g | Protein: 18g | Sugar: 4.8g | Cholesterol: 0mg

608. Ripe Banana Pudding

Preparation Time: 5 minutes | **Cooking time:** 25 minutes | **Servings:** 8

Ingredients:
1 pound (½ kg) of white/square white bread, in thick slices
1 can of condensed milk (14 oz/396 ml)
1 can of evaporated milk (12 oz/354 ml)
1 cup coconut milk
3 beaten eggs
½ cup Marsala wine (optional)
2 ripe bananas chopped into small pieces
½ cup pecan nuts (optional)
1 teaspoon vanilla extract
1 teaspoon ground cinnamon
½ teaspoon nutmeg powder
1 teaspoon whole wheat flour (optional)
Oil spray

Directions:
Chop the bread into medium cubes. Place it in the bowl, and pour half of the condensed milk, half of the evaporated milk, and half of the coconut milk. Stir well.

Add the beaten eggs, wine, bananas, nuts, vanilla extract, cinnamon, and nutmeg. Combine and let the bread absorb the mixture for about 15 minutes.

Meanwhile, in the pot, mix the remaining 3 kinds of milk (evaporated, condensed, and coconut), and cook for 8 minutes at medium temperature, or until they begin to thicken. Stir occasionally. If you need thickness, add whole wheat flour.

Preheat the skillet over medium heat for 2 minutes, sprinkle oil spray and add the bread mixture.

Reduce the temperature to low, cover, and cook for 18 minutes.

Remove the pan from the pot and let stand for about 5 minutes.

Serve and pour a little of the milk mixture in each serving.

Nutrition:
Calories: 288 | Carbohydrates: 47g | Fat: 10g | Protein: 4g | Sugar: 34g | Cholesterol: 6.5mg

609. Picositos Brownies

Preparation Time: 5 minutes | **Cooking time:** 15 minutes; | **Servings:** 8

Ingredients:
3 cups brownies mix
2 eggs
1/3 cup of milk
½ teaspoon cayenne pepper
1 teaspoon cinnamon
1 teaspoon vanilla extract
¼ cup chocolate sprinkles
Liquid candy to taste (decoration)
Chocolate sauce to taste (decoration)
Oil spray

Directions:
In a bowl, stir the following ingredients until a homogeneous mixture is obtained. Be sure to add them little by little, in the same order: mix for brownies, eggs, milk, cayenne pepper, cinnamon, vanilla, and chocolate sprinkles.

Preheat the skillet at medium-high temperature for 2 and a half minutes. Cover the pot with the spray oil and reduce the temperature to low. Make sure the oil does not start to burn.

Add the previous mixture immediately, cover with the valve closed and cook for 15 minutes. Turn off the pot, remove the pan from the burner and let it sit for 3 minutes. Carefully invert the brownies on the Bamboo Cutting Board, slice them, and serve with caramel or chocolate sauce.

Nutrition:
Calories: 539 | Carbohydrates: 54g | Fat: 33g | Protein: 8g | Sugar: 29g | Cholesterol: 115mg

610. Fruit Crepes

Preparation Time: 5 minutes | **Cooking time:** 15 minutes | **Servings:** 4

Ingredients:
Crepes:
1 cup wheat flour
2 eggs
1¼ cups of milk
1 teaspoon vanilla extract
2 tablespoons melted butter
a pinch of salt
Powdered sugar to taste (powdered sugar)
Olive oil spray
Filling
2 cups of strawberries, sliced
½ cup sour cream
¼ cup brown sugar
1 teaspoon vanilla extract

Directions:
In a bowl, combine the flour and eggs. Add the milk gradually. Then add the vanilla extract, butter, salt, and icing sugar. Beat well until you get a homogeneous mixture.

In the other bowl, combine the filling ingredients well with the help of the Spatula.

Preheat the skillet at medium-high temperature for about 2 and a half minutes and immediately lower the temperature to low. Cover the pan with olive oil spray.

With the help of the ladle, add approximately 1/8 cup of the mixture to the pan. Tilt the pan slightly to allow the mixture to spread evenly across the surface.

Cook the crepes for 40 to 45 seconds per side, or until lightly browned. Use the Silicone Spatula to flip them.

Repeat steps 4 and 5 with the remaining mixture. Add more spray oil, if necessary. Fill the crepes and serve with syrup.

Nutrition:
Calories: 101 | Carbohydrates: 17g | Fat: 1.4g | Protein: 6g | Sugar: 5g | Cholesterol: 43.4mg

611. Crème Caramel

Preparation Time: 1 hour | **Cooking time:** 1 hour | **Servings:** 12

Ingredients:
5 cups of whole milk
2 tsp vanilla extract
8 large egg yolks
4 large-sized eggs
2 cups sugar, divided
¼ cup 0f water

Directions:
Preheat the oven to 350°F
Heat the milk on medium heat until it is scalded.
Mix 1 cup of sugar and eggs in a bowl and add it to the eggs.
With a nonstick pan on high heat, boil the water and remaining sugar. Do not stir, instead whirl the pan. When the sugar forms caramel, divide it into ramekins.
Divide the egg mixture into the ramekins and place in a baking pan. Add water to the pan until it is half full. Bake for 30 minutes.
Remove the ramekins from the baking pan, cool, then refrigerate for at least 8 hours.
Serve.

Nutrition:
Calories: 110kcal | Carbs: 21g | Fat: 1g | Protein: 2g

612. Galaktoboureko

Preparation Time: 30 minutes | **Cooking time:** 90 minutes | **Servings:** 12

Ingredients:
4 cups sugar, divided
1 tbsp. fresh lemon juice
1 cup of water
1 Tbsp. plus 1 ½ tsp grated lemon zest, divided into 10 cups
Room temperature whole milk
1 cup plus 2 tbsps. unsalted butter, melted and divided into 2
Tbsps. vanilla extract
7 large-sized eggs
1 cup of fine semolina
1 package phyllo, thawed and at room temperature

Directions:
Preheat oven to 350°F
Mix 2 cups of sugar, lemon juice, 1 ½ tsp of lemon zest, and water. Boil over medium heat. Set aside.
Mix the milk, 2 Tbsps. of butter, and vanilla in a pot and put on medium heat. Remove from heat when milk is scalded
Mix the eggs and semolina in a bowl, then add the mixture to the scalded milk. Put the egg-milk mixture on medium heat. Stir until it forms a custard-like material.
Brush butter on each sheet of phyllo and arrange all over the baking pan until everywhere is covered. Spread the custard on the bottom pile of phyllo.
Arrange the buttered phyllo all over the top of the custard until every inch is covered.
Bake for about 40 minutes. cover the top of the pie with all the prepared syrup. Serve.

Nutrition:
Calories: 393kcal | Carbs: 55g | Fat: 15g | Protein: 8g

613. Kourabiedes Almond Cookies

Preparation Time: 20 minutes | **Cooking time:** 50 minutes | **Servings:** 20

Ingredients:
1 ½ cups unsalted butter, clarified, at room temperature 2 cups
Confectioners' sugar, divided
1 large egg yolk
2 tbsps. brandy
1 1/2 tsp baking powder
1 tsp vanilla extract
5/cups all-purpose flour, sifted
1 cup roasted almonds, chopped

Directions:
Preheat the oven to 350°F
Thoroughly mix butter and ½ cup of sugar in a bowl. Add in the egg after a while. Create a

brandy mixture by mixing the brandy and baking powder. Add the mixture to the egg, add vanilla, then keep beating until the ingredients are properly blended

Add flour and almonds to make the dough.

Roll the dough to form crescent shapes. You should be able to get about 40 pieces. Place the pieces on a baking sheet, then bake in the oven for 25 minutes.

Allow the cookies to cool, then coat them with the remaining confectioner's sugar.

Serve.

Nutrition:
Calories: 102kcal | Carbs: 10g | Fat: 7g | Protein: 2g

614. Ekmek Kataifi

Preparation Time: 30 minutes | **Cooking time:** 45 minutes | **Servings:** 10

Ingredients:
1 cup of sugar
1 cup of water
2 (2-inch) strips lemon peel, pith removed
1 tbsp. fresh lemon juice
½ cup plus 1 tbsp. unsalted butter, melted
½ lbs. frozen kataifi pastry, thawed, at room temperature
2 ½ cups whole milk
½ tsp. ground mastiha
2 large eggs
¼ cup fine semolina
1 tsp. of cornstarch
¼ cup of sugar
½ cup sweetened coconut flakes
1 cup whipping cream
1 tsp. vanilla extract
1 tsp. powdered milk
3 tbsps. of confectioners' sugar
½ cup chopped unsalted pistachios

Directions:
Set the oven to 350°F. Grease the baking pan with 1. Tbsp of butter.

Put a pot on medium heat, then add water, sugar, lemon juice, lemon peel. Leave to boil for about 10 minutes. Reserve.

Untangle the kataifi, coat with the leftover butter, then place in the baking pan.

Mix the milk and mastiha, then place it on medium heat. Remove from heat when the milk is scalded, then cool the mixture.

Mix the eggs, cornstarch, semolina, and sugar in a bowl, stir thoroughly, then whisk the cooled milk mixture into the bowl.

Transfer the egg and milk mixture to a pot and place on heat. Wait for it to thicken like custard, then add the coconut flakes and cover it with a plastic wrap. Cool.

Spread the cooled custard-like material over the kataifi. Place in the refrigerator for at least 8 hours.

Strategically remove the kataifi from the pan with a knife. Remove it in such a way that the mold faces up.

Whip a cup of cream, add 1 tsp. vanilla, 1tsp. powdered milk, and 3 tbsps. Of sugar. Spread the mixture all over the custard, wait for it to harden, then flip and add the leftover cream mixture to the kataifi side.

Serve.

Nutrition:
Calories: 649kcal | Carbs: 37g | Fat: 52g | Protein: 11g

615. Revani Syrup Cake

Preparation Time: 30 minutes | **Cooking time:** 3 hours | **Servings:** 24

Ingredients:
1 tbsp. unsalted butter
2 tbsps. all-purpose flour
1 cup ground rusk or bread crumbs
1 cup fine semolina flour
¾ cup ground toasted almonds
3 tsp baking powder
16 large eggs
2 tbsps. vanilla extract
3 cups of sugar, divided
3 cups of water
5 (2-inch) strips lemon peel, pith removed
3 tbsps. fresh lemon juice
1 oz of brandy

Directions:
Preheat the oven to 350°F. Grease the baking pan with 1 Tbsp. of butter and flour.

Mix the rusk, almonds, semolina, baking powder in a bowl.

In another bowl, mix the eggs, 1 cup of sugar, vanilla, and whisk with an electric mixer for about 5 minutes. Add the semolina mixture to the eggs and stir.

Pour the stirred batter into the greased baking pan and place in the preheated oven.

With the remaining sugar, lemon peels, and water make the syrup by boiling the mixture on medium heat. Add the lemon juice after 6 minutes, then cook for 3 minutes. Remove the lemon peels and set the syrup aside.

After the cake is done in the oven, spread the syrup over the cake.

Cut the cake as you please and serve.

Nutrition:
Calories: 348kcal | Carbs: 55g | Fat: 9g | Protein: 5g

616. Almonds and Oats Pudding

Preparation Time: 10 minutes | **Cooking time:** 15 minutes | **Servings:** 4

Ingredients:
1 tablespoon lemon juice
Zest of 1 lime
1 and ½ cups almond milk
1 teaspoon almond extract
½ cup oats
2 tablespoons stevia
½ cup silver almonds, chopped

Directions:
In a pan, combine the almond milk with the lime zest and the other ingredients, whisk, bring to a simmer and cook over medium heat for 15 minutes.
Divide the mix into bowls and serve cold.

Nutrition:
Calories 174 | Fat: 12.1 | Fiber 3.2 | Carbs 3.9 | Protein: 4.8

617. Chocolate Cups

Preparation Time: 2 hours | **Cooking time:** 0 minutes | **Servings:** 6

Ingredients:
½ cup avocado oil
1 cup, chocolate, melted
1 teaspoon matcha powder
3 tablespoons stevia

Directions:
In a bowl, mix the chocolate with the oil and the rest of the ingredients, whisk well, divide into cups, and keep in the freezer for 2 hours before serving.

Nutrition:
Calories 174 | Fat: 9.1 | Fiber 2.2 | Carbs 3.9 | Protein: 2.8

618. Mango Bowls

Preparation Time: 30 minutes | **Cooking time:** 0 minutes | **Servings:** 4

Ingredients:
3 cups mango, cut into medium chunks
½ cup coconut water
¼ cup stevia
1 teaspoon vanilla extract

Directions:
In a blender, combine the mango with the rest of the ingredients, pulse well, divide into bowls and serve cold.

Nutrition:
Calories 122 | Fat: 4 | Fiber 5.3 | Carbs 6.6 | Protein: 4.5

619. Cocoa and Pears Cream

Preparation Time: 10 minutes | **Cooking time:** 0 minutes | **Servings:** 4

Ingredients:
2 cups heavy creamy
1/3 cup stevia
¾ cup cocoa powder
6 ounces dark chocolate, chopped
Zest of 1 lemon
2 pears, chopped

Directions:
In a blender, combine the cream with the stevia and the rest of the ingredients, pulse well, divide into cups and serve cold.

Nutrition:
Calories 172 | Fat: 5.6 | Fiber 3.5 | Carbs 7.6 | Protein: 4

620. Pineapple Pudding

Preparation Time: 10 minutes | **Cooking time:** 40 minutes | **Servings:** 4

Ingredients:
3 cups almond flour
¼ cup olive oil
1 teaspoon vanilla extract
2 and ¼ cups stevia
3 eggs, whisked
1 and ¼ cup natural apple sauce
2 teaspoons baking powder
1 and ¼ cups almond milk
2 cups pineapple, chopped
Cooking spray

Directions:
In a bowl, combine the almond flour with the oil and the rest of the ingredients except the cooking spray and stir well.
Grease a cake pan with the cooking spray, pour the pudding mix inside, introduce in the oven, and bake at 370 degrees F for 40 minutes.
Serve the pudding cold.

Nutrition:
Calories 223 | Fat: 8.1 | Fiber 3.4 | Carbs 7.6

621. Vanilla Cake

Preparation Time: 5 minutes | **Cooking time:** 23 minutes | **Servings:** 12

Ingredients:
Flan:
1 cup of condensed milk
1 cup evaporated milk
3 eggs
1 teaspoon vanilla extract
Cake:
2 cups of chocolate cake mix
2 eggs
¾ cup of nonfat milk
Oil spray

Directions:
Flan:
Blend condensed milk, evaporated milk, 3 eggs, and vanilla extract for 2 minutes. Reserve this mix
Cake:
In the bowl, combine the cake mix, eggs, and milk with the help of the Balloon Whisk. Reserve this preparation.
Preheat the pan at medium-high temperature for 3 minutes; Remove the pan from the stove for 1 minute and lightly spray the spray oil all over the surface - including the walls of the pan. Add the cake mixture to the pan. With the help of a spoon, pour the flan mixture evenly. Put the pan back on the pot, reduce the temperature to low, cover with the valve closed, and cook for 23 minutes.
Let the pan rest for a few minutes. Turn it carefully, so that the cake falls on a plate or flat surface. Slice it and serve.

Nutrition:
Calories: 84.62 | Carbohydrates: 1g | Fat: 7.02g | Protein: 3.71g | Sugar: 0.64g | Cholesterol: 97.43mg

622. Vanilla Pastry Cream

Preparation Time: 5 minutes | **Cooking time:** 5 minutes | **Servings:** 4

Ingredients:
2 cups low fat milk
2 lightly beaten eggs
¼ cup sugar
¼ teaspoon salt
½ teaspoon of vanilla
Nutmeg
1 cup of water

Directions:
Combine milk, eggs, sugar, salt, and vanilla and pour into individual cups for custard. Sprinkle with nutmeg.
Cover each cup firmly with the foil. Pour the water into the pot. Position the cups on the rack of the pot.
Close and secure the lid. Place the pressure regulator on the vent tube and cook for 5 minutes once the pressure regulator begins to rock slowly.
Cool the pot quickly. Let the cream cool well in the refrigerator.

Nutrition:
Calories: 137

623. Small Pumpkin Pastry Cream

Preparation Time: 5 minutes | **Cooking time:** 10 minutes | **Servings:** 8

Ingredients:
1 can of 16 ounces of prepared pumpkin
1 14-ounces can sweetened condensed milk
3 beaten eggs
1 teaspoon finely chopped polished ginger (optional)
1 teaspoon ground cinnamon
¼ teaspoon ground cloves
1 cup of water

Directions:
Mix the pumpkin, milk, eggs, cinnamon, ginger, and cloves. Pour into individual cups for custard. Cover each cup firmly with the foil. Pour the water into the pot. Position the cups on the rack of the pot. Close and secure the lid.
Place the pressure regulator on the vent tube and cook for 10 minutes once the pressure regulator begins to rock slowly. Cool the pot quickly. Let the cream cool well in the refrigerator. If desired, serve with whipped cream.

Nutrition:
Calories: 207

624. Tapioca Pudding

Preparation Time: 5 minutes | **Cooking time:** 20 minutes | **Servings:** 6

Ingredients:
2 cups low fat milk
2 tablespoons quick-cooking tapioca
2 lightly beaten eggs
⅓ cup of sugar
½ teaspoon of vanilla
1 cup of water

Directions:
Heat the milk and tapioca. Remove from heat and let it stand for 15 minutes.
Combine eggs, sugar, and vanilla. Add milk and tapioca, stirring constantly.
Pour them into individual cups for custard. Cover each cup firmly with the foil. Pour the water into the pot. Position the cups on the rack of the pot. Close and secure the lid.
Place the pressure regulator on the vent tube and cook for 5 minutes once the pressure regulator begins to rock slowly.
Cool the pot quickly. Let the pudding cool well in the refrigerator.

Nutrition:
Calories: 113

625. Mango Mug Cake

Preparation Time: 5 minutes | **Cooking time:** 10 minutes | **Servings:** 2

Ingredients:
1 medium-sized mango, peeled and diced
2 eggs
1 teaspoon vanilla
1/4 teaspoon grated nutmeg
1 tablespoon cocoa powder
2 tablespoons honey
1/2 cup coconut flour

Directions:
Combine the coconut flour, eggs, honey, vanilla, nutmeg, and cocoa powder in two lightly greased mugs.
Then, add 1 cup of water and a metal trivet to the Instant Pot. Lower the uncovered mugs onto the trivet.
Secure the lid. Choose the "Manual" mode and High pressure; cook for 10 minutes. Once cooking is complete, use a quick pressure release; carefully remove the lid.
Top with diced mango and serve chilled. Enjoy!

Nutrition:
Calories 268; | Fat: 10.5g; | Carbohydrates: 34.8g; | Protein: 10.6g | Sugars 31.1g

626. Chocolate Coffee Pots de Crème

Preparation Time: 10 minutes | **Cooking time:** 15 minutes | **Servings:** 6

Ingredients:
1 teaspoon instant coffee
9 ounces chocolate chips
1/2 cup whole milk
1/3 cup sugar

A pinch of pink salt
4 egg yolks
2 cups double cream

Directions:
Place a metal trivet and 1 cup of water in your Instant Pot.
In a saucepan, bring the cream and milk to a simmer.
Then, thoroughly combine the egg yolks, sugar, instant coffee, and salt. Slowly and gradually whisk in the hot cream mixture.
Whisk in the chocolate chips and blend again. Pour the mixture into mason jars. Lower the jars onto the trivet.
Secure the lid. Choose the "Manual" mode and cook for 6 minutes at high pressure. Once cooking is complete, use a natural pressure release for 10 minutes; carefully remove the lid.
Serve well chilled and enjoy!

Nutrition:
Calories 351; | Fat: 19.3g; | Carbohydrates: 39.3g; | Protein: 5.5g | Sugars 32.1g

627. Almond Cherry Crumble Cake

Preparation Time: 5 minutes | **Cooking time:** 10 minutes
Servings: 4

Ingredients:
1/4 cup almonds, slivered
1/2 stick butter, at room temperature
1 teaspoon ground cinnamon
A pinch of grated nutmeg
1 cup rolled oats
1/3 teaspoon ground cardamom
1 teaspoon pure vanilla extract
1/3 cup honey
2 tablespoons all-purpose flour
A pinch of salt
1-pound sweet cherries, pitted
1/3 cup water

Directions:
Arrange the cherries on the bottom of the Instant Pot. Sprinkle cinnamon, cardamom, and vanilla over the top. Add the water and honey.
In a separate mixing bowl, thoroughly combine the butter, oats, and flour. Spread topping mixture evenly over cherry mixture.

Secure the lid. Choose the "Manual" mode and High pressure; cook for 10 minutes. Once cooking is complete, use a natural pressure release; carefully remove the lid.
Serve at room temperature. Bon appétit!

Nutrition:
Calories 335; | Fat: 13.4g; | Carbohydrates: 60.5g; | Protein: 5.9g | Sugars 38.1g

628. Black Forest

Preparation Time: 5 minutes | **Cooking time:** 23 minutes | **Servings:** 8-10

Ingredients:
1 box of chocolate cake mix; use 2 cups
1 cup skim milk
2 eggs
2 cups of double cream (heavy whipping cream)
1 teaspoon icing sugar (powdered sugar)
1 teaspoon vanilla extract
¼ cup unsweetened cocoa powder unsweetened cocoa powder
24 jar maraschino cherries (12 cut in half and 12 whole to decorate)
1 cup cherries juice
½ cup grated chocolate (chocolate shavings)
Oil spray

Directions:
In a bowl, add the cake mix, milk, and eggs. Combine well.
Preheat the skillet at medium-high temperature for 3 minutes; Remove the pan from the pot for 1 minute and lightly spray the oil spray. Pour the cake mixture into the pan, cover with the valve closed, lower the temperature to low, and cook for approximately 20-23 minutes, or until a knife is inserted, it comes out clean.
In the other bowl, add the double cream, sugar, and vanilla extract. Beat until it thickens. Divide this cream into two equal parts. Mix one of the parts with the cocoa powder, and the other with the cherries in halves.
Slice the chocolate cake into two layers and drill holes in each with the help of a knife. Pour the cherry juice into both layers.
Spread the cream mixture with cherries over the bottom layer. Place the second layer on top and cover with the cream and cocoa mixture. Garnish with whole cherries, grated chocolate,

and cocoa powder. It can be served immediately or refrigerated for 30 minutes.

Nutrition:
Calories: 539 | Carbohydrates: 54g | Fat: 33g | Protein: 8g | Sugar: 29g | Cholesterol: 115mg

629. Greek Cheesecake with Yogurt

Preparation Time: 20 minutes | **Cooking time:** 0 minutes | **Servings:** 12

Ingredients:
1 teaspoon vanilla extract
9 oz. digestive biscuits
3 ½ oz. butter, melted
5 oz. Greek yogurt
16 oz. cream cheese
2 tablespoons honey
4 oz. icing sugar
280 ml double cream
1 cup any jam

Directions:
Add the biscuits to a blender and pulse until crumbled. Transfer the crumbs to a bowl and add the melted butter. Mix well until the crumbs are well coated. Add to the pan and press into the bottom. Refrigerate.
Add Greek yogurt, cream cheese, icing sugar, vanilla, and honey to a bowl. Beat with a mixer until smooth. Add the double cream and beat until well combined.
Add the mixture onto the biscuit crust and top the cheesecake with jam. Refrigerate overnight. Serve.

Nutrition:
402 calories | 27 g fat | 36.1 g total carbs | 5.2 g protein

630. Greek Yogurt and Honey Walnuts

Preparation Time: 5 minutes | **Cooking time:** 10 minutes | **Servings:** 6

Ingredients:
½ cup honey
2 ½ cups strained Greek yogurt
1 cup walnuts
¾ teaspoon vanilla extract
Cinnamon powder

Directions:
Preheat the oven to 375 F.
Add the walnuts in a single layer onto the baking sheet. Toast for 8 minutes. Transfer the walnuts to a bowl. Add honey and stir to coat well. Cool down for 2 minutes.
Mix vanilla extract and Greek yogurt and divide among bowls. Add the honey-walnut mixture over the yogurt and add cinnamon powder on top. Serve.

Nutrition:
284 calories | 16 g fat | 26.7 g total carbs | 11.8 g protein

631. Healthy Coconut Blueberry Balls

Preparation Time: 10 minutes | **Cooking time:** 10 minutes | **Servings:** 12

Ingredients:
¼ cup flaked coconut
¼ cup blueberries
½ tsp vanilla
¼ cup honey
½ cup creamy almond butter
¼ tsp cinnamon
1 ½ tbsp chia seeds
¼ cup flaxseed meal
1 cup rolled oats, gluten-free

Directions:
In a large bowl, add oats, cinnamon, chia seeds, and flaxseed meal and mix well.
Add almond butter to a microwave-safe bowl and microwave for 30 seconds. Stir until smooth. Add vanilla and honey in melted almond butter and stir well.
Pour almond butter mixture over oat mixture and stir to combine.
Add coconut and blueberries and stir well.
Make small balls from the oat mixture and place them onto the baking tray
Serve and enjoy.

Nutrition:
Calories 129, | Fat: 7.4g, | Carbohydrates: 14.1g, | Sugar: 7g, | Protein: 4 g, | Cholesterol: 0 mg

632. Chocolate Matcha Balls

Preparation Time: 10 minutes | **Cooking time:** 5 minutes | **Servings:** 15

Ingredients:
2 tbsp unsweetened cocoa powder
3 tbsp oats, gluten-free
½ cup pine nuts
½ cup almonds
1 cup dates, pitted
2 tbsp matcha powder

Directions:
Add oats, pine nuts, almonds, and dates into a food processor and process until well combined.
Place matcha powder in a small dish.
Make small balls from the mixture and coat with matcha powder.
Enjoy or store in the refrigerator until ready to eat.

Nutrition:
Calories 88, | Fat: 4.9g, | Carbohydrates: 11.3g, | Sugar: 7.8g, | Protein: 1.9g, | Cholesterol: 0mg

633. Creamy Yogurt Banana Bowls

Preparation Time: 10 minutes | **Cooking time:** 0 minutes | **Servings:** 4

Ingredients:
2 bananas, sliced
½ tsp ground nutmeg
3 tbsp flaxseed meal
¼ cup creamy peanut butter
4 cups Greek yogurt

Directions:
Divide Greek yogurt between 4 serving bowls and top with sliced bananas.
Add peanut butter to a microwave-safe bowl and microwave for 30 seconds.
Drizzle 1 tablespoon of melted peanut butter on each bowl on top of the sliced bananas.
Sprinkle cinnamon and flax meal on top and serve.

Nutrition:
Calories 351, | Fat: 13.1g, | Carbohydrates: 35.6g, | Sugar: 26.1g, | Protein: 19.6g, | Cholesterol: 15mg

634. Chocolate Mousse

Preparation Time: 10 minutes | **Cooking time:** 6 minutes | **Servings:** 5

Ingredients:
4 egg yolks
½ tsp vanilla
½ cup unsweetened almond milk
1 cup whipping cream
¼ cup cocoa powder
¼ cup water
½ cup Swerve
1/8 tsp salt

Directions:
Add egg yolks to a large bowl and whisk until well beaten.
In a saucepan, add swerve, cocoa powder, and water and whisk until well combined.
Add almond milk and cream to the saucepan and whisk until well mixed.
Once saucepan mixtures are heated up then turn off the heat.
Add vanilla and salt and stir well.
Add a tablespoon of chocolate mixture into the eggs and whisk until well combined.
Slowly pour the remaining chocolate into the eggs and whisk until well combined.
Pour batter into the ramekins.
Pour 1 ½ cups of water into the instant pot then place a trivet in the pot.
Place ramekins on a trivet.
Seal the pot with the lid and select the manual setting and set timer for 6 minutes.
Release pressure using the quick-release method, then open the lid.
Carefully remove ramekins from the instant pot and let them cool completely.
Serve and enjoy.

Nutrition:
Calories 128, | Fat: 11.9g, | Carbohydrates: 4g, | Sugar: 0.2g, | Protein: 3.6g, | Cholesterol: 194mg

635. Decadent Croissant Bread Pudding

Preparation Time: 5 minutes | **Cooking time:** 15 minutes | **Servings:** 6

Ingredients:
1/2 cup double cream

6 tablespoons honey
1/4 cup rum, divided
2 eggs, whisked
1 teaspoon cinnamon
A pinch of salt
A pinch of grated nutmeg
1 teaspoon vanilla essence
8 croissants, torn into pieces
1 cup pistachios, toasted and chopped

Directions:
Spritz a baking pan with cooking spray and set it aside.
In a mixing bowl, whisk the eggs, double cream, honey, rum, cinnamon, salt, nutmeg, and vanilla; whisk until everything is well incorporated.
Place the croissants in the prepared baking dish. Pour the custard over your croissants. Fold in the pistachios and press with a wide spatula.
Add 1 cup of water and a metal rack to the inner pot of your Instant Pot. Lower the baking dish onto the rack.
Secure the lid. Choose the "Manual" mode and cook for 12 minutes at high pressure. Once cooking is complete, use a quick pressure release; carefully remove the lid.
Serve at room temperature or cold. Bon appétit!

Nutrition:
513 Calories | 27.9g Fat | 50.3g Carbohydrates | 12.5g Protein | 25.7g Sugars | 3.8g Fiber

636. Poached Apples with Greek Yogurt and Granola

Preparation Time: 5 minutes | **Cooking time:** 15 minutes | **Servings:** 4

Ingredients:
4 medium-sized apples, peeled
1/2 cup brown sugar
1 vanilla bean
1 cinnamon stick
1/2 cup cranberry juice
1 cup water
1/2 cup 2% Greek yogurt
1/2 cup granola

Directions:
Add the apples, brown sugar, water, cranberry juice, vanilla bean, and cinnamon stick to the inner pot of your Instant Pot.
Secure the lid. Choose the "Manual" mode and cook for 5 minutes at high pressure. Once cooking is complete, use a natural pressure release for 5 minutes; carefully remove the lid. Reserve poached apples.
Press the "Sauté" button and let the sauce simmer on "Less" mode until it has thickened.
Place the apples in serving bowls. Add the syrup and top each apple with granola and Greek yogurt. Enjoy!

Nutrition:
247 Calories | 3.1g Fat | 52.6g Carbohydrates | 3.5g Protein | 40g Sugars | 5.3g Fiber

637. Jasmine Rice Pudding with Cranberries

Preparation Time: 5 minutes | **Cooking time:** 15 minutes | **Servings:** 4

Ingredients:
1 cup apple juice
1 heaping tablespoon honey
1/3 cup granulated sugar
1 ½ cups jasmine rice
1 cup water
1/4 teaspoon ground cinnamon
1/4 teaspoon ground cloves
1/3 teaspoon ground cardamom
1 teaspoon vanilla extract
3 eggs, well-beaten
1/2 cup cranberries

Directions:
Thoroughly combine the apple juice, honey, sugar, jasmine rice, water, and spices in the inner pot of your Instant Pot.
Secure the lid. Choose the "Manual" mode and cook for 4 minutes at high pressure. Once cooking is complete, use a natural pressure release for 5 minutes; carefully remove the lid.
Press the "Sauté" button and fold in the eggs. Cook on "Less" mode until heated through.
Ladle into individual bowls and top with dried cranberries. Enjoy!

Nutrition:
402 Calories | 3.6g Fat | 81.1g Carbs | 8.9g Protein | 22.3g Sugars | 2.2g Fiber

638. Orange and Almond Cupcakes

Preparation Time: 5 minutes | **Cooking time:** 20 minutes | **Servings:** 9

Ingredients:
Cupcakes:
1 orange extract
2 tablespoons olive oil
2 tablespoons ghee, at room temperature
3 eggs, beaten
2 ounces Greek yogurt
2 cups cake flour
A pinch of salt
1 tablespoon grated orange rind
1/2 cup brown sugar
1/2 cup almonds, chopped
Cream Cheese Frosting:
2 ounces cream cheese
1 tablespoon whipping cream
1/2 cup butter, at room temperature
1 ½ cups confectioners' sugar, sifted
1/3 teaspoon vanilla
A pinch of salt

Directions:
Mix the orange extract, olive oil, ghee, eggs, and Greek yogurt until well combined.
Thoroughly combine the cake flour, salt, orange rind, and brown sugar in a separate mixing bowl. Add the egg/yogurt mixture to the flour mixture. Stir in the chopped almonds and mix again.
Place parchment baking liners on the bottom of a muffin tin. Pour the batter into the muffin tin. Place 1 cup of water and metal trivet in the inner pot of your Instant Pot. Lower the prepared muffin tin onto the trivet.
Secure the lid. Choose the "Manual" mode and cook for 11 minutes at high pressure. Once cooking is complete, use a quick pressure release; carefully remove the lid. Transfer to wire racks.
Meanwhile, make the frosting by mixing all ingredients until creamy. Frost your cupcakes and enjoy!

Nutrition:
392 Calories | 18.7g Fat | 50.1g Carbohydrates | 5.9g Protein | 25.2g Sugars | 0.7g Fiber

639. Bread Pudding

Preparation Time: 5 minutes | **Cooking time:** 25 minutes | **Servings:** 4

Ingredients:
4 egg yolks
3 cups brioche, cubed
2 cups half and half
½ teaspoon vanilla extract
1 cup sugar
2 tablespoons butter, softened
1 cup cranberries
2 cups warm water
½ cup raisins
Zest from 1 lime

Directions:
Grease a baking dish with some butter and set the dish aside. In a bowl, mix the egg yolks with the half and half, cubed brioche, vanilla extract, sugar, cranberries, raisins, and lime zest, and stir well. Pour this into a greased dish, cover with some aluminum foil, and set aside for 10 minutes. Put the dish in the steamer basket of the Instant Pot, add the warm water to the Instant Pot, cover, and cook on the Manual setting for 20 minutes. Release the pressure naturally, uncover the Instant Pot, take the bread pudding out, set it aside to cool down, slice, and serve it.

Nutrition:
Calories: 300 | Fat: 7 | Fiber: 2 | Carbs: 46 | Protein: 11

640. Ruby Pears

Preparation Time: 10 minutes | **Cooking time:** 10 minutes | **Servings:** 4

Ingredients:
4 pears
Juice and zest of 1 lemon
26 ounces grape juice
11 ounces currant jelly
4 garlic cloves, peeled
½ vanilla bean
4 peppercorns
2 rosemary sprigs

Directions:
Pour the jelly and grape juice into the Instant Pot and mix with lemon zest and lemon juice. Dip each pear in this mix, wrap them in aluminum foil and arrange them in the steamer basket of the Instant Pot. Add the garlic cloves, peppercorns, rosemary, and vanilla bean to the juice mixture, cover the Instant Pot, and cook on the Manual setting for 10 minutes. Release the pressure, uncover the Instant Pot, take the pears out, unwrap them, arrange them on plates, and serve cold with cooking juice poured on top.

Nutrition:
Calories: 145 | Fat: 5.6 | Fiber: 6 | Carbs: 12 | Protein: 12

641. Lemon Marmalade

Preparation Time: 10 minutes | **Cooking time:** 15 minutes | **Servings:** 8

Ingredients:
2 pounds lemons, washed, sliced, and cut into quarters
4 pounds sugar
2 cups water

Directions:
Put the lemon pieces into the Instant Pot, add the water, cover, and cook on the Manual setting for 10 minutes. Release the pressure naturally, uncover the Instant Pot, add the sugar, stir, set the Instant Pot on Manual mode, and cook for 6 minutes, stirring all the time. Divide into jars, and serve when needed.

Nutrition:
Calories: 100 | Fat: 2 | Fiber: 2 | Carbs: 4 | Protein: 8

642. Peach Jam

Preparation Time: 10 minutes | **Cooking time:** 5 minutes | **Servings:** 6

Ingredients:
4½ cups peaches, peeled and cubed
6 cups sugar
¼ cup crystallized ginger, chopped
1 box fruit pectin

Directions:
Set the Instant Pot on Manual mode, add the peaches, ginger, and pectin, stir, and bring to a boil. Add the sugar, stir, cover, and cook on the Manual setting for 5 minutes. Release the pressure, uncover the Instant Pot, divide the jam into jars, and serve.

Nutrition:
Calories: 50 | Fat: 0 | Fiber: 1 | Carbs: 3 | Protein: 0 | Sugar: 12

643. Raspberry Curd

Preparation Time: 10 minutes | **Cooking time:** 5 minutes | **Servings:** 4

Ingredients:
1 cup sugar
12 ounces raspberries
2 egg yolks
2 tablespoons lemon juice
2 tablespoons butter

Directions:
Put the raspberries into the Instant Pot. Add the sugar and lemon juice, stir, cover, and cook on the Manual setting for 2 minutes.
Release the pressure for 5 minutes, uncover the Instant Pot, strain the raspberries, and discard the seeds.
In a bowl, mix the egg yolks with raspberries and stir well. Return this to the Instant Pot, set it on Sauté mode, simmer for 2 minutes, add the butter, stir, and transfer to a container. Serve cold.

Nutrition:
Calories: 110 | Fat: 4 | Fiber: 0 | Carbs: 16 | Protein: 1

644. Pear Jam

Preparation Time: 10 minutes | **Cooking time:** 4 minutes | **Servings:** 12

Ingredients:
8 pears, cored and cut into quarters
2 apples, peeled, cored, and cut into quarters
¼ cup apple juice
1 teaspoon cinnamon, ground

Directions:

In the Instant Pot, mix the pears with apples, cinnamon, and apple juice, stir, cover, and cook on the Manual setting for 4 minutes. Release the pressure naturally, uncover the Instant Pot, blend using an immersion blender, divide the jam into jars, and keep in a cold place until you serve it.

Nutrition:

Calories: 90 | Fat: 0 | Fiber: 1 | Carbs: 20 | Sugar: 20 | Protein: 0

645. Berry Compote

Preparation Time: 10 minutes | **Cooking time:** 5 minutes | **Servings:** 8

Ingredients:
1 cup blueberries
2 cups strawberries, sliced
2 tablespoons lemon juice
¾ cup sugar
1 tablespoon cornstarch
1 tablespoon water

Directions:

In the Instant Pot, mix the blueberries with lemon juice and sugar, stir, cover, and cook on the Manual setting for 3 minutes. Release the pressure naturally for 10 minutes and uncover the Instant Pot. In a bowl, mix the cornstarch with water, stir well, and add to the Instant Pot. Stir, set the Instant Pot on Sauté mode, and cook compote for 2 minutes. Divide into jars and keep in the refrigerator until you serve it.

Nutrition:

Calories: 260 | Fat: 13 | Fiber: 3 | Carbs: 23 | Protein: 3

646. Key Lime Pie

Preparation Time: 10 minutes | **Cooking time:** 15 minutes | **Servings:** 6

Ingredients:
For the crust:
1 tablespoon sugar
3 tablespoons butter, melted
5 graham crackers, crumbled
For the filling:
4 egg yolks
14 ounces canned condensed milk
½ cup key lime juice
⅓ cup sour cream
Vegetable oil cooking spray
1 cup water
2 tablespoons key lime zest, grated

Directions:

In a bowl, whisk the egg yolks well. Add the milk gradually and stir again. Add the lime juice, sour cream, and lime zest and stir again. In another bowl, whisk the butter with the graham crackers and sugar, stir well, and spread on the bottom of a springform pan greased with some cooking spray. Cover the pan with some aluminum foil and place it in the steamer basket of the Instant Pot. Add the water to the Instant Pot, cover, and cook on the Manual setting for 15 minutes. Release the pressure for 10 minutes, uncover the Instant Pot, take the pie out, set it aside to cool down, and keep it in the refrigerator for 4 hours before slicing and serving it.

Nutrition:

Calories: 400 | Fat: 21 | Fiber: 0.5 | Carbs: 34 | Protein: 7

647. Fruit Cobbler

Preparation Time: 10 minutes | **Cooking time:** 12 minutes | **Servings:** 4

Ingredients:
3 apples, cored and cut into chunks
2 pears, cored and cut into chunks
1½ cup hot water
¼ cup honey
1 cup steel-cut oats
1 teaspoon ground cinnamon
ice cream, for serving

Directions:

Put the apples and pears into the Instant Pot and mix with hot water, honey, oats, and cinnamon. Stir, cover, and cook on the Manual setting for 12 minutes. Release the pressure naturally, transfer

Nutrition:

Calories: 170 | Fat: 4 | Carbs: 10 | Fiber: 2.4 | Protein: 3 | Sugar: 7

648. Stuffed Peaches

Preparation Time: 10 minutes | **Cooking time:** 4 minutes | **Servings:** 6

Ingredients:
6 peaches, pits and flesh removed
Salt
¼ cup coconut flour
¼ cup maple syrup
2 tablespoons coconut butter
½ teaspoon ground cinnamon
1 teaspoon almond extract
1 cup water

Directions:
In a bowl, mix the flour with the salt, syrup, butter, cinnamon, and half of the almond extract and stir well. Fill the peaches with this mix, place them in the steamer basket of the Instant Pot, add the water and the rest of the almond extract to the Instant Pot, cover, and cook on the Steam setting for 4 minutes. Release the pressure naturally, divide the stuffed peaches on serving plates, and serve warm.

Nutrition:
Calories: 160 | Fat: 6.7 | Carbs: 12 | Fiber: 3 | Sugar: 11 | Protein: 4

649. Peach Compote

Preparation Time: 10 minutes | **Cooking time:** 3 minutes | **Servings:** 6

Ingredients:
8 peaches, pitted and chopped
6 tablespoons sugar
1 teaspoon ground cinnamon
1 teaspoon vanilla extract
1 vanilla bean, scraped
2 tablespoons Grape Nuts cereal

Directions:
Put the peaches into the Instant Pot and mix with the sugar, cinnamon, vanilla bean, and vanilla extract. Stir well, cover the Instant Pot, and cook on the Manual setting for 3 minutes. Release the pressure for 10 minutes, add the cereal, stir well, transfer the compote to bowls, and serve.

Nutrition:
Calories: 100 | Fat: 2 | Carbs: 11 | Fiber: 1 | Sugar: 10 | Protein: 1

650. Chocolate Pudding

Preparation Time: 10 minutes | **Cooking time:** 20 minutes | **Servings:** 4

Ingredients:
6 ounces bittersweet chocolate, chopped
½ cup milk
1½ cups heavy cream
5 egg yolks
⅓ cup brown sugar
2 teaspoons vanilla extract
1½ cups water
¼ teaspoon cardamom
Salt
Crème fraîche, for serving
Chocolate shavings, for serving

Directions:
Put the cream and milk in a pot, bring to a simmer over medium heat, take off the heat, add the chocolate and whisk well. In a bowl, mix the egg yolks with the vanilla, sugar, cardamom, and a pinch of salt, stir, strain, and mix with chocolate mixture. Pour this into a soufflé dish, cover with aluminum foil, place in the steamer basket of the Instant Pot, add water to the Instant Pot, cover, cook on Manual for 18 minutes, release the pressure naturally.
Take the pudding out of the Instant Pot, set it aside to cool down, and keep it in the refrigerator for 3 hours before serving with crème fraîche and chocolate shavings on top.

Nutrition:
Calories: 200 | Fat: 3 | Fiber: 1 | Carbs: 20 | Protein: 14

651. Refreshing Curd

Preparation Time: 10 minutes | **Cooking time:** 5 minutes | **Servings:** 4

Ingredients:
3 tablespoons stevia
12 ounces raspberries
2 egg yolks
2 tablespoons lemon juice
2 tablespoons ghee

Directions:
Put raspberries in your instant pot, add stevia and lemon juice, stir, cover, and cook on High for 2 minutes.
Strain this into a bowl, add egg yolks, stir well, and return to your pot.
Set the pot on Simmer mode, cook for 2 minutes, add ghee, stir well, transfer to a container, and serve cold.
Enjoy!

Nutrition:
Calories 132, | Fat: 1 | Fiber 0, | Carbohydrates: 2, | Protein: 4

652. The Best Jam Ever

Preparation Time: 10 minutes | **Cooking time:** 5 minutes | **Servings:** 6

Ingredients:
4 and ½ cups peaches, peeled and cubed
4 tablespoons stevia
¼ cup crystallized ginger, chopped

Directions:
Set your instant pot on Simmer mode, add peaches, ginger, and stevia, stir, bring to a boil, cover, and cook on High for 5 minutes.
Divide into bowls and serve cold.
Enjoy!

Nutrition:
Calories 53, | Fat: 0 | Fiber 0 | Carbs 0, | Protein: 2g

653. Pistachio and Fruits

Preparation Time: 5 minutes | **Cooking time:** 7 minutes | **Servings:** 12

Ingredients:
½ cup apricots, dried and chopped
¼ cup dried cranberries
½ tsp. cinnamon
¼ tsp. allspice
¼ tsp. ground nutmeg
1 ¼ cups unsalted pistachios, roasted
2 tsp. sugar

Directions:
Start by heating the oven to a temperature of around 345 degrees F.
Using a tray, place the pistachios, and bake for seven minutes. Allow the pistachio to cool afterward.
Combine all ingredients in a container.
Once everything is combined well the food is ready to serve.

Nutrition:
Calories: 377 | Carbohydrates: 24.5 g | Fats: 5 g | Proteins: 16 g

654. Avocado Sorbet

Preparation Time: 5 minutes | **Cooking time:** 10 minutes | **Servings:** 4

Ingredients:
¼ cup of sugar
1 cup of water
1 tsp grated lime zest
1 tbsp honey
2 ripe avocados, pitted and skin removed
2 tbsp lime juice

Directions:
Combine the sugar and water in a small pan over medium flame. Continue until the sugar dissolves completely and then remove from the flame.
Place the avocados in the food processor. Add the sugar and water mix along with the honey, lime zest, and lime juice into the food processor. Process until you reach a smooth consistency.
Place the mix into a baking pan and cover with foil. Place the mix into the freezer until completely frozen.
Upon serving, process the food in the food processor until you reach a smooth consistency.

Nutrition:
Calories: 390.3 | Carbohydrates: 19 g | Fats: 6 g | Proteins: 10 g

655. Cioccolata Calda

Preparation Time: 5 minutes | **Cooking time:** 10 minutes | **Servings:** 2

Ingredients:
1½ tbsp sugar
1 tbsp cornstarch
3 tbsp unsweetened cocoa powder
1½ cups plus 2 tbsp milk

Directions:
Mix the cocoa powder and sugar in a little frying pan. Add one and a half cups of milk while mixing. Start with medium heat and gradually lower until the sugar is fully dissolved. The entire mixture should simmer.

In a separate container, mix the cornstarch and the remaining two tablespoons of milk. After being mixed add to the cocoa mix on the frying pan.

Continue mixing until the entire mixture reaches a thick consistency. Serve while hot.

Nutrition:
Calories: 427 | Carbohydrates: 22 g | Fats: 4 g | Proteins: 12 g

656. Chocolate Pudding in a Mug

Preparation Time: 10 minutes | **Cooking time:** 70 seconds | **Servings:** 2

Ingredients:
2 eggs
1 oz almond Flour
1 tbsp xylitol
2 tbsp unsweetened cocoa powder
4 oz almond milk
1 Tbsp olive oil
½ tsp baking powder
1 tsp espresso powder
Whipped cream for topping

Directions:
Mix almond flour, xylitol, cocoa powder, espresso powder, eggs, coconut milk, olive oil, and baking powder in a bowl.
Pour the mix into mugs ¾ way up and cook in a microwave for 70 seconds.
Remove and swirl a generous amount of whipping cream on the cakes and serve.

Nutrition:
Calories: 200 | Fat: 3 | Fiber: 1 | Carbs: 20 | Protein: 14

657. Healthy Fruit Salad with Yogurt Cream

Preparation Time: 10 minutes | **Cooking time:** 0 minutes | **Servings:** 4

Ingredients:
1 1/2 cups grapes halved
2 plums chopped
1 peach chopped
1 cup chopped cantaloupe
1/2 cup fresh blueberries
1 cup unsweetened plain nonfat Greek yogurt
1/2 teaspoon ground cinnamon
2 tablespoons honey

Directions:
In a large bowl combine the grapes, plums, peach cantaloupe, and blueberries. Toss to mix. Divide among 4 dessert dishes.
In a small bowl whisk the yogurt, cinnamon, and honey. Spoon over the fruit.
Sprinkle yogurt with sugar and drizzle with honey. Serve fruit with yogurt mixture.

Nutrition:
Calories (Per Serving): 74 | Fat: 0.7g | Carbohydrates: 16g | Protein: 2g
Summertime Fruit Salad | **Cooking time:** 0 minutes
Preparation Time: 30 minutes | **Servings:** 6

Ingredients:
1-pound strawberries, hulled and sliced thinly
3 medium peaches, sliced thinly
6 ounces blueberries
1 tablespoon fresh mint, chopped
2 tablespoons lemon juice
1 tablespoon honey
2 teaspoons balsamic vinegar

Directions:
In a salad bowl, combine all ingredients.
Gently toss to coat all ingredients.
Chill for at least 30 minutes before serving.

Nutrition:
Calories per serving: 146 | Carbs: 22.8g; | Protein: 8.1g; | Fat: 3.4g

658. Banana Shake Bowls

Preparation Time: 5 minutes | **Cooking time:** 0 minutes | **Servings:** 4

Ingredients:
4 medium bananas, peeled
1 avocado, peeled, pitted, and mashed
¾ cup almond milk
½ teaspoon vanilla extract

Directions:
In a blender, combine the bananas with the avocado and the other ingredients, pulse, divide into bowls and keep in the fridge until serving.

Nutrition:
Calories 185 | Fat: 4.3 | Fiber 4 | Carbs 6 | Protein: 6.45

659. Cold Lemon Squares

Preparation Time: 30 minutes | **Cooking time:** 0 minutes | **Servings:** 4

Ingredients:
1 cup avocado oil and a drizzle
2 bananas, peeled and chopped
1 tablespoon honey
¼ cup lemon juice
A pinch of lemon zest, grated

Directions:
In your food processor, mix the bananas with the rest of the ingredients, pulse well, and spread on the bottom of a pan greased with a drizzle of oil.
Introduce it in the fridge for 30 minutes, slice into squares, and serve.

Nutrition:
Calories 136 | Fat: 11.2 | Fiber 0.2 | Carbs 7 | Protein: 1.1

660. Strawberries Cream

Preparation Time: 10 minutes | **Cooking time:** 20 minutes | **Servings:** 4

Ingredients:
½ cup stevia
2 pounds strawberries, chopped
1 cup almond milk
Zest of 1 lemon, grated
½ cup heavy cream
3 egg yolks, whisked

Directions:
Heat a pan with the milk over medium-high heat, add the stevia and the rest of the ingredients, whisk well, simmer for 20 minutes, divide into cups and serve cold.

Nutrition:
Calories 152 | Fat: 4.4 | Fiber 5.5 | Carbs 5.1 | Protein: 0.8

661. Sweetened Grapes

Preparation Time: 10 minutes | **Cooking time:** 10 minutes | **Servings:** 4

Ingredients:
2/3 cup stevia
1 tablespoon olive oil
1/3 cup coconut water
1 teaspoon vanilla extract
1 teaspoon lemon zest, grated
2 cup red grapes, halved

Directions:
Heat a pan with the water over medium heat, add the oil, stevia, and the rest of the ingredients, toss, simmer for 10 minutes, divide into cups and serve.

Nutrition:
Calories 122 | Fat: 3.7 | Fiber 1.2 | Carbs 2.3 | Protein: 0.4

662. Compote Dipped Berries Mix

Preparation Time: 10 minutes | **Cooking time:** 10 minutes | **Servings:** 8

Ingredients:
2 cups fresh strawberries, hulled and halved lengthwise
4 sprigs fresh mint
2 cups fresh blackberries
1 cup pomegranate juice
2 teaspoons vanilla
6 orange pekoe tea bags
2 cups fresh red raspberries
1 cup water
2 cups fresh golden raspberries
2 cups fresh sweet cherries, pitted and halved
2 cups fresh blueberries

2 ml bottle Sauvignon Blanc

Directions:
Preheat the oven to 290 degrees F and lightly grease a baking dish.
Soak mint sprigs and tea bags in boiled water for about 10 minutes in a covered bowl.
Mix all the berries and cherries in another bowl and keep aside.
Cook wine with pomegranate juice in a saucepan and add strained tea liquid.
Toss in the mixed berries to serve and enjoy.

Nutrition:
Calories 356 | Total Fat: 0.8 g | Saturated Fat: 0.1 g | Cholesterol: 0 mg | Total Carbs 89.9 g | Dietary Fiber: 9.4 g | Sugar: 70.8 g | Protein: 2.2 g

663. Popped Quinoa Bars

Preparation Time: 10 minutes | **Cooking time:** 10 minutes | **Servings:** 3

Ingredients:
2 (4 oz.) semi-sweet chocolate bars, chopped
½ tablespoon peanut butter
½ cup dry quinoa
¼ teaspoon vanilla

Directions:
Toast dry quinoa in a pan until golden and stir in chocolate, vanilla, and peanut butter.
Spread this mixture in a baking sheet evenly and refrigerate for about 4 hours.
Break it into small pieces and serve chilled.

Nutrition:
Calories 278 | Total Fat: 11.8 g | Saturated Fat: 6.6 g | Cholesterol: 7 mg | Total Carbs 36.2 g | Dietary Fiber: 3.1 g | Sugar: 15.4 g | Protein: 6.9 g

664. Almond Orange Pandoro

Preparation Time: 10 minutes | **Cooking time:** 0 minutes | **Servings:** 12

Ingredients:
2 large oranges, zested
2½ cups mascarpone
½ cup almonds, whole
2½ cups coconut cream
½ pandoro, diced
2 tablespoons sherry

Directions:
Whisk cream with mascarpone, icing sugar, ¾ zest, and half sherry in a bowl.
Dice the pandoro into equal-sized horizontal slices.
Place the bottom slice in a plate and top with the remaining sherry.
Spoon the mascarpone mixture over the slice.
Top with almonds and place another pandoro slice over.
Continue adding layers of pandoro slices and cream mixture.
Dish out to serve.

Nutrition:
Calories 346 | Total Fat: 10.4 g | Saturated Fat: 3 g | Cholesterol: 10 mg | Total Carbs 8.5 g | Dietary Fiber: 3 g | Sugar: 2.4 g | Protein: 7.7 g

665. Mint Chocolate Chip Nice Cream

Preparation Time: 5 minutes | **Cooking time:** - minutes | **Servings:** 1-2

Ingredients:
2 overripe frozen bananas
Pinch salt
1/8 teaspoon pure peppermint extract
Pinch spirulina or natural food coloring (optional)
1/2 cup coconut cream
2-3 tablespoons chocolate chips

Directions:
Pop all the ingredients into your blender and whizz until smooth.
Serve and enjoy.

Nutrition:
Calories: 601 | Net Carbs: 130g | Fat: 12g | Protein: 8g

666. Creamy Berry Crunch

Preparation Time: 10 minutes | **Cooking time:** 0 minutes | **Servings:** 2

Ingredients:
2 cups of heavy cream for whipping
3oz berries, fresh if possible
The zest of half a lemon
0.25 tsp vanilla extract

2oz chopped pecan nuts

Directions:
Into a large bowl, whip the cream until stiff
Add the vanilla and the lemon zest and whip for a few seconds longer
Add the nuts and the berries and stir in gently
Place plastic cling film over the top of the bowl
Serve!

Nutrition:
Carbs - 3g | Fat: - 27g | Protein - 3g | Calories - 260

667. Creme Brûlée with a Gingerbread Twist

Preparation Time: 5 minutes | **Cooking time:** 5 minutes | **Servings:** 4

Ingredients:
cups of heavy cream for whipping
2 tbsp erythritol
4 egg yolks
2 tsp pumpkin spice
0.25 tsp vanilla extract
4 ramekin glasses

Directions:
Preheat the oven to 180C
Separate the eggs, with the whites in one bowl and the yolks in the other. You can save the whites for something else
Cook the cream in a pan and allow to boil lightly, before adding the pumpkin spice, vanilla extract, and the erythritol
Pour the mixture a little at a time into the egg yolks and whisk continuously
Take small ovenproof bowls (ramekins) and place them into a large dish with sides to hold everything in place
Add water into the larger dish
Add the mixture evenly to each small ramekin
Cook in the oven for around half an hour
Once finished, remove the ramekins, and place them to one side to cool
Serve warm or cold

Nutrition:
Carbs - 3g | Fat: - 28g | Protein - 4g | Calories - 274

668. Mandarin Cream

Preparation Time: 20 minutes | **Cooking time:** 0 minutes | **Servings:** 8

Ingredients:
2 mandarins, peeled and cut into segments
Juice of 2 mandarins
2 tablespoons stevia
4 eggs, whisked
¾ cup stevia
¾ cup almonds, ground

Directions:
In a blender, combine the mandarins with the mandarins' juice and the other ingredients, whisk well, divide into cups, and keep in the fridge for 20 minutes before serving.

Nutrition:
Calories 106 | Fat: 3.4 | Fiber 0 | Carbs 2.4 | Protein: 4

669. Pumpkin Cream

Preparation Time: 5 minutes | **Cooking time:** 5 minutes | **Servings:** 2

Ingredients:
2 cups canned pumpkin flesh
2 tablespoons stevia
1 teaspoon vanilla extract
2 tablespoons water
A pinch of pumpkin spice

Directions:
In a pan, combine the pumpkin flesh with the other ingredients, simmer for 5 minutes, divide into cups and serve cold.

Nutrition:
Calories 192 | Fat: 3.4 Fiber 4.5 | Carbs 7.6 | Protein: 3.5

670. Minty Coconut Cream

Preparation Time: 4 minutes | **Cooking time:** 0 minutes | **Servings:** 2

Ingredients:
1 banana, peeled
2 cups coconut flesh, shredded
3 tablespoons mint, chopped
1 and ½ cups coconut water

2 tablespoons stevia
½ avocado, pitted and peeled

Directions:
In a blender, combine the coconut with the banana and the rest of the ingredients, pulse well, divide into cups and serve cold.

Nutrition:
Calories 193 | Fat: 5.4 | Fiber 3.4 | Carbs 7.6 | Protein: 3

671. Watermelon Cream

Preparation Time: 15 minutes | **Cooking time:** 0 minutes | **Servings:** 2

Ingredients:
1 pound watermelon, peeled and chopped
1 teaspoon vanilla extract
1 cup heavy cream
1 teaspoon lime juice
2 tablespoons stevia

Directions:
In a blender, combine the watermelon with the cream and the rest of the ingredients, pulse well, divide into cups and keep in the fridge for 15 minutes before serving.

Nutrition:
Calories 122 | Fat: 5.7 | Fiber 3.2 | Carbs 5.3 | Protein: 0.4

672. Chocolate Lava Cake

Preparation Time: 5 minutes | **Cooking time:** 10 minutes | **Servings:** 4

Ingredients:
2oz butter
0.25 tsp vanilla extract
3 eggs
1 tbsp butter
2oz dark chocolate
4 greased ramekin glasses

Directions:
Preheat the oven to 200°C
Take four ramekin dishes and grease with butter
Cut the chocolate up into very small pieces and add to a saucepan with the butter, allowing it to melt
Add the vanilla to the chocolate once melted, and stir well
Take the pan off the heat and set it to one side to cool down
Crack the three eggs into a bowl and beat for around 3 minutes
Pour the chocolate mixture into the eggs and mix well
Pour into the prepared ramekins and cook in the oven
Turn the oven down to 175°C when you place the ramekins inside, and cook for 6 minutes
Serve whilst still hot

Nutrition:
Carbs - 4g | Fat: - 16g | Protein - 4g | Calories - 180

673. Coffee Mocha Ice Cream

Preparation Time: 5 minutes | **Cooking time:** 0 minutes | **Servings:** 4

Ingredients:
2 cups of heavy cream for whipping
3oz chopped dark chocolate
6 egg yolks
2 tbsp coffee powder (instant)
0.75 cup of erythritol powder
2 tsp vanilla extract
0.5 tsp salt
6 drops of liquid sweetener
1 drop of peppermint extract
For this recipe, you will need an ice cream maker

Directions:
Take a large saucepan and warm up the cream, stirring constantly
Add the dark chocolate and keep stirring until it has all melted
Add the egg yolks into the pan and stir constantly
Once warm, add the erythritol powder, coffee powder, and combine well
Keep stirring until a custard consistency is achieved
Remove the pan and place it to one side
Add the salt, peppermint extract, and vanilla extract to the mixture and combine
Add the liquid sweetener and combine once more
Place the pan into the refrigerator to cool completely

Transfer the mixture into the ice cream maker and follow the instructions to create delicious ice cream.

Nutrition:
Carbs - 5g | Fat: - 40g | Protein - 7g | Calories - 422

674. Chocolate & Pecan Thins

Preparation Time: 5 minutes | **Cooking time:** 10 minutes | **Servings:** 4

Ingredients:
4oz dark chocolate
0.5oz pecans, chopped
0.25 tsp vanilla extract
1 tsp liquorice powder
Baking tray lined with parchment paper

Directions:
Warm-up a pan on low heat and melt the chocolate, or place it in the microwave as an alternative
Add the liquorice and the vanilla extract and combine well
Take a baking tray and grease it, lining it with parchment paper
Pour the mixture onto the tray and add the pecans over the top
Allow to cool or place in the refrigerator if you want it faster!
The mixture should set to a completely hard consistency - snap to break up, to around 15 pieces, and enjoy!

Nutrition:
Carbs - 3g | Fat: - 5g | Protein - 1g | Calories - 60

675. Banana Blueberry Blast

Preparation Time: 4 minutes | **Cooking time:** None | **Servings:** 2

Ingredients:
½ cup oats
1 ½ cups plain nonfat Greek yogurt
1 cup blueberries
1 banana
5 walnuts

Directions:
Add all the ingredients to a blender and blend until very smooth. Enjoy!

Nutrition:
Calories: 300 | Carbohydrates: 22.5 g | Fats: 4 g | Proteins: 5 g

676. Sweet Yogurt Bulgur Bowl

Preparation Time: 10 minutes | **Cooking time:** 0 minutes | **Servings:** 4

Ingredients:
1 cup grapes, halved
½ cup bulgur, cooked
¼ cup celery stalk, chopped
2 oz walnuts, chopped
¼ cup plain yogurt
½ teaspoon ground cinnamon

Directions:
Mix grapes with bulgur, celery stalk, and walnut. Then add plain yogurt and ground cinnamon. Stir the mixture with the help of the spoon and transfer it to the serving bowls.

Nutrition:
123 Calories | 12.3g Protein | 33.4g Carbs | 19.3g Fat

Conclusion

The Mediterranean diet is not a short-term course that can be jam-packed with hours of exercise and a small portion of tasteless dishes to ease your hunger. The diet is a way of life, a completely different way of thinking, and a unique way of approaching diets than what has been sold to all those desperate to shed the pounds.

The Mediterranean way of eating is a simple one to follow—no more counting calories. If calories were a subject in school, I am sure we would all have doctorates in it by now. Get rid of those unhealthy fats and eat more healthy ones.

The good kinds of fat are hidden in olives and nuts, foods that have been shown to promote longevity and boost health.

The frozen food aisle will no longer be your most frequented stop when grocery shopping. The fresher, the better, the more seasonal—sensational.

The good news, you do not have to say goodbye to bread, either. White bread, unfortunately, has to go. Most modern diets will target the bread and carbs first as items destined for the chop. But whole-grain slices of bread are there to enjoy—in moderation, yes, but around enough in the diet to not want, nor need, nor miss it.

Another marvelous revelation that comes with this way of eating is that the variety of foods that you can eat are endless. Your menu can change from week to week and is versatile enough to switch out ingredients for others without hampering the flavors and tastes.

Because the Mediterranean is so diverse, foods from Italy, France, Morocco, Spain, Turkey, and Greece can be explored. There is plenty of room to get creative in the kitchen—and, as all good Mediterranean do, include your family and friends.

Just as the cuisine is varied, so is the list of herbs and spices that you can include when whipping up something delicious. Herbs and spices are a fundamental part of living in the Mediterranean. Many of the herbs are also rich in minerals and nutrients, meaning it would be wise to stock up on them.

In all honesty, simple is the way to go, even when preparing food. Remaining true to your ingredients and keeping them as unrefined as possible are a few fundamentals. We all live busy lives, and it is hard to want to come home and still have to think about a meal—let alone a healthy one—to make for the family and yourself. Cooking in the Mediterranean way is less complex; choosing to keep the produce as close to unrefined as possible. How well does a mezze platter sound with a glass of wine? There's your dinner problem solved for one evening, and it ticks all the right boxes when it comes to the diet.

It is a lifestyle, a way in which to embrace a new way of eating, exercising truly, and living. It is about achieving equilibrium in what we put into our bodies and how to stay happy.

You will never feel hungry, which is guaranteed—most, if not all, of the foods allow your body to digest them slowly, meaning you will stay fuller for longer.

It brings me to my final point. All of the above sounds too good to be true, but it is not—best of all, eating this way can help you lose weight. Feeling content and satisfied in life leaves you less room to stray, as conventional diets do. Lastly, your heart will thank you, as all the foods on the list support its function and will keep it beating steadily along.

The Mediterranean diet is not new to us, though it sounds like it. If you think about it, this diet is about tradition. It focuses on how we lived when we were younger, or perhaps the way our parents did when they were kids.

Now, does that not sound like the life you want? Well, it's the Mediterranean way, and you can start following it right now.

Here's to living a good life—salute!

Printed in Great Britain
by Amazon